My Colour-Coded Life

Living with Schizoaffective Disorder

MEGAN JACKSON HALL

 FriesenPress

Suite 300 - 990 Fort St
Victoria, BC, V8V 3K2
Canada

www.friesenpress.com

Copyright © 2020 by Megan Jackson Hall
First Edition — 2020

All rights reserved.

No part of this publication may be reproduced in any form, or by any means, electronic or mechanical, including photocopying, recording, or any information browsing, storage, or retrieval system, without permission in writing from FriesenPress.

This is a true story but most of the names have been changed.

ISBN
978-1-5255-7182-4 (Hardcover)
978-1-5255-7183-1 (Paperback)
978-1-5255-7184-8 (eBook)

1. Biography & Autobiography, Personal Memoirs

Distributed to the trade by The Ingram Book Company

Contents

2008 11
2010 39
2011 105
2012 153
2013 157
2014 179
2015 185
2016 235
Inventions or Creations 237
2017 249
2018 261
More Creative Dreams 315
What Makes a Good Parent? 319
More Creative Ideas 321
Yet More Creative Ideas and Dreams 327

They say in sickness and in health. Well my husband is definitely living through the in sickness part with me. George, my husband, who has stood by me through all this, has always said that I should write down my thoughts on the computer and today I have started. Now that I have, I feel that I should not have because one can never erase from a hard drive. One who knows the workings of a computer is likely always able to retrieve what they want. In the end I am very glad I did!!

It just takes one event for one to lose what they once cherished. In my situation, it is my mind. Losing faith and perhaps trust in what you held dear is all it takes to send one spiraling into a whirlpool of what one feels to be right.

Perhaps the reasons for my demise should be left unsaid and yet according to my doctor had I not had a predisposition to my problem or illness my reactions to given circumstances would have been different, yet, here I go again.

It is said by many that I should let go of things that are or were real incidents and move on. However, I look at the present and still so certain with what I see make it so difficult to let go. Am I caught in a game? Am I caught in an undercover sting? Am I part of some sick reality show? Am I merely ill with thoughts that are my own? On the other hand, did I agree to be a subject in research where no one would know during one of my discussions in my Master's Degree? I vaguely remember something like this.

First, let me say that I have been going to Duncan Mental Health since October 2005. I had first sought a psychiatrist through my family doctor but had no rapport with that person. George is the one who got me into Duncan Mental Health after my first trip to Serenity Hospital where I was first diagnosed with schizophrenia in 2005. The first trip they were not sure that I had schizophrenia and thought I was too old to have it.

Where do I begin to unravel all that sits in my mind? The best place perhaps is at the beginning, though personal and private. It all began in the year 2000. Living in our first house in North Duncan after being intimate, our eldest, Darcy, woke up at 3:00 a.m. and was nearly passed out after having come from the bathroom. She was twelve years of age. I ran to her and asked my husband to call 911, but he did not want to and did not. He proceeded to take the sheets off our bed and the towels out of both bathrooms and do the wash AT 3:00 a.m. I did however; call 911 and they took her to the hospital. I went with her in the ambulance but never knew the results because soon after the girls had a female doctor.

This only began my turmoil and questioning as to what was going on around me. Why do the wash at 3:00 a.m.? I still have no clear answer that serves to quench my curiosity; hence, for years later I began to wake at 3:00 a.m. This was only the precursor of what was yet to unfold.

I began to question things that I had taken for granted. I felt that my husband was having an affair or somehow into drugs. I thought I was losing him. Was this just my paranoia? It was just a gut feeling. I had no proof.

One day I emptied his side of the closet and realized that some of his pants were missing. When I questioned him on this the next day, he told me they were in the closet, and low and behold, they were. He did not take anything to the Dry Cleaners, so how did this happen; I knew better than to pursue the issue. This is but one incident.

My parents always mentioned how they had difficulty getting out of our couch sets, so one day, thinking about replacing them I had looked inside and low and behold these custom-made couches and chair were made with an old mattress which had little zippers everywhere where things could be hid inside the mattress. It totally freaked me out!

He had refused for years to replace these couches and I began to think this was why. He was always so proud of these couches that had been custom made for him by Sandy's furniture. I know very little about couch making, but I am certain they do not stuff them this way. The funny thing is, I think these mattress innards were added while we were on Saber Road, our first house here that we owned here in British Columbia, because in my mind they did not sink down as much as they had previously. Whose mattress was it? Where did it come from? He said we never had it reupholstered and this fits with my recollection as well.

Having it stuffed in this manner with zippers must have been for some illegal purpose and I have absolutely no tolerance for illegal activities and want no part of it. When I questioned him on it, he said that I should not be bothered by it, that's how it was made. One might think that this too is part of my delusion; however, I showed them to my sisters. Was this just in my head? Our niece now possesses them and they still haunt me. I do not speak of them to anyone for fear they will think negatively about me.

George has not always been a patient man and often lost his temper at the beginning of our marriage. He would not tolerate any expression of jealousy on my part. Moreover, after the girls were born, he would storm out of the house during any disagreement. It appeared that being newly married and having a family was difficult for him.

We had moved several times in our marriage. First we lived in North Dakota, then back to Canada, specifically, Treble, Ontario when I had a complicated pregnancy. When I became pregnant with Darcy, we moved to Brampton and when he lost work and we had both Darcy and Jessica, he wanted to move back to British Columbia, even though I had been offered a permanent teaching position, at the school I was substituting at. He argues I was not offered a permanent position.

I was not opposed to adventures, so I agreed. Now I did not think about friends or anything. Although I like British Columbia, I miss having friends here. I thought I would be closer to my sisters-in-law and that George would have some friends, but no. I was fortunate that mom and dad were able to afford to come and visit every summer! Dad took us on all our summer trips. My parents never travelled together because they did not have a great marriage. They decided to stay together for the kids I guess.

When we moved to British Columbia, we lived in his mothers' condominium, then a rented house and later the home on Saber Road where we resided for a decade before moving to Gage Lane for three years and to the present house on Wade Avenue. George decided to have one of our cars driven to our new location by strangers. They wrecked the car in Lonsdale I think and we lost the crib and all our old tapes even the one George had made me.

The stress of that initial move from Ontario and the fact that we had no jobs at our destination affected George. One night while the girls were rooming in the same room in his mother's condo they had difficulty falling asleep because they were not used to sleeping together, anyhow, one night Darcy, who had bowel problems hadn't done Number two and George was getting mad. He was at the bathroom door and didn't want her to come out. We fought about it; he ranted, and left.

He always liked things, just so, which was the reason for Jessica's problems when she was young, because while I returned to work, Jessica was taken care of by George. Jessica is our youngest daughter. We have two. We sought professional help for her because frankly, I thought someone had molested her and I even thought it might have been George. Perhaps this was my paranoia talking. She woke up in the middle of the night one day and screamed while on the toilet, where she wiped herself furiously and was upset that she could not get herself dry enough. During meals, she would get extremely upset if the utensils or plates were not placed in a particular way. Her psychologist said that she did not show signs of being sexually abused, which was a great relief, but said that her obsessions were her way of dealing with George's need for preciseness. The psychologist gave Jessica a tape to listen to, to calm her, and taught to blow bubbles when she was worried or stressed about anything.

While living at his mother's condo I had applied to all the public schools because his sister, Paula, suggested I do. However, it was July and they had done all their hiring. I saw an ad in the newspaper for the Catholic Schools and discussed with George that perhaps I should apply because I taught under the Catholic system in Ontario. I did apply and was hired in 1991. For years I was the main breadwinner.

When the girls were young and we were living on Saber Road, they were goofing around George's truck and found a pack of cigarettes. Therefore, they cut out some pictures of themselves and placed them in his visor. They were scared to tell me because they knew I had no tolerance for smoking, they did however confide in me. When I brought it up with George, he said that it belonged to one of his customers who left it in his truck. He assured me that he was not smoking even though he reeked of it when he came home. This was because many of the people working in the shops he visited smoked.

All of a sudden, while living at Gage Lane, he no longer had that customer. I felt that he was going somewhere and showering or taking his clothes to the Dry Cleaners, because we seemed to accumulate so many blue and white hangers that appeared to have been spray-painted. I was the only one taking things to the cleaners, so I had no idea where these were coming from because my Dry Cleaner does not use coloured hangers. Well I have never seen the blue ones. His sister Paula would sometimes pass down some nice clothes, but even these were not on coloured hangers and those were the only two sources. This freaked me out so much, that when we moved to this present house I got rid of most extra hangers.

We had lived at Saber Road for ten years. When they built the houses behind us, I just could not stand it, so we began to look at other houses which I regret. I liked the house on Gage Lane, for its vaulted ceiling and view, as well as the price, but the house seemed too much for George, after a while. The only help he offered when unpacking was to flatten the boxes and put them in the garage. This was when I first lost the diamond in my wedding band.

This move was different from all the others. He spoke to the girls, and I of the stresses involved and yet we had been in much more stressful situations. I thought that it was affecting him, yet in the end, it was me. I thought it strange that he even brought it up.

While cleaning up his bathroom downstairs on Saber Road I noticed some brown stuff smudged around the bolt of the toilet on the left as you look at the toilet. I used our cleaner to try to clean it off but it would not come off. I thought it was hash or something. I also found some powder in the bathroom drawer under a piece of paper with a long toothpick. I stupidly tasted it. I wondered if it was cocaine but it could as easily been talcum powder. There was also the smudgy stuff in the cupboard on the bottom shelf.

What fed my delusion was George's reaction when after seeing our former family doctor who made me tell George. He wanted to know what cleaner I used, as if it mattered to him because he used the stuff. In addition, because I was so "manic" at the time, he tried to soothe me telling me, everything was going to be okay and he was used to bringing people down.

Prior to seeing the doctor, I had taken the Echinacea looking pills, which looked like dark brown honey or small pellets of pooh and smelled sweet, that I had found in his truck to a co-worker whose husband worked for CSIS. She said her husband would have to make a formal report to have them analyzed so I said forget it. I then took them to the local police department and they dismissed me without telling me whether I was mistaken.

While we were living on Saber Road, we would occasionally have visits from a friend of George's whose brothers and himself were into dealing drugs according to George. On one visit, apparently he propositioned George in getting involved with trafficking drugs implying that with all of George's trucking connections it might prove profitable. George told me he flatly refused. Since then we have not seen or heard of him. George believes it to be because George sold a car that he had given to him and subsequently sold, but sometimes I think it could be because George is involved, therefore, face-to-face communication has to stop. Awful thought, I know.

My illness (?) seems to have brought about a more tolerant, peaceful man. I can tell him things and he takes them in his stride. I have been very open with him since I have been told to check my reality through him. I wondered why he was not affectionate or receptive to affection because he does not seem to reach out for me in bed or for hugs during the day. He will hug back though when I go to hug him. I also said I thought that he might be seeking sexual gratification somewhere else because of his reactions to me being more sexually aroused. I felt like I was on some sex drug.

Once, while living on Gage Lane, I went to a sex shop to buy some things to make George more responsive and he was not interested in any of it. I bought some likable oils and some fancy lingerie but I remember I approached George the night before we were leaving for Leroche Lake and he turned me down. I was so hurt that the next day in the car I was very quiet. When we stopped at the grocery store he got very angry and called me a f'n bitch and a few other choice words. The time there was awkward in many ways.

He blew up at me because I could not give an answer fast enough as to which meats we should get. He shouted at me, and was angry that I was not being as good at conversation as he would have had me. I was scared. I had not seen him blow up like that since we were living in the States and he banged his fist on the table when I told him I was jealous of his secretary.

That whole summer was weird for me sexually. I thought that I was actually on some sort of drug. I was so oversexed that I phoned George to come home from work, which he did not. I also phoned my girlfriend about it and her suggestion was to masturbate. I did not but I was confused as to why I was feeling this way. It was not only me behaving oddly. He was hot and cold toward me.

Yet, still the memories of being told that I must have total trust, even if he were walking with a gorgeous blonde still press on my mind, since I am a jealous person.

Now, although I am told to have full disclosure with George, I find he does not see the same things I do. There is a saying that everyone has a double and perhaps everyone does. I know they do for Television and stunt doubles.

Although I believe it to be the incident with my daughter passing out that caused my demise. The following incidents could have also triggered my illness: the loss of my father which happened November 27th 2000, a hysterectomy I had to have because of precancerous cells or not being involved in the purchase of our second dog.

My youngest, Jessica, seems angry with me most times. Is it because of my illness (?)Alternatively, is it because she feels that she is not seen by me, whom she expects to know her inside and out? I recall so many uncomfortable situations while we were living on Gage Lane. I recall her coming to me while George was sitting beside me near the fireplace saying something like, you know me, don't you, not this stranger. In addition, she pointed to George.

I look at her and one day she has light brown hair longer bangs and problems with pimples, yet another day, her bangs are shorter, her hair darker and her complexion clear, then back it goes again another day.

Why do I focus in on her so much? I do because she seems so distant and we were so close before. She has every reason to be distant though. When she was younger and assessed by the child psychologist they said that she was very bright, in fact, gifted, and that we would have the tendency to talk to her like an adult and unfortunately when I felt things go sour with George while living at Gage Lane, I turned to her. She tried to help in her own sweet way and printed off some material on Feng Shui. I even went to her school and asked her counselor to watch over her. She somehow interpreted that or the fact that George arranged a visit for us to a marriage counselor as a sign that we were getting a divorce and phoned me at work in tears to ask me. I merely told her that it was up to her Dad. I was of little comfort.

Jessica was not the only one I turned to. I also spoke to Darcy while she was watching TV and she said that I should tell Grandma because she would pay for a private investigator

I notice Jessica's clothes, come and go; she lives at different places, that, I do believe because she has so many sleepovers. I guess it is like in the Bible when the father celebrates the return of his son who squandered all the money and left the fold. I just want her respect again. Then there is her not wanting to be touched or hugged and I recall how I thought that people would comfort another with a hug but do nothing to help. (I think I even mentioned while online during my Masters that that was the case.) I know I need her affection. Just as I need it from my husband, whom I feel is distant in that department unless it is the night to be intimate.

I believed there was a competition between hugs and taking action. While at school there was an incident where everyone was comforting the person with hugs but no one was helping. I felt that I needed someone, anyone to take action in my life. I needed someone to believe what I was going through with my husband.

So, where am I in search of my mind? I look at my eldest, Darcy, and I see differences there too. I fear that I may be losing it again. All the things that swarmed my mind and meant different things are creeping back into the forefront.

When I was at my weakest, we moved to this house on Wade Avenue and I could barely function. I could not decide what to wear because every colour had a hidden meaning. Hence, the same was true for the new couch set we have which replaces the haunting one that went to our niece. It comprised of a blue couch, a yellow chair and a red chair. I found myself surrounded by the colour, the very colours that were bothering me so I lay huddled on the wooden floor, which had no meaning at all. The couch set, though colourful, in retrospect was a poor purchase and impulsive. Jessica had said she liked the couch set in the store and George decided we should get it.

MY COLOUR-CODED LIFE

I could not read, watch television or listen to music, for everything had hidden meanings to me. I do not want to revisit that place in my mind again. I am not faltering on taking my medication because I also fear that awful ward in the hospital. Signing papers, the second time saying that I was being admitted involuntarily scared me, and attending a meeting there with a former student was embarrassing. Then, there was something surreal there; they let me have my needlepoint. It surprised me that they did, but I was gratified at the same time.

While there, there was a man on the top of the next building fiddling with what looked like camera equipment and he reminded me of what George used to look like. It was unnerving. A big part of my delusion believes that George is not the person I met in The Keg so many years ago. George has blue eyes and I feel that he should have brown eyes and curly hair. I wish he would grow his hair to prove it to me…but even if he did I probably would not be satisfied. The second time in the hospital was scary and I was even put in an observation room with a video camera…not really sure why, but I was able to go home every day, which was nice. I had to sleep there though. Honestly, I think they admitted me the second time because I had revealed how I felt about George. He scared me. Perhaps it was protection from him, who knows. George also said to me that if I was not nice he did not have to take me home for visits, so I had to make sure that I did not disagree with him.

The first trip to the hospital was more pleasant. The hospital had a ping-pong table, there was a patient that reminded me of what George should look like, and we played ping-pong together. I also played with George when he came to visit.

The medication though causing my depressing weight gain, grants me sleep at night, which I am thankful for.

As I unload and sort out my thoughts onto paper, I am reminded by the time I was sleeping at Gage Lane, our last house, and was woken by words spoken by my father "Bring George home". I was startled. I have never dreamt of my Dad, nor do I dwell on his loss, but it did appear as if he was trying to reach me somehow.

There is no doubt I was close to my Dad though. He loved to come and visit and always took and paid for all of our vacations each summer.

He was also, so proud, of how our girls helped their Dad when he fell off the ladder. He was instrumental in our lives and though he never had the opportunity of higher education, something I know he would have enjoyed, he instilled the need for higher education in us. It is through his gift after he died that afforded me the opportunity to obtain my Master of Arts in Education with a focus on Curriculum and Technology through the University of Phoenix. I know he would have been proud because he was so proud of all other accomplishments.

While living on Gage Lane, food had different meanings, so I had a hard time eating. I felt if I ate certain food that I had assigned to different family members that I would hurt someone's feelings.

I have struggled hard to swim to the surface and breathe again and in many ways I know that I am a survivor and so is George for that matter or whoever is living with me.

I find it odd that my sister-in-law showed me a family picture of George several months ago standing behind me while we were married and I did not recognize him. That was so weird to me. How could that have happened? I have expressed all these thoughts and many more concerns to him and he has taken them in his stride as if distanced from it. He has survived all that has been concerning me. Is this what happens to a mind when filled with so many hidden fears? I am told, no, only to minds that have a predisposition to falling apart.

Through all these struggles to the surface, our girls are struggling with theirs. As I hope for them to look to me as a role model, I fear that I have let them down. Through it all though I hope they know how very proud I am of them…we both are.

My next appointment is on Thursday, and I wonder whether I should wait until then. I should have phoned today…Is it the stress of Report Cards and Christmas Concert that has me so uncomfortable or is it bigger than that?

2008

Wednesday, January 2, 2008

Well my appointment with Doctor Argle has come and gone. I unloaded my thoughts of not being sure who was who and why? In an effort to enjoy my vacation, she gave me some "as needed" extra Seroquel, which I did take, but to no avail. It did not seem to work, anyway I see her tomorrow.

One day I admitted to George that I was seeing certain things and many things were coming to the forefront again, like his lack of memory for things. He told me, one of my problems before was staring at people. I said I did not think I was staring at anyone. I was surprised because the only one who had complained that I was staring at them was George.

While on the return flight back from Mexico, we watched Ratatouille again. To me, it seemed we were watching a different version since some of the scenes were different. However, I never said a word to anyone. It seemed to me that a message was being sent to me that I should do more cooking at home. In addition, it brought back a memory of how my Dad used to call us his little petootee. With this, it strengthened the idea in my head that someone was trying to find the true me; that somehow, someone was posing as me and I was being sent messages to trigger the past and to gain information about various things, a very classic schizophrenic action or belief. I cannot deny this.

As much as I fear being schizoaffective which my diagnosis is, I feel this has been thrust upon me for a greater purpose. Messages are often sent in bizarre ways in code sometime, and certain people may be more sensitive to these. Watching the movie and a presentation on purple rain helped bring back and cloud my thoughts again. The presentation of a man with a floppy cape reminded me of George with his open shirts and the black and white umbrella stood for how I had expressed that things were always black and white with George, and that this black and white umbrella was keeping me from the purple rain. *Although I do not remember what all the colours and food stood for before, I will try:*

- † Black and White- represented George's negative characteristics.
- † Green – represented my Dad and actions being taken against George and his criminal activities.
- † Yellow – represented Darcy and my music.
- † Red – represented Jessica and caring.
- † Royal Blue – represented my Mother and my dream of opening an online school.
- † Tan – represented my thinking that George was not interested in me.
- † Grey – represented my staying married to George.
- † Pink – represented me because it was my favourite colour
- † Purple – represented the Catholic Church. They wanted me to have a miracle cure.
- † Fine/Good-points were gained by responses. At first everyone said good in response to "how are you" then when I was grocery shopping with Darcy one day I remembered how Chief Dan George said "Fine" in his book…then "fine" was added to the equation.
- † Hello/Hi-points were gained somehow by these responses too. Fancy George would often announce his entry by shouting, "Hello" when he entered the house..
- † Water- represented religion and I wrote about how my favourite song was Water! Bring me Water by Shania Twain during my online courses. The words just expressed everything.

MY COLOUR-CODED LIFE

† *Cows meant something but I don't remember what. George's story of being chased up a tree by a cow and dairy I guess.*
† *The colour messages on the TV and in the stores, medical offices and street give me hope, make me feel like I have friends and there is hope. Even on the turbans worn by those whom I think are East Indian. They make me feel strong and more confident. He kept isolating me from people and friends.*
† *In my mind there was a competition between Starbucks and Tim Hortons. Dad stood for Tim Hortons and George stood for Starbucks. It started when Dad wanted me to take a picture of him under the Tim Hortons sign. I always thought that was odd.*

What I do remember is that somehow I was to come into some money and people wanted me to spend it on different things. Jessica (Red) wanted me to give it to charity, Darcy (yellow) felt I should spend it on getting my songs recorded, Mom (blue) felt I should spend it on getting my idea for an online school off the ground. George also wanted a cabin on a lake but I kept getting ideas that said I would be lonely living on a lake with George. These colours and purple are what really affect me. Purple stood for the school I taught at and Religion. Over time I believed that if I just believed that purple would let all my dreams come true, then, I didn't have to choose between them. However I don't believe God intended the Catholic Church to be the way it is. I feel that I am on a journey to hopefully change the Church as well. There is only one Pope and no superior for any other church, like Anglican or United, which means to me maybe there is only one faith and that is Catholic and we are already united.
What you must understand is that no one verbally said where they wanted this sum of money to go. It was all in my head.
   Over time I realized it was me that desperately wanted a place on a lake to hand down but just not with George. I dream of it being on Lake Muskoka.

With all the colours and food representing different things, I had difficulty dressing myself and eating. It would take forever when I was at my worst to make a decision thinking that I would hurt someone by my choice.

Therefore, unlike all the schizophrenics mentioned in the news and on television, none of my thoughts are so out there to cause me to do harm to anyone. Moreover, let me tell you, watching such shows, as Criminal Minds was very difficult when I was able to watch television again, for as TV utilizes stereotyping, they always had scenarios of schizophrenic paranoid people being the bad person. Like Spencer's mother needing to be institutionalized. People just like me, apparently. I honestly think that TV writers should seriously think about what they air if they want to break the stigma of Mental Illness. Now (2015) I watch Criminal Minds to see if it's changed because I like the idea of the show. I think they should focus on criminals that are more sophisticated like white collar crime.

Though it appears that Jessica is supportive of George and is closer to him, I think in some way that she is allied with Darcy and they are both trying to get at the bottom of this. As much as I think, he is trying to make me out to be paranoid/ill. It is he/ his (twin) who is trying to protect me by having me appear schizophrenic. Wednesday, September 14, 2016 I now believe that all The Georges I see that are acting as my husband are bad.

Darcy is an angel through all of this. She has stuck by me and answers any queries I may have. She does not seem bothered by my emotions at all. They seem to have no effect on her.

Wednesday, January 8, 2008

I went to see my psychiatrist on January 3 and expressed everything that has been happening. She suggested I take a "time out" and visit ECE. ECE is an emergency short stay residential treatment centre for psychiatric patients in crisis. I spoke to a social worker at her office, Becky, who set up the visit. I stayed on a voluntary basis. Scott drove me there and I stayed Thursday and Friday night January 3 and 4th. I was overwhelmed and needed to ensure that I could discharge myself. I was not keen on going because it was Jessica's birthday but Dr. Argle has assured me that Jessica would be happier that I was taking care of myself. I am not so sure. I texted her Happy Birthday when I was there but never got a reply. I think she was angry. It appeared that many of the people there were new and most were smokers, or at least appeared that way. Smoking was allowed in the back and must have wafted into the room they first had me in. The nurse was kind enough to transfer me into a much fresher room (room 9).

I attended the "talking" session Friday on anxiety and was pulled out to meet with Dr. Teagen. He really did not have much to say but did ask questions that other doctors had not. When I mentioned that my husband thought perhaps I needed a change in medication, he upped it. It appeared that it was to satisfy my husband in some way.

When I mentioned this to my mother, she was a little miffed that George would have a say in this matter. Anyhow anyone I had spoken to (friends and family) seemed to think that I sounded in control of my situation and very lucid. In fact, my husband was surprised that I had agreed to go to this place; he had not found anything wrong with me, even though I had admitted to him that many things were coming back.

(My first sign that I was slipping was when the children were lining up in the hallway for the school Christmas Concert dress rehearsal. They were dressed in black and white and somehow I felt the colours stood out to me more than they should have.)

While there, at ECE, I suggested to George that he take me out to dinner on Friday. He thought it was a wonderful idea. He came to pick me up at 5:00 p.m. and to my surprise, Darcy was with him. I was so happy she was there! We stayed out until 7:00 p.m., and then I returned to ECE. When I returned, the door was locked and I had to wait for someone to let me in. I noticed that this did not happen with any other person there.

On Thursday night they gave me 250 mg Seroquel, after seeing the Doctor I was given 300mg that night. When I said I was ready to be discharged, Emilie suggested I leave and see how it goes for the day (Saturday) at home. During our conversation, I had mentioned that I saw my former caseworker, Eva and that I got along well with her. Anyhow, she said that she would be working Saturday during the evening shift. Shift change is at 3:00 p.m. Emilie thought that at this time, I could have a nice chat with Eva.

On my way to ECE, around 7:30 p.m., after the whole day at home and having lunch at the local Japanese restaurant with George, I decided that I would discharge myself. When we arrived at ECE, again the door was locked. I had expected Eva to want to chat with me, but she appeared nervous. George introduced himself to her, which I thought was odd because he had met her before in our living room, and I said as much.

Eva quickly guided me to the nurses' board and showed me who would be my nurse. I told Eva that I had planned to leave. All of a sudden, my nurse appeared (and she smelled of smoke.-yuck!) Eva said that I was more organized now and more aware and that I was leaving. Eva told me she would get things ready while I gathered my things from the room. When I returned, she had me sign the form and gave me all my pills. She asked me if I was seeing my doctor and I said that there had not been an appointment made, so she said to phone Jemma and request an appointment with Dr. Argle for Thursday. She said to tell Doctor Argle about my stay and how I felt about the "as needed" drugs.

I phoned on the Monday to book an appointment. Jemma confirmed an appointment for January 10 at 2:00 p.m.

During the weekend, George downloaded all the pictures from the Hawaii and Mexico trip to Darcy's computer. (According to Jessica, Darcy had already downloaded them two weeks ago) I digress. After he downloaded them to her laptop, we watched them. He printed one picture of us in Hawaii, apparently of the two of us, but let me tell you, the picture looks airbrushed. I have never had a tan like that! Anyhow, we viewed the pictures of Mexico and I saw that there were two pictures that really stood out. George had wanted me to lean over the stone that indicated Villa 71, when I asked why, when our villa was 72. (In fact, our room with two separate double beds was room 7212 and that the girls adjoining room was 7211.) He said because it gave a better view. When I said we should take a picture of the other one too. He said it was unnecessary. However, when we viewed the pictures in a slide show, low and behold there is one of me apparently leaning over the stone indicating Villa 72.

Now, a person cannot remember everything, granted, but I thought it odd at the time and thought it better to do the 72 one than the 71 one, but

I went along. This sticks in my mind. I am right! He wants me to think that I have forgotten. Why?

On the 11th we were to have our second Twinrix shot for Hepatitis A & B, however, I am to be at an all-day in-service regarding the FSA's, which are provincial exams given to grades four, seven, and ten, so I phoned the family doctor Monday, to change the appointment. The secretary said that he works on Monday at the clinic so we could go there. He did not start until 2:00 p.m., but we did go and get them done. While there, he asked me about my ECE visit and I told him a little about how I was feeling, even about the pictures. Anyhow, I thought it was nice that he inquired. (Tuesday, April 13, 2010 as I think about and read this I still think that maybe Twinrix was a sign that George has a double.)

George came home today and asked how I felt. I told him "a little confused". He asked me when my next appointment with Dr. Argle is and he wanted me to ensure that I told her about the pictures that made me uncomfortable.

What is going on?

Except for Eva (whom was a little off) everyone acts as if everything is normal.

When we were last at the family doctor's office George asked for some "assistive" medication, so our doctor recommended Levitra. Anyhow, today, while on vacation, I decided to read the directions and discovered that in addition to the one we had used, one had been torn off. When I asked him about it, he stared at me with no expression then suddenly, with amour in his eyes, he said he had one in his wallet, for a time when I might be in the mood and we were not at home. But we were not at home, so I do not put much credence into this answer.

The funny thing is he is supposed to stay away from grapefruits too. I find this so odd, when it is just grapefruits and no other citrus fruits. He used to call my breasts "grapefruits" – not "little Sarah's"! Every time I hear the name Sarah used on the TV, it reminds me how he grabbed them at Gage Lane while standing in the hallway and called them "little Sarah's".

Something is going on, but what I worry about is whether George has been playing this trick and splitting his life with someone else that looks like him for a very long time. Have I been going to bed with another man?

For how long has this been going on? Has he been taking advantage of me? Perhaps he calls them "Little Sarah's" because he has been given misinformation so I will know it is not the real George.

Now, are people getting back at him by seeing whether he can truly see the girls and me?

The other day, (yesterday) we were in Starbucks and I mentioned how they, ECE, asked me questions about when I had been admitted to the hospital. He said, like them, that I had lost some of my short-term memory. Perhaps, I just categorize what I will remember. Somehow, we got onto the subject of his mother and the time she stayed at our house convalescing after her surgery. He said I was wrong about the facts and said he did not want to play this memory game anymore. Clearly, either he is losing it, or is someone else.

Another thing that is bothering me recently is the amount of times my mother is calling. It is annoying, especially when she ends her conversations by saying "Good Luck". Today I told her it really bothers me and I would like her to stop. It is as if I have something to win. She never used to say that, why has she started?

Wednesday, January 9, 2008

Monday night I was kept awake from excruciating pains in my left leg. I had already been experiencing pain before. It was so bad Tuesday morning that I took one of the Methoxisal pills that Dr. Twill had prescribed for me when I injured my back previously. It worked like a charm. Last night I took 300 mg of Seroquel and had a fantastic sleep, my legs ached though when I awoke. Thankfully, the pain is easing as the day is wearing on.

When I got out of bed and came upstairs, George was still in his slippers, and I noticed that he was shorter than I was.

This morning Jemma phoned to confer. Oddly the call display on my phone said unknown name and number. We talked and I told her about the pictures, Levitra and finding him shorter than I was.

A few weeks ago, Jessica received her renewal for car insurance. What I found odd was that it said something like; when not in use at 6791, our home on Wade Avenue, it is downtown. I asked George about this and he said they just want to cover their bases. Does he think I am stupid?

My mother called after dinner and again, wished me luck! When I was at the height of whatever is going on, in addition to not being able to read, listen to music, or watch TV, I could not use the computer, talk on the phone, or play my guitar. I began to doubt that the people on the phone were actually who they claim to be.

Technology is really advanced and it would not take much for someone to tape someone's voice inflections and have some gizmo attached to someone's throat and have the voice sound like the actual person. A sci-fi notion and likely did not / is not happening, but I bet technology could do that.

Last night I asked Darcy to print the pictures in question, but one of them was different from what George and I viewed in the video show, nonetheless it helps ground me to realize things are not right. After a little frustration, they were printed with George's help.

In addition, when Jessica came home from Chambray's, one of her friends, she had bags of clothing and she was not too pleased that I saw her, though she said nothing. I've known about this clothing thing for quite a while.

This morning while vacuuming, I discovered a reserved parking tag for Jessica for during the week from 8:00 a.m-3:00 p.m. I doubt very much that they supply her with this for parking at the church beside her high school. I could be wrong though.

I also recall a phone call to Darcy from George one day a few years back where he was talking about her people and me. *I had no idea what that meant?*

Of interest, as well, was the phone call we received during the night while in Mexico. A man called regarding suntan lotion. Apparently, there was another George and Megan at the resort. Well that just sort of jives with everything I was thinking? It did nothing to ease my thinking.

Thursday, January 10, 2008

Yesterday George got home about 2:00 p.m. and he had spent a couple of hours at the cabin before coming home. When he walked in the door, he suggested we go out for coffee. He asked me which Starbucks I wanted to go to and I said the one by Chapters. We ended staying several hours because once again we ran into Marilyn. I had taught her boys. She was with her daughter-in-law, Carly. I have not seen her in years and lately we run into each other a lot. Darren also walked into the coffee shop and I waved at him. He came over for a brief moment and then left. He was waiting for his daughter. His wife teaches kindergarten and I taught several of their children.

I had phoned my brother the other day and left him a message regarding the usage of another card for purchases via the computer. We had GM Visa for years that we did not use, but had accumulated many points on the card. I phoned and they suggested I switch to the Gold Travel Card, which I did and they would waive what we owed on the GM Visa. I told this to George, but he paid for the GM Visa anyway, so now, we have a credit on the card that he wishes me to cancel and around 200.00 dollars toward travel. I feel it silly to cancel when we have dollars that we can use toward travel. As the girl said, use the travel points than cancel the card. I will ask George what he wants to do. In 2015 I was rereading my book and noticed multiple changes. I believe that someone was altering my book. I do not recall any phone call about the GM Visa. However I remember this happening to my brother with another credit card and he coming to visit Louise and I to use his points.

My brother told me I did not need it. I did not cancel the card! I rely on him a lot because George comes up with some adventurous ideas that I sometimes worry about. The latest was selling this house and purchasing five more; renting out four.

We went shopping after dinner to get more of the ingredients to make more muffins using his recipe. The funny part was when we bought more yogurts. I was looking for more Blackberry and Blueberry, which is what we bought and used the other day to make the muffins. He wanted me to choose the strawberry because he said he would not like the Blueberry and Blackberry. That struck me as odd, since he knew what we previously bought and used them. We ended up with the strawberry because they had no more of the other; however, we still have some in the fridge that I could use.

Last night when Darcy came home, I had to tell her to make changes on her Facebook page that we were made aware of. She thought her Dad hacked into her account and did not believe me that someone had told us.

In addition, Darcy is taller than I am today. Last night we were out visiting George's sister and brother-in-law and it was nice to just sit and chat. Sometimes I think, maybe it is all in my head, but then, I have tangible proof; the pictures.

This morning taking a good look at Darcy, I see that it is her and her hair does not look as dark.

Wouldn't it be terrible if a person were able to pull off having someone look just like them and be able to fool family and friends for years? With all that has happened to me, I admit my mind goes in many directions. Sometimes I think that this has happened to make me aware of the differences and that this gathering of information from me is disguised as something else. There were times when I thought I was being protected and a part of some governmental study. I repeat I thought that perhaps the University of Phoenix through whom I got my Masters completely online was doing it and the result of something I had signed up for inadvertently. These thoughts could definitely be classified as schizophrenic thoughts I guess, paranoid at the very least.

Yesterday, I was reminiscing over the time when George fell off the ladder while cleaning the second story windows at Saber Road. I was not there, but I was told everything that had happened. It still surprises me where he landed considering the position of the ladder. It is also interesting how I do not remember the roof being broken where he fell through. He also had no broken bones or problems with his arms.

Of note, on Gage Lane, his right arm could not straighten above his head; he explained that this was a result of his fall that crushed one of his vertebrae. However, when I asked him the other day to show me he had no problem. I noticed a few days ago he used his right arm to grab onto his right to stretch.

The impairment that he had on Gage Lane would have been present while living on Saber Road, yet it was not a problem.

On the last couple of episodes of Criminal Minds, they have coined the phrase of their work being "victimology" and proceed to outline what the room of a certain person portrays; then I think of the girls' rooms that I painted while they were at camp. Darcy's I painted green and white and Jessica's was blue and white. Plus I had George install new white wire closet systems in their closets. Darcy's favourite colour used to be green and Jessica's was blue.

Now George wants me to bring this to Dr. Argle's attention today. Why?

Tomorrow Friday, I am supposed to attend an FSA in-service. It is interesting that now parts of the test are being done through the computer. I remember mentioning in my courses that that would be a useful way.

Friday, January 11, 2008

Yesterday I had a lengthy session at 2:00 p.m. with Dr. Argle. Jemma also attended the meeting. We discussed the pictures that I had printed off and they really did not show anything. It was the same picture that George had taken twice, one in nighttime mode. I do remember this…but as I said before this picture was not printed from the folder that George had downloaded in my presence and saved under the title Grand Bahai Principe. If he had not labeled it that, it would have been labeled with the day's date that it was downloaded. When we printed it, she said we had labeled it with December 2007. This is incorrect because I had suggested that that be added so we would remember when, but George did not want to do this. I am certain there was one of me leaning over the Villa 72 sign. Now, of course, I doubt myself and perhaps my eyes were playing tricks on me. However, I also remember George getting a text message from Jessica at the same time, so maybe I need to check her picture folder. Now George was saying it has something to do with it being saved in two different places on Darcy's computer but the URL stated where it would be located and I am sure it was to be in My Pictures.

We discussed many things and I told her that I cannot deny that things are resurfacing and mentioned the relationship between looking at pictures of Darcy and then listening to a song on the radio "You and I were meant to fly"" in George's car as we went for coffee. It felt like there was this connection between her and I through the music but it was not the same vibes when we were physically together.

Overall, we concluded that it would be best for me not to go back to school for a while. Since I was a little intimidated about Duncan Mental Health contacting my employer, I chose to have our doctor write a note for me to fax in. I raced up there around 3:30 p.m. because he does not work Friday's. The note reads, "Ms. Hall is unable to work due to medical illness. She will be re-assessed in three months."

As suggested by Dr. Argle, I have continued with 300 mg of Seroquel last night and will take the same amount tonight. Saturday I will up the dose to 350 mg.

However, I have been experiencing pain in my knees, more so in my left knee. In addition, as mentioned before after my work out the pain all through my left leg was terrible which precipitated my taking Methoxisal. Well, again, last night in bed the pain began again. As a result, I got out of bed at 7:30 a.m., so that I could move about. If I were a bigger woman, I would have pulled the railing out of the wall; that is how much I was relying on it to pull myself upstairs. It resulted in my having to take another Methoxisal at 9:20 a.m.

George and I went to Whittle Head for coffee and then walked out to the end of the wharf. My leg loosened up a bit, but I am not getting the same relief that I had the other day. I think that our doctor will be seeing me again in the near future regarding this,

I phoned Jemma regarding what I should do about my leg. She suggested going to the clinic, so I did. The doctor said it was not neurological and to take a couple of Advil which is what George had suggested. When I got home around **4:30-5:00 p.m.,** I took two Advil. My leg felt better after the tea that George made. Usually, I make the tea, but since I was aching, he did.

The pain began to localize and felt like a muscle pain from my outer hip to my knee and then my knee and ankle were aching. Something is up, only I do not know what.

While at the clinic, there was a small pair of mittens sitting on the ledge. I reminisced again about the time George fell off the ladder and Jessica had placed her mittens underneath her Dad's bleeding head. When I went to see him at the hospital, he was lying on a board with his head braced on both sides. Funny though I do not remember any wounds or bumps on his head when he came home and he was not in the hospital very long, from what I recall.

Saturday, January 12, 2008

I had hopes of going to the Weight Watchers meeting at 8:00 a.m. this morning but neglected to have George set the alarm. I did not get up until after 9:00 a.m. I prefer to go to morning meetings than evening meetings and being weighed after a full day of absorbing food…looks like I might be joining online after all.

This morning George asked me what I wanted to do, so I mentioned that it would be nice to go to Gaivota Island. For lunch, we went to Bugle House. We had been there before, he thinks it was one-2 months ago and I remember it being in the summer time or maybe September, October. When we left, he still asked me if I wanted to go to Gaivota or if I had another idea. Seems I have to dictate the day. How fun.

While at Gaivota, we stopped in the hat store and I picked up a hat, he almost picked up another for himself, but did not. I saw some fantastic native paintings but did not buy them, instead I bought a set of four soft-boiled cups that came with spoons and he bought me some Maple butter.

On our way home Darcy called, just as I was thinking that I should check Jessica's picture folder, and said that the lights went out at the cabin because they had blown a fuse. They were cooking corn dogs in the microwave and when her male friend went to turn the light in the bathroom on the fuse blew. He told her what to do. However, there I was making some connection to corn, which to me somehow relates to the school. This memory seems flawed to me as I never recall Darcy spending time at the cabin with a boy. I believe this was another alteration.

At about 3:00 p.m. we stopped at Esquires near our house. We got into the conversation regarding my sister, Louise, and when she was diagnosed with Bi Polar and was at the hospital. I thought it was while we were living at Gage Lane, but I was way off. (I checked with her when we came home) it was while we were living at Saber Road. That makes sense to me now because she was diagnosed with it before she came to take care of the kids when I had the hysterectomy in 2000, and she already had all her specific pills when she came to visit us at Gage Lane. I remember phoning her house when she left because she left her pill pack at our house with some pills left in it. Gabe answered, asked her about it and they were not necessary pills, so I need not worry.

However, what was most strange about our afternoon together is the following. First, this morning when he was suggesting Bugle House for lunch, he had said, "**apparently** we had liked it". I didn't question him on his phrasing because he would have some excuse for it, but these Freudian slips often do make sense and this word leads me to believe that he had been told this information. Second, while we were in Esquires and we spoke about **Riverview**, he said it was for the criminally insane and that he was not sure it existed anymore. Well we have driven past it several times over the years and there is controversy (discussion) as to whether to reopen it. I know that if I had been taken there. I would have been really scared! Therefore, he, George or one of them anyways knows that the building still exists. Third, during our drive home, I was saying something regarding Jessica and then **Mama Mia** played on the radio. (This is significant because Jessica used to call me mama.) Just like the strange connection, I was feeling with Darcy. However, in reality Jessica wants nothing to do with me most times. In addition, when I spoke of the boats to George and how that was the first time I had seen that part of Gaivota. The last thing that I was surprised at is that he wanted to go out at all today, because yesterday he did not want to go out to lunch because we had to watch our P's and Q's. For those of you not familiar with the term, it means we had to watch our money.

Now just look at how I am nit picking everything I hear and see.

I had been bothering George about making his Bran muffins and the other day he piped up that we should make them together. Well, I have already told you about the yogurt incident. Well, today while we were in the kitchen store where I found the egg cups he was drawn to the muffin tins. I told him I like what we have; afterwards he wanted to go grocery shopping for specific ingredients to make the muffins again. I find this strange. In addition, I woke up one morning and both he and I remarked on how several of the **muffins** were missing. I was certain Jessica had taken them. However, today, when George asked her she said she did not like muffins.

Yes, Jessica also does not like chocolate though Nutella is being eaten here "supposedly by her" like it is going out of style. When she was small, she began to dislike chocolate and preferred that the Easter Bunny bring her candy so I always did.

I used to be disturbed by the missing dishes and glasses at our place on Gage Lane. Well now, George has noticed it too; **three** *missing bowls,* **3** *missing bread plates and* **2** *dinner plates…enough to set up another roost. The kids know how I feel about missing dishes so I am certain they would tell me if they got broken. Where are they?*

Jessica for the longest time has said that her favourite street where we live is PRINCESS. Is that somehow related to Darcy's black sweatshirt that went missing on Saber Road that had PRINCESS written across the front in red letters or am I just making that connection in my head?

George always said that she must have left it at one of her friends' house. Well, Darcy and I always doubted that because she really did not have that many friends back then that she visited and so it was not hard to check and she came up empty.

At 6:30 p.m. Jessica is telling George that she and Leslie, her girlfriend, were going out for Sushi. George asks if they would like to go bowling. Jessica said that with some advance notice she would go, when he mentioned maybe the four of us could go she said, "No way, not a family thing."

When I go over my conversation with Dr. Argle regarding personal care, I had never thought that it could get to the point for someone where they were unable to shower because they thought that it was a part of their "reality show" or whatever. I do remember however, that I in some strange way thought hair and makeup were a part of some point system, as was saying Fine or Good in response to the phrase **"How are you?"** I used to have trouble responding because of it and this has slowly crept in again.

I sometimes think that people are asking only to trip me up…but that is so silly.

I recall how in 2005, when the present grade 7's were in grade 4 that during the student –led conference, one of my students, had made a note for his Mom with the same phrase with Fine or Good as the answer and she checked **Fine**. *In addition, this same student drew a picture of a man sleeping at the back of the church and a woman praying in the front pew with a computer on the bench behind her. Somehow, I felt this was depicting my husband and I.*

One day while in the computer lab I recall another student saying to his neighbour **"remember it doesn't matter what they say, it's the points"**, *again, I related this to all the words. Understandably, he could have been referring to something else, but this is how I interpreted it.*

Now, all this information has never left my memory bank, this is just the first time I have put it into print. Most of it I have spoken about over time with Dr. Farsi and Dr. Argle.

Sunday, January 13, 2008

Last night I took my recommended dosage of 350 mg of Seroquel, but I am still noticing and doubting certain things that I am seeing.

This morning George played some of our old home movies. However, I saw our trip to Disneyland, our Kinter Valley trip and Tofino as well as Kevin's visit recorded for the same summer 1996. Kevin is George's cousin. George said that it said the year 2000 for our trip to Disneyland, but this is not right because Dad's last trip out here was that summer, just before he died. He turned eighty-eight years old and I had given him a song I wrote for him thanking him for everything he had ever done for me. I do not recall on going on a major trip that summer. As I reread this journal entry I do not recall watching any movies. I do not remember George taking any videos and I was not able to find the video recorder my mother bought us. I believe this was another alteration.

After lunch, we went on a hike with Kaiser. We went to Elgin Park. We have never gone there before. It was nice. Unfortunately, the Historic Stoneville House was closed. I have never been there either.

Tuesday, January 15, 2008

Yesterday he asked me what I wanted to do, so I told him that I wanted to go to a wool shop in Saguenay, a wool shop we had gone to when we lived on Saber Road. George did not remember it when we got there. Anyway, I wanted to check what kind of classes they have and decided to sign up for one, for something to do during the week.

Yesterday Jessica opened her mail from UNBC, University of Northern British Columbia. She was all excited and showed it to George and Darcy. George then asked if she had shared the news with me. I said no, but she did with Darcy. He proceeded to tell me, so I went to congratulate her. She was all angry and told me that she had been accepted a couple of weeks ago. I told this to George and his facial expressions were those of confusion.

This morning Jessica was making her lunch and low and behold, she packed **a bran muffin**. George was downstairs and I sure was not going to bring the subject up. The funny thing is I do not think she is lying.

I went to see our family doctor regarding the pain in my left leg. He sent me for blood work and x-rays of my knee and ankle and gave me a prescription for Celebrex. He also gave me a prescription for Pensaid when I saw him at the clinic, the day we got our Twinrix shot. I have not filled them yet because I would rather know what the results of the test reveal. Of note I use to break words up so Pensaid meant pen said and Twinrix meant twin Georges.

Our doctor also said that my pain could be a result of my increase in weight and that I need to lose weight. Well at 154 Lbs., I fully agree with him. I am 9 pounds heavier than I was the last time I joined Weight Watchers.

Due to my inability to get my act together to go to the Weight Watchers meeting, I finally decided to go the ONLINE route and signed up yesterday. I had to cancel though because they did not honour Lifetime Members.

I took the IRP's (British Columbia's Curriculum Guides) to school and met with Jocelyn and Carolyn. Apparently, they had a staff meeting regarding me that very morning. I found that interesting.

I was given two more gifts from the students, one was a box of chocolates and the other was a second gift from a student, who had already given me one. It was a Christmas tree ornament of an Angel with the word Faith on it. I somehow feel that this is another message to me to have 'faith" that all will turn out well. On that note, I am optimistic.

When Carolyn said I was so advanced and had received some very special training, I do not think that anything I did in Social Studies with the computer is beyond her means and when I offered to help her with it, she did not seem interested.

I did offer to them that I would do some marking for them…perhaps that is not a wise idea. I do not know.

During dinner, I told everyone that I had joined Weight Watcher's Online. George and I got to talking how thin I got. I told him I remember people remarking about it. He said there was a movie from when we were living at Gage Lane that shows how slim I was and he wanted to show it to me.

This particular film was made for a contest where they were looking for big spaces to renovate. I really did not look that thin in the film and true to form, I began to doubt whether it was me. However, I do remember making this film for the contest. They really wanted the whole family in it, but George said it would not matter; even he did not really want to participate in it, he only wanted to film. Therefore, I was the main character and Kaiser joined occasionally. Part of my delusion believed that people were renovating our house on Gage Lane for me.

Tonight Jessica asked George to deposit her cheque from Ocean Spray and then write her a cheque in that amount so that she could go snowboarding with her class to Whistler (5 times). I questioned him on the date of the cheque and he said it was for the pay period ending October 20, 2007. I said that that was odd because she has not been working at all since September. He said that obviously I was wrong.

Wednesday, January 16, 2008

This morning I am going to the 10:30 a.m. Yoga class at Cowichan Aquatic Centre, a local recreation centre.

As I think back to the film George showed me yesterday I am wondering why we have it. We hand delivered that to a place downtown. **How is it that we have the tape? We did not make a copy.** We never heard from the people regarding our submission and I never saw the show on TV either.

I am almost getting myself excited. Is it possible that they are doing major renovations inside to make the house more suitable? Did we in fact not really sell the house, but these people are making technological and structural changes to it and it is just taking many years to get it completed?

I remember when we were living there that Jessica suggested the B&B I wanted to open be named **"Megan's Point of View"** because of the view of the place. The B&B idea dissipated because I had different ideas as to how it should look. George did not like my ideas and we could not agree hence no B&B. Plus the city had certain laws regarding how many individuals you could host at one time. I wanted to follow the laws, but George said we could have more than allowed.

These may just be thoughts of grandeur. *Nevertheless, I remember that I used to think that there was some sort of competition between my School and George that the girls were supporting. Plain Cheerios supported George, which Jessica supported and Honey nut Cheerios represented the school because of the honey, as did Plum Sauce, which Darcy supported. I felt like there were people who wanted the money spent on the school and others wanted it spent on our own family. When I was at school before I felt every time I mentioned George's name people walked in the opposite direction.*

At some point, I was receiving the message that if I opted to move to a cabin with George, that I would be isolated and lonely. Essentially, George wanted the cabin, Jessica wanted our Gage Lane house and Darcy wanted us to move to Tinsel Town. Wow, are these thoughts ever wild. I was spinning because I did not want to let anyone down. It was the same with the furniture when we moved to Wade Avenue. Each of the family members wanted money to go different places. The red chair stood for caring which Jessica represented; charity, the yellow chair was music, which Darcy represented and the blue couch represented the internet that MOM stood for. Our green leather couches which I had planned to buy and weren't an impulse buy directed by George as the other set was, represented my dad and action against George. I did not know who to support so I could not sit anywhere.

I began to think that one of the reasons that the boys (previous owners) took so long to move out of this house, Wade Avenue, was because they were setting up this house for secret monitoring. I also thought, especially since the man from Future Shop actually came here to set up the TV that we were being limited to what we could actually see. Perhaps that is why we never saw that show about decorating large spaces. The name of the show has slipped my memory bank.

I also felt that that was true with the stereo, especially the one in the Living room, since you cannot change stations and oddly enough George cannot show me how. So, I was restricted to listening to one station.

I asked George why we still had the tape that we made for the contest. He told me that we had to make a VHS tape out of it, which is why we still have the original. ..That makes sense to me.

Thursday, January 17, 2008

I gathered all the white and blue hangers in our closet, and I put them into the spare cupboard. There were plenty. I have no idea how many. I am slowly trying to buy proper plastic hangers for everyone, so this problem disappears.

I just came back from Dr. Argle and spoke about all the things that had caught my attention this week. Consequently, she has upped the dosage of Seroquel again. She suggests that I take 400 mg for four nights and 450 mg for 3 nights. I have been following her advice even though I do not like taking pills. I do not want someone to say to me later that the relapse was because you did not take your medication.

The last time I was in Chapters, I looked for books on Psychosis and there were none available at the store. I was also looking to see if there were any autobiographies regarding it. Perhaps I can tap into a new market, but I do not know who to contact regarding my writing a book about my experiences.

The other night George asked me if I had looked for any properties on Quesnel Lake. I had not at the time, but I started to. I found a remote one on Robertson Island near Charlotte City. We looked at it and he said it would be fun to go up there this weekend. Therefore, I phoned the people and got more specifics.

To get there by plane would take two hours. One would take Air Canada Jazz, which leaves the airport once a day and lands in Sandspit. The trip is two hours long. Then you have to take an airport limousine to Charlotte City, which is about $15.00 each. What was strange is that the flight there leaving this Friday would be $256.00 each and $175.00 return, whereas next week both the flight there and back is $175 each. I find it strange that it is cheaper next weekend over this weekend to get there.

Anyhow, George came home and said it is pointless to go since we do not have the money. Although some of his questions regarding garbage etc. make sense, and perhaps finding something closer to home would be better, I am tired of his having me look into these things and then bursting my bubble.

Since I had phoned the owners and spoke with the man I asked George to phone to say we were not going. He did not want to phone right away but I told him the man was expecting a call back when our arrangements were finalized. Moreover, I was afraid that he would make out that I had phoned because of my illness. As it was he did imply this when he told the man we could not afford it, but it was a pipedream of ours. I do not like it when he implies that it is my fault when he is the one who encourages me to look for a place. Now he is telling me not to bother.

He had a good ole conversation with the man on the subject too. Push comes to shove once again we are not taking a trip up the coast.

Wednesday, January 23, 2008

It has been almost a week that has gone by since I have written down anything in this journal, but that does not mean that things have totally disappeared either. As suggested after 4 days of taking 400 mg of Seroquel I began taking 450 mg Monday night. This morning I am finding it difficult to concentrate, even though I am drinking coffee. I feel as though I am coming off a general anesthetic.

A couple of times this week, I noticed a couple of things that were strange regarding my pills. First, I use one of those weekly containers for my pills. I just open the proper day and dump it into my hand. However, on Monday night when I went to take my pills I noticed one Seroquel tablet sitting in the open Sunday night box. I just do not see how one pill would not come out when I turned the box upside down. I have been so careful to take the right medication. A terrible thought went through my head, one of which I am ashamed to record, but I thought maybe someone had a narcotic made to look like my Seroquel pill. However, that is a paranoid thought; so, I just put the pill in with all the rest in my Seroquel bottle. On another day, when I went to take my pills, I think Tuesday night, I noticed that the Celexa pill for that night was missing. I had to grab another from the bottle. I find this so strange because I have been so careful with my medication. I also noticed that my Xenical was disappearing faster than I had used them, so I moved them. Maybe my thinking my Xenical is disappearing is all in my head, nevertheless, I still moved them. It is times like these that I would like hidden cameras to decipher whether I am making up these mishaps.

Darcy had her boyfriend over for the weekend. He, Carlos, stayed over, in another room, Sunday and Monday night. I feel no issue with them, but yesterday Jessica came home and asked if a boy was living in our house over the weekend. George answered that in fact there was. I found it odd that she would say this because to everyone else Jessica definitely was here the whole time and knew what was going on.

A few weeks ago, George and I were in Esquires by Dr. Argle' office. They often have pictures there that one can bid on. Robert Bateman called the print, In the Oak - The Great Horned Owl. George thought it would be cool to bid on it, so we did. As it turns out, ours was the winning bid. It was delivered Monday. It is not a real painting, or a limited print but it is a Robert Bateman. It is not my favourite picture of his but what it does remind me of is the owl my brother caught on Muskoka Lake in Bracebridge.

Carlos by the way appears to be a very nice person. What I admire is that he seems to like Darcy a lot. He cuddles her more than vice versa... that is something that is missing in my relationship. Seriously, George is more into cuddling with the dog.

What was disappointing was how both George and Jessica felt the need to show off in front of Carlos. George went too far and made himself look small and someone who is disrespectful to his wife. George is a person who laughs at everything. I, on the other hand, am fussy with what makes me laugh.

We were watching a show last night that surrounded the use of baseball bats and it reminded me how disturbed I was with how many kid **baseball bats** *we had. There was a small red plastic one, two normal size black plastic ones and a yellow and black foam coloured one plus a whiffle ball. What is odd is that I do not remember either of us playing baseball with the girls at all. I noticed them all while we were living on Gage Lane. The thought that George had a child out there that I knew nothing about crawled through my head. There is no point asking him about them because he would say that we used them with the girls and I just have forgotten.*

This past week, at the risk of repeating myself, I inquired about joining a painting class and previously I had inquired about a knitting course.

This morning I had wanted to go to Yoga, but unless this wonky feeling disappears, I will not be using the car.

On Saturday night some friends invited us to a pub night at the Pub. We had a great time. I was surprised that George wanted to leave at 9:00 p.m. He felt things were winding down because most people had stopped drinking. I did not quite understand his reasoning because I had been drinking Diet Cokes the whole night.

Yesterday I went to the school and delivered my vote on the Benefits package. While there I spoke about Georges arm with Bess, the secretary, and about what I was not able to do before with Tim, the principal. Informing him that it was I who noticed things were going wonky again. He smiled through our whole conversation, which made me wonder. I would have thought that people would react the same way as when someone is telling them they have cancer. Since most people have taken this lightly makes me think there is more to it then I realize…but what? In addition, if they are smiling then they must think I am involved in something interesting.

Even though I feel more comfortable here, it's still unnerving to be constantly wondering if George is an imposter or not. He tries to go out of his way for me that much is certain. However, I can't help but wonder whether it was indeed George whom I was with when we moved from Saber Road? If it wasn't George himself signing all the moving papers, then are they legal? I hope my assets are being protected.

One of the main reasons why I doubt George is who he says he is, is because I do not understand how one can be diagnosed with a crushed disc causing the impairment to his arm and then it not impair his ability to use his arm at all. I mean maybe exercise could take it away. I am not sure. He told me it was permanent.

(2015 Plus now I think it was planned that I meet George at the Keg in Tuckerville that night and I'm not sure but I think it began at my birth.)

Well, the fact of the matter is, I am either really sick or insightful and not sick at all. Yesterday, I worked at filling out the long-term disability papers and contacting the necessary people. Now Dr. Argle has her portion to fill out and the part that scares me the most is whether she thinks I am competent enough to endorse a cheque. Having financial responsibilities taken away from me is frightening. I would feel that I would have no say in anything and I would definitely feel disheartened, hurt, angry and even resentful, especially toward George, who would likely be given all responsibilities which he talked to Ben, Paula's lawyer friend about.

At the cost of about $16,000 we are having all the windows replaced here. In fact, some window guys came over last night to take the actual measurements. Some of our windows are bad because they leak.

I am definitely able to unload all my thoughts and feelings and are given pills to cope, I guess. It astounds me though that everything I say seems to be taken like a grain of salt. I guess nothing that I was concerned about matters, but it must.

Monday, March 24, 2008

It has been a long time since I have written anything down, perhaps that is because my brain has settled down. I am not sure.

I still wonder about George's couches that we had for years and wonder why George's niece and her husband never ask about why it is stuffed with old mattresses with zippers. Why does this only bother me? I am set against drugs and as I told George the other day when he said he thought that his friend stopped contacting him because he did not want to get him involved in his illegal affairs. I told George that I thought he was involved and that is why contact was stopped. I never brought up the couch again though because I did not want to get him mad.

Right now I am on 20 mg Citalopram, 300 mg Seroquel, and 50 mg Loxapine. Slowly the Seroquel is being phased out of my system. I am feeling less like there are "imposters" around playing the role of family members. (George, Darcy, Jessica)

I am so thankful that Darcy is accepting of me and still is willing to hug, as does George. However, he accepts hugs but does not give them. I do miss Jessica in my life though. She treats me like I have cooties and wants nothing to do with me.

Last night after celebrating Easter dinner here, both girls helped clean up. I am not certain whether Jessica was helpful to help me or just to look good to the rest of the Hall family, George is always chief cook and he prefers it that way. Even when the girls were small he wanted me to entertain and watch the kids whether it was in the kitchen or on the road. Because his sister Paula always feels so sorry for him, it makes me look bad. Little do they know how our family works?

Thankfully we were at home last night because George passed out in front of the fireplace before dessert…talk about not knowing your limit. He tried to disguise it, as being over tired, but it was very transparent to everyone that he had had too much.

On another note my principal wanted to start making plans for the rest of the year and asked how I was doing and what my plans were. Consequently, George went with me to meet Dr. Argle and discuss what should be done. It was decided that it was too soon to return to the classroom. When I emailed my principal with this news he sent me a lovely email stating that I will be missed and that I was an important part of the staff. This email made me feel much better about everything. I do not recall George accompanying me. I believe this is another alteration.

My next meeting with Dr. Argle is on April 3, my birthday, and I plan to discuss with her my idea of asking my principal about a webmaster position. When the present webmaster started he wanted one of the staff to take over the responsibility. I am thinking on asking my principal if it is possible to make it a paid position, that way I could work part time in the classroom and part time as the webmaster.

At this meeting she wants to talk further about my trip to Tinsel Town for a grade school reunion and to visit my Mom, my younger sister and her family, and my brother Sam and his family.

According to my recollection, I went and met my girlfriends Carly and Roxanne and stayed in a hotel with Mandy, I did not see the rest of the family so obviously there is something very strange going on. I am not ill. The master of my life and the writer helping me with this journal is telling what my other self is doing. Sometimes I am able to pick up on the differences and sometimes I am not because I can't remember clearly enough.

Saturday, March 29, 2008

At my last meeting with Dr. Argle, she told me about craft classes at a nearby studio that is sponsored by the FHA, Fraser Health Authority, so it is free. I attended the jewelry making class yesterday and made a bracelet, which I finished and a necklace, which I started. I was not really into it because most of the beads were kiddy beads. However, I am looking forward to the Mosaic and painting classes. 2015 they were a bust there was not enough direction in the classes.

Well, I have booked my flight to Tinsel Town. I leave on Thursday, April 24 and return Thursday, May 1. Mandy is not so swift on leaving Thursday but I need the breather before meeting everyone. It will be a little stressful knowing where to go and taking care of taxi fares. For these are things I have always relied on someone else. However, if everyone else can do it, so can I. I have to view it as a growing experience.

I spoke with Charlotte, my friend, the other day, a grade school friend and she seemed very happy that I was coming for the reunion.

Today George is at his younger sisters' tearing apart their kitchen. Darcy and I are going shopping.

2010

Tuesday, January 19, 2010

Well, it is over a year and somehow my mind and I have synchronized together. I returned to work in September 2008 as the Learning Resource teacher and resigned in June 2009 because I could not stand the position and there was no class position that I could have. I lasted the entire year without incident. No colours or paranoia to speak of; nothing seems to be jumping out at me and I have accepted George as George because he is who is living with me. However, I did have to take several days off work because the stress of going to work was too much. My medication has been reduced to 5 mg of Loxapine and I do not even take that regularly. It makes me wonder about my diagnosis and how to view everything I have experienced. Was it the switch from Seroquel to Loxapine that allowed reality to realign itself? Alternatively, was it like one of the nurses at the hospital said-menopause?

When I first started seeing all the doctors and given medication people kept telling me it is like having diabetes. I think it is more like someone who has been blessed.

I have to believe that I can carry on without medication to keep my head working. I plan to be medication free…so far that plan is working out. It was not what my psychiatrist believes but then again she is the one who changed my dosage from 10mg to 5mg…that is a good sign!

As much as I wonder about why George wants sexual gratification in bed when he barely reaches for me during the day, he has stuck by me through all this mess. I must admit if he only showed me some more affection during the day when we are at home, I would probably feel more interested. Oh well…Perhaps it is a catch 22 if he gave more, he would get more, who knows?

This year has been a major one for us though. Darcy got pregnant and now has a baby girl, Cassie, who is as cute as a button and Jessica has begun talking to me again…a little bit.

Thursday, January 21, 2010

Fancy today is my best friend Elizabeth's birthday and my confidante through my whole experience.

I went to see Doctor Argle today and things went very well. She asked me how it was going with my medication and I was honest. I told her that I had not been taking it religiously. When she pressed for more specifics, I told her about three times a week. So now she has told me to take the medication only as needed. Yippee! I am off the medication! To be honest I am a little scared though. Anyway now I have a follow-up appointment on February 4 with Jemma to discuss symptomology. They need George's input, so when I told him he either has to write down his thoughts of what he thinks signs of my slipping are or attend the meeting. He did neither.

George was a little worried when I told him that I now only take the pills when needed. On the other hand he knew what my goal was.

I feel like I have won something and to know its full control of my mind is elating. I do fear now that George will be watching me like a hawk and anything might set him off. I understand that he is the one who sees me the most, so Jemma and Dr. Argle rely on him but it is still unnerving. I wonder if they can decipher when it really is a symptom or something that just rubs George the wrong way.

I told Dr. Argle that I have plans to write a book about this whole experience and she was quite surprised, if not a little impressed, so was Jemma.

I asked for the dates for when I was admitted to the hospital. The first time was the end of March beginning of April in 2005 and then again in September of 2005. The first time we were still living at Gage Lane. We moved that summer. (2015 According to my memory this can't be right because I never spent my birthday in the hospital.)

I found it interesting that the first time I went to the hospital that I was able to play ping-pong etc., but the second time they really did their best job to scare the living day lights out of me. I was petrified! They took me in a wheelchair, which reminded me of the time I went into isolation when I was younger, and wheeled me down this dingy hallway. I was not allowed my purse this time but I managed to take some pictures out. However, why was I allowed to do my needlepoint? I thought my having something sharp they would have been afraid.

I also discussed with the doctor about how I thought it might have been hormones/menopause that played a key factor in what happened to me and she said that it could have been but wouldn't go so far as to say that I didn't need medication. I'm not sure that I doubt her on that because by refusing to take my medication the first time is probably what led me back to the hospital the second time. However, I in my case maybe taking HRT medication would have had the same positive result.

I would not have liked to take HRT (medication for menopause) because of all its cancer-causing agents but at least I would not be labeled schizoaffective and had to live with that. (2015 I did not have a female doctor and it was a nurse that suggested to me that it could be menopause.)

I brought up the topic about going back to work and told her that the reality is most boards are cutting back hiring and I do not come cheap because I have my Masters. In addition, I am a little reluctant going back because I dislike field trips and how it is not a 9:00 a.m.-3:00 p.m. job. In the end, I told her I am feeling a little burned out.

I did tell her that I was thinking about staying home and taking care of Cassie while Darcy goes back to school, but I am not sure that I have the stamina for that.

I also discussed how much money I would get if I went on disability. So Jemma gave me some numbers to call and I am supposed to get some papers from EI to have them filled out by the doctor. 2015 I never contacted EI that I remember. I just went from being covered by Great West Life to CPP. Although I remember Dr. Argle having to fill out forms for me.

Wednesday, February 17, 2010

George did not attend the meeting with Jemma to discuss symptomology nor did he write anything down. He said I seemed fine and did not know what to write. I cleared up what Jemma was suggesting for funding. I had been on CPP disability. I had been on it before and she said that too much time might have passed and that I should apply again. I went to get the application but I also called the woman who was in charge of my case for CPP and asked her what I needed to do. Since it had not been that long I just had to apply for reinstatement of my benefits. There is a short form for both Dr. Argle and myself to fill out. I told Jemma that I never pursued this earlier because I was not sure whether it was my disability that caused me to quit. She believes it was. So I will bring the forms with me to my appointment with Dr. Argle tomorrow.

Recently there was an advertisement for Vice Principals and Principals on the School Board website. The applications had to be in by February 15. I did not tell George about it because I was not sure what he would say, but I did not want to feel pressured. Anyhow, I did not apply because I have not been going to Mass for some time and getting a letter might be difficult. George does not like to go to Mass anymore and I do not like going alone.

I have noticed that one thing over the last few years. I once had the confidence to go anywhere on my own, but now I tend to fear more. I do not even like to travel to the drugstore. I managed to go to work and back and to the doctors and back, but I do not venture out anymore. I suppose this is also a symptom. I feel fine regarding delusions and everything but my self-confidence has just disappeared. As much as I would like to have the prestige of being a Vice Principal, I fear that I might not be able to handle the stress and that goes with just being a teacher as well.

Monday, March 1, 2010

I have started noticing symptoms again.

I saw Dr. Argle on February 18 and gave her the CPP form. I got a phone call from the lady at the CPP office the other day saying that she had the form from the doctor and me and that I was accepted. They will pay me retroactively from July since I resigned at the end of June. It will take about seven weeks.

I also talked about joining the Wellness Group in South Duncan and Jemma was going to look into that for me. I followed up this past week and found out that you have to be a South Duncan patient to participate. She is still looking for something for me.

What I am finding now is that I still remember things that used to bother me or I will be in a situation and think when I was messed up I would have thought a certain way. For instance, today I remember how I used to think there was some sort of competition between Black Bell Trucking (George's employer) and my school and Darcy and Jessica's high schools. I used to think that every time Georges name was mentioned at my school everyone would walk the other way.

Also, when we were at the bank today depositing the cheque from my Uncle Chuck's estate it was like having a déjà vu. I was thinking that if I were sick with the way things were said and how quickly things were done I would have thought that these people were protecting me and looking out for my interests. Well they are you say, but I would have thought they were making sure George did not squander it and were protecting me from him. This is a ridiculous thought when you think of how much he has had to go through with this so-called disability and me. 2015 He made me use my uncle's money to go towards paying for the backyard renovation. That was such a waste of the money. He also cancelled the life insurance policy my father gave him and payed off the Mercedes. I thought that was a silly thing to do.

George and I had coffee before going to the bank and he feels that if I had a job, any job, then Darcy would not rely on me so much regarding her going back to school. As much as I want to fill my days, I am also a mother and a female who is filled with guilt if she does not help.

I am definitely feeling closed in at home. This morning I went for a run. I was out for a total of 10 minutes and probably ran five....not bad for a start.

Tuesday, March 2, 2010

Another coincidence happened last night that if I were sick I would have thought people were reading what I write here as I write it. Weird. No sooner did I write about the bank visit yesterday, the bank phoned and asked to speak to George. They were asking about the late payment to the line of credit, which we have for our condominium in Kinter Valley. He had paid it, but two days late. The girl checked and it was there but George found out that the actual due date for payment is the twenty-first of the month, not the end of the month as he had thought. So our next move is to go to the bank and set up an automatic withdrawal. It was a good thing they called but it was timing nonetheless.

That was not the only thing that I realized would have bothered me if I were sick. Last night we were watching a show, Super nanny, and the actor's name was, the same as our daughter's nickname. Well that is normal I know but I would have thought it was some way for her to let me know that she cared about me since she does not really talk to me. It was like, no sooner did I mention that we tried that technique of time outs matching their age in our house that her name appeared on the screen. In reality, it is nothing but it would have bothered me and meant something.

That is not all. As I said before the colour red represented caring and Jessica. It dawned on me that the main colour of these Olympics has been red. If I were sick, I would have related that to meaning that somehow everyone was looking out for me and that perhaps the Olympic theme song, "Believe", was a message to me as well. Now these are some grandiose thoughts and definitely indicative of schizophrenia, if that is indeed what defines schizophrenia.

One other thing I have noticed since I have stopped taking medication; I am getting more headaches. They are different from the migraines I used to suffer from but I take Tylenol migraine to manage them and that seems to work. A couple of weeks ago though, the Tylenol did not work and I had the headache for 4 days. It is different now because before every headache was a migraine but this one still allowed me to function, before only Zomig rapimelts worked and I went through a lot of those.

I suffered from bad migraines right after I gave birth to Darcy and they only increased in frequency until I was diagnosed with a mental illness. Even second hand smoke use to trigger them. Thankfully it does not anymore.

I don't remember whether or not I have mentioned this or not but I remember that I used to feel that there wasn't enough action when things went wrong and that people usually comforted others with hugs. I used to feel a kind of struggle between hugs and action. I also used to think that there was some competition between my dad and George. Dad represented Tim Horton's and George represented Starbucks. It got so bad for me that I could not enjoy going out for coffee.

As well, it became difficult to eat. Corn, fish, and Honey nut cheerios represented Darcy and my school and regular cheerios represented Jessica and George. I even remember how it used to bother me that one of the sponsors for Tom Petty and his car race was Cheerios. Weird. So weird.

I got another call from the lady at CPP as I am writing this entry just telling me what she had said the other day. She had forgotten that she had already talked to me. Glad to see someone else is losing it. Anyway, in my twisted mind I would have read into that.

As well, my daughter Darcy just told me that Capilano offers the course she is looking for online. That would be totally cool, if affordable. Sometimes online courses are more expensive. But what I also want to point out is that I would have made a connection somehow between that and the blue couch, which meant technology or something. I still have not figured out what the technology stood for. Is it I working teaching online? I am really trying to make sense of it.

Funny how now I remember that somehow with this competition between my school and George that I felt somehow George was trying to protect my interests, so I was not taken advantage of by my school, regarding some big money. I also remember when we lived on Gage Lane and my sister Mandy came to visit, (at George's request) that I was afraid to go out for a walk with George because it somehow represented agreeing to live at a cabin up north with him. I was not sure that was the best thing to do for I was receiving messages over the radio that I would be all alone and lonely. I also felt that George was trying to win and really did not care about me. The only thing was that I was key to all that was going on so he had to care. Logically there must not have been messages; it is just what I was taking from the music. Truth is I would feel lonely up at a cabin I think unless we made some friends and we have not been very good at that even before I was sick.

I felt somehow that he was trying to make me look schizophrenic or out of my mind to win, win what I have no idea. Nevertheless, if he were so bad why would he encourage that I write everything down? As much as he is not really a romantic or very affectionate, he has lasted through this ordeal. I wish he were more affectionate though and more willing to help resolve the queries I have that have gone unanswered.

All these colours and everything really happened to me so was I over stimulated or what? I already do not like rereading this book because it makes me feel uncomfortable, plus I feel someone has been editing it to make more sense. I feel this because at times the facts are wrong. It is difficult to make sure that I am not repeating myself and that it flows in some logical manner. I am also wondering why I am so sensitive to what I would have thought weird before. It is a strange feeling to be thinking about what used to bother me and seeing new things that would have bothered me before. Am I just aware or is this the beginning of slipping again?

On another note, Jessica came down this past weekend with three of her male friends. They came down Friday and left Saturday night. It was so nice to see her. Her friends were also very nice. I am so glad that kids who are university bound surround her. Anyway, about a week ago she emailed me saying that she would like to learn guitar and would like mine. I had to think about it for a while because at first I was ticked that the first time she initiates a text with me, it's to ask for something. But, later I realized that I have two guitars and I would have liked to pass them down anyway. I was actually pleased that she wanted to learn. Unfortunately, both guitars had broken strings, so I gave her the one that I thought she would have more fun with. I gave her the one that you can attach a strap to and stand playing the instrument. The one I used at school, liturgies, and the Teachers Drama Club where I played the Sultan. I sent her a message before she came for the weekend that I couldn't ship it to her but that I would pass one on to her. She just had to make room for it in her car. When she arrived, I asked her if she still was interested considering it had a broken string and I did not have time to get it fixed. She said yes. I gave her the book (From Linda, my families housekeeper) I began teaching myself on back in grade six when I first got my first guitar (the other one), a sheet of chords and after I learned she liked Neil Young, I gave her my book too. After she left, I sent her another email telling her that these guitars meant a lot to me I only ask that she take care of it and keep it in the family.

My guitar was my form of expression; I used to write my own songs. I played my guitar a lot when we were at Gage Lane. I would sit in our bedroom and sing my heart out thinking I was on some sort of stage. After a while, especially when we moved here, when everything began to become overwhelming, and I couldn't read, watch TV, listen to the radio, make decisions on clothing easily or sit in the furniture, I tried playing my guitar, but I could not. All the words had hidden meaning, so I couldn't play familiar songs. I couldn't write new ones because I was too emotional. I just was not able to write anything. I would say I was at my very worst once we moved to this house on Wade Avenue …just before the second time I was admitted to the hospital.

I will have to get my guitar fixed and play again…maybe even take lessons, but then I will have to decide which type of lessons to get, classical or folk…decisions are hard for me to make and I like both types of playing.

You know I see these ads for identifying people who have had to overcome great odds get awards for having the courage to come back. I keep wondering if I have had the courage or will have the courage to do the same.

It is no wonder Jessica has trouble relating to me. I remember I had some intimate conversations with her when we lived on Gage Lane. I remember expressing my fears about George to her and she in her own little way trying to help and gave me a printout of Feng Shui to enhance sexual relations or something like that. When things got weird for me, I even went to her school and left a message for her counselor to look out for her. She ended up phoning me at work in tears and asking if George and I were getting a divorce. I am afraid I was not too reassuring at the time; all I said was that it was up to her dad.

I remember having a conversation with Darcy at Gage Lane too. She suggested I hire a private investigator and she said that Grandma would pay for it. We never talked about it again.

When things were weird back then George and I went to some marriage counsellor that George found that I hated. I think we went once. Apparently he phoned George and said that I needed help and from rereading and reminiscing over some of this stuff I sure did. I was overwhelmed, but I still resented the fact that I did all the talking and when he said that, the next time George would have to do it we never went back again.

I remember at Gage Lane that I was really quite stimulated sexually and remember phoning my girlfriend, Elizabeth about it. One day I even phoned George and asked him to come home, how weird is that? So weird! He said that that was a side effect of my schizophrenia or psychosis. I think I will ask Dr. Argle. I felt like I was on some sort of drug. Probably what it feels like to be on ecstasy.

When I spoke to Dr. Argle about it, it is actually the reason she says that I am schizoaffective rather than schizophrenic, because I had a mood episode, (feeling very sexual) but I do not always. This mood episode only happened the first time not these last two times.

Before I forget, when I was in the drugstore last to fill my prescription for Zopiclone to help me sleep when I need it, I remembered how I used to feel safe there getting my prescriptions filled. One of the reasons was that they had all these billboards with advertisements from Aviva and that is the company my brother works for, so, in some way I felt that he was watching over me.

Also worth mentioning that when I was in the thick of things, I remember going to Dr. Browns, our optometrist's office and being struck by the colour of the office uniform, which was grey.

It was so difficult to go anywhere because the colours were everywhere. Once when George and I were in the car at a stoplight I remember cars surrounding us that were representative of several of the colours. You can see how overwhelming things can become. When I started getting better, I wanted to go out but was afraid to. Once I made plans to get together with a colleague that had gone through breast cancer, to meet at the coffee shop in Whittle Head, but when it came time to go I could not get in the car. I was afraid to go out and I was afraid to use the phone. SO strange…yet I still battle with this going out in the car by myself thing. I do go out and feel good when I do, like getting my hair done or going to the doctors, but it does take an inner push.

Wednesday, March 3, 2010

Although I am not at all sure of the privacy of this, it is a way for me to get out what I need to get out. Last night while watching NCIS-LA on TV, it reminded me, or maybe I have written it out before, but toilets use to haunt me. Why would toilets haunt me you ask? When we were living on Saber Road, I was cleaning George's bathroom downstairs and noticed that the cover over the bolt holding the toilet down was loose. One of those bolts had some junk smudged all around it and it made me suspicious so I scrubbed and scrubbed to try and get rid of the substance. No big deal, really, only when I had to tell George about it he made a big fuss over what cleaning agent I used. I never understood why. I also found some powder in his cabinet and tasted it, which is a totally a stupid thing to do. It was his reaction to Darcy fainting that really got me mistrusting him. I guess I am dwelling on the past.

Anyhow, I remember being at the cabin and George, Ben (Paula's boyfriend who happens to be a criminal lawyer) and her son were replacing the toilet there. At the time, I kept thinking it was because of everything I had said before about the toilet at Saber Road. I remember it was some celebration day in the States, like July 4th. I had never seen so many people down at the beach. George never went down, I went by myself. It was packed with people in boats and even horseback riders and planes flying overhead.

You know when I was in the thick of things I used to think that George was being impersonated and his identity was being stolen. I used to try to figure out when this might have happened, when he fell off the roof, when he passed out in the ditch, or when he had his hernias removed. Silly to think this way, but I did. I also used to think that someone was trying to imitate being me.

But here is the decisive factor, last night while watching The Good Wife there was a part where the star and a man had to enter a house and when they knocked on the door, the woman answered and immediately said she was not interested and closed the door in their faces. The man said something like you might want to try another name or something and then I thought that the woman of the house reacted just like I did when a woman came to the door pushing the Holy Bible. Just as I thought that, the star of the show said that works. Now I know in real life people cannot read your mind but I thought that it was my thinking that got them in the door. Now that can't be, so why did I think it? In addition, during the same show, George brought my attention to the kitchen cabinets, and later an actor on TV walked in as part of his script saying, "so these are the kitchen cabinets" and carried on with his piece, which had nothing to do with the kitchen. It was coincidental that they spoke of cabinets at the same time, but not to my fragile mind.

Although my concentration stinks, I noticed that the sum of money that they were referring to in the show was the same amount that we had deposited into the Spousal RRSP ...coincidence I know. In addition, it seemed to me that at some point, they were talking mutual funds and then nothing came of it. I also felt weird when they had a part on Sarah Palin. The resemblance of the other woman to her was uncanny and I kept thinking about my situation and all the thoughts I had about people looking like members of my family but not being them. It made me feel uncomfortable.

February 2015 I feel that there are Georges and that the daughters in my life right now are undercover agents.

Also of note was the fact that I was feeling anxious last night and when I told George this he asked, "Why because its tax time?" I told him I am not sure but inside I feel because all my discomforts are rising. Anyway he then told me that I hadn't washed a pot in the sink and when I told him that I couldn't because I cut my finger he responded by saying if he had known that he wouldn't have cooked dinner.

This morning George wore a shirt over a T-shirt, which he has been complaining about not being able to do because he has gained so much weight. He's been wearing sweaters. He never wears his company shirt, which I thought was mandatory now. Perhaps he is just cold and does not want to wear the short sleeve shirts they supplied even though he says he does not wear them because of his weight. I am not even sure why I care anyway.

I know things are not right so I phoned Jemma to move up my appointment with Dr. Argle. I told her how things are, by going over my list for Dr. Argle and she's going to email her right away to see if she can squeeze me in tomorrow, if not then the 11th. In the meantime, Jemma suggested that I take the PRN (as needed pills) prescribed by Dr. Argle to calm things down if I need to.

Another thing that I think is pretty weird is if I thought we were being watched in the house, or at least I was, then why I never incorporated my new lenses for my cataracts into my paranoia. I never thought they could see things for other people or anything like that. I find that interesting. 2015, I definitely think my cataract surgery has a lot to do with helping me now see colours and signs, also helping others see what I see which I used to pray for.

I went out with Darcy and the baby and felt a little weird, so I decided to take a pill at about 4:00 p.m. What strikes me as weird is why I am recognizing so quickly when things are not right.

Anyway, at the risk of repeating myself I wanted to say that I am still concerned over the burgundy couches that we used to have. George always bragged how they were custom made for him by Sandy's furniture company. But for some reason I checked inside the cushions and discovered that the insides were made of mattresses. The strange thing was that these mattresses also had hidden zippers where you could place things. Why were they made that way? Whenever I questioned him, he just said that was how they were made. However, reputable furniture companies do not make furniture that way that much I know for I even phoned the furniture store. What hasn't he told me? I know that what I saw was real. I found them so disturbing that I showed my sisters while we were living on Gage Lane.

When I spoke to Mandy, my sister, about it at the time, she said that maybe I should just let it be. But, how do you fully trust someone when that lurks in the back of your brain. I want to be rid of it. I am rid of the couches but not the why.

Below are notes I made to my psychiatrist. I just could not write twice and my mind is racing.

Thursday, March 18, 2010 adjusted to Thursday, March 4, 2010

- † Beginning to recognize things that would bother me if I were sick
    - † TD Bank. I felt I was getting signs they were helping protect me while we were having a conversation with Bennett to go over my portfolio.
    - † TV show Supernanny-Jess: The super nanny's name was the same as Jessica's nickname.
    - † Olympics-Jessica –red-caring- grandiose. I felt Jessica was reaching out telling me she really cared. 2015 Now I see it as many people reaching out to me showing that they really care

- † Remembering more things that used to bother me
    - † Black Bell Trucking vs. my school vs. High schools:
    - † Starbucks vs. Tim Horton's
    - † Food: corn, fish cheerios
    - † Aviva
    - † Intimacy- is being over sexual a symptom?

- Couch

- First signs: The Good Wife
    - Entering the house
    - Kitchen cabinets
    - Amount of money-coincidence
    - Anxiety-

- Georges reactions that bother me
    - Anxiety, taxes, Kitchen cleanup, pot washing etc.

- Headaches- why such a drastic cut in the amount of migraines I used to get before being on the medication

- Some group to join

Thursday, March 4, 2010

I took that 5 mg Loxapine and boy did it wipe me out. I was zonked for the rest of the night. I had never really felt how sleep inducing it really was until yesterday.

I am back on medication.

I went to my doctor's appointment this morning at 9:30 a.m. and brought a printout of things to discuss and those were just some of the things I needed to discuss, or rather unload. Making that list helped me though, so I think I will keep doing that. She told me to start taking 10 mg of the Loxapine and she will get permission for some other kind of drug to use with me that she will discuss next week. Although, admittedly I was not as relaxed as I have been it felt good to have somewhere to go and tell someone my burdens. The medication really must have helped keep my concerns at bay.

I told Dr. Argle and Jemma, she was in on the conversation, that I was also surprised by George's reaction yesterday. He did not ask why I was so sleepy. I was definitely not myself, but he did not say a word. He did expect me to help Darcy though when she was experiencing stomach pain. I was totally zonked on the couch when he said, "Dear, Darcy is experiencing pain", or something like that. So, I asked her if it was like when she had her appendix out. She said she did not remember, so I suggested that she try jumping up and down. She got up and did it on both feet when I suggested doing it individually, but she said she didn't want to…fair enough. She then asked to lie on the couch. I told her that if it got bad, to let her Dad know and he could take her to the hospital and I would stay home and take care of the baby.

I was very tired so I took the blanket and went to lie on Jessica's bed. I heard him ask her a couple of times how she felt. She ended up going to bed at 8:30 p.m. and so I went back to the family room to lie down. George had American Idol on and as we were watching that, rather I was trying to stay awake to watch it, a contestant by the name of Di Di (pronounced DD) came on and at the same time Darcy texted her dad saying that she felt better.

Another coincidence happened to me this week that I just recalled today. My brother called the other day to tell me that he was experiencing trouble with Mom. He mentioned that she did not trust him and that she had plans to cut him out of the Will if he broke into her briefcase again. Apparently, she has some briefcase and it is broken and now held together with a belt and that in fact she had asked Sam, my brother, to replace the briefcase, but told Louise, my sister, something different. He wanted to let me know or to find out if she had said the same thing to me…she has not.

His mentioning this briefcase though makes me dwell more on the briefcase that I had bought for George, that never did get broken, and where it might be now. I had it engraved with his name on it. What strikes me as strange is that even George has asked me where it is? I cannot remember the last time I saw it. Maybe he kept the briefcase in the garage at Gage Lane. I remember doing some snooping and found some notes on I think it was the Blue Angel Cafe restaurant. I cannot remember the contents now. I would have thought he would take better care of a briefcase that was engraved just for him. Sad when you think about it.

It is also sad that he never does anything for me for Valentines either. I remember sending some singing women to his place of work as a surprise.

He never goes out of his way. I once had flamingoes placed on the front yard to celebrate his fiftieth. He did have a surprise party for my fiftieth at Paula's, but I wonder whose idea that really was? I believe it was Paula's. But I really wasn't surprised. Ben called the house and he never calls and then I saw Jessica's car. I used to enjoy surprising him with things like sending him all over the house to find his Christmas present with riddles. He already knew where it was but he played along, but now I have lost that enthusiasm. I don't even like going shopping for presents anymore because I'm afraid of the money issue…the joy is gone …zapped…kaput!

After I met with Dr. Argle and Jemma, I met with only Jemma. Apparently, my symptoms are more schizoaffective. When I tried to understand the difference between schizophrenia and schizoaffective, by having her explain it, I still do not understand. All I know is that they were pleased that I was able to call at the first signs of things going awry.

I was teary-eyed thinking about Jessica but was happy about her visit. I told them how she wanted my guitar and when I found out she liked Neil Young I gave her my guitar book of some of his songs and that the weird thing was Neil Young played at the Closing Ceremonies for the Olympics! The book was called Harvest.

I did ask Jemma if anyone had any worries about me taking care of the Cassie because Dr. Argle had asked how things were with her. I told her I was thinking the same thing the other day and was saying to myself while I was holding her that she had better not start changing on me. Jemma said no. I told her that I am supposed to take care of the baby tomorrow during the day for a couple of hours and was curious about whether I should or not. She suggested I have a back-up person and the only person is George.

Since I am supposed to tell George about all this I suggested maybe he might stay home as back up.

I phoned him when I got home from my appointment and he wasn't sure that he could…I didn't tell him why…I just told him that I needed to talk to him and he asked, " face to face?" I said it was probably better that way. He asked if it could wait until he got home and I told him it could.

I worry about taking care of the baby more out of these headaches I have been experiencing.

Friday, March 5, 2010

Well I did what I had to last night. I told George everything that I told Dr. Argle, even more. I actually told him I thought it was him that might have caused Jessica's behaviour when she was young. I thought she had been sexually molested. He said that it was all a part of my psychosis and perhaps he is right. I told him I thought it was more a sign of mistrust, but he disagreed with me. When I told him about everything, I was quite amazed at how strong I was. I was also very surprised at his "unshakable" face. His eyes expressed no caring or worry at all. It was at this time when I almost wished that my eye lenses were really windows and that others could see what I was seeing. The only time he seemed to show any reaction was when I mentioned about the kitchen and having to clean the pot.

I also asked George where or why he brought home the blue and white Silk flowers and he could not even remember bringing them home. I told him I thought maybe the flowers were a sign to me that he just wanted to be friends because they are blue and white like the hangers I found in the closet.

The first show we watched of the evening was CSI and I remember how surprised I was when Sarah, the actor, mentioned a mattress being a part of a criminal investigation. We were eating dinner; I only had a cup of rice, so I could not really follow the plot. I did remark to DeeDee (Darcy) that it was a coincidence that we were just talking about how few new episodes there are for some of these shows and low and behold, we were watching a new one.

George had watched American Idol last night so he wanted to see the finale tonight. I was very anxious watching this show. It seemed like a direct message to me. When I noticed in my mind that the background was all red a gold bright light appeared in the background. This gold bar only appeared twice. George was speaking about a blonde haired girl who was exceptional and learned how to play a 12-string guitar in a week. Now that is amazing, but I connected the focus of the guitar to Jessica wanting my guitar. I also noticed that when the contestants, DiDi and Megan were competing, that George thought that DiDi should be kicked off and I was wondering why…was it really her singing…or was he somehow kicking his real Darcy out. I remember when Darcy was so afraid of her Dad when we lived at Gage Lane. He also had a good temper back then and on Saber Road…but I digress. He also kicked off the girl who was dressed in black and white. I say he kicked off because he not only predicted it but I thought they should let him make the decision.

Danny Kokey performed and played an uplifting song that I felt was directed to me. George said he never liked him but I said I did. Anyhow, while he was singing, he seemed to get more energetic or excited by thoughts that I was having. Weird right? He really made me feel that this was not only in my head and that better days were ahead. When I thought that I didn't need my pills but would take them anyway to help calm me… he seemed excited. All sorts of multi-colours showed up in the background.

What was tense for me was how different this show was. Parents were proudly displayed and there were so many tears. It really felt like they were feeling for me and I was feeling for them. I even felt that the panelists were ticked off and I thought they were ticked off with George. I even began to think that maybe the fact that Ellen DeGeneres was on the show was another sign.

At one point during the show, I started thinking about Darcy and how pretty her voice is. She was so confident singing after her voice lessons. But she did not like competitions so she never tried out for Canadian Idol. I also thought that maybe that was why there was no more Canadian Idol.

We also watched Ghost Whisperer. It was a repeat and I thought maybe I might get a message from the show too. What I did remember was that when we were living at Gage Lane I was woken by a dream…now I rarely have dreams I remember…but this was haunting. I heard my Dad say, "Bring George back".

I told George about the golf balls for stocking stuffers while at the store, so, he bought everything for golf in my stocking. He bought tees and a hat in pink as well. Everything was pink! I somehow thought that maybe this was a sign that he wanted me to be independent and not married to him.

Later we saw the Mentalist on TV and what struck me a lot here was that they were focusing on salt, which I had mentioned to Dr. Argle today, and rice that George had mentioned at dinner. These things meant something to me but I do not remember what they stood for. I was also getting the message from the TV show, that George has a lover. Then, I remembered the elementary sized blue pencil that I found at my desk on Gage Lane, (this pencil is important because I taught an intermediate grade and never used them and both of our daughters didn't use them either). This pencil seemed to verify that someone was in our home that I did not know of. The show started to pick up and green napkins appeared on the table. When I remembered this, the man in the show mentioned how he liked the napkins.

George left today in the cashmere burgundy sweater that I bought for him. I would have thought that too nice a sweater to wear to dirty grease shops. So I wonder again. Maybe someday I will be strong, not care, and not always doubt.

I noticed my cousin posted a movie clip on the Tooth fairy on Facebook and it reminded me how last night George started talking about Jessica's wisdom teeth. He seemed to think she should get it done in Kinter Valley, after all he suffered on his own and I said that she would probably feel better at home.

It also made me think about how awful I was as a tooth fairy. The girls had special pillows for their teeth and I remember that sometimes I would forget and have to quickly find a sneaky moment in the morning and put it somewhere where I thought they had not checked. Anyway, the crazy thing is I kept all their baby teeth. I even have my own. They were never handed down to me or anything. I just lost a tooth and saved it. I Imagine, some might think that was gross or bonkers. Right? But growing up I was not led to believe in the tooth fairy or Santa Clause.

Today Darcy had on a show that I came into watch that somehow struck me. The plot of the show had a girl/mother named Jessica whose nickname was Jess she had a daughter named Tara and she left her daughter with her brother. Tara did not attend school when she should have so Social Services were going to take her away. Her brother ended up taking her to his father's ranch where they had some horses. The Dad was very mean and was quite abusive to Tara and Jessica's brother. The brother said that it was Jessica that had the problem with their Dad not him, but in the end when the Dad threatened him with a shovel and started in on hurting Tara. He flew into a rage, hit his Dad with a shovel, and killed him.

At one point, I felt that my Jessica was telling me that she and her sister were not with their Dad anymore when the actress spoke. The brother said, "What does Dad have to do with this?" She said, "She did not know." It seemed to me that the conversation on TV was more a reaction to what I was thinking because what they were saying did not seem to fit the storyline.

I also felt that my brother was talking to me when he left a message for Jessica saying that this was the first day of the rest of her life or something like that.

I was also fascinated by a PBS show on electronics for the car. It was interesting and I thought that maybe such devices were used to track people's whereabouts.

Although I felt awkward, I asked George if he wanted to come with me when I took Cassie for a walk. He said yes. I was surprised. He spoke of one of his co-workers sending some sort of official document to all his former customers at his place of work saying that Volvo would now service them where he now works. When I asked him if he saw the letter, he said that it was faxed to the house. I told him all I read on the fax was the word Fleet guard, after that he dropped the subject.

He told me that his boss was going to California this week and we started talking about our trip. One of the things I reminisced was Darcy getting her first period and her not saying anything about it. George did not remember and thought we went when the girls were 8 and 10. I do not remember the ages they were.

I feel so awkward. I feel that this is all about identity and finding out who is who and who remembers what. I also remember his cold face when I talked to him and got almost scared. He acts like everything is normal today…but how can George feel that way? I still do not have my answers. He said that that was an expensive couch. How do I know whether that is how they make them if the company no longer exists like he says?

I told him about all the times he gave me flowers. Twice. The last roses were at St. Anne's with the words I am sorry on his business card. Sorry for what? So much went on.

I have also always wondered about the vandalism to our pool at Saber Road. I remember George having a conversation with his friend about it and no sooner, while George is recovering from his surgery, our liner is knifed and one of the big foot rocks were thrown in the pool. I always wondered about it thinking his friend might have arranged to have it done.

I feel the need now with this computer to write down everything…so I will. I remember going to Dr. Moran about George's drinking and he suggested a book called, "Codependence No More." I remember reading part of it. George used to treat me so badly after he would drink…he would not hit me or anything but, it was not fun nonetheless. I am one who believes you should not drink and drive, so it bothered me when he did. What kind of role model is he if one drink per hour or whatever is ok? I often had to drive back from family events because he never agreed to not drink and he knew I feared driving in the dark. I have always feared the border crossing too, and have never crossed myself, so one time, a year or so ago we were stopped at the border and hauled inside because of George's drinking. He was not charged. I had not drank so when I agreed to take a Breathalyzer, he asked why I wasn't driving. I told the officer I wasn't driving because I fear the border. He did request I drive us home.

We even went to a party at our neighbours and when I went to look for him no one knew where he had gone. I found him at home passed out. He had left me behind.

One thing that has haunted me is how connected I felt to some guy at the hospital that I played ping-pong with. He reminded me so much of what I thought George looked like….so weird. This man looked like he had befallen on hard times and I thought George had stolen his identity and that the powers that be were letting me get a glimpse of the real George. He left as quickly as he had come. I wanted to go with him.

Saturday, March 6, 2010

I have been having frequent headaches and last night I developed one during the night, so I got up early.

We watched some new shows last night, Ghost Whisperer, Medium and Numbers. Certain things really bothered me but they seem hazy now. I remember that one scene of Numbers I had seen before, a long time ago.

Last night though I thought it was strange how the star of the show's brother called him Mr. Good, right when Rose, our neighbour called. Earlier in the day, I had been thinking how he is always so pleasant to other people and cuts their grass and everything but when I tell him of this stuff, he was so cold the other day.

Earlier yesterday, we watched a talk show and somehow I felt like I was being assessed. They were doing three-second evaluations on what the audience thought about the four people on the show, two girls and two guys. George did not really do the assessment he quickly went to play with the baby. When it was over he gave an overall evaluation and then asked what I thought and I told him. Basically I remember looking at one girl and thought how green and black, the colours she was wearing, reminded me of the book mark Jessica made me out of beads when we were living on Gage Lane and how one guy George, I thought looked handsome. I also liked his modesty, but I did not tell George that part. The bookmark read LOVE.

This morning I woke up and found dental floss on the kitchen stove. It bothered me. I thought about what I wrote yesterday. Then I began to think about how I do not remember George flossing his teeth back on Saber Road…why? When we lived on Gage Lane, I also found this picture and felt the person looked like George and that he had had dental work done. I mean serious dental work. I thought George's imposter living with me had his teeth made to look like George's.

This morning I checked my Facebook and was bothered by Darcy's hair. Of course, it could just be how pictures transpose, but her part was on the left when she came home and on the right in her picture.

Another thing that bothered me and caused me to think that George was into drugs somehow was the large containers of baby powder I found in the girls' bathroom at Gage Lane. When I asked them about it they said it was not theirs. George never used it either.

Thursday, March 11, 2010

Things I used to notice:

- † Silverware were missing
- † Plates were missing
- † The staff were wearing Grey at Dr. Brown's
- † The Street sign on my street on Wade Avenue Drive said Street maintained by Lady Bug Production (Still see, still there) I was haunted by the millions of ladybugs that appeared in our bedroom I thought the next door neighbor was using them for drugs and contacted the Mayor.

Things I am curious about:
- † Briefcase – brother, Mom, the one I bought for George. Where did the briefcase I bought for George go? I even had it engraved.
- † Elementary blue pencil – primary pencils kept showing up in the office and I never brought them from school and the kids weren't in the grades to use them as well. So where did they come from?
- † Jewelers rouge. Why did George want me to buy it when we were in North Dakota? He rarely ever shines our rings now.
- † George's socks- he used to get little holes at the big toe…but not anymore. He told me once that you could take a certain drug by using small pieces of material, specifically cotton.
- † Baby powder – A large container found in the girls' bathroom that no one used

George's reactions to things:
- † Going to Tinsel Town-and saying he would only go if he could go golfing with my brother-$ Uncle Charlie-married obligations/visiting Tinsel Town etc
- † My telling him everything about our previous doctor appointment-Jessica's psychologist

Things that concern me
- † Rings- why did he have us sit down with the girls and ask them what rings they wanted?
- † Why did he give his family ring to Darcy at such a young age?

MY COLOUR-CODED LIFE

- † Jewelers' rouge- which is used to clean jewellery…he asked me to buy it in the States while we were living there. He used to clean our rings with it.
- † Forged Signatures –while we were in the States, we went to visit someone that showed us how to forge signatures. I later wondered why. The picture I have that Pierre Trudeau signed when I wrote him a letter when I was young – the picture looks wrong
- † TV telling me that perhaps I'm hanging around George for company
- † What's really going on at the Bank-is it real-scam-protection. While I was there, I thought about all the bonds I had put away for the girls 2015 I now feel that they are protecting me!
- † He keeps talking about the bonds that his mom gave them but I had saved their family allowance and bought several bonds for them too.
- † Darcy and Jessica's first bank accounts. George decided it was best to keep their first bank account books in his dresser. They were pink with white bunny heads and those accounts were with TD. Where was their money transferred to?
- † I think about my GIA account and why the lady at the bank put me on the spot and asked me why I opened it in front of George. I opened it because I did not trust George. I wanted some money he couldn't touch in case I needed to escape. I opened it with dad's estate money.
- † Why George wants cheques of substantial sums only deposited at the main bank we use?

Things I notice:
- † **I am doing a lot of reminiscing.** I've been thinking about Old boyfriends, sailboats, my family etc. It seemed when I thought about one memory about an old boyfriend regarding a swimming pool and lights, George appeared very understanding to me when I came upstairs
- † **Sunday, February 18, 2015 I am still doing a lot of reminiscing**
- † I've been making a lot of name connections
- † February 18 the name connections are not strong

- † Babyliss- I saw this written on the electric curler set at my hair salon and I thought it meant that Darcy really did not have a baby.
- † Used to only have headaches as a kid…migraines only for years…. now I was getting headaches that have turned themselves into neck pain. I think my pain is being controlled…fuzzy arms…hands etc
- † Jason, from Duncan Mental Health, asked me if I was hearing voices. No. I heard George's cough and a door bell when there was neither.

Thursday, March 4, 2010-

- † American Idol: I feel the songs directly relate to my situation and are chosen because of me. The colours on the show used to send me messages too
- † Ghost Whisperer-Bring George back
- † Mentalist Salt-Water
- † Kaiser- seemed to be two dogs
- † TV reacting to what I think and sometimes to what George says and does during his day; It even reacts to what Darcy says sometimes
- † My lenses at the Bank. While there I was able to see better without my glasses. My vision was clearer both short and long distance while in the office.
- † Bank- things that stood out:
    - † The folder he Bennett, our financial planner at the time, handed George had changed: from green with a green with a little bit of grey with the words Financial Planning to all grey, Dark grey with a little bit of light grey with TD Waterhouse (Price Waterhouse) Shania Twain-water
    - † in one investment –it was titled, Sr B (which meant Dad to me) it was also labelled, research in motion (University of Phoenix), and the pie charts with all the same colours that stood for things to me: blue green purple red
        - † Bay Street-Dad's office
        - † Fidelity Investments

- † The other investment-I-had a lot of banks and government with future dates
- † They both had RBC-Royal Bank of Canada
- † The information all seemed to be some sort of indication that this was not real and all a part of a sting operation on George. What I was noticing-were messages to me.
    - † I thought about Manulife that day and George scratched out Manulife which Bennett had written down
- † December 31, 2009-haircut
- † Feel like what I write on the computer is sometimes used on TV-Academy Awards
- † I am interested in reading the paper again, but all sorts of connections are there to whatever I do or think
- † Playing cards was difficult for me which George suggested.
    - † Black and white deck and red and white deck-couldn't pick- George picked Black and white- Darcy came upstairs and put the bottle of milk for the baby upside down. This meant that someone had been hurt by the choice we made.

Friday, March 5, 2010

- † Some show with the actress Jessica.
- † Tyra Show-3 second evaluations
- † Darcy's picture –transpose, part left visual, right picture

Tuesday, March 9, 2010

- † American Idol – felt like Simon was talking to me
    - † First girl sang and though it made me emotional and the idea of breaking away, he said it was the wrong song choice
    - † Randy was wearing black and white and beads

- † Two girls played with guitar : acoustic and electric –seemed as soon as I thought about my nephew, Keith, the judges thought the performance was outstanding
- † Randy (one of the judges) wore black and white which is what George made me pick in cards
- † The Good Wife – stacks of money in show-I thought about the mattress and then they said something like, with a hint of marijuana. I felt like it was a reaction to what I thought
- † Street signs-turning right (Wednesday, February 18, 2015 I know that right and left meant something too only I can't remember what)
- † DD turning off the music when she saw it made me cry
- † His kissing me and saying, "Is that all?" something I had been thinking about before. He always only pecks me.

Wednesday, March 10, 2010

- † Norton did an update and the only thing without a check, is this saved document, which is blue with arrows. Why? Later it was green and after George downloaded the Tax files to a flash drive it went to blue again
- † Darcy came upstairs, we were talking about her shirt with the ND huskies, I thought of George's Alaskan Malamutes, and all of a sudden, she says her boyfriend said it was snowing in Ladysmith. Also, I thought about whether this place was real or not and she talked about Cassie's mattress, which made me think about the couch again.
- † I even noticed how the correction tool on my laptop made me doubt my own entry and whether Darcy was who she was. I clicked for the correction and was going to add something to it when it just left what I wrote the way I had it
- † I feel the computer is testing my teaching knowledge. –incorrect verb

- † He whistled to the dog today. He never whistles. I had reminisced about him whistling. Then I thought of my childhood and my old neighbour whistling.
- † banana cake- the one my mother made me for my birthday… bananas and fruit used to mean something but I do not remember what
- † Bicycle- Why did George encourage me to sell my bike while living in Brampton? Why did we never go bike riding with the kids after they won their bikes?
- † My trip to the hairdressers-The girl in the magazine looked like the girl in American Idol

Extreme Makeover – hair, hair dresser,

Song: Signs, Signs Everywhere a Sign
Going left and being strong and asking for a divorce

    I noticed things while watching American Idol during boys' night. George slept through the show. When one of the guitar players played during the show, I noticed he was using a capo and I remembered I have no idea where my capos are…they are both missing. When I thought that Ellen De Generous got up and gave the contestant a hug.

    They began to play all guitars until I thought about their show last week, which I did not see, Ryan Seacrest said unplugged. (I guess this means that they were playing unplugged.) The pretty woman with the long brown hair, (I still do not remember her name even though they're introduced each time. I used to know it) began to cry when I thought about the red handkerchief in his pocket. I remember I did not know what those red and blue bow ties of George's were for or where they were from. Even if he got them from his dad and kept them hidden. Why? We don't have the lifestyle where he would ever wear them. I began to think that he was wearing them out of the house. I had never seen them until we were living on Gage Lane

    After the contestant sang for some reason, I began to think about how George says he always listens to the melody and not the words and I had focused on so many other signs. Then he sang again it was like …here…in your face…when the show ended it was like okay Megan make a choice…like the t-shirt I found downstairs that said "HERESTOYOURCHOICE.COM"

CSI: NY – There were a few things I noticed to…more like an educational test

Mac Taylor was Mac, maybe not, perhaps he represented Mac Makeup or Mac computers

His son Reed was wearing a colourful scarf when I thought his name could be used for the apparatus used for a clarinet he loosened his scarf. When I thought about George's new shirt and tie, Mac buttoned his shirt and was going to put on his tie.

When he and a friend were writing, back and forth as #39 and #40, I began to think how Dad had numbers for us and the horns honked. I was #2.

In my Masters course, I said my favourite drink was water because of how George had been behaving…but as a little girl I had to have jugs brought to the table just like Connor (a friend of George's) new wife Beth. I thought she was having so much water because of what I wrote in my Masters course. The water only tastes good here sometimes for a little while. We have a filter on the fridge that doesn't help. I think that is controlled too. I asked for bottled water and George thinks that is silly. Hopefully we can go out and get some today.

Thursday, March 18, 2010

Things I used to notice:

- † Buttons/button box from his grandmother I was finding little buttons all around the house and thought George was using them for drugs
- † Donald Trump's ties changed colours. I felt he was supporting me.
- † A student having a sign for his Mom- How are you feeling today Good or Fine
- † Another student saying it didn't matter what we said it was only for points

† That George was getting mail on his CPP contributions and I wasn't so I phoned them

Things I am curious about

† Darcy used all my saved safety pins for her jeans and now she doesn't…she's crying and I feel sad
† Why Jessica was in a different room than where she said she was when we last Skyped
† Why Kaiser is more obedient and listens to commands
† Why my mom said she had my brother catch a bat in the basement of our house when I was small. It was in the yellow bathroom. I verified with my brother and it really happened
† What happened to all the Wesley Disney Books my mother had bought the girls? My favourite picture that I took of Jessica when she was a toddler was when she was sound asleep with these books open and all over her bed. I still have that picture. It depicts her personality perfectly! The only thing I query is why there are Dalmatian sheets on her bed when hers were Mickey Mouse. Darcy's was the 101 Dalmatian sheet set.
† How my Dad did certain renovations to the house that were so advanced for the time…and so many trips to all sorts of places even here. How did he afford it?
† How my Mom afforded to do the things she has done for us
† How did my grandmother Jackson die
† Why I never heard my brother shoot the Patterns of five into the wood in the basement that I was told he did
† Why I never saw him play with his large toy gun collection
† Why I never saw Sandra's obituary(George's mom)
† Why I never saw Eddy's obituary (George's dad)
† How we used to file things in North Dakota, Mississauga and Brampton addresses. We didn't.
† Why I do not remember us filing taxes for years? We definitely did not do it together while living in North Dakota, Treble or Brampton. I am certain we did not hire anyone.

- † How I used to take care of our bank account until Treble, when he felt he wasn't in control
- † I chose paint and rollers to paint the girls room at Saber Road in their favourite colours. Jessica's was blue and white and her walls looked like clouds and Darcy's was green and white which looked like marble. They turned out looking that way unintentionally. I have never seen rollers like that before or since. The roller had two sponges that you dipped into a divided tray
- † How you can have constipation when you are younger and frequent painful bowel explosions when you are older for some years, be diagnosed with IBS and everything be fine now
- † 2015 I wonder whether Jessica is really studying to be a dentist. I saved a note from her saying that she wouldn't marry until she had been one for a year.
- † Why when George apparently presented an idea of having scanner codes attached to garbage cans they didn't think it was a good idea. I am glad they did not like the idea. You should never have to pay to get rid of garbage.
- † Why my DAD wanted his picture taken in front of the Tim Horton's sign
- † Whose genes you get hair from…your dad or mom
- † Did my brother really take boxing lessons
- † Why is this street said to be maintained by ladybug productions

George's reactions to things:

- † Trying to encourage me to take my Ativan rather than telling me

Things that concern me

- † Echinacea-I went searching George's truck while living at Gage Lane several years ago and found an Echinacea bottle that had some rat shaped pooh pellets, which were like his present Coenzyme Q10 vitamins, but they were much darker and smelled sweet. I had talked to Elizabeth about what hash or something might smell like.

February 20, 2015, they look nothing like the same type of pills he has now!!
- † I took them to the police station first to find out what they were and they dismissed me. I took them to my family doctor, Dr. Moran and he said he could commit me and that I had to tell George. I did and he threw them out. No other Echinacea pills we bought smelled as sweet as the ones I found in his truck and they were all lighter. If I was wrong, why did he throw them out?
- † I also took them to a co-worker whose husband works in some sort of Special Services (CSIS) I thought he could identify it but she gave it back to me and said I would need to make a formal complaint before he could do anything.
- † I do not remember if I went to my co-worker or the doctor's second.
- † Why when I went to show George what I found in the false ceiling at Gage Lane …a cigarette package…he told me to leave it there
- † Why there was a hidden fuse box in the false ceiling. Why did George tell me to ignore it when I showed him?
- † On Saber Road-How George could fall from a second story window and land on the cement and not come home with a bandage on his head or anything. I do not understand the trajectory of the fall and how he narrowly missed the fence. I do not understand how he went through the roof that he said he went through and landed with his head in the position he landed. Why didn't he have a concussion? Was it this that had him have a grand mal seizure in the hydro right of way years later? Why didn't he have another seizure? (Holmes on Homes helped remind me to write this March 18, 2010)
- † Why he wanted to make a Path through the brush to the stairs at Gage Lane? A path we never used.
- † Why there were so many ladybugs in our bedroom at Gage Lane. It was eerie.
- † Remembering that apparently Dr. Rob said that the girls needed to take fluoride here because they didn't add it to the water like they do in Ontario

- † Remembering that when we had Barclay that we used to put her in a kennel when we went away…Why don't we do the same with Kaiser? Why is Kaiser so pampered?
- † We gave her things that smelled liked us and some favourite toys one that I remember…and now George always wants someone to take care of the dog, like a friend of Jessica's. Barclay tore up the things that George left in her kennel. Perhaps if I left her something she would have felt better!
- † Where certain kids play things went
- † Where Barclay's wire kennel went
- † Why it took so long for Dr. Moran to call me in regarding my pap smear results
- † Why I had to go to a specialist for tinnitus when I never had to before or since
- † Remembering how George grabbed my breast at Gage Lane and called them little Sarah's when he used to say they were the size of grapefruits
- † Why when I asked George on Saturday morning if he remembered whether I took my pill or not he said to check the number of pills. He figured out the math for me and seemed to know I only had seven pills in the bottle. I did not even notice that. Did he look in my bottle? I do not remember him looking at the bottle label. The only other way is if he prescribed it…weird
- † The little brush George had to clean the fireplace at Gage Lane had a green dot on it. I don't remember that brush from before
- † Why George had a whole bunch of UPC codes adhered to a bag of screening material
- † Why he had his grandmothers sewing machine when he never sewed
- † The colour of my daughters' eyes are blue but somehow I remember George's being brown
- † The colour of my sister Louise's eyes. They are brown.
- † What are the colour of my eyes…they are supposed to be blue.

- † My mom on the phone always says GOOD LUCK and it frustrates me. I don't remember my mom always saying that and it sounds like I have something to win
- † All the shows on HGTV seem to react to what I think…things move so fast now they're hard to record
    - † PVC piping I thought only came in white…they are shown in black
- † I feel like I am getting information sent back to me in black saying they from HGTV and George and Darcy got the information I thought.
    - † Tupperware containers-George bought $90.00 worth from a mom at my school selling them. Where did they all go?
    - † PVC Pipes-Mike Holmes
    - † Organ/piano Why did George get rid of my organ from my Uncle
- † American Idol- What stood out the most for me last night was the opening song and the Grey scarf…props…that signified things to me…The song sounded really nice and sort of was like a reaction to what you (Dr. Argle) and I had spoken about…only the words that stood out were "I just haven't met you yet"
- † That you, Dr. Argle wore orange when I thought about George having chosen an orange blouse for me to wear one time. I do not wear orange. This is when orange entered into the mix. At first it represented my psychiatrist but she did not want to be involved so I made it represent health. (As I read this for my final edit, I do not recall orange entering into the mix this way. I remember a man coming to the door at Wade Avenue wearing an orange T-shirt. Then I received messages from the media that British Columbia was happy because now the BC Lions could be a part of whatever is going on too. Now all the sport colours were represented.)
- † Mammography exam reminder came right after I thought about it

Saturday, March 13, 2010

- † Para Olympic Ceremony: All the colours that I spoke about were there.
  - † The people had to wear certain colours; and then there were pompoms, which reminded me of Jessica and her pompoms when she was a cheerleader. I also thought of me trying out for cheerleading and my sister becoming head cheerleader. I couldn't become one because I did not know how to do a cartwheel.
  - † They had songs and red and yellow lights which reminded me of the girls.
  - † They had children doing the speaking which I thought surprising and well done as with all the choreography which reminded me of school
  - † I could barely wear my cape
  - † The book was so inspiring and when I reached the Braille part, I thought of the CNIB and how when I was little I wanted to volunteer there. It was across the street close to the Granite Club of which my family were members growing up back in Tinsel Town
  - † They had butterflies, planets that reminded me of Grade six
  - † It was overwhelming when I saw the red twinkling lights at the Olympics ceremony. It was so overwhelming that I cried and Paula, George's sister never said a word. If it wasn't for Paula we never would have gone to anything for the Olympics. She also invited us to the Cirque de Soleil as well
  - † There was even orange in the same lights. After they shook it the pompom now had orange twinkling lights
  - † One of the speakers name was Clara too which reminded me of my cousin
  - † Even the bathroom had double blue and green tiles with grey square tiles; the stall I used also had one tile with brown in the middle and white on either side…I thought of George washing bathrooms at my school

MY COLOUR-CODED LIFE

- † The Canada line platform had the sign with a picture and the word damper and they didn't jive with what I thought a damper was…from what George told me about his days as a Chimney sweep a damper is inside the fireplace
- † The subway also had yellow poles you could hang onto which still means music and Darcy. I know it also means caution on the stoplight
- † I kept expecting to see my family, especially my Dad when Nikki Yanofsky who sang the Olympic song "Believe" sing …"Rise Up Again"
- † They spoke about Terry Fox – cheerleading- Jessica did her cheerleading at the Terry Fox High School-I used to receive quotes on the computer while taking my Masters for my graduate degree.
- † Rick Hansen was there …was it really him? It sounded like him. I tried to read his story to the class before I had to leave because of my health, in retrospect it was probably too heavy a book to read to the students. He was also at Ted's funeral
- † All the athletes were wearing the colours too,
    - † a lot of black and white
    - † The athletes wore Canadian sweaters with deer's on them. The deer reminded me of me and my nickname "Dear".
- † Even my sister in law, Paula's place, had the colours and a lot of things I've written or thought about…though it sounds like her …I would think this would be hard for her to really be her
- † They didn't Tear off the stubs of the tickets at the Para Olympic ceremony…they didn't scan it
- † The tickets said XO1 and I kept thinking of kiss and hug #1 and the only ones I could think of that represent that were maybe #1 Dad that Darcy sewed on the back of George's shirt and #1 dad written on my dad's headstone …#1 husband…#1 sister …when I thought that, the only thing I remembered #1 for me was on the butt of the

black pants Jessica gave me…as soon as I thought that a yellow light in George's car flashed
- † I cried through the whole ceremony
- † There was even a dance that created the shape of an eye
- † All the colours downtown even on the clock of city hall and now we seem to get yellow lights when we travel through
- † Remembering seeing Archbishop Raymond once and thinking, he looked like George too.
- † Going places and seeing square symbols which meant something after I realized the last prescription you, Dr. Argle, gave me
- † I enjoyed the Cirque de Soleil that we went to with Paula. George and I went to one in Las Vegas called "Love Love "with Beatles music and George said it was the best one. I beg to differ, there were hardly any acrobats.
- † That Nando's the restaurant has the same name as my cousin's son. I remember going there and the food being too hot for us. We've never been back since
- † I'm having trouble using the internet and trusting it…email…Facebook,
- † I'm having trouble believing people are who they should be on the phone again
- † I feel my teaching knowledge is being tested in addition to everything else that is going on

Noticed that while watching a movie the signs seem to have almost disappeared

Sunday, March 14, 2010

- † I noticed the first night I took the 5:00 p.m. pill that I became tired and could barely stand up to take my night pills but George said I should. I have been sleeping better…they feel like sedatives.
- † Going grocery shopping with George I thought of Jessica. While thinking how she likes certain noodles, she called George while we

were in the store…she hadn't been in contact with him for quite a while and that just seemed a bit uncanny

Monday, March 15, 2010

- † I had the strength to choose a pair of glasses…George was with me
- † I saw the colours at the Pacific Eye Doctor's as well…and at the BCAA
- † (I forgot to say that I noticed I was able to see far away with my reading glasses on at the TD Bank…so weird)
- † I had a rough morning looking through our recipe file. There were recipes there I had no idea where they came from
- † In case you didn't understand Babyliss which was a sign on some curlers at the hairdressers-I took it as a sign that Darcy really does not have a baby (Baby-less)
- † I have not been able to drink the water in the house from the fridge. In fact, ever since I bought the bottled water I have not been able to get enough of it. I'm drinking it like I did when I was small… So weird
- † I am still noticing things on the radio and the TV but they do not seem to bother me as much. I find I think something during the day and it shows up in a commercial or TV show

Tuesday, March 16, 2010

I was having a hard morning all by myself yesterday even after a really good night's sleep and really broke down a couple of times looking at **recipes** I was sure I didn't have of my Mom's. I called her even though I did not think it was her and talked to her. She said I would have all my **favourite recipes** but I do not. I forgot to ask her about Grandpa Jackson. George came home unexpectedly while I was talking to her so I cut off my conversation with her.

Canadian Tire- George had to go to Canadian Tire. Earlier I had thought about where in Yorkville I used to get my hair done and I could not remember the name of the salon but he went and stood at the counter and low and behold, it was on the box behind the counter, the name was Monroe's.

Another important piece of information to add here is one year I bought George a red Timberland golf shirt. He said he would not wear it because he would look like an employee of Canadian Tire. Several years later he discovered that Timberland was an expensive brand. He started wearing it.

BCAA- We went to get the insurance for the cars and I remembered I never went with him before we got the green van. Which was our third car. I also saw Sandi Renaldo wearing glasses and thought how I was just thinking how I need glasses. I also saw a name Boland that reminded me of a family that lived in the community I grew up in.

Pacific Eye Doctor's-I had the strength to buy glasses today with George. I do not think he has come with me before to choose glasses. Anyway, they took tests different from what I am used to…Anyway these glasses reminded me of the ones I had seen at Gaivota.

This reminds me of the first time I stayed with George in Tuckerville, I had a new pair of glasses I quite liked. He was quick to tell me that he did not like them. The frames were quite different and I have never seen a pair like them since.

I had noticed all the uniforms the girls were wearing were black this time. Last time I went with George and Jessica (two separate occasions) they were grey.

Bones – George and I talked about his old girlfriend Sue at BCAA and his ex-wife Mia whom the girls know nothing about. One of the names they used on the show was Sue. They also showed a red car and I had thought about the fancy red car George had had.

Tic Tac- Mom always gave the girls a lot of Tic Tac's

Darcy and Greg came home from a day out with black fuzzy die wrapped around Cassie's carseat, which means to me that they got the message and I am right that my Darcy does not have a baby. I had not thought of black until I saw these die. This is when my mind defined solid black.

I also have noticed that Darcy is the only one to redo the paint on the bedroom walls since we moved from Saber Road much like me when I grew up. I also noticed that she used purple in both rooms and last time she hand painted yellow flowers

I am still reminiscing and making name connections

HGTV seems to only play when Darcy is here; it was not on at five yesterday.

I still get many signs on HGTV and it reminds me of things I want to write about

I had thought about my sister, Mandy, playing Violin at a hall in Tinsel Town and the next day or so George bought a bottle of wine called Masi that reminded me of the name of the hall George Massey

Sometimes I think George and Darcy are also coaches or undercover to help me remember my past.

Cassie and Darcy seem to wear the colours and signs of purple and pink

I do not understand why Darcy can back into the garage sometimes and not others….and why she says Holy Moses when I hear Holy Crap most of the time.

Even Cassie seems to wear the colours

American Idol- This show is hard for me to watch sometimes because I like it and do not want to offend anyone

- † I was noticing what people were wearing and all the lights. All the judges were wearing some form of Grey but Randy he was wearing a light blue cardigan. He was still wearing the multi-coloured beads
- † The guys were all wearing chains around their necks and one was wearing a cross
- † All the contestants were wearing some form of black which is sort of a sign to me that things I'm thinking are right
- † I noticed all the red, purple and yellow lights which I think are a sign to me

Wednesday, March 17, 2010

† BOWEL PAIN, GAS, I used to suffer from this for years while first married but no longer…they said I had IBS, if I did why did it disappear?

I remember some competition between a wedding, a new home and my music too

I feel like the title of the HGTV Show Extreme Makeover is meant for me. Not only the colours mean something but their actions too…they started dancing after I had thought about dancing. The title also matches what I feel is happening to me.

Even my computer underscores things in colours that mean something to me.

I have noticed my face is dry as well as my lips and I am more thirsty than hungry, although I will start eating around dinnertime usually.

Thursday, March 25, 2010

Things I used to notice:

Things I am curious about

George was wondering whether I should have an MRI considering the brain flips I have had in the past…Maybe it is related and I have a tumor or something. I thought so when I had the flips…but I have only had two.

If being over sexual is a symptom, than why hasn't it happened to me again?

George's reactions to things:

Thursday, March 18, 2010- George said he bought his Whistler Blackcomb sweatshirt in Whistler but the only clothing we bought were turtlenecks when he first took me to Whistler. When I told him that, he started coughing and said he was coming down with some sort of cold and should stay away from us. When he coughed like that, I thought he was signalling someone I could not see.

Friday, March 19, 2010- George has no cold today and he did not stay away from us. George did not mind buying bottled water for me even though we hooked up the water to the fridge for me. The water here still tastes Terrible. When we first had water installed at Saber Road we had big canisters under the sink…now we do not.

Saturday, March 20, 2010 When George and I went to shop for golf shoes we stopped off at Tim Horton's and he seemed surprised they had the roll up to win on when they had it the last time we went.

When George said, he planned to shoot some golf balls this afternoon he did not automatically tell me he planned to go with his brother-in-law, until I asked him if he wanted to go alone. I was going to ask if I could tag along when he told me…this is not like him. He said that his brother-in-law is in rough shape and was going to let him know at 1:00 p.m. … they went.

Things that concern me

- † Remembering I said something at school or home about hugs vs. action. I was reminded of this on Friday, March 19, 2010 show of Extreme Makeover
- † Saturday, March 20, 2010 Holmes on Homes episode reminded me how as much as I liked our house at 7535 Gage Lane I was also unsettled by it. I thought it would make the perfect drug house because of how private it was from every angle. I used to be concerned about the unnecessary amount of time George spent outside. He even had me cook dinners 3 times a week because he would rush outside. It was unnecessary no matter what he says. I was concerned about the open ground I found under the kitchen. I got so upset I borrowed Jocelyn's (a colleague from school) Holy Oil to sprinkle in every room. There was a hidden fuse box above a false ceiling, a

hidden package of cigarette and access to hidden plastic bags. When I showed George he said I should not be concerned. I was and still am.

Because of these hidden plastic bags and their possible use I thought we should rid society of them. I thought maybe the recycling movement was started because of me.

Things I notice:

Saturday, March 20, 2010-remembering about my Dad's brogues when George showed me some shoes he was interested in buying.

- † Also saw yellow soles in some golf shoes I liked, but I wasn't ready to buy shoes
- † HGTV's show Curb Appeal reminded me how George chose our paint colour for the outside of the house on Saber Road all by himself and chose a painter that had one hand. We chose the same painters for inside the house when we were ready to sell but I chose the paint colours and had a terrible time choosing. He also let me choose the paint colour for outside Gage Lane and again I had to look all over the neighbourhood before I found the shade of green I liked.
- † We never did any updating to our house in Brampton, other than draperies, air conditioning and a homemade jungle gym out back and that house George sold by himself through Peartree. I cannot remember how we sold our house in North Dakota. My recollection is different from George's. I thought we rented to own that place and we just got out of it. I do not remember any real estate agent, visitors or buyers.
- † George wanted me to deposit my cheque through the machine but I wanted to do it at a teller. He said that was a waste of time so he would not go with me. I went with Darcy, there were cop cars there, and no one was allowed in the bank. I would've gone to the other bank but George specifically likes me to use this one

specific branch…While in the car I saw a girl going towards the bank wearing a dark blue t-shirt and on the back it said this is my game…I didn't know what that meant….but I didn't deposit the cheque.

Sunday, March 21, 2010

I still am uncomfortable listening to the radio station. George usually has it on FUN FM, which I have never heard of before. Sometimes I think they called it that because I sing to Cassie and tell her to dream and have some fun. Listening to music emits many emotions…sometimes I think they are telling me something and I just do not want to hear it and think they are wrong. We used to wake to Fred and Cathy Latremouille at Gage Lane who coincidentally have the same last name as my grade 8 teacher.

I took my first Ativan today because George thought I should. I was remembering about meals out and times together as a family. I think George in his way has isolated us from family and friends.

Monday, March 22, 2010

Remembering how I used to go to my dad when I had a bad dream made me think of our girls and how they never came into our bedroom. When we lived at Gage Lane Jessica used to sleep in her sisters room for comfort. Darcy never wanted me to put my arm around her when I lay beside her to say goodnight when we lived at Saber Road. I am worried something bad might have happened to her too. Why did Jessica cry when Darcy and I left for school? She still had her dad.

While in Safeway I was wondering again, about why they call the ham I have been buying black forest when I saw for the first time they had regular cooked ham. While walking out of Safeway I noticed the rug cleaners they have called The Rug Doctor and thought how our rug doctor used to be The Mighty One carpet cleaners when the girls were small…I connected that to a T-shirt I had made for an old boyfriend that said the same thing.

I also noticed today that after thinking about the various ways my name is spelled while at Delta Municipal Hall, TD Waterhouse sent mail with my name misspelled.

Tuesday, March 23, 2010

I wonder whether it was planned that George walk up to me in the bar of the Keg in Tuckerville…after all, he was apparently having dinner with thirteen other women. Did my dad have something to do with it? It strikes me as odd now why me out of a crowd?

The radio in the house still seems unreal to me. They are giving away tickets to groups that have ceased performing on dates that have passed and I cannot change radio stations.

I checked the inside of our couch cushions here and they are made of yellow foam, so Sandy's could not have made it with mattress.

I am still making name connections and, since I know what all the colours mean and see the colours everywhere, even on Cassie's bottle caps. I connect them to the person they represent. So, when I see yellow, I will say in my head "Darcy". The same is true with the other colours.

I am not as emotional, my left leg hurts, and I feel somewhat sad that everything is fading somewhat…music still has an impact on me when I hear certain songs.

Thursday, March 25, 2010

We talked to Jessica the other day on Skype. As usual, I had nothing to say because I was afraid to speak, but I noticed she was drinking out of a water jug with a straw. It turns out she has strep and is taking Echinacea. When I heard that I thought she in some way knew what I wrote in this book because as far as I remember she did not take Echinacea even though George always used to promote it. We do not have any here and have not had any for years.

I sometimes feel a little like St. Bernadette because nobody believed her but on the other hand, I feel everybody believes me and is trying to help me in some way. They do say that thoughts like believing everyone is supporting me are grandiose thoughts and a psychotic symptom.

I do not believe what I see on the news.

Now my doctor has asked that I make a list of Pros and Cons of my situation but I am not sure how to go about it, so I am not going to.

Saturday, February 21, 2015

As I reread my book, I will try to express the Pros and Cons of living with my mental health situation.

PROS

- † The colours and music help me dream of many things. A big house on the lake like a log home where I can hang paintings made by my favorite artists like Roy Henry Vickers and Robert Bateman. A real wood fireplace (no idea how to get the wood chopped) and items like a totem pole carved by Bill Reid, plus a house near my kids in the city, my own central music system that I can access my own music too in both homes!! Maybe Mike Holmes could be instrumental in these. It would also be nice to have a beautiful stone home in Tinsel Town, which has room for my dog to play, a female boxer. I would like my home in Tinsel Town to be in Rosedale or Moore Park. Each has to have a house cleaner, a gardener and chef. All to pass down to my girls. Or relocate my entire family to where I now live in British Columbia and set them up with homes and work if they want to work. And if possible relocate my friends here too and give them work if they want. Perhaps even an income property that Scott McGillivray would renovate or someone just as good. All homes I would want wire free with lots of light. I would like a craft room and a new piano like I saw at Tom Lee but to have it look like a grand piano with all the doodads like the organ my uncle gave me.

I would like to enable my girls and their significant others not to have to work unless they want to. A car that is techy and advanced made just for me with first nation designs on the side, meeting Oprah and share my story, publishing my book, having it made into a movie, having my guitar songs published and recorded, especially the ones that are good. I like my song, Souls Design but I also like the one I made for dad. Any they deem good, even the one I made for Carol before she was born, and my Teacher Teacher song.

† Having a big bash with music and movie stars whom I feel have all been guiding me like Ariel Birkhead, Josh Groban, Katy Perry and Taylor Swift, Paul McCartney, Whitney Houston, Beyoncé and the guy who sings the Happy song, Pharrell Williams and Elton John. I would love to hear Candle in the Wind. I love Celine Dion's style of music but they are all love songs and I don't feel that way toward my husband. I would like Gary Barlow to also be there and many more that have helped me. I want Gary to be my happy ever after!! I want to be his girl forever!! I would love to hear symphonies too. We will dance!!

† The colours and music seem to make me feel special, intelligent and made for a purpose I have yet not fulfilled

† The colours and music make me feel like I have a lot to look forward to and be thankful for now. I remember having a retreat with St. Anne's and feeling I had nothing to be thankful for. Until recently I had stopped dreaming.

† My first conference was completely inspiring when the choir sang and the one song that stuck to me was If We Dare to Hope by Bobby Fisher.

† I dream that my home on the lake would have a dock that attracts no leeches. That it would have a speed boat with water skiis and tubes and such. Plus fishing rods for fishing on the lake and a canoe with native designs. Maybe another boat specific for trolling. I loved Lake Muskoka I wish there was a lake like that close by. I would love it to be a log home.

† The colours have helped me think and create things

    † Like entering your house with a palm print or fingerprint

MY COLOUR-CODED LIFE

- † Having public places use hand sanitizer that dispenses with the wave of a hand to rid them of most sinks and towels and dryers. These can also be used in homes
- † Use finger prints to enter cars ridding the need for keys and auto shops would have to have a universal entry system to access all cars but they would have to undergo criminal record checks
- † Ridding the country of the need to carry currency and credit cards by everyone registering their fingerprints. The stores' terminals can be a reader of the fingerprint where it automatically connects to their bank. The customer can choose which method they would like to pay. This system can be used for parking as well and travelling on the sky train (subway). This system could be applied worldwide.
- † Having heat sensors around cars that detect people – from what I overheard Greg say to George, this has already been developed
- † I also think that a fingerprint could run pay parking as well, and have access on your phone to extend the time if necessary.

CONS

- † That perhaps none of this is real
- † That now both girls won't talk to me
- † That their eyes are not opened to their dad
- † That I never get justice for what George has put me through
- † That it all disappears and I am left with nothing but an unhappy life
- † That my dreams and creations will never come to fruition
- † That I never get to create and be a part of an online school for grades Jk-doctorate for both Catholic and public schools
- † That I don't get to work with the technology giants like Apple and Microsoft and Google
- † That perhaps Donald Trump doesn't help me

- † That I won't get to meet George Clooney, Winston Reckert, Morgan Freeman, Oprah or the many musicians that have helped including Robbie Williams who seems to get so emotional over the whole thing.
- † That Catholic schools don't get 100 % funded by the government
- † That I don't get my doctorate
- † That I will never be with a man that truly loves me (touches me) and helps me live
- † That I will never have a wedding surrounded by all my colours like Darcy's with all my relatives
- † That I will never have a father daughter dance-perhaps my brother can take his place
- † That I will never go dancing again with the man who loves me
- † That this book never gets published and made into a movie
- † That my songs never get released
- † That I never live in a grand home on a lake surrounded by all the things I love that I can pass down through generations including a totem pole and perhaps a huge place in the city where I am connected to the bank and computer tech guys like ED and Aziz from the computer store.
- † That my girls don't get their own homes they like and have room to be themselves and decluttered
- † That if I live where I want that I am not isolated from friends and family
- † That Jessica and I will never be close, go shopping, talking, going to coffee shops
- † That my girls are never proud of me
- † That I am actually not working now
- † Or that I won't be paid for lost wages
- † That I am restricted access to TV, internet, home phone and cell phone
- † That I won't be able to have a proper nickname like Mimi or Mickey. Each has pros and cons. Mimi was given to me by my niece which I love but it is George's cousin wife's name. An old boyfriend gave Mickey to me and the girls used it eons ago, although it represents

MY COLOUR-CODED LIFE

Mickey Mouse it also represents a mickey of booze! I'm not decided on which I like best. I just don't like "Dear" I have decided that I like Mickey. I want to be connected to Wesley Disney! I will leave Mimi as private with my niece and her parents

† That I won't be able to afford the mortgages on my dream places. I dream that they are all paid for.
† That I won't get a Boxer pup. I would like a fawn female boxer whom I would call Mocha unless she came already named through her pedigree as Barclay was. I'm just not sure how to get it as well trained as Barclay was because I want her as a puppy just like Barclay and Kaiser were
† That I won't get eye contacts that gradually go dark with the sun and go clear during the day without removing your eye colour, if that's even possible.
† That the changes I hope for the Catholic Church will never happen.
† That I won't find a good place to train my new dog like the kind of training Barclay got.
† That I won't be called Grandma instead of Nana
† That I won't be able to connect with all the students and people I have been name connecting about…all my students, colleagues and people I know from my past.
† That my family and I will not have to go through hoops to go over the border or travel. That now I am a trusted traveler that I am not hassled going over the border or have to go through so many hoops to renew the Nexus pass or passport. I think they should just update your photo for these things perhaps but it should not be necessary to fill out the papers again. When I think about it with facial recognition you should not even need a picture.
† The passport office should contact you when your passport is going to expire. There should be no need to go in and update it. In fact there is no need for the passport or Nexus card.
† That I will not have the credit or rights for my creations, songs, book, book to movie, or technology and urban planning ideas.
† That I will not reap the financial benefits from my creations

- † That my computer will stop functioning so well and I won't get a new updated one
- † That I will stop getting super service by Daryl at Future Shop and Aziz at Best Buy
- † That I will never find a velvet long sleeve black little dress again
- † That I won't get a new wardrobe and feel pretty enough to wear clothes other than jeans.
- † That I won't get off this medication
- † That I won't become slim again
- † That I won't have a house that gives me room for my shoes and a special place to put on my makeup and keep my jewelry that is easy to store and get to.
- † That I will never know what my First Nation totem is
- † That I won't get a native button blanket with a button for every student I taught.
- † That I won't see the students I keep name associating. It's like I'm calling everyone I know by name by being reminded by names on the TV. For instance if the name on TV is George, I will think of all the people I know named George including students and come up with their last names. The same is true if I see a last name I recognize, I will think of the first names.
- † That I don't have big money for my favourite charities: Heart and Stroke, Canadian Mental Health Authority, Ronald McDonald House.
- † That I will never see a Canucks or Maple Leafs game live
- † That I will never again experience the thrill of attending live events for the Olympics
- † That I won't be able to see the musicals I am interested in
- † That I can't have a family reunion with my side in a pretty place where we all hang together and do fun things together
- † That I won't be able to see another live baseball game like my brother gave us seats to in Tinsel Town
- † That I won't see another live football game of the BC Lions or the Tinsel Town Argonauts

- † That the park I initiated for Darcy in Brampton Ontario is never named after me for inspiring its makeover in her name. I was so heart-broken to see the sign on the park when I visited years after.
- † That I never get to try and ride a horse again
- † That I never get to go deep sea fishing like my dad always wanted to do. I doubt it's as crazy out there as George says.

Saturday, March 27, 2010

I went out to lunch with Darcy, Cassie and George and still saw so many signs.

George said he had no previous plans that we would go to the restaurant that we went to…but with all the colours, it sure seemed like it. It was decorated in red, so although Jessica was not there I felt she was. I also felt that the whole restaurant cared about what was going on. I had never gone to the bathroom in the restaurant Charlie Don't Surf before but I have been several times. In the bathroom, they had purple draperies and a light right over the toilet. They even had a couch in the restaurant, which was red. I have not had very good lunches when I have been out with George before but this was an exception. I had their West Coast Bouillabaisse, which reminded me of the soup I would have at the restaurant in Steveston when we went with Dad.

Friday, April 2, 2010

(50 mg loxapine-10 mg in morning, 10 mg at dinner and 30 mg at bedtime) I was taking 10-15-25 but taking 15 mg at dinner wasted me for the rest of the evening. This sedative feeling makes me believe that that is exactly what this medication is, and not an anti-psychotic. I was also given 0.5 mg lorazepam to take twice a day as needed if I feel nervous. Sunday, February 22, 2015 I feel the same way with the 5 mg of Saphris I am taking now. I believe that it is a sedative of sorts coming from within like an iDoc that is implanted in you, just like what I read about in a novel. I am sleeping better

now that George is not sleeping with me. It's either something inside me controlling my body heat, sleep etc. But I strongly feel others are in control of what I see, taste, and how I sleep, I also think they are controlling my access to the TV, internet, radio and cell phone. They all don't seem to work properly.

Sadly, a lot of the stimulation has disappeared and I do not cry as often. I did cry today, once, when I heard the beginnings of Born in the USA play by Bruce Springsteen on George's phone. It made me think of our little girl that was conceived in the United States and had to be therapeutically aborted. I began to cry when I thought back as to why George left me to go back to work. He flew away and I was still overwrought. My dad comforted me.

We went to Petra's, which is a coffee shop, today and when I looked around I noticed so many things that make me think that I'm not crazy… like painted starfish. George used to throw starfish into the water…I even saw an owl…which represents my brother because he caught an owl on a fishing hook when he was younger.

On Monday, George and I left for Tofino, the last place we vacationed with Dad. We stayed at the Wickaninnish Inn in Room 209 with an amazing view of the ocean! It should have been a romantic retreat but for me it was just a retreat where stimulation was at a minimum. It was nice to bundle up and let the rain fall all around me. The only time I became emotional was after going through Roy Henry Vickers Art Gallery. I really like his work…but I have become fussier, you could say, with what I like. I would like the colours of some, but not the content, and some appeared very lonely. What did strike me was one that was entirely yellow with a pair of eyes that he called "The Warrior". I began to think about how sometimes in native lore natives go on a journey to find what their totem will be, an eagle, owl, bear etc. I wondered what mine would be. Also, the painting being yellow made me wonder whose supposed to represent this warrior… Was it supposed to represent me because I keep looking and trying to figure things out?

I talked to my sister tonight and Liz, my girlfriend the other day, and they both are pleased with how cognizant I am about everything. This may be true, but it saddens me because with part of this delusion comes so many hopes, dreams and expectations built by what I see around me and every time I think they're going to appear…they don't. My birthday is tomorrow, maybe then they will appear.

Saturday, April 3, 2010

As much as I said that I have not really thought about my dad, I really have this time around. I even had hopes of seeing him on my birthday and he died 10 years ago on November 27, 2000. I even had high hopes that my daughter Jessica would phone me today, but she has not really spoken with me in at least 5 years, so why would I think today would be different. Because when I was at the Olympic celebration and I saw all the twinkling red lights in the pompoms, I felt it was a message saying that she really did love me. It hurts that she goes out of her way for her dad but really ignores me.

Some of my delusions that I feel sad to not be true were to have an extreme home makeover. A house filled with custom native art. A brand new wardrobe and to have my music published especially my song to George called Soul's Design. I think it is a neat name. Even my song to my dad would be neat to be published, and then maybe he would hear it.

I have been doing the laundry for five years now at Wade Avenue and not one of George's socks have developed holes at the big toe. He used to say it was because of his big toe. I used to think it was because he was using it for drugs or something. Even little squares were cut from my Manhattan T Shirts that I really liked.

Monday, April 5, 2010

I am still on 50 mg Loxapine and as needed Lorazepam

As much as I would like to play my guitar again, I look at old songs I wrote and feel someone has adjusted them in some way. I also do not have a copy of the song I first wrote George when he was living in Utah and when I asked him what happened to it he said he does not know. He also did not remember me writing songs for him on our nineteenth anniversary that I sang to him and recorded. He has not appreciated the music and effort put into the songs I created for him and it hurts.

I must admit that everything seems to be fading now. I am not making the same connections nor are the colours making such an impact. My life just seems to be my life, with dreams just that …dreams…not dreams becoming reality. It is all coinciding with the drugs I am taking but I am too stubborn to admit it is the drugs, because I really do want to be caught up in something where I will eventually get answers and where Jessica and I will once again feel comfortable talking to one another and she might actually like hanging around me. Right now I feel scared around her even though I desperately want her around because I do not know what to say. I am afraid she will bite my head off. It is terrible feeling so torn by your own daughter.

It is terrible feeling isolated in your own home where you are not sure who is who. Right now, George and I are doing the 2009 taxes and I am still not quite certain he is my husband, but I go along with it.

Wednesday, April 7, 2010

I have been taking my medication religiously and I must admit that I am no longer feeling as connected to the TV shows that we watch. I am no longer feeling like there is something for me to figure out…some message. I feel a little more confident but I feel sad at the same time. Because when things are real, I am no longer someone special whom good things are going to happen because I have persevered through all this.

I must have part of my mind intact though if I was the one who noticed my symptoms and not someone else.

On Friday April 10, we leave for Kinter Valley. We probably would not be going if I did not suggest it. As much as I want to go I am afraid to be around Jessica for fear that she will ignore me. I am usually quiet around her now, so I am hoping she talks to me.

Sunday, April 11, 2010

Our trip to Kinter Valley was uneventful. I took a Lorazepam pill when we were going to meet Jessica for dinner on Friday at the Cabana, which is connected to the condominium we own at The Playa Del Sol. I was admittedly nervous. She was nice, though she did not go out of her way to initiate a conversation with me. I broke the ice by asking her if she liked my glasses. She responded positively and the rest of the meal was fine I actually felt normal. The next morning Jessica and George went golfing and Darcy and I went shopping and met one of her friends. I was actually able to buy clothes. The colours did not bother me and there seemed to be no messages to decode.

Saturday night though, the night of April 10th we had a barbecue at the condominium with Jessica's roommates. Her boyfriend whom we found out about because I asked the previous night and Fraser and Dave who are two of her roommates' boyfriends were good hosts. I found it difficult to converse with her and her friends and talk, partially because they were glued to the TV and two, I just felt awkward. Although, I had taken two lorazepam pills, I found they were of no use at all! I wish we had just connected as a family and Jessica could have invited her boyfriend if she had liked.

George wanted to get together with Tara and her husband who are friends of his. Tara used to be married to Connor, but I just was not into it. I preferred staying at the bar at the Eldorado and relaxing there. I also feel jealous that we always see his friends and never see mine!

Even baby Cassie was an angel on the trip. She slept most of the drive and was never cranky except for a little bit when we were at the Cabana, but that was it.

I guess you could say that I am back to normal, which makes Dr. Argle glad…, but as I tell her, it saddens me because I no longer feel special. I still have problems that are deep rooted with George and I am in no way ready for any intimate contact.

Tuesday, April 13, 2010

Perhaps I am not normal. I am not getting messages but I want them! I want Darcy to be childless. I am not ready for it, yet the more I am grounded with this medication the more I feel that her soap opera is my life too! She got pregnant by a boy that I used to teach and in fact, they were both in the same grade four class when I taught them. I am angry with the mother for allowing them to be in the same room at her house! I am embarrassed by the whole thing and want it all to disappear, even though the baby is cute and sweet I cannot help but be resentful at the same time! Actually she brings sunshine into all our lives!! Cassie is so special and I am also happy she is in our lives!!

I want to write a book about my experiences with all this but who is going to help me decide what is better to leave out.

I tried talking to Darcy about writing the book and all but, she was so distant that it was hard to be frank. When she is so disconnected like that, I really feel that she must not be my daughter at all but because she plays my daughter, I trust her in some weird way. I mustn't be too hard though because she has a lot on her mind regarding custody of the baby. However when I told Jessica of my idea she was very receptive of me publishing a book.

Darcy took me out so I could run some errands. I still do not feel confident driving and running errands myself. We went to the eye doctors so I could have my glasses adjusted, then to the drugstore. We also went to R&R music where I bought a set of classical guitar strings. I was awestruck with how cheap they were…maybe it is a trick or something. George used to be able to string my guitar; maybe he can show me how. February 21, 2015-It seems he doesn't know how to do it anymore.

I also took Darcy out to lunch. We went to the a local pizza place. I wanted something to stimulate my taste buds and they certainly delivered! We have never gone there so we both thought at the same time that it would be nice to try. I am sure glad we did…even the music they played was refreshing and upbeat! Once again, Cassie was an angel and a pleasure to be out with.

Wednesday, April 14, 2010

What I do not understand is how my intuition can be so far off! As much as my husband demands full trust, how can I trust him when he doesn't have clear answers for me, especially regarding the couch! I want a husband who hugs me, not just when asked for one! As much as I want a new dream house, I want trust and love back in my life!

I am still reading into things on the TV. I saw a commercial for Miracle Whip and remembered what it meant. It said they were not going to give up sending me messages! Miracle Whip meant the Catholics wanting me to have a miracle cure!

Also of interest is the tissue paper of George's birthday gift to me, it was blue and white!

Thursday, April 15, 2010

I had my appointment with Dr. Argle today and she does not think we need to see each other for another 2 weeks. We talked about how things went well in Kinter Valley with Jessica and about George and my discomforts and how counseling might be in the cards when I am better.

Friday, April 16, 2010

I had a great morning with Darcy and Cassie in Whittle Head this morning. The weather was gorgeous and we goofed around for a couple of hours. It was great to be out of the house! We were actually out early because Darcy wanted to talk to a counselor at the courthouse regarding the papers she was served by Robbie (Cassie's dad) and his Mom. She totally forgot that they were not open today, hence our beautiful morning in Whittle Head!

This afternoon while Darcy was out with Cassie, I took the opportunity to give Liz, my girlfriend a call and we spoke for about 2 hours! It was great! She is such a solid good friend! It's just she never wants to come and stay with me and it's so hard to connect face to face. (February 22, 2015 I would like to get away to somewhere warm with my girlfriends.)

George came home all excited about a truck that he went and got a quote for. I do not want a truck and do not see the need for one at our age. It will just be used by other members of the family for things. I do not want one, unless he got a truck and I got a car.

Saturday, April 17, 2010

We had an appointment to go see the truck at 9:30 but I guess George changed his mind after my voicing my opinion. I also told him I do not think this is the time we should be making big purchases considering all that is happening to me.

We picked up my dry cleaning and while I was there, I noticed the owner handing back shirts to another man on white hangers. So if they do use white hangers they likely use blue hangers. Such a story I have spun. Truth must be I am schizoaffective and I feel like tearing my brain out! February 21, 2015 - My head feels so clear and I am able to formulate my thoughts. I think there is something big out there for me.

George left this afternoon to go watch my brother-in-law build a deck and as he was leaving I stopped him and said, "You don't kiss me good-bye anymore" His response was "You don't kiss me in the morning" There's no winning with him. (February 21, 2015 Truth be told I have lost interest in him).

I am sad. I have lost the one thing I held so dear, my brain! The pills have brought some semblance to my life, granted, but it has not built my confidence yet and I need that. It also has not helped with my comfort of reading either. I still cannot find a novel to read! I need to feel accomplished and I feel so useless. (February 22, 2015 I don't think it's the pills that settle me I think it's the external things that change.)

I am supposed to meet with Jason; he works at Duncan Mental Health, about some community social worker meeting with me. I am not sure whether I like the idea, but maybe I should take advantage of all the help I can get. I am not depressed but I am sad. And it makes it worse when I see people who are physically challenged and I think about all the challenges they must face. It makes me feel like such a wimp!

I had a melt down after writing the last paragraph. I started crying and asked for a hug from George. When Darcy saw, she joined. I asked for my old brain back and George said he wishes it were back too. He was not very comforting. I tried to phone my Mom and vent but she cannot hear, does not understand and tends to repeat herself in one conversation.

Monday, April 19, 2010

George and I went out to dinner at the Keg last night. He started talking to me about vehicles again. I am concerned about getting a vehicle, especially another big one. He says four-wheel cars cannot take us to where we can go fishing and he knows that is something I would like to do again. That is not enough of a reason to get a big truck! I do not care how cheap it is especially if I can't have a small car.

He knows I am not comfortable driving right now and especially at night. He also knows how I feel about drinking and driving, and went ahead and not only ordered a double Keg size scotch, but a glass of wine too. He may have had more if I had not asked him about his plans as to who was driving home. As it is, I took the keys!

Before we left for dinner, we watched the Junos, or the last night of it. We apparently missed it on Saturday night. I somehow felt connected to the show and the only songs I recognized were from Mitch Bublé. I did not realize that the song I had heard on American Idol "I just haven't met you yet" was his song.

There are things on my computer that do not make sense as well. When I punched in the website for music counts that they advertised during the Junos it wouldn't come up and finally it came up with "Did you mean www.musiccounts.ca?" and that's exactly what I had typed. Another thing that is weird is that when I found the new website for St. Anne's the URL's did not match the grade page I was visiting. I did not check all of them but the grade four page had the URL for grade three.

Jason phoned this morning and changed our appointment from 10:00 a.m. this morning to the afternoon. I chose 1:00 p.m. I am interested to know what it is all about. From what I got out of what he said in Dr. Argle's office; there is paperwork that needs filling out for me to go for coffee with a community social worker. What I do not understand is that Dr. Argle said Angie wouldn't go out for coffee with me because she is the case manager. Well since Angie is taking over for Jemma and so did Norma, why did Norma go out with me? I do not understand Jemma's job, all she does is sit in meeting with Dr. Argle and me. Even Eva came over to the house.

I met with Jason and we have signed me up for this person to be my community support worker to get me out of the house. I am not sure how I feel about it. It is not like having a real friend …this is their job! I will try to keep an open mind.

I went out for coffee and a walk in Whittle Head with George, Darcy and Cassie. It was a beautiful day!

Wednesday, April 21, 2010

Every time I go on the Archdiocese's website I keep thinking about how I had talked about the board having a website and connecting all the schools and no sooner had I wrote about it in one of my papers for my Master's, it happened.

I also am proud of the fact that the school is continuing to use Teacher Web to communicate with parents. I do think the school should put the money out and have either Teacher Web do the School site page or have a company do it because it still lacks pizzazz and there is no school picture!

I look back on my Master's thesis and wonder why we had to write it as if we were going to do it. I am just glad I was able to at least accomplish my action research and it meant something. I just hope they continue to use Teacher Web and really find it useful. I have been so out of loop for so long it would be a learning curve for me to learn all about it again for Teacher Web has evolved so much.

I asked Darcy the other day since she spends so much time with me to let me know when she thinks things are weird with me. She did not notice anything this past time until I asked her a month ago about her dad falling off the ladder years ago and wanting minute details. I was way into my episode by then so it is a good thing I notice things myself when they go weird. Both George and Darcy did not notice anything until after I told them things were weird again. Go me!

Let me explain what happened when George fell off the ladder. Many years ago when Darcy was four and Jessica was three and playing in the backyard, George was washing the bedroom windows in the backyard which were on the second floor. He fell and hit the cement. Darcy called 911 and Jessica put her mittens under his head, I was told. I was at work.

What bothers me as I look back is that he had no broken bones and the trajectory does not make sense to me.

Thursday, April 29, 2010

(50 mg Loxapine at bedtime)

I saw Dr. Argle today and there's no change in medication because things are going well. I have been very good about taking my medication all along. It was only the first time after I came home from the hospital that I stopped.

I met Angie today who is taking over for Jemma while she is on maternity leave. She is going to meet me on Monday and we are going for a walk I think. Anyhow, Dr. Argle and I had a very nice chat and for some reason the toilet episode came up and she said I had never told her. So I explained everything to her.

We talked about work and brought Angie up to speed on my work situation with my school. Dr. Argle suggested that I talk to Shelagh at her office to discuss what other work situations that my skills might match, since I am not sure about returning to teaching and she already has met with me before and done some testing. Shelagh is not back until May 10 so I will wait to check in with her. (February 22, 2015 Teaching and learning is my passion but I want to use technology. I was so burned out and deflated about the Catholic Church and all the extra-curricular things teachers have to do. I do not want to coach teams. I want to cheer for them. I get stressed taking kids on field trips. Those were my roadblocks! George influenced me to leave because he felt my school never treated me properly but they were like my second family. I used to be uplifted by their music at the conferences. I was awed the first time I went. However, I was stressed in knowing how to get to the venue each year. I used to love the band that played "Don't quit your day job" it was fun to dance with a co-worker, just to dance again.)

One thing that I found interesting during our talk was Dr. Argle saying it was good that I was assertive in telling George that I did not want a truck. I told her that George had come home a couple of weeks ago wanting us to look at a truck that he was interested in getting. I told him I did not want a truck so we did not end up going to look at it. The next week he looked at a Subaru and we went out in that. This week he looked at a Mercedes Benz and he took it for a drive. I'd rather the Mercedes of course. No matter what we will still have to wait before we can afford it on our line of credit. Any way I just thought it was odd that she mentioned that it was good that I was assertive, like she knew how I was at home. I did not think that she knew about that but I guess she did. Interesting.

Today Darcy went out to visit some friends so I grabbed my courage, drove myself to the drugstore to pick up my prescription, and then went clothes shopping. Overall, it was a successful day!

Saturday, May 1, 2010

Jessica drove down last night!

Today was fantastic! George, Jessica and I went car shopping. We went to see the Mercedes, a Lincoln and an Audi. I even had the guts to test-drive the Lincoln because we took side roads. Afterwards we went for lunch at the Blue Angel Cafe. What was great about today is the fact that Jessica actually conversed with me. It felt great. I feel great because she was so nice. Darcy did not come with us because she was at a birthday party with Cassie.

Tuesday, May 4, 2010

Today is Tuesday. On Sunday, Jessica and I went shopping to get her some things from the drugstore. The fact that she was willing to have me take her was amazing ...and we actually conversed. I am sooooo happy! I do not know what brought about this turn around. I am just glad it has happened.

On Monday, yesterday, I met with Angie and I drove to the offices myself. (I am starting to drive more, which is great!) We did not go walking because the weather was not nice. Instead, we went to Esquires, which is right across from the parking lot. I shared with her the history I have had with Jessica and how much this weekend has meant to me. We also talked about teaching, my old school, and what I would like to do. I felt it was a very productive talk and feel it might actually lead somewhere. She is a very nice person and very easy to talk to. I meet with her again next week on Tuesday at 10:00 a.m.

2011

In January, we bought a Mercedes GLK. I just went along. I would have settled for a much cheaper car. In fact, I am a little embarrassed to be driving this car. Anyway, George thought it would last us a long time and likely, the last car we will need to buy. He really wanted a four-wheel drive for drives up to Kinter Valley. Anyway, I picked out the colour, a special grey, from the slim choices that they had. He just drives it on the weekend, and I am still so reluctant to drive that he is registered as the principal driver. If I get a job or anything, then it will change.

Thursday, May 26 2011

I have been healthy for some time now but I have to say I am sad. My sister Louise passed away suddenly on Sunday May 22, 2011 she was only 61 years old. I will miss her terribly! She and I would talk on the phone nearly every day this past year. I am so glad we did. She was such a big part of my life. She died of a blood clot. I blame the hospital for not prescribing blood thinners for her when they discharged her.

Jessica has offered to go to Tinsel Town with me because Mom is in the hospital. I think we will wait to go later in the summer when my brother-in-law buries Louise on top of Dad. I need to be there for that. By that time, Mom will be in a nursing home and settled in. That way I will have a mental image of where she is.

Jessica ended up going to Tinsel Town on her own to visit her boyfriend and I went on my own for the service and stayed with my sister Mandy for 2 weeks. During the first week, Mandy drove to Montreal and I was able to see my Aunt Dorothy and my cousins, Clara and Helena. I had not seen my cousins in about 40 years! It was so nice of Mandy to do that. I did not get to see my Aunt Laura or my uncle Jacob. Plus I did not get to see all my cousins.

The next week I was thankful that my brother-in-law, Gabe, and niece, Carol, were there because they helped fill my days while Mandy went to work. I think Mandy thought I would be more independent than I am and go off and do things on my own using a taxi or something.

Earlier on in the year, I visited the Open Door Group, which is an agency that helps people with disabilities find work. The woman who is helping me suggested I take some psychological testing to see what other areas I would be good at other than teaching. I agreed and Open Door paid. The results were hard to take. They said that the disease and the medication have affected my memory and that I do not have the skills indicative of someone with the amount of education that I have. They said it would be better to stick with what was familiar, teaching, and to work part time. This is hard to do because no one is hiring.

Tuesday, July 26, 2011

We met with our new financial advisor today. He is going to revise our retirement plan for 2014. I am not ready to retire if it means golfing every day. We will meet again to transfer over my RRSP with Great West Life through the Archdiocese to the TD Bank, go over George's Insurance Policy that Dad set up and give him a breakdown of our expenses to help with our retirement plan.

Wednesday, August 24, 2011

My doctor changed my medication. She would rather change it then reduce it. I believe we are doing this because the testing showed I appeared flat to others. Before I was on 20 mg of Loxapine, now I am on 15 mg Loxapine and 10 mg of Abilify.

Saturday, August 27, 2011

We celebrated everybody's summer birthdays including George's sixty-fifth. I felt strange because I had nothing to do with the party. In fact, I resent the party because we always have a big celebration for George's birthday and rarely for Darcy or me. Anyway, I have to admit that the colours came alive for me while there but I think it was more out of stress because they were not prominent when we were in Christina Lake from August 29th to September 5.

Anyway, while at the party I noticed how his younger sister made George dress in yellow (yellow stands for Darcy and she and Cassie were in Kinter Valley) and how Paula made mention how there was no red... but there was also no purple. The red was significant because Tammy, his younger sister's card to George was weird to me and significant to the colour red. It had pictures of creams and lotions on the front which said eliminates aging, eliminates puffiness, eliminates fine lines, eliminates sagging, eliminates wrinkles and on the inside had the picture of a beer can that said eliminates caring. I understand the card now but I did not before and took it to mean eliminates Jessica and what she stands for. This does not make sense though because George really gets along well with Jessica.

While at Christina Lake for Linda's wedding (Darcy's best friend), nothing jumped out at me. Colours were fine. On our way home, George and I stopped off in Kinter Valley (Sept 5) to drop things off to her since she was not with us at Christina Lake. We also took her and her boyfriend out to dinner. It was a very nice dinner and was uneventful for me in that no colours jumped out at me. I think I was aware of them and what they stood for but that was it. Sunday, February 22, 2015 I just remember Linda chose pink for her bridesmaids and I did not know what to wear and asked Darcy if it would be okay for me to wear my pink dress with jacket and she said "sure". But at the reception line I had the feeling by what her mother said to me, she was a little miffed.

When I came home, I reread parts of this journal and thus became more aware of what used to bother me.

Today I signed up for the contest to be a medal bearer on May 20 in Whittle Head during the Rick Hansen 25th celebration. They wear yellow. I wonder if there is any significance for that Colour for them.

Tuesday, September 13, 2011

I noticed an ad in the local paper on the eighth. It was about the YWCA accepting applications for affordable housing for single moms and their children. The paper indicated they had openings at Ash Place in Saramin. I thought I would look into this for Darcy for when she is determined to move out. I looked at their website and no such place exists. Weird.

Thursday, September 15, 2011

I went to see Dr. Argle today and Angie was there too. I gave Angie the short story I wrote to enter into a contest to get her feedback. I told Dr. Argle about how the colours came back to me at the summer birthday party we celebrated for George's 65th. I also told her what George said to me when I said I did not want sex at Christina Lake. He said, "I don't know dear, this is a one-sided relationship." I told her I just was not interested and wanted to assert myself this time. I have not been interested in sex for some time now but always say yes anyway. I did not tell her that. I should have. Anyway, she thought it was weird that he would say that.

With me more focused on George right now and the colours presenting themselves at the reception she put me, back to 20 mg Loxapine and 15 mg Abilify. The plan is to reduce the Loxapine once things stabilize and see how Abilify works for me. We are trying this, one because I wanted to reduce my dosage of Loxapine and two because I did not want to appear flat. Dr. Argle did not want to reduce the Loxapine because she is not sure that my decision-making skills may have been at their best for I was on a lower dose when I resigned from my school. I forget what I was on when I said I would do Learning Assistance…that was definitely a poor decision!

I have not told George or Darcy about the change in medication but Dr. Argle suggests that I do, so I will tell them tonight at dinner.

Friday, September 16, 2011

I told George and Darcy about the change in my medication and I was surprised George did not ask why the change. Instead, he remarked that he guessed the doctor wanted me to tell them in case they saw a change in my mood. I said yes, and that was it.

Today I thought I would start seeing messages and almost am looking for them in the TV…but nothing. The only thing I have is doubts about George again which could be the start of another episode. If that is true, I am surprised that Dr. Argle did not up my Loxapine to 50 mg since she knew that that worked last time. I am pleased she is trying something new, Abilify, but I am already on 15 mg and I want to be on a low dose of whatever drug I take.

Maybe I cannot forgive George for some of the things like the couch because his answers do not make sense. (Sunday, February 22, 2015-I now realize that distrusting George and being awake to my unhappiness is actually healthy and seeking counselling is wise. I just don't know where it will go. Carl (our marriage counsellor) seems to have no advice just questions. He is receptive to what I say. It is nice.

I think I have learned over the years not to ruffle George's feathers and have lost some of my personality, like arguing or saying what I really mean or want. I used to play the middle man for the girls so they would ask him things at a good time.

Sunday, September 18, 2011

We found out yesterday that Donald's mom passed away from an aneurysm in her stomach. It comes as quite a shock. Everyone thought that his dad would be the first to pass away.

I also found out that my Aunt Laura was diagnosed with ovarian cancer that has spread to her liver. This year is a terrible year for loss and bad news!

I still keep looking for messages…but nothing. Everything seems normal but the reawakening that George should look different. However, I am living with him and Jessica, and Darcy find things normal….so it just must be this darn illness.

I wonder how I did with that facial recognition test that I took at the psychological services. I should ask.

Funny how I look at George's back and I notice that his mole seems to be in the wrong place. I remember it being on his left side closer to his spine.

Tuesday, September 20, 2011

Yesterday I met with Angie and this time I did most of the talking, which is unusual. I am not sure if this is a result of the Abilify or the nature of the disease. I've been on 20 mg of Loxapine and 15 mg of Abilify since Thursday when I saw Dr. Argle so you'd think that any symptoms I have would have disappeared by now but no. I still feel uncomfortable around George, which is sad in a way because most of the time he is so understanding and does not expect a lot from me.

Yesterday I had the guts to phone Lindahl Aluminum Railing to get a quote to do our railing out back.

Today we meet with our financial advisor at the bank. I decided to keep the appointment because I have been able to manage my discomfort and if George is really supposed to be my husband than we need our affairs in order. In addition, I want all my RRSP's to go to the bank and be in one place. Therefore, I am transferring what I had invested from Great West

Life through the school to the bank today. I hope that was a wise decision. It's better than having things all over the place.

Wednesday, September 21, 2011

Well we met with Mark, our new financial advisor and got all of our affairs in order. He is going to spend a lot of time on our budget and see where we can trim our expenses.

It is funny though I am on all this medication and I am still doubtful about George. I even had a fleeting thought that maybe Mark was an undercover cop…what a silly notion. I think I watch too many crime shows!

I went out with George for coffee today at Esquires where I go with Angie. George again told me that he thought I was more alert, aware and confident. He had first said that after our meeting with Mark. He had asked me how I thought I was on the new medication. I told him and he agreed. I still have not told him that I have doubts about him. One because I want him to notice things and two I don't want to hurt his feelings or have a discussion about my medication with him.

Thursday, September 22, 2011

Well a week has gone by on this medication and I notice no difference. I accept George but that is about it. I still feel he should have brown eyes. I wonder what is going to happen in another week when I meet with Dr. Argle.

I still receive no messages from the TV or vice versa but I have noticed that they are wearing more vivid colours especially on HGTV. There is a lot more purple and oranges, pink, blue, yellow, and green. However, the orange really surprises me.

Mark gave me the name of a person who does his income tax, Bobby. Therefore, I contacted him and told him he could expect us in the spring. He sounded nice. I feel so much better having a professional do our taxes especially after the mess up we had this year.

Friday, September 23, 2011

Well another day and nothing has changed. I hang around George but I still feel uncomfortable around him at the same time. The more I read over my journal the more uncomfortable I become. I am getting good at masking my own feelings. He has no clue, neither does Darcy.

I just weighed myself and I weigh the lowest I have in well over two years. There must be something wrong with my scale. I weight 129.8! I sure do not look that weight. After all, 125 was my goal weight with Weight Watchers several years ago and I am a Lifetime Member because I did reach my goal weight! I am going to try to start an excel spreadsheet on my weight to see how this medication affects it! Maybe I can insert it into this document. I am also going to ask Angie the next time we have a meeting if she can give me a workout for my stomach that I can do at home. I am on 20mg Loxapine and 15 mg Abilify.

George came home at lunchtime and we went to BCAA to take advantage of George being the principle driver and sixty-five. It will change if I get a job. We also went to David Hunter to see where our order of Arugula was for the backyard. They did not find it written down even though we watched the girl do it. Anyhow, today a lady helped us and we chose Japanese Spurge for the area by the stairs to help with soil erosion.

Saturday, September 24, 2011

Well I can see it now; Dr. Argle is going to increase my medication because I still feel there is something off with George. I still feel uncomfortable around him yet I hang around him.

This morning Darcy, George and I took Cassie to Roaming Rascals at Cowichan Aquatic Centre, which is a local recreation centre.

We came home to have lunch, grill cheese sandwiches that Darcy suggested we have. I cut the cheese, George put margarine on the bread and when I proceeded to put and make them the way I always do, they both came at me saying I was doing it wrong. Therefore, I put up my hands up and said, "Okay you do it. I'll play you." I proceeded to go into the living room and read the paper while they finished up. The reference to "I'll play you" referred to how George reacted to most things.

At noon, George left for his company golf game. I was supposed to go too but I had promised Darcy I would babysit and honestly, I could not remember who asked first.

I am thinking about publishing my story again. Maybe that is a bad sign. I had given Angie a first draft for a contest but she suggests I wait until I am better. Funny thing is I feel better, more confident. As I said before is this the disease or the medication, Abilify?

One thing that frustrates me about George is that his memories about our life on things I want to know are the same as mine. He is unable to fill in the blanks. Today I asked him if he remembered about the man in Tennessee showing us how to forge signatures. I wanted to know why we were there etc. but all he remembered was the same as me. Frustrating.

Sunday, September 25, 2011

Yet another day and things have not really changed. I feel I am receiving no messages at all. I only have one delusion regarding George. I still think he should have brown eyes. Weird! Is it a delusion?

Today we are going to Donald's mom's funeral from 2-4.

It was a touching service with people getting up and talking about her. It does not make any sense to me why my gut tells me something is wrong with George when all his relatives have no problem with him. Also, I thought it strange at the service, with her loss, there were no tears or crying. Tammy and he reminisced about old dogs they use to have. What is wrong with me? Why don't these pills work?

I asked George how we came up with Dear and Dar as nicknames for ourselves but he did not remember. I told him he used to call me Mickey but he said no way. I found an old letter and proved it to him. He was surprised.

I remember going to Donald's sister's husband, Ted's funeral it was like a colleagues husband's (Darren). Ted was a teacher and Darren was a principal therefor there were so many in attendance. My only regret is that I was not in the church to hear how Darren's went. I only went to the reception at Darren's. Somehow I don't think Ted is dead because I am pretty sure we would have been invited to the burial or wherever they lay him to rest, the same with Donald's mom. No one cried at Ted's funeral either.

Monday, September 26, 2011

I wonder if I am slipping into some other form of illness where my delusion is fixed. I read on the internet today that that can be a symptom of psychosis. Nonetheless, I still feel awkward around George. What will Dr. Argle say?

I am supposed to go to the Notaries Public to get a notarized copy of our marriage certificate but I feel awkward making the appointment and doing it. I guess I am not that confident yet.

Well George came home for the afternoon at lunchtime. He did not want to work anymore. He wrote a letter to Desjardins to cancel the life insurance policy my dad set up for him just to pay off the car. I feel uncomfortable with this decision.

George and I went out to Starbucks for coffee and bought some outfits for Cassie's doll for her birthday. We discussed what we could get her as a big item as well. I told him she needs more play-acting toys and he suggested a kitchen centre. I am sure he will change his mind if they are too pricey. Anyway, I suggested we go out this weekend. (Sunday, February 22, 2015 I am sure George never suggested a kitchen Centre)

While there I discussed my writing a book and he is all for it even though I told him he may have a hard time getting past his part in my problem. I found a book that can help writing creative non-fiction but I would have to order it. I will discuss it with Dr. Argle before I order the book. (February 22, 2015 I recall he said that an author has discretion as to what they want to put in.) Well I'm holding back.

On the way home, I verified that he was okay with me writing a book and he said anything that will keep me busy is good especially if I'm not going to work. He also piped in that I started to write poetry but gave that up. I told him no I did not write a poem, meaning in regards to my mental health. I told him. I only wrote one poem and that was for a very specific purpose, the genetic termination of our first child. He could not even remember why I wrote the poem. I find it unbelievable that he would forget about my writing the poem. He asked to see the poem so when we got home I showed it to him and he said he never knew. I was so happy it was in print I shared it with him! I even tried to share it with Brenda another colleague but she did not seem interested in reading it. I cannot believe he forgot! Perhaps the poetry he might know about are the poems I wrote in high school, but I have no idea where those are and I never brought that up to him.

Tuesday, September 27, 2011

This morning I went out with Darcy. She bought a membership to the YMCA. Afterwards we went to Home Sense and I bought a shower curtain liner for her bathroom and some white sheets for Jessica's bedroom just in case Mandy decides to stay here during her visit on October 4 and 5th.

These pills are not working. I feel no different.

Wednesday, September 28, 2011

I still feel anxious around George. Nothing else is bothering me. I wonder what Dr. Argle will say? I am going to bring her the prescriptions print out for Abilify so she can read for herself what I told her.

I wanted to check out Ellen DeGeneres' website but my computer keeps freezing. I told George about it and we are going to take it in on the weekend. Ellen had an interesting video I wanted to watch on what is real and fake but it did not work. I also wanted to check out the link on nominating a deserving person who might need Ellen's help. I am considering reaching her to get out my message. Maybe she can get an interior decorator in here so these couch sets would change especially the red, yellow and blue one, find me a house with a proper dining room, or renovate so I have one…maybe even get me a job.

I tried her site again and it worked. It would be too weird to nominate myself but I wish I could be nominated but then again she may not help a Canadian. However, she might because her show is international.

(Sunday, February 22, 2015 I no longer have the coloured couch set made with the cheap material and have moved yet again into a town house and finally have a new dining table but none are my dreams. They are much better and I would prefer to stay in the townhouse than move into a condo if my dreams can't be reality.)

On another note, I woke up with a sore baby toe on my left foot.

Thursday, September 29, 2011

Last night I was lying on the couch and got up to get some juice. While I was there, I felt dizzy and asked George to come and help me. He held me up and started taking me to the family room but **I fainted.** George had Darcy phone 911 and I woke up while she was on the phone. After a while, I sat up and they helped me to the couch where I waited for the ambulance. The paramedics came, asked all sorts of questions and left. I did not need to go to the hospital! My foot was still sore though but they thought nothing of it.

This morning Darcy took me to the clinic and the doctor said I have gout. After, Darcy took me to my appointment with Dr. Argle. She increased my medication by 5 mg, so now I am on 20 mg of Loxapine and 20 mg of Abilify. It was not a pleasant visit. It was rushed.

Darcy took me to the drugstore to get my prescriptions plus the 75 mg of Voltaren (Diclofenac Sodium) to reduce the inflammation of the toe joint. We had to wait close to 45 minutes for the prescription and the funny thing is the pharmacist checked to see if he had enough Abilify and said he did, but when Darcy went back in the store to pick it up they only gave me 4 tablets and owed me 38 more…so I have to go back! Again! This happened the last time two weeks ago too. They never seem to have enough of this drug.

Once I got home, I had something to eat and took the pill for what the doctor thinks is gout. By early afternoon, I could walk again. The pain was nearly gone after just one pill! The doctor said I would feel better and boy was he right!

When George came home, we went out to Art Knaps to get some bark mulch for the backyard. On our way there, George asked me about last night with the paramedic and wanted me to clarify what I had said about him. I did and told him that I had had doubts about him again. He asked me if I told my doctor and what she said. I told him I did tell her and that she upped my medication. He took it all in his stride and said that this is how it started last time. I told him I knew and have insight into all of it. What he doesn't understand is that when I'm stable on my medication I still feel uncomfortable around him. I always put on a brave front.

It is probably not true, but it pacifies me thinking that they keep me medicated in order to satisfy George in some way. I prefer to think that they are doing some sort of investigation than believing I am just plain sick and delusional! Sometimes I prefer to think that I am doing research on the effects of different medications. None of this is likely true but it gives me comfort and keeps me taking my medication. It gives me hope!

Friday, September 30, 2011

Darcy kept Cassie home today and they both took me to the clinic at 8:30 in the morning to have the blood tests done that Dr. Argle ordered. Unbeknownst to me she ordered an ECG as well. I have never had one of those.

Afterwards we went to Superstore because she wanted to look at snowsuits, then we came home.

At 10:00 a.m., a principal called and said he was in desperate need for a sub for today for grade 7 for his school. Three things made me say I could not do it. First, my medication is not stabilized, although I feel fine other than my doubts about George. Second, the gout in my left foot has not gone away and I do not think I could stand for the whole day and third, I was a little scared that it was for grade 7. I should not be afraid though when I asked Marian, a former principal, several years ago what grade she thought I would be good at, she said grade 7.

I felt so good that someone from the Archdiocese called me and wanted me. I did not even know I was on some sort of sub list. Maybe he called downtown and got my name knowing that I am looking for work…but I rather want my next employer to know my illness. I am afraid they will not hire me though.

I weighed myself today and I now weight 129.6. I have gone down .2 of a pound!

I suggested to George the other day that we have Thanksgiving here and celebrate Cassie's birthday at the same time. He thought it was a good idea. I found out that Robbie has Cassie for the weekend so we would have to celebrate on the Monday. Paula and Ben are out of town but his other sister and her family are still here. I left George to invite them even though I am embarrassed about our house and the way it looks. It is so cluttered.

When George came home from work, we went to get more bark mulch and then went out for coffee at the best doughnut shop. Darcy and Cassie met us there. While there, we got to talking and the topic of Jessica and her visit to a psychologist when she was young came up. George wanted to know all about it. I told him and Darcy that the reason Jessica reacted the way she did was all him. It was his need for preciseness that caused Jessica to need to have the table set a certain way or the chair in a certain position. The doctor said it was because of him. I did not make that up. She gave her bubbles to blow her troubles away and a tape to listen to that took her to a fantasyland. He just laughed at the thought that it was his fault. He did not laugh back then.

(May 10, 2018 If George was really the one who was living with me while living at Saber Road why would he not remember when he was the one to find the psychologist for her. Whom was I living with if not a doppelganger?? My question is how many doppelgangers did I live with?? Also why while living at Wade Avenue would Jessica make fun while setting the table and put the fork where the knife goes and the knife where the fork goes? Was she a doppelganger?)

While we were driving to the doughnut shop George called his younger sister to ask her about Thanksgiving. We got her voicemail.

By the way, I have enough Abilify for tonight and I have not heard from London Drugs yet about the remaining tablets they owe me. So far, the pills are not helping, I still feel uncomfortable around George and his poor memory about important events does not help!

At dinner, I told George and Darcy that I was waiting to hear from London Drugs. George said I should call them and then said he wanted to go to Home Depot to check on shelving for his customers. I suggested we go to London Drugs and check on my medication. He preferred I call but I said I did not want to deal with an automated answering system. We ended up going to the drugstore first and they had the medication, they just had not gotten around to calling me. While we were there, he took a picture of some shelving and we went to Home Depot where he took some more pictures. I saw him email the picture from London Drugs but not the pictures taken at Home Depot.

Saturday, October 1, 2011

Angie got back to me yesterday on the question I had for Dr. Argle. I wanted to know if I could take Melatonin to help me sleep; Angie said I could and that it was not habit forming. Therefore, last night I tried one and so did George. George kept me up all night snoring. It definitely worked for him but not for me. I will try again tonight but ask George not to take one. (February 22, 2015-It was only after we moved to Gage Lane that George started snoring. He never used to.)

We went to get more bark mulch and George worked in the backyard spreading it out. Later we went to a nearby store and bought Cassie her birthday gift. We bought her a cardboard playhouse that she can draw on. Then we went to Toys r Us to buy some play food to go with the toy sink that Darcy found at a garage sale.

Afterwards we went for coffee, but I had tea.

Sunday, October 2, 2011

I decided not to take the Melatonin last night. My sleep was okay but George's snoring kept disturbing me.

I am still trying to feel comfortable around George. I think it is mostly the questions I have that makes me most uncomfortable. I think I need something to boost my libido and maybe things would be better. Maybe I will talk to my family doctor. I just do not like how George reacts in the bedroom when he wants sex and I am not sure about him. He still insists on it. Maybe it is not an up in medication I need but something else, perhaps a marriage counselor for my bedroom issues.

Constantly upping my medication will not help my libido any especially since I am going through Menopause as well.

This morning we are going to David Hunters sale to see if we can buy some plants for the back 40, our backyard.

I told George that I do not think we sent anything to Nancy when Ted died. I checked and we did not. Could I have been so out of it? Why didn't George think of it? I feel terrible.

I am also wondering why we have not received the tax receipt for our donation to the Cancer Foundation in memory of Donald's mom that we sent to his dad. They said we would get it in a couple of days. Was it a fraudulent site? Was a note sent to his dad?

I also find it funny why George's receipt for the donation to Jessica running in the CIBC Run for the Cure does not look as legit as mine.

Monday, October 3, 2011

This morning, as usual, I took care of Cassie while Darcy went off to school. She was an angel. I also made an appointment for Thursday morning at 10:00 to see me family doctor for my annual check-up. I will ask for a flu shot, all about gout, and what I can do about my libido.

George got home around noon and had some lunch.

He asked Darcy if she wanted to take Cassie to the company Christmas party on December 10. That is the weekend that Robbie, her dad has her so I guess we will see. George also said that he was asked to be Santa. (He was also asked to be the emcee at the adult Christmas party). I told him that is just like when Jordan, a colleague of his and his wife played Santa and Mrs.

Clause. Therefore, he said I could be Santa's helper. I told him I would be Mrs. Clause.

I feel sad that I am not a part of some school where they would ask me to do things as they did when I was emcee.

He kissed me good-bye because he had to go back to work and told me not to sit around. I hate sitting around too but my reluctance or fear to do things gets in the way. I would like to work out like Darcy, but I would like company, just as she goes with a friend. I never used to need a friend before but now I seem to and I hate that about myself! To tell the truth I prefer active things to keep fit like dancing and racket sports.

Now onto these pills, I do not feel much more confidence with them even though I am taking 5 mg more a day. As far as my feelings for George go I am still a bit anxious around him, but as I said, I do not think it is because of any present delusion but unanswered questions. After all, maybe he always had blue eyes and I never noticed. It is possible, I guess. In any event, it must all be in my head because as I reread some of my entries it sure sounds off the wall.

George got home around 3:00 p.m. and we went out for tea at Starbucks near Chapters. He got a phone call so I put the order in and paid. The cashier was a former student of mine, Bess! It was so nice to have her remember me and be so excited! (April 2016 I remember seeing Bess when I was out with Jessica at Starbucks, at another location. It was the store near London Drugs. I do not remember at all being with George when I ran into Bess.)

After George and I had our tea, he actually wanted to look for more presents for our granddaughter, Cassie. I was surprised! Therefore, we bought some crayons, a water paint activity and a clock from Chapters. All gifts I would have liked to have bought her, so it was great! They even do free wrapping there which was better. Funny thing was that he forgot that we had already bought Cassie some clothes for her dolly. He has a great memory for work, I guess, but a poor one for home-related things.

Tuesday, October 4, 2011

I think these pills make me feel more anxious because I can feel my heart pumping still! I wonder what the ECG will say.

George still seems strange to me. Why just him? It does not make sense. I do not want any more medication! I have until October 20 for things to get better for that is when I see Dr. Argle again.

Gordon from Lindahl Aluminum came to measure the backyard for the safety railing. I dealt with him, which I guess is good for me.

George came home around 3:00 p.m. and we went to Crescent Beach for tea. He worked nearly the entire time there.

Wednesday, October 5, 2011

Last night Paula's son, Jim came over and picked up the turntable we had. We gave Jessica ours that replaced the one she got from her aunt, so we gave her aunts to Jim.

As usual, I did most of the listening and said very little.

I tried another Melatonin last night but I did not notice much change so I am not going to use it again.

Thursday, October 6, 2011

I went to see me family doctor today. He said all my test results were normal and so was my uric acid level. He gave me a requisition to get a halter to monitor my heart for palpitations, but I have not noticed them so far today and it is 2:30 p.m. It is the first day that it has gone so long.

I still feel uncomfortable about George but that is because I keep thinking that he does not tell me how he feels about me other than when he wants to have sex. Then I remember again how he acted strangely and made me feel uncomfortable when I did not recognize him…that was 5 years ago but it has scarred me. The worst thing is he felt justified. He never said he was sorry. Then there was the time on our trip to Mexico where he behaved inappropriately and said that how I felt didn't matter!

Just because I have these feelings is not a good enough reason to up my medication…so I hope she does not.

Friday, October 7, 2011

I still have feelings but I have no delusions.

I spent today looking at online graduate programs I could take.

George came home at lunch and we went to the cabin to shut the water off, than coffee at nearby coffee shop.

Jessica comes home tonight and is bringing her boyfriend to stay for Thanksgiving weekend so I probably will not make an entry in here until after the weekend.

Sunday, October 9, 2011 THANKSGIVING

Well I found some time to write in here. Everything is going fine. Jessica has been nice and has actually spoken with me a bit. They are out at a brunch right now. Everyone is busy preparing for tonight's Thanksgiving dinner.

I applied for a grade four teaching position at Ladner Elementary that is full time. I was honest about my condition in the covering letter and do not expect to get a call back. I actually have butterflies in case I do.

Monday, October 10, 2011

It is 11:30 a.m. and Jessica and her boyfriend just left. She said her good byes but it is so evident that she cares for her dad more. She barely touches me when she hugs, but at least she hugs! I am so thankful for that! I miss her already and it brings tears to my eyes that the next time I will see her she will be off to Malaysia!

Our Thanksgiving dinner was great! I was quiet but maybe I am normally quiet compared to others. I do not know anymore. I remember how my sister used to hesitate to speak because of her medication, I do not want the same to happen to me, and I think it is. Sometimes I rehearse in my head what I am going to say, deciding whether I should say it or not. This has been going on long before I started the Abilify.

About these pills, I think they work as best as they are going to. I have no delusions. I take things for as they appear. George still thinks they give me more confidence…I would like more…confidence that is! I am anxious to be on one pill!

Tuesday, October 11, 2011

I have spent the morning looking into online programs I can take. I need to do something!

George drove me to an appointment at the Outpatient Care and Surgery Center for an MRI. Dr. Beckett, a specialist, had scheduled it for me back in April for my right shoulder. I am sure they will not find anything because it feels so much better.

Today George received the check from Desjardins, which cancels his policy. He plans to pay off the Mercedes and put the rest into an RRSP, so I made an appointment with Mark for Friday at 1:00 p.m.

Wednesday, October 12, 2011

Today at noon, I have an appointment to have a **24-hour ambulatory holster to check out my heart palpitations**, which I still have. I hope it shows something because I am definitely feeling funny with them. I am a bit anxious because I have to take myself today to get it hooked up and lately I have always had someone else drive me.

I had to keep a record of all my activity and like before I only notice them when I am at rest. They were not as bad today as they were before.

I guess we will see what the results are. I have to return it tomorrow at 9:50 a.m.

Thursday, October 13, 2011

I do not think 20 mg of Abilify made any difference from 15 mg as far as George goes because it is not a delusion that is bothering me. It is old stuff that I reread in this journal, which brings all my doubts to the forefront and makes it hard to let go. I wonder if Dr. Argle will get that. Otherwise, I accept things the way they are. What does strike me funny about George is that he does not know how to spell his own parents' name. When asked security questions on TD he can never remember. Weird!

Friday, October 14, 2011

Today I emailed the Art Gallery about volunteering there…that is a big step for me.

George and I are going to the bank at 1:00 p.m. and then maybe to the home and design show. Tonight we are going out with Tammy and Donald to dinner and then the casino.

We did go to the home show and we both bought cashmere scarves that were at a ridiculous price of $25 each! I could not pass it up! Later we went to Tammy and Donald's to go to dinner. We went to a nice restaurant near Bright Angel Regional Park. Afterwards we went to the Casino. It was fun to be out but I was so conscious about how quiet I am. It really bothers me! I am anxious to see what I would be like just on Abilify!

Saturday, October 15, 2011

Last night we got home about 12:30 a.m. After washing up I asked George if he wanted to fool around…Yes, I did, but not because I was in the mood or anything. I just felt if I was his wife I should show some interest. He got all excited and it was the best time we have had having sex in a very long time!

My conversation with my family doctor really helped where he told me that many women feel no desire and lack libido even women who are not on any medication! (Sunday, February 22, 2015 I have no interest in doing that again! He needs to earn intimacy from me and he does not!)

Sunday, October 16, 2011

This morning we have Cameron helping spread bark mulch over our backyard! We are paying him $20 an hour plus gas. Cameron is Donald's daughter's husband.

My heart still is pumping funny. The ECG was normal but I wonder what the heart holster will read?

Jessica called last night and I answered the phone but she did not want to talk to me. She wanted to talk to her dad and share the good news about her scholarship. She did say in the end to her dad that she loves us both but I never get to hear it. I wonder if one day she will realize how much it hurts, not to be spoken to.

Tuesday, October 18, 2011

Yesterday I sent an email to the CMHA (Canadian Mental Health Association) about volunteering. She suggests that I make an appointment with her for next week. I am a little anxious about it and there are a few things I want to know first. I want to know if they are a separate entity to what I am a patient at now or are they the South Office. I want to know if the volunteer opportunities are with the CMHA or in the community.

I am so bored but I am afraid that if I volunteer that will inhibit me from finding a job. I am also anxious about getting out there period but I must do something. I wish I knew myself more. I think I would rather work than volunteer my time because the hoops you go through to volunteer are the same as for a job.

Wednesday, October 19, 2011

Today Cassie is two! We will be celebrating at home.

I hope tomorrow that Dr. Argle is not rushed! I am in such a quandary now as to what I should do regarding volunteer work. I could volunteer to be a docent at the Art Gallery or I could volunteer with the CMHA where they know about my disorder and might better be able to fit me back into work. I think I might have to put myself into an uncomfortable position regarding the Art Gallery, but then again it would put me in contact with kids again. I am not sure what I should do. I need a career coach!

Thursday, October 20, 2011

Well I had to wait 30 minutes for my appointment today. She was really backed up. **She raised my medication. I am still taking 20mg Loxapine but she maximized the Abilify to 30mg.** She raised it because I was telling her things about George. I told her how he did not remember about the poem and his reaction bothered me. I also told her how he does not know how to spell his parents' names and of course, I brought up the good old couch. From this, I think that she will say that Abilify does not work for me because I never forgot about the couch I just chose not to bring it up again. It will be interesting to see what she thinks in three weeks' time.

Angie told me they have a vocational counselor to replace Sheena. Therefore, instead of waiting for Angie to talk to her I phoned and left a voicemail. We will see how long it takes her to get back to me.

I phoned Angie this afternoon to let her know that my left arm was twitching.

Friday, October 21, 2011

I weighed myself this morning and I weigh 129.6! Now I have to break this barrier.

Angie phoned me this morning to talk to me about the twitching and when it started and what I wanted to do because Dr. Argle said we could get rid of the Abilify but not the Loxapine. I told her I wanted to see how I do on the Abilify because I think it makes me more alert. Even George has noticed this. Therefore, my goal is to be only on Abilify.

She also had to fill out a referral form for me to be able to see Melissa the vocational counselor. She did it over the phone and signed my name to it.

I hope that it does not take too long before Melissa contacts me.

Sunday, October 23, 2011

Friday night George wanted to do something so he took me out to dinner at The Old Fork. While we waited, we went bowling. He played as if he never stopped playing. I lost both games…so it was fun but not fun! We were also intimate in bed.

I chose to take the 30 mg Abilify in one tablet as opposed to three but I find I have trouble swallowing it.

Saturday we went to the mall to get a new battery for my watch also to try on some jeans. I was disappointed because they did not have my size in jeans. We went to Duncan City Square. I think I will try Granger Square this week.

In the afternoon, George and I went to go hiking. We have not done that in 20 years or so.

Today George and I are going to the beautiful gardens while Darcy has her birthday party for Cassie.

Monday, October 24, 2011

I want to send, my former principal an email updating him on my situation and ask for a job, but I do not know if that is wise. Therefore, I have a call into Angie for her advice.

Today we are having a man come over to show us his central vacuum system and whether it would work here. I think storing and lugging the hoses will be too much! The name of the company is Divac.

Tuesday, October 25, 2011

Therefore, for us to get the central vac just the way we like it, it would cost $1,600. I am not completely sold on the system and since George barely vacuums anymore, so it would be my decision really. I know it would be great for resale but we have to do so much prep work to find places for the hoses etc. that I am not so sure it is worth it.

Today I have a tickle in my throat and it feels like I may be coming down with something. In addition, George is still sick with his Bronchitis, He has gone through two courses of antibiotics and he still has it. Therefore, he has an appointment for tomorrow at four, which meant I had to cancel our appointment with Mark for 5:00 p.m. I am trying to reschedule for Thursday instead.

This morning Darcy and I are going to Duncan Village Mall to see if they have some petite jeans in the style I tried on in the weekend. We will see. George said he was coming home around 10:30 a.m. or 11:00 a.m. to relax.

Thursday, October 27, 2011

Yesterday George stayed home sick.

I wish this never happened to me. I had a good job teaching grade four at a school that was close. I am beginning to feel that there is no hope of me finding another job, any job that will suit me. I am also beginning to think that Melissa will not be able to help me. I am feeling so useless.

Today we have a meeting with Mark to go over my fund transfer from Great West Life and our budget.

Friday, October 28, 2011

Today I weigh 131.6. I am up 2 pounds. It simply is not fair! I am on 20 mg Loxapine and 30 mg Abilify! I really do think it is the pills that are working against me. I am going to have to bring this up with Dr. Argle.

Wednesday, November 2, 2011

I met with Angie today and she said I seemed more stable now. Interesting. While we were at the Esquires coffee shop, I saw that Sandra the pharmacist that deals with me at London Drugs was there and we said hi to each other.

I also met with Melissa the vocational counselor at Duncan Mental Health. She told me things I already knew but am afraid to do, like contact the principals. I think I need someone to hold my hand and walk me through it. She is going to look into other educational options for me as well though. We will see. I think teaching is too narrow a field to branch out. She talked about teaching at college level, which I would like, but I do not think I have a specialty. We will see what she comes up with.

I also applied for a position as a **Classroom Solutions Product Director**. I would work from home and likely do some promoting of the product. It would put me way out of my comfort zone but if it is a product I can stand behind, maybe I could do it. The job is posted until the November 17, 2011 so I do not expect to hear from them before that. It would all depend on whether or not they have training.

Thursday, November 3, 2011

One thing I noticed looking over my journal is that I did not write in it for the entire year of 2009, my year as a Learning Assistance Teacher. I wonder why I did not. I must explain how I became the Learning Assistance Teacher. I was on long term disability and anxious to get back to work as the fourth grade teacher. My principal called to meet with me and I had a gut feeling that he wanted to ask me to take the Learning Assistance role for the intermediate grades. Again my gut told me to say no but my case worker told me to check my reality with George. So I did. He thought I should take the position.

I was very unhappy and wanted back in the classroom but my principal believed it takes more than one year to know if you are happy in a position. So, I resigned. Darcy was pregnant and I felt it was a good time to move on.

My advice to anyone suffering any kind of mental illness is to stick with what you know and stay with your position.

Angie seems to think that it is not a good idea to go back to my school. It is a step backward. Melissa seems to think it is okay to get me back into the workforce. I feel awkward though because I have not spoken with anyone since I left and I feel awkward going to Mass knowing that George hates it. I need him to be stronger for me in this regard. I like how people know me there and the more we are away from it the more out of touch I feel.

I think I am afraid to contact, the present principal at the school, because I am afraid of rejection and afraid of not being able to do a good job and communicate properly.

Today I have an appointment at 1:45 p.m. with Dr. Beckett to go over my MRI results. I am sure it is just to see if I am okay, which I am. Time is a great healer! I drove all the way there using the TOM TOM, which was great! (February 22, 2015 I don't recall using the TOM TOM on my own at all.)He did say that I had a tear in my rotator cuff and that is why my shoulder hurt so much. It mended by itself though.

Friday, November 4, 2011

Today I weigh 129.6. I am back to my lowest. I want to weigh 115 lbs.! Maybe when I am off the Loxapine it will go down. All the literature I read on both medications says they may cause weight gain or loss. Well I know Seroquel caused weight gain so maybe these do but not as bad.

I have noticed that I have had to urinate a lot more.

Today George came home at noon and has been busy on the phone all afternoon with work related problems.

It is too bad I live so far from Tinsel Town. Considering I am out of work, I could see Mom more often. Sam feels he needs a break and Mandy is so busy she barely has time.

Saturday, November 5, 2011

This morning we all, George, Darcy, Cassie and I all walked to a local school to go to a craft fair. Cassie sat in her stroller the whole way there. On the way, back though she walked and ran the whole way. Unbelievable! At the fair, Darcy bought some earrings and I bought a pretty necklace made with a silver rose broach. George did not like it but since he rarely buys me jewelry, I decided to get it.

Last night I wore my blue nightgown to bed and we made out. It was great! His eyes actually went bug eyed when he saw me wearing it. It was nice! I had him wear his black boxers…the only one he has. Am I just getting used to his presence? Everyone says he is George and the man I married. My mind is torn.

Tuesday, November 8, 2011

Yesterday I applied to **St George's School for the Director of Learning** position. It would be full time and encompass overseeing the teachers as well. It would be a challenging but stimulating position at a very prestigious school. I do not think I have a chance since I have had no leadership experience and I have been out of the work force for a few years but nothing is lost in trying. The posting closes December 15, 2011 so it would be awhile before I heard anything.

I really wish Melissa would give me her email. I have these people helping me but I get the funny feeling that it is all up to me to find a job. I have a funny feeling that I will not get the help I am looking for because they have something else in mind for me.

I really wish this disorder never fell upon me. One might say it is for the best and everything happens for a reason but I do not know what that is yet. I could better understand it if I had grown from the experience but I have not. Nothing good has really come out of it. I do not have a different career path or anything. I am merely in limbo and it is not because I have not tried.

Thursday, November 10, 2011

George came home with white t-shirts from The Bay and new dark socks for everyday wear. This is strange because he has always worn sports socks. He also bought new underwear not too long ago. I mentioned to him that I heard on a few talk shows that the telltale sign that a man is cheating is that he buys new underwear. He did not have much to say and said nothing to reassure me. When I asked him about why he bought them and did not put them on his Christmas list he said he had to know exactly which T-shirt he liked and had to go right where he bought the last one. It sounds fishy to me; he just had to look at the label of his shirt to know what to ask for.

Thursday, November 10, 2011

George wore his new shirt and socks today without having them washed which is new for him. Strange. He even showed off his socks to me this morning. He normally likes to have everything washed before he wears anything.

I had an appointment with **Dr. Argle** today and told her of my suspicions and what I thought was weird. I also mistakenly got dressed up today. She thinks I am still unwell so she has decreased the Abilify and increased the Loxapine. So now, I am on **25mg of each.** Maybe I just need to stay quiet besides she has no words of advice. She thinks the Abilify is not working as well as she would have liked. I am fed up of these pills and have an inclination of stopping them altogether!

Saturday, November 12, 2011

Today started off with a bang! I asked George if he was taking a shower and he said he was and I told him so was I. He said we best say good-bye to Cassie before Darcy took her to Robbie's for the day…so we did. By the time, I got downstairs, he had already started the shower and since I did not want to wait, I got naked too. He was surprised. We had a very nice shower and he finally said we should go to the bed all wet. I was surprised! We soaked the bed and then finished our shower. He seemed in kind of a rush. Anyway, what surprised me more was that by the time I finished blow-drying my hair and got out of the bathroom he had made the bed. I thought for sure he would take the wet sheets off the bed because his side was soaked! Anyhow, I decided to change the sheets anyway myself!

I know I am a little suspicious of George and that is why Dr. Argle adjusted my medication. He could not still cuddle and make love to me if he was seeing someone else, could he?

Today we set up the bed for Cassie, went out, and bought her dresser. Tonight should be an interesting night! I hope she likes her bed, it is Jessica's old one and I hope she is a good girl and stays in her bed!

I am not feeling good about my hair recently. It appears all dry and I do not know what is causing it. I cannot wait until the November 23 when I can ask my hairdresser, because if this is permanent than maybe I should have shorter hair!

Monday, November 14, 2011

Saturday night after dinner, George wanted to go out. He was getting frustrated with Greg, Darcy and Cassie…too much action and business for him. We went to the bank to withdraw some money out than London Drugs where he bought some toothpaste. Afterwards he surprised me by going to Earls. We had a drink and talked. I told him about the change in my medication and why. I also told him how I would like more affection but he said he is comfortable with the way things are and probably will not change. I asked him why when I am needing something he cannot try, but he said the same thing. When I told him how he used to lie behind me on the couch and cuddle but now he wants to lie in front, citing he gets too hot he said, "People change". I do not think we resolved anything. I did not argue my point well enough.

Friday, November 18, 2011

Wednesday I met with Melissa about work. Thursday I met with Sarah (Sunday, February 22, 2015 I don't remember meeting anyone named Sarah) about work and I was very teary-eyed. I do not know why. I ended up telling her about what George said to me about affection. She is going to contact Melissa about my case.

On Wednesday, I noticed black smudges on the mat in our bathroom. They were powdery and on the closet floor too. George said he must have stepped on some of my black makeup. I do not believe him. I only have black mascara and eyeliner and they would not do that. I am suspicious!

George came home before lunch on Wednesday all stuffed up and not feeling well. He went to bed. Thursday he went out in the morning to work and then came home at lunch. Today he has gone off to work this morning and should be home by lunch.

Funny thing he asked me if I had eye makeup remover pads to take off the spots in the closet. I told him I did not have pads but lotion and when I looked today, I notice that one of my containers is gone and the other looks like it has been filled with water. Too weird!! I asked Darcy if she borrowed it and she said no, that leaves me with more suspicions! (Sunday, February 22, 2015 I don't remember him asking me for makeup pads)

Today I finally went to get my eyebrows done and she talked me into buying an exfoliant for my skin. She said Neutrogena would not work and it has not, so, I purchased it even though it was expensive. She said that George could use it too.

Saturday, November 19, 2011

Yesterday Jessica phoned the house looking for George because she could not reach him. However, while I had her on the phone he was calling her so she said she would call back. She did! She called in the evening to talk to me, nothing special, just to chat. It was so nice! She apologized because she said she forgot but she remembered and that is all that counts. I was surprised she even said she would call back! (Sunday, February 22, 2015 I have no recollection of her ever calling me to chat. This would be an important moment for me so if I don't remember it I have to wonder that maybe something is blocking my short term memories.) (April 2016 although I don't remember this phone call I do remember her calling me one night asking for advice for one of her friends who was experiencing mental health issues.)

Tuesday, November 22, 2011

I just found out on the weekend that my Aunt Laura passed away on November 5. She was a special person and although we got out of touch over the years, I will miss her! I had asked her to be my sponsor for Confirmation but since she could not make it, she sent me a beautiful gold medal of Mary from Brazil, which I still wear today when I can wear religious jewelry. It sometimes chokes me because of my discomfort with the Catholic Church. She was also whom I wrote and sought out boy advice when I was young.

Yesterday Darcy and I did some Christmas shopping. I bought George some new undershirts and underwear in black, which I hope he will wear. It is a sexier choice than always white. The t-shirts are not exactly like the ones he bought for himself but I hope he will wear them.

George came home yesterday at about 1:30 p.m. for lunch. Darcy and I had just got home. He stayed home the rest of the day. We went to Bright Angel Regional Park with the dog, and had coffee at a nearby coffee shop.

No dosage of these pills seems to help with the feeling of fear I have for venturing out on my own. It was so helpful to have a woman help me find everything for George. It was like a godsend and so unusual for The Bay.

I went looking for the photo album I made for George before we were married and I cannot find it! I was merely looking for a specific picture showing my hairstyle then but now I am worried about where the album is.

Angie finally got a hold of me. I had phoned her last week about being teary eyed after I met with Sarah. She also mentioned how I was teary eyed when I spoke with Melissa. Therefore, something is up. Angie and I spoke about my suspicions and his reaction when I told him I wanted more affection. She suggested a marriage counselor or maybe see Dr. Argle. She is going to let me know what Dr. Argle says on Friday when I see her next.

I know I am sad about all the death that is happening but I am tired of blubbering like an idiot when I see these women! Something is not right.

Thursday, November 24, 2011

Yesterday I got my hair streaked and cut and I am happy with it! I also decided to spend the extra money and have her wash and blow dry it on Saturday for the Christmas party at George's work.

George also called and took me to Esquires for coffee yesterday. We had a good talk and I told him about my fears. He said I should join Toastmasters to gain some of my confidence back…maybe I should and if they had an afternoon one where you did not have to dress up I probably would. He also said I should look at working at Work Safe BC and the Ministry of Education. But the Ministry of Education is in Victoria!

I looked into both and there is nothing for me.

This morning Darcy and I went to Granger Square again. I was going to exchange George's black t-shirts that I bought which are classic for the stay cool ones he wears. I decided not to because the classic ones feel a lot nicer. I just hope they fit the same. I also went to Sears to look at their bread makers. I wanted some help, and wouldn't you know it as soon as Darcy and I talk about not having help, a woman appeared. She did not know the product and could not help me with my questions but she did say that the

Black and Decker was the most popular and it was on for $89.00 plus tax and it can make a three-pound loaf! Therefore, I got the extended warranty on it so it is covered for four years. I really hope he likes it. I hate going Christmas shopping late so now I have him done, and we did Jessica, I just have to wait on him for shopping for Darcy. Maybe he will go on Sunday, I will ask. (Sunday, February 22, 2015 He hated the machine and got rid of it. To tell the truth I used the old bread-maker the most yet it was him that had spoken of getting another.)

Friday, November 25, 2011

Today I met with Angie and she had her hair coloured and makeup on, even her eyebrows were darker. We had a good talk and it sure appears that she gets where I am coming from concerning George. She said Dr. Argle thinks it is a good idea that he come to my next meeting.

Once Angie left the coffee shop, I stayed a little longer and decided to check my phone. To my surprise, I had a text and it was from Jessica. I was so touched by her text and that she responded to my letter that I cried! I debated all day whether I should respond by text or write another letter. I decided to text her so she would not think I did not read it or get it. (Sunday, February 22, 2015 Funny I don't remember this either.)

George came home for lunch and I told him that he was invited to attend the meeting on December 8, 2011. I thought he would ask me questions but he merely said okay and recorded it in his blackberry.

George called Mitch our original real estate agent trying to get a contact in Kinter Valley to sell the condominium. The contact called back right away, Ariel. I told George this is the second time he has gone ahead with Mitch without thoroughly talking it out with me.

After lunch, we took a trip to Ladysmith to check out the Travel Lodge to see if we could stay there Saturday night instead of driving home after his Christmas party. I do not see the point of that if he also thought we could get other people to drive us home. We also went Christmas shopping for Darcy and he was a bump on a log. We went into Sears to look at bread makers and now he knows how much the one I bought will be. I just hope it is a good one. He told me not to spend that much money on him because he finds it a waste of money. I told him I already bought for him. I hope he gets more in the mood for shopping for Darcy as he was for Jessica and I hope he spoils me too!

Saturday, November 26, 2011

This morning I got my hair styled for the Christmas Party. When I came home and asked George how he liked it he said it was parted on the other side, meaning left and he liked it better on the right. Finally, he said he liked it but I somehow doubt it. I think that was a funny reaction!

George is baking oatmeal chocolate chip cookies, which I find strange. He has not baked cookies in a long time.

Last night Mani from Future Shop phoned and said the camera we picked out for Jessica was in so we picked it up. I told him that that was quite an expensive present and I would think it would include her birthday as well. He agreed. Since we bought her a case and a card for her camera as well we will give that to her on her birthday so she has something to open! As far as Darcy is concerned since we spent $600.00 on the camera, I told George that, we should spend $300.00 on Darcy for Christmas and $300.00 on her birthday. He agreed. It will just mean that Jessica will have one present to open and Darcy will have more. I hope that goes over well. I do worry that Jessica will change her mind and not want a camera.

Although, I did not think the camera we bought, that apparently Jessica wanted, was what we should buy because it was too big, George got his way and we bought it.

I am nervous about tonight at the Christmas party because I have a funny feeling we will be sitting with the big wigs, since no one else George hangs with will be there. I barely know anyone and am not very talkative anymore so it has me a bit scared. Usually I get scared, nothing happens, and everything is okay.

Funny thing, I am looking for a document Darcy helped me name when I was going to submit a book. We called it something like My Colour Coded Life and I cannot find it on my computer!

Ariel got back to George and told him now is not a good time to sell. I was worried when we invested in it, but George was sure we would make money on it. It has not turned out that way so far. I just hope everything works out in the end when we need to sell it. I think we should continue to rent it and see how it goes now that we have it. Maybe we can rent it for more than we are getting now and cover the added costs. We will see.

(All I know is that George did not factor in the Strata fees when setting the rental fees for Jessica's roommates, so we did not make money!).

Sunday, November 27, 2011

Last night went pretty well. We sat with some nice people at the Christmas party. A couple of the men introduced themselves to me, which was nice. George did a good job being an emcee and keeping up with everything that had to be done. I could tell he was nervous though even though he said he was not because he read off his sheet.

George wanted to leave and I wanted to dance even though there was no one on the floor but the DJ was playing lousy music. All of a sudden when his co-worker Brad came over to talk, George heard a song by Led Zeppelin and decided now was the time to dance. I did not care for the song. I wanted George to go up to the DJ and ask for something from the Beach Boys but he said he had to know the name of the songs and so would not do it. I almost had the guts to do it myself. I almost felt that he jumped up to dance because he saw this other girl get up to dance. There go my suspicions again!

I also decided to drive home because he had 2.5 beers and I just felt it was best. When we got home I initiated lovemaking again. It all went well and he said I was hot, (and I did do a better job of letting him know what I wanted him to do but I found there was little foreplay and I was disappointed that afterwards he wanted to wash up to go to bed instead of cuddling. Therefore, for me it was not so great. There has to be affection for the sex to mean anything. (Sunday, February 22, 2015 I do not remember this at all. (April 2016 I still do not remember this. Ever since George made me feel so terrible about initiating sex way back when, I have lost the desire to initiate. Frankly, I just feel he should want to touch me if he feels it is a healthy relationship. That is why I sought a marriage counsellor because I feel our life isn't healthy and to tell the truth I'm not sure anymore that I want to be touched by him. Maybe I would if he made me feel good about myself.)

Monday, November 28, 2011

Darcy found my document last night it was titled Short Prose Entry! I would have remembered that if it had shown itself but I could not even see that. It was not there when I looked. Somehow, I wonder whether I should trust this computer and whether I should write things down on it.

Yesterday George and I did some Christmas shopping. He was more involved, which was good! We went back to Future Shop and we bought Mom a digital picture frame! Darcy is going to help me load the pictures. Then we came home and watched the Lions win the Grey Cup!

Tuesday, November 29, 2011

Yesterday while Greg was putting up all the Christmas Lights in the house, George asked him to be a witness to me relinquishing all rights to George's pension when he dies. I wonder what he would have wanted me to do if it had been a more substantial amount. Right now, it amounts to about $30.00 dollars a month until he dies. (Tuesday, May 21, 2013 I asked George about this today and he totally denies this and says everything I wrote down is wrong. However, he says I have to prove it to him rather than him proving it to me. He did finally pull out the papers but neither of us understands them and the document states that my birthday is May 4 when it is April 3.)

We also discussed the line of credit. Now I know we borrowed for the condominium and I made him pay insurance on it just in case, which is a good thing because right now we cannot sell it because the market is not good. It is not turning out to be the investment George thought it would be. I am a little scared we will lose money on it. I have asked him to check into the other rental management companies and compare.

However, back to the line of credit, he said that even if we paid off the condominium we would still owe $200,000.00! I do not understand how. The only major thing we did was the backyard, that was $50,000.00, and I even used the $8,000.00 I received from Uncle Chuck's estate! I bought all the inside and outside furniture with my inheritance from dad as well as my Graduate degree. So where does all the money go that he makes or I have made over the years? Here go my suspicions again! I do not trust him.

The only furniture we have bought together for this house is the office furniture and the new girls' bedroom suites. In addition, the grey cabinets and the used glass dining room table. I wish the girls knew what I think, but I just cannot tell them! When the girls were young Darcy had my childhood bedroom suite and Mom bought Jessica's. Both were white. I never saw these furniture sets leave the house because I was at work.

Thursday, December 1, 2011

George and I talked some more about our line of credit and he paid for the windows using it too. I did not know this. He wanted to see if we were on the same page regarding when to sell the condominium in Kinter Valley and move out of this house. I think we should hold onto the condominium until we can sell it for a profit. In addition, I am not ready to move from this house to a townhouse yet and that is what I told him! It bothered me when we bought this condo for Jessica and her friends to move into while attending university. George added Jessica as an owner which stops her from being able to apply for a first homeowners grant in the future. She, I'm sure, didn't understand the consequences.

Last night he actually initiated us making love and he actually cuddled… things are looking up!

Yesterday I saw Melissa and she gave me a lead for a job but when I came home, I found a job that seems to be perfect for me at St Anthony of Padua teaching grade 1 part time. They are even looking for someone with background knowledge in technology. I am a little rusty but I am sure I could handle it so I applied via email.

I am in the process of sending an email to my former principal asking him to continue to be a reference and to ask for a position at the same time. I am hung up on what the subject line should be so I have a call into Melissa.

Melissa just called and suggested that I put "request" as the subject line. Good idea!

I sent off the email! Now I wait with baited breath!

Saturday, December 3, 2011

I went Christmas shopping with George again at Madewell Square. Boy I like that mall! We had lunch at Blue Angel Cafe and I found out that George told Tim, my former principal, I had psychosis. I never knew that. He also phoned Elizabeth and told her, I never knew that either!

I must admit I found it quite weird that the shopping mall parking lot was packed only eighteen minutes after the store supposedly opens!

Monday, December 5, 2011

Saturday night while I was creating a letter to Elizabeth and her family, George came inside and asked me if I wanted to go to the 5:00 p.m. mass? I was surprised and pleased but told him I would rather go to the 11:30 and hear that choir. Therefore, we did and it was nice! When we went there and got the bulletin, I discovered that Father Larry was no longer the Pastor. I was disappointed.

Right before we went to Church, I noticed I had lost the diamond out of my engagement ring, George told me to search the house and I phoned Mom and asked her to pray too. She also told me the insurance should take care of it. When I mentioned this to George, he said the deductible would be too high and it would not be worth it, but he does not remember the value of the ring or the diamond. I told him that I would phone the insurance people if he would not and find out what I need to do. I feel naked without it.

I plan to go to the local jeweller if possible to have it replaced because they give certificates stating the value of the ring. They gave me one for the ring I had made for George! The jewellers where we had the rings made did not give us one for our wedding bands. Otherwise, I would have them! Therefore, while I am at my favourite jewellers I will have my Great Aunt's ring assessed. I sure hope all goes well! This is the second time this has happened to me. It has never happened to George!

Jessica phoned on Saturday and asked if I would drive her to work while she is here. I said, yes, because I figure it will be good for us. I was surprised she asked. She said the price of a transit pass is $100.00. I know the price of gas will be more but she will have to make too many changes to get where she needs to go.

Wow! I just was called for an interview at St. Andrews! I just hope I heard the girl right and she said Tuesday and not next Tuesday. I emailed Melissa first and she phoned right away. We talked and she suggested I Google interview questions.

Tuesday, December 06, 2011

I am so nervous God! I have questions prepared but am I ready. In many ways, I want them to know about my disorder, than I do not have to worry if something happens, if they hire me. It would be nice to know that I was hired.

Right now, my computer is acting weird so I will take it into Future Shop for a check-up. I think it is still covered. It just shuts down and flashes black.

Wednesday, December 14, 2011

I phoned Daryl, and set up an appointment to bring my computer in to Future Shop and he gave me great service! He met me there on his day off and told me it would only be a few days. I had to bring in my software because they had to reinstall windows because I had three viruses. When he called me into the shop to pick up my computer he called me into the back to make sure all my documents were in the right spot. It felt so strange to be invited back there. I've never seen anyone back there before but I've not paid close attention to that either. While I was back there, Fred, another employee, helped me transfer everything. Now I do not have to go through so many layers to get to my documents! While I was there, Daryl had me check a recent document that I frequent and low and behold, it was not the updated version of my journal, so he did a search for it and found it. I also noticed that they cleared my computer of all of Darcy's files! They made me feel so special!

Daryl even walked my computer to the car! However, no sooner did I take it home and open it on Saturday the 10th of December it immediately went to a blue screen, so I put in a call to Daryl. He told me to transport it so that they could see the blue screen. Daryl passed me onto Alli who told me it might be a hardware issue. On Tuesday, I phoned again to check on the status and Daryl asked me if it was connected to a USB drive. Alli phoned me back and said it was ready and I could pick it up but when I opened it up I had problems and now it is flashing black again. I am afraid I have a lemon.

George got me connected to a browser and I thought I would try Google Chrome now I am afraid I will have Favourites in two places if I save some more. I also think the way it downloaded or synchronized my Favourites was weird. It put them in a folder.

I had my meeting with Dr. Argle and George and I thought it went well. I told Dr. Argle afterwards about the black powder that I told Angie about. I had found black smudges on the bathroom rug in front of George's sink. He said that it must have come from my makeup, but I had not been using anything black. I also told her I was beginning to see differences again, or notice them anyway. I told her how I noticed Darcy's hair was very frizzy one day. **She upped my Loxapine to 30 mg and lowered the Abilify to 20mg.**

I also talked to her about the Advent Wreath; how Darcy brought it upstairs and I started to read it at dinner. (Monday, February 23, 2015 I remember bringing it up myself) However, I noticed George acting weird so I asked if it bothered them. George said "yes" and he preferred that I read it to myself. I did not pursue it and Dr. Argle said I should, so the other day I asked him and he said he does not believe in it or Church but will go for me. I am glad he comes with me.

When we got to Mass, I felt there were more changes than were written on the card and I had a hard time believing everything. A visiting priest was very easy to understand over Father Dennis and he was very informative with why we now say AND WITH YOUR SPIRIT. I got teary eyed though when I thought about everyone who has passed away, even that was different at Mass there was no time to mourn for others than parishioners.

George told me to go ask Mr. Dowell which Mass they were going to do for Christmas because he knew I wanted to know, but I told him I was too shy or afraid so he went to ask for me. They are doing the 11:00 a.m. Mass on Christmas Day. George said he would not go because of the turkey and Darcy said she would not go because Cassie is too squirmy and not used to it so I do not know what will happen. It makes me sad.

I am starting to notice things again and feel that the TV can read my thoughts. Things do not make sense yet I have them under control so far!

I met with Melissa today and she had nothing for me but we talked. I told her that I feel like Saint Bernadette, in that nobody believed her.

The other day I found the appraisal from the jeweller we had our rings made regarding my great aunts ring but it was in a place I would not have put it…so it does not make sense to me.

We have our wedding bands back and I decided to keep the new diamond rather than replace it with the one that Greg found after I prayed to St. Anthony. Imagine it was actually found! I now plan to use it in the necklace I plan to have made for Darcy on her 25th birthday. I will buy another diamond for the necklace I plan to have made for Jessica on her 25th. (Monday, February 23, 2015 The TV helped me remember that the symbol I really wanted to make for Darcy was two thumbs up. How could I have forgotten? They are so right because I recall perfectly wondering how it could be designed. The only block I have is why it was special. Anyway I went to the local jeweller to have it designed and the whole process is going to be different than it was for the others. The lady who took my order was so memorable she wore many rings just like my grade four teacher).

Right now, I am waiting on the local jeweller to create my Aunt's ring with a setting I prefer and is safer. I followed my gut instinct to get that ring checked and low and behold, two of the diamonds were loose. The only thing that made me sad was that having it made this way made it worth less. The way it was made by the jeweller we had our wedding bands made, it was worth $8,000.00, now it is worth only $5,000.00. It looks prettier this way though!

I went for my interview at St. Andrews and I told them about my disorder. I notice when I looked at the Archdiocese's website that the position is no longer advertised and they did not call. That does not make sense to me. Of course, they would contact me and let me know one way or the other…something is not right in Kansas☺

Thursday, December 15, 2011

The strangest thing, I am doing exactly what I did before. I am taking people's names and identifying them with people that I know from my past. The television is identifying with things that I do. I notice it right now on The Chew. I am not scared this time though. I feel that things are going to work out for me.

Monday, December 19, 2011

I am noticing things again and again. I am uncomfortable with George. He seems bothered by the little things I do. He wanted me to get an appointment with Dr. Argle, which I tried, and Angie is not in until tomorrow. I asked him to tell me exactly what concerns him and he said, the way I connect people's names and significant others. I noticed this too and told him. I also, look at TV credits and link the first or last name to someone I know or a student I have taught. He is also bothered by the fact I will think about things in the past and ask him if he remembers. However, he has been doing the same; my lack of concentration is another thing that bothers him, which I agree with.

He told me last night that the girls were worried about me so I asked them separately what bothered them. Darcy mentioned how I was quieter with the family. Maybe, I have not noticed. Jessica said I was doing what I was doing before but would not be specific. She said I was mean, which is total bologna. I do not know where she got that! I guess she felt she had to say something. Right now, I am getting up early to get her to work.

The other day while picking up my ring at my favourite jeweller I thought he would phone back, complain about the appraisal, which is what bothered me, but he phoned back, and complained about whether we were compensated for the larger amount of gold there was in the former ring. I must admit I am shocked that the ring is not worth more. It is worth less than when I received it from my mother by about 1,000 dollars.

Yesterday I was a little frustrated because Jessica asked her dad to go to Cowichan Aquatic Centre and I was not invited. However, while they were away I decided to phone my old can mate where I graduated Teacher's College, Marilyn whom I have not spoken to since we met at the airport when she moved to Nova Scotia. She was critical in my meeting George! It was so nice to hear her voice again and to talk to her. She was very accepting of my disorder when I told her.

It is strange though my intuition tells me that something bigger than I is going on. I think that the ANDERSON show is called that to remind me of her. So too do I think that my favourite jeweller filed our appraisals under her name by accident for a reason.

I even think that Listerine's new Total Care Rinse is purple for a reason… telling me that purple is total care. It will take care of all my worries. Therefore, I am more comfortable with my religion now. I feel there is no longer a struggle between them. I sometimes feel that we are a part of a show.

I feel stronger though because I can play my guitar and the songs do not bother me. I must admit I wonder why George is so complacent when it comes to the songs I have written him. Where did the one I first wrote him that he said went to Utah go?

I get comfort from all the songs I wrote and would like someone else to sing them one day…maybe one day they will be recorded and on You Tube and the radio. I can understand why he did not like the songs I wrote him in 2002 but they expressed how I felt and still do in some ways. I was trying so hard to reach him!

I wonder if dad ever listened to the song, I wrote him. I pray and really hope he did!!!!

When my dad passed away I was so saddened that there was no singing. My dad had sent me a clipping of how Pierre Elliot Trudeau's son got up and spoke at his funeral. My dad hoped for the same sort of celebration. I was so upset by my dad's service that I wrote the Archbishop of Ontario at the time venting my feelings. He wrote back and had the audacity to say that I had taken my dad for granted. I at no time took either of my parents for granted. I was so upset by his response that I forwarded the letter to my brother. He probably threw it out.

Thursday, December 22, 2011

I am so livid! George's real personality is coming out. The highway or my way! The other night Jessica suggested we replace the glass table with the wooden one he refinished. I thought it was the one on Saber Road, she suggested, so I agreed. Last night I blew up at George because he had plans to bring up the one that belongs to the set of his grandmothers. I hate that set! He knows that and had the audacity to say, "Maybe it will grow on you." Again, he wins his way! Well I told him I would not sit at that table and I will not, not even at Christmas! I feel like a stranger in my own home! When it comes right down to it, he does not care about my feelings at all!

Ten to one they all think my blowing up has something to do with my medication. I just tried to stick to my ground! You might call this sulking or being stubborn but I will not sit at that table unless I decide to change my mind while Carol and Gabe are here, but I doubt it.

Health wise I am doing a bit of name matching but I have not noticed much else. I see the colours but that is all. There are no messages of support except for maybe I really identified with the songs from X Factor, especially Melanie Amaro's songs and Chris Rene's message Believe.

Well to no surprise, George called Duncan Mental Health unbeknownst to me and I got an appointment to see Dr. Argle. To put it briefly she upped my **Loxapine to 50 mg and lowered the Abilify to 15 mg.** I personally think that name matching is no big deal nor is my raising my voice. I do not think I am sick.

Wednesday, December 28, 2011

Well Gabe and Carol have come and gone. We had a good time especially Christmas Eve when we went to the Festival of Lights. Jessica was very helpful and did most of the cooking. Darcy was supposed to do the turkey but I guess George forgot. I feel displaced in my own kitchen.

Little do the girls know that it was George who decided to do all the cooking because he did not want to deal with the girls when they were young. I in many ways wish it were me who did all the cooking than maybe they would be closer to me too, but it is a little late for that.

I was quite upset that I got phone calls over the weekend on Friday and Monday night checking up on me. I did not like it one little bit!

When you listen to all the inspirational music, they say all you have to do is Believe. Well I believe that I am right. This will mean an increase in medication just the same but I believe that I am involved in something bigger than everyday life. I do not exactly know what it entails but I am sure that people are using my colours more on TV than they used to. I also believe that the TV reflects my life or what we do, read or talk about…it is too coincidental. I believe that I will get my dream job and that George will have to pay for his covering up overt situations regarding that couch! It is hard to trust him when his answers are so vague to things that really bother me. Why was he so proud of that couch?

Do not get me wrong I am not receiving messages from the TV! I just notice the colours. If the colours bothered me, the Festival of Lights would have been unbearable!

I still have wishes though. I wish that Mike Holmes could have fixed up our house on Gage Lane and we could have had a bed and breakfast there since George wants to retire soon.

Thursday, December 29, 2011

I am sad. George bought me earrings he would have bought for Darcy. They would have been nicer without the red bobbles and the latch at the back, which makes it harder to wear. I cannot get this type of earring in my ear. I do not think I will wear them. I wonder when he will ever surprise me with something real.

Today I went to see Dr. Argle again. She kept my medication at 50 mg Loxapine and reduced the Abilify to 10mg. She had the audacity to give me the drug Benztropine to deal with the shakiness. I had told her it did not work last time so she upped it to taking 1 mg twice a day. Forget that noise! Give me a pill that does not give me the shakes! I am not going to take a psychotic medication and then something else to combat its side effects! I hate taking pills! This problem would have been better for George he does not mind taking pills!

2012

Sunday, January 1, 2012

Last night I did not take the Abilify and I slept until 6:30 am. I took the Abilify in the morning as Dr. Argle suggested. I will try it until Thursday when I see her again and try to keep track of when I wake up.

This afternoon George went golfing with Donald. I hope it is not too cold for them.

Thursday, January 5, 2012

I saw Dr. Argle today and she has kept my medication at 50 mg Loxapine and 10 mg Abilify. She asked me if I noticed anything different about the family and I just mentioned how Jessica seemed sad yesterday on her birthday. At dinner, she looked like she was going to cry. What was surprising is that she did not want to go anywhere for dinner apparently and ended up making it herself, and it was tasty.

I am not sure that these pills are working. I still think something is up. How could the girls afford such a lavish Christmas present for me?

They got me a manicure, pedicure, European facial and an infrared sauna. It must have been so expensive that I am afraid to use it. What I do not understand is why there was no certificate. In addition, I at times am still not sure of George and that blasted couch.

I applied to some job openings that the principal of Star of the Sea posted. They are for a new school, St. Marvins. I hope I get an interview and more importantly get a position. I am tired of staying home. I just pray that I am mentally healthy enough to feel that I am in the real world and that the real world is not spinning around me, which is sometimes how I feel.

Friday, January 6, 2012

Today I let Jessica have the car to get to work. I was tired and needed a break from the silence in the car and I get stressed driving there to pick her up. For some reason driving home is no big deal but leaving the house to pick her up is.

Friday, January 13, 2012

I have let Jessica have the car Wednesday, Thursday and today. I feel less stressed when I do let her have it, although, I am bored out of my tree with nothing to do.

I am feeling level headed and I see now how silly it is to believe that I was right about the colours. One thing though I still feel that I am going through this for some other reason than being sick…maybe a drug trial. I cannot believe it has been six years since I was diagnosed and the doctor still has not figured out my medication. It is frustrating to take what you are supposed to and apparently have it not work.

Monday, January 16, 2012

On Friday, I phoned St. Anne's to verify Tim's email and to get Brenda's to see if they would still be a reference. I decided to take a chance, see if Tim was there, and talk to him. He was and I did. It was a great conversation and it left me hopeful! The only thing I worry about is my medication causing me not to be as energetic as I was. I think I can handle everything else.

Due to Dr. Argle's suggestion to take Abilify in the morning because it might be what impedes my sleep, I have been taking it in the morning. The trouble with that is that I do not always remember.

George and I went to the 5:00 p.m. mass on Saturday and I noticed I was shaking but I do not notice it now. I am so worried that this will be permanent!

Monday, January 23, 2012

I think I know why I did not write in this journal while I was working, it is because I did not feel the need or feel it was safe… that is how I feel now. I probably never should have put this on the computer.

I am so bored, yet I am afraid to do stuff! Jessica has the car for work, which only makes my claustrophobia worse…but it will not be for long.

I really hope that I get a job teaching long term somewhere. I will be heartbroken if I do not even get in at the new school, St. Marvin's!

I am supposed to go to my sister's in May but as much as I am looking forward to seeing her, I am not looking forward to seeing all moms' stuff in her house!

George has made me promises of having an interior decorator and then when the time comes he will say we have no money. If only we just let Jessica rent! It is too late now though. I want to wait until the market goes up before we sell. I know George does too.

Monday, January 30, 2012

I just noticed the Archdiocese's website posted another opening for St. Marvin's-a grade 2 position. Interested candidates have to apply by February 10. That must mean that interviews will follow shortly after. Please God let me get an interview and let it go fantastically! I really need this position to feel satisfied. Please let me get it.

I have noticed that being on 50 mg of the Loxapine has steadily increased my weight! I do not like that!

I am procrastinating booking my flight to London because I was freaked out last time and I am worried about going to the reunion.

I am lucky to have a man like George who takes care of me and puts up with my mental illness. However, why does he, when he shows such little affection? Which begs the question Why? Maybe it's because few women would put up with such lack of affection. (Monday, February 23, 2015 I have a message into one of our lawyers, Peter to look into an annulment and to change my Will.)

Monday, February 13, 2012

I feel totally fine and Dr. Argle lowered my Loxapine to 45 mg. plus 5mg Abilify.

Jessica is in Malaysia now and staying in touch by emailing her Dad. I wish, just for once, she would get in touch with me too.

I really want a job at St. Marvin's so I am praying constantly and doing my best to get the job. First I need an interview and need to do well. This time I will not disclose my illness.

I am going to get my hair cut on Wednesday but I am not sure what I want done. Decisions!

2013

Friday, April 5, 2013

We are moving into a new townhouse tomorrow! George wants to pay down the line of credit but we still have modifications to make to the new place like Built in wall units to make this place look nice. It was a crazy time to move because Darcy gets married in July.

    I think I am handling the move quite well. In fact, I am the one taking care of cancelling and getting new services for the place. I am far more involved in this move. (Monday, February 23, 2015 finally I got my cell phone transferred into my own name!)

    Although I am handling things well I must admit that I am bugged about those couches again! We went couch shopping for our family room at the new townhouse and I never thought a thing of it until we went to Sandy's which I thought did not exist anymore. However, low and behold there it was and I was shocked to find out how high end it was.

    I was really triggered when Mark our financial advisor at the bank brought up our shopping for furniture and specifically brought up Sandy's. I reminded George that that was where he had his couches made and was about to say how they were made strangely, when George cut me off.

Thursday, May 2, 2013

Yesterday I did a search on First Nations and low and behold, the topic appeared on CSI last night and in the headlines of today's paper. Is this just another coincidence? Another thing that seems to bother me is that sometimes Darcy puts on makeup and her complexion is clear and at others, I notice the red. Is it the way she applies makeup some days? That would be the logical thinking. However, my thinking is not logical. I put myself on 5 mg of Loxapine with Dr. Duran because I had myself on 10 mg for a very long time.

I do not want to say anything to anyone because I want to see if it will settle down. These are real things I am noticing, like Darcy's makeup and George's memory and so far, I see the logical side of things.

Jessica was down for Darcy's bridal shower and was nice to me. Well, she let me take her shopping for some running clothes at Sport Check. She suggested we go to Starbucks and pick up a coffee. Low and behold Bess, a former student served us. It was nice to see her. When she asked if I still worked at the school, it broke my heart to say, no.

Recently I applied to two positions at Immaculate Conception because the school is very close and that would be another great school to work at. There was a grade one and two position opening. I wanted the two because it was more permanent but to be honest, grade two is a hard year because it is a sacramental year and perhaps I am not up for that. I do not know. I did not get an interview. I just know I liked grade four because that is what I am used to. As Tim said, "We are creatures of habit." However, I have been applying to everything just to get back in.

I applied to the Boys and Girls Club to volunteer there once a week. Apparently, volunteer positions can lead to full time work. Maybe this is a road I need to go down if they will not let me back in to teach. Anyhow, this morning I am going to the Police Station to have a criminal record check done.

Tuesday, May 7, 2013

I filled out the papers for the record check and it will take 2 weeks. While there, a nice man named Kevan told me that I would make a good Commissionaire and gave the name of someone to contact. I might but not yet. I am feeling a bit shaky.

What was interesting about my discussion with him is that he could tell that I was a teacher by how I filled out the forms. He also seemed to know that I was a teacher's pet and deliberately got into trouble.

To be honest I do not trust George. Although I have nothing to base what is normal in a marriage, except my parents', and theirs was not a good one according to conversations I had with them. Now that I see how Greg treats Darcy, I feel that I am missing something. George can go 6 months or more without being physical and I can now go forever. I do not enjoy it. During the day, he just pecks me good morning and good-bye and another peck good night. No hug, nothing and then he expects me to want to be intimate. I always agree but I hate it.

I wrote a few songs a few years back called "Souls Design", "Windows to the Soul" and rewrote "I Want You to Want Me" that expresses how I feel about our being intimate. These are the songs I shared with him in 2002.

He does not seem to like the things I like. I like to go to plays, musicals and concerts and he does not seem to want to go to anything I might like. The only concert we have gone to is the Rolling Stones.

In addition, I am beginning to have those same doubts about him. I think that I should call Grace, my new caseworker. I took 10 mg last night of my medication to see if I go back to what I was taking, if that would help because Dr. Argle always gave me extra just in case so maybe it will work.

I am thinking that George and I do need to see a marriage counselor and, I need to see someone about all my negative feelings about the male anatomy. When I was in grade 13 my first boyfriend was in first year of University. I took the subway to his residence once and he chased me across the bed when I said no, I was scared. I remember thinking about him when George did the same thing when I did not recognize him. When I dropped out of University, I started going out with a truck driver. One day his brother gave me a ride and forced me to put my mouth on his penis and help him come. He also tried to make me laugh because it stimulated him afterwards. When I told, my boyfriend, at the time he said it was my fault. I never told my parents. We were parked in the middle of nowhere. I was trapped and more afraid of what would happen if I ran away. Another time I was in an elevator in his building and I pressed the wrong floor, a man, a complete stranger grabbed my breast and said it was because I had big breasts. I reported that one to the police but nothing came of it. When I was in high school, in grade 10, one of my math teachers used to single me out and leave notes on my desk. The next year I was in his class I sat at the back and he forced me to sit in the same seat I had the last time I was in his class. In teachers college I was naïve and not too confident and my drama professor singled me out. He made it so that he went to all my practicums and wrote my evaluations. I was thrilled but I look back and thought how wrong that was for him to single out a student. He gave me the love of Drama but made me feel guilty for many years. Now I have George who is awkward around me during the day. I need something better in my life. I need to feel beautiful. It is hard to feel beautiful when he is constantly criticizing other women from what they wear, their size or how much makeup they wear. I've stopped dressing up. I only wear jeans. He never notices me.

I took Kaiser to be groomed today. George was home so we went to pick her up together. We first went to my favourite jeweller to get his family's signet ring engraved for Jessica's graduation gift, then we went for coffee at Starbucks. I wanted something sentimental engraved but George said no. I told George that Father Larry was now a Vicar and he DID NOT KNOW WHO FATHER LARRY WAS. I find this very strange since I worked for him for about 10 years!

It will be hard for Darcy when her sister gets the signet ring because she received the original when she was far too young for it and lost it.

About Kaiser, she is not my favourite dog. George picked her out by himself and it was as if he knew nothing about dogs. I was not involved in the picking of the breed or the dog! When he took me to pick her up, she was not well. I could tell right away. When I took her to our Vets, she had dual ear infections and crystals in her urine. I would rather have no dog than not have a boxer! Jessica and I took Kaiser for training lessons. Darcy never came nor did George. In addition, it was George when we had

Barclay in North Dakota that told me to never pick the dog up, always go down to the dog. That rule did not apply to Kaiser. He picked her up and let her on the couch!

Friday, May 10, 2013

Okay something strange is going on and frankly, I feel more empowered than sick. Yesterday I made an appointment with Grace, my new caseworker, to tell her about all my abuses mentioned above and to get a name for a couple's counselor and to tell her about my lack of sleep, but low and behold she wanted me to go to the hospital to get evaluated. I did because I wanted to learn more about the system and to see what they thought. I saw a psych nurse and had to tell my story to her than I had to wait quite a while for the emergency doctor to check my thyroid etc. His name was Dr. Salter. Then I had to wait forever for the psychiatrist and he has me talk to a med student who was working with him. After I relayed my story to him again the psychiatrist, Dr. Dagle walked in, the student relayed it to him, and he said I was sick and needed to be on 25mg of Loxapine and 250mg Divalproex or Epival, which is a mood stabilizer. He used some scare tactics to get me not to lower my own dose. He scared me but maybe I should stand my ground. Scare tactics is mild; he threatened me! After all, Jessica's friends have a saying that goes something like if you do not stand up for somethings, you will fall for anything. I wish I could remember it properly. I just want to be a role model for my girls. I am not afraid of getting medication injected into me but I do not like the hospital. If Grace asks me again if I will take a trip I doubt I will unless I will be forced.

It is hard to believe Dr. Dagle when Dr. Argle said that there was nothing she could do to force me to take my medication. There were no laws. If there were laws forcing medication, why would so many people be on the street that the papers claim to be mentally ill? The papers always imply that all the homeless are mentally ill and drug addicted.

Grace asked me if I felt if I would be famous one day and to be honest I do…one day. I still feel that my computer is trying to teach me, and it does act weird…so does the television.

I do not feel scared I feel people are doing this to help me. I just do not know when it will come to fruition.

Saturday, May 11, 2013

I took the family to Stars on Ice last night and I loved it! Of course, there were colours there and they all stood for something but it did not bother me. We took the sky train which was a nightmare coming home. The line-ups to get tickets were crazy! Our trip on the sky train was uneventful for me and no colours really stood out.

One thing that I was surprised at was their promotion of World Vision. It reminded me of when I was in the throes of whatever is going on, I thought it would be nice for the girls to have someone to write to, so, I signed up for a little boy. George finally wanted me to cancel it. I was motivated again to sign up for one last night but George said no.

Anyway, I took my medication last night for the first time. I did not take it Thursday night because they had already given me 20mg of Loxapine, which is now called Xylac that made me sleepy. Strange how it made me sleepy when I have been on that dose before and have felt no effect. Anyhow last night I woke up at 3:00 a.m., went to the washroom and fell back to sleep quickly. I woke up at 6:30 a.m. when the dog barked and fell back to sleep again and finally woke up around 8:00 a.m. Overall, an improvement in my sleep, I was not tossing and turning all night long!

I have been really trying to make an educated choice with the upcoming election that I somehow do not believe is real and not let the colours influence my choice but I am not a fan of any parties' platform in British Columbia. I am intrigued with the green party folding private and independent schools into public. I would be interested in learning more about that. It would be more in keeping with Ontario. None of the websites seem legitimate as with the websites connected to the Archdiocese, which makes me wonder whether the changes in saying the mass are real. I think I am going to exercise my right not to vote.

I just found the curriculum for teaching first Nation studies to k-12 students but it is difficult to follow. It would have to be printed which is a waste. It would be better to be interactive than you can click and go to where you want to go.

I think the ministry should have all of them interactive and have it so that teachers can show more than one subject on a screen at once for instance being able to see the IRP for science at the same time as another to make creating short-term plans easier. It would be ideal to be able to have the word document open on the screen while being able to see more than one IRP as well. This way teachers can see the correlation between different subjects and make, I forget what you call it, but teach a bunch of subjects under one topic of study. Oh yeah, a theme based unit.

The document written for first nation art I disagree with, it says it is not necessary for the students to learn the specifics of the elements of design but I had my student learn the names and shapes of the ovoid, U, split U and S, I think they were. I had them name them and incorporate them into their own designs using the colours most often used in native design. We made pictures, painting, masks and cedar plaques. I think it is important for them to know the basic elements and apply them. They were proud of their accomplishments and so was I!

Seeing the native blanket reminded me of the native blanket I made for my class I tried to get every student I ever taught to sew a button on it but unfortunately it never worked out and I left it in the classroom.

I love first nation artwork and some of my treasured pieces are from my students and one I chose when we picked up Jessica from camp of two hummingbirds. I now have a favourite Robert Bateman print of whales I got from the Variety Show.

Sunday, May 12, 2013

Well I slept even better last night! I woke up at 3:00 a.m. perspiring like crazy on my neck and face but went back to sleep without having to go to the washroom. I finally woke up at 7:30 a.m.!

Today is Mother's Day and Darcy and George surprised me with a Kobo! Greg was able to get it working for me.

We all went to the Bugle House but unfortunately the service was bad and Cassie was acting up. I think I will try to find another buffet that offers more variety of food.

I wrote a letter to Father Larry, who was the former priest at my parish today but George suggested that I wait a week before I send it. I was thinking that too. See if this medication changes my mind. I wrote about all the changes I would like to see in the Catholic Church especially in this year where their focus seems to be about Bringing Catholics Home (back to the Church). I am trying to effect change in my life.

Monday, May 13, 2013

I have to say that I really do not think many of the sites I visit on the internet are legitimate. I really feel that my computer is trying to teach me in some way. I am trying to apply the knowledge I learned in my Masters in Curriculum and Technology. It seems the more I do the more I doubt the sites I am looking at. I am not sick! (Monday, February 23, 2015 I still feel the same way and I have been on my medication for a month. I feel in some way that I am working perhaps on my Doctorate, wouldn't that be nice!!)

Hurray! I slept through the night! I went to bed at 11:00 p.m. and did not wake up until 7:00 a.m.! I have not slept through the night for well over a year or more.

With all the exploration, I did on the internet regarding the political parties I found it interesting that they presented a checklist outline for their parties and articles on persuading people to vote. The Liberals want to have a 10-year plan for the teachers but they have not outlined what that would look like.

One thing I have forgotten to mention is that I have the gift of music back. I have downloaded iTunes and have downloaded some of my favourite music, which inspires me, like Josh Groban and Nikki Yanofsky and her Olympic song "Believe". It is so nice to have the gift of music again and yet they say that I am sick again. It is not the medication that gave this gift of music to me. I did all this before I met with Grace my new caseworker at Duncan Mental Health.

Well, all I can say is that this medication has allowed me to focus and edit this book today.

Tuesday, May 14, 2013

Today I woke up at 3:00 a.m. again but only for five minutes and then woke up when the alarm went off, so it is getting better but obviously three is still bothering my subconscious.

I remember when we were living in Ontario George bought me beautiful gifts. One year he bought me a red dress but I felt so uncomfortable in my own skin that I returned it with him. Instead, he should have said I was beautiful in it and persuaded me to keep it. I have always missed it and he never bought me a dress again. (Monday, February 23, 2015 He also gave me a blue saphire ring, which he said was very cheap, for our first anniversary, but when I wanted diamonds or something more permanent for our 30th anniversary he said no. He preferred going on an expensive vacation and during it he was too cheap to have a private romantic dinner on the beach.)

This morning I had an appointment with my new psychiatrist, Dr. Mullard. Grace came to pick me up because it was in the South Office rather than the North Office and she did not want me to stress in how to get there. He was a very nice man and we decided together to up my Loxapine to 50mg. Perhaps this will help me with my unsure feeling towards George and that he is not who he says he is.

I mean what father would not keep, in a special place, the tiny article written in the National Enquirer about his daughters helping him. In addition, what father would not care to keep a coffee mug with his daughters' pictures on it or the portrait that I had made for him of the girls?

Not that I want it right now, but just like last time I became sick, George has stopped kissing me. I thought maybe Grace had said something to him about my being bothered about him just pecking me on the mouth good morning, good bye and good night and then expecting intimacy, so I asked her. However, no, she had not said anything. Why then, if he cares about me does he pull away, it does not make sense to me. Is he mad that I am "having another episode"?

This afternoon was very productive. George and I went to vote then he dropped me off back home and I went out. I went to the drugstore to fill my prescription of the extra 25 mg of Loxapine, which will mean I will take a total of 50 mg. I like Dr. Mullard, he reasoned with me. Afterwards I went to my favourite jeweller to pick up Jessica's graduation gift. The signet ring that we had engraved with Grad 2013 was not exactly the word choice I wanted. I would have added Love Mom and Dad but he did not want to. He said she was not mushy. While I was there, I asked them about the pendants I ordered. They said it should be ready Friday! It sure is a good thing that I ordered it in March because it has taken quite a bit of time. What was exciting is that the woman helping me gave me a sneak peek as to what they look like. They were not polished yet but they looked great! I feel great!

Wednesday, May 15, 2013

I took my 50 mg Loxapine and my 250 mg Epival last night. This time I woke up at five for five minutes. However, last night's sleep was restless nonetheless, I keep dreaming of the election and how I voted. It seems all connected to the internet.

This morning I tried to enter Darcy in Walmart's Mother of the year but the site did not work well and it did not work. I finally did it but it said I nominated myself. Truth is I would like to be nominated for something too.

Thursday, May 16, 2013

I slept very well but again I woke up at 5:00 a.m. and fell back asleep quickly.

Today would have been George's Mom, Sandra's birthday. I wonder if he will think about her.

This weekend is a long weekend and Paula invited him to play golf on Saturday with Ben as well. Ben also wants to play Sunday so George for the first time will spend Saturday night there without me. I was invited to come and stay at the cabin or likely sit in the cart but I am not interested.

I have noticed some massive bruises on my legs so I have a call into Grace to see what I should do about my medication.

She returned my call saying that she checked with the pharmacist and this is not a side effect.

One thing I have noticed ever since I went shopping with Darcy; the stores sell a full array of colours. All my colours I have spoken about are in the stores. Because it is the fashion, there are more vibrant colours showing up on TV. However, I somehow feel responsible for this. A very grandiose thought. However, it is like, let us see what happens if we overload her with colours. None of it scares me anymore.

I am feeling good about myself. I signed up for a course through Delta Continuing Education. They allow people to sign up online and that is what I did. I signed up for a course called "Triple Your Reading Speed". It takes place Wednesday May 22 from 7:00 p.m.-10:00 p.m. in South Duncan. This is a big deal for me to go out on my own, especially at night. We will see how strong I feel once the time comes.

Friday, May 17, 2013

Last night I slept very well. I slept until 5:50 a.m.!

I am so excited today the pendants for the girls are supposed to be ready!

In addition, to make sure I make a wise decision I am going to send my letter to Father Larry for my brother to read. I want his input. (George will not read my letter). It has been almost a week now and I still feel the need to send it.

(November 14, 2019- I cannot find where I was sure that I mentioned that while living here at Diamond Head, the townhouse, when I was into getting deeper into my computer, it asked me if I trust Jessica. I said, "Yes." Because of this I feel strongly that she is behind helping me with my book/manuscript editing. I also believe she is aligned with my mother in getting my school off the ground by helping Darcy have the musicians perform to raise money for my school.)

I picked up the pendants and chose some chains. They are beautiful! I cannot wait to give them. How will I ever be able to keep Jessica's a secret for two years? I cannot wait to give Darcy hers! (Monday, February 23, 2015 I feel like a fool for having given Darcy the wrong symbol.)

This afternoon while watching TV, I was surprised that we got so many more channels, like DIY, W, TLC and Vision. While watching Vision TV I was able to watch my favourite show ever Touched by An Angel, then The Waltons came on. I have not seen that show in years. It has been well over a decade since I have seen it. I am not even sure the girls would know what I was talking about if I mentioned the show to them.

I did email my letter to Father Larry to my brother so now I wait to see what he says.

Saturday, May 18, 2013

My brother got back to me and said that I should not send the letter but that I should stay true to my beliefs and that he would talk to me further about it with me this weekend.

Last night I did not have a great sleep and that is because George got up and I heard him at about 3:00 a.m.

George has left for the cabin so I am spending the day with Darcy. I am miffed with him because I asked him to take Kaiser and he did not.

Today Darcy and I went and had a manicure and pedicure done. Then we went to Target where we both bought Jessica a graduate card and I bought a purse. Afterwards we went grocery shopping at Save On and ran into Steven and his friend. Steven is our next-door neighbor. Steven is getting married tomorrow.

Darcy was going out with Greg for her birthday dinner since Cassie is at her dad's this weekend. I did not want to have a cheese sandwich, so I went to my favourite Japanese restaurant for dinner all by myself. That is huge progress so why do I keep thinking about the couch and I am still uncomfortable with how George treats me physically. This medication has not kicked in.

Sunday, May 19, 2013

Although you would think I would sleep terribly because George was not here; I had the best sleep that I have had in years! I woke up at 8:19 a.m. to Darcy making some noise.

One thing that I must mention here is that when I saw the American Idol finale for the season last week I thought it strange or coincidental that they should have Frankie Valley and Aretha Franklin sing and all the songs were from the golden oldies. I thought it coincidental because just that day I was listening to the jukebox oldies on the TV and they were not playing anything familiar. American Idol was terrific!

Another thing that I find weird or strange is when I started to edit this document, the word "déjà vu" was printed in French with the accents. I never knew how to put the accents on and when I tried on my computer a week ago, it would not fix itself but low and behold today as soon as I write it, it types itself properly.

George came home and asked me if I wanted to go to our favourite Japanese restaurant for dinner but I said the Pad Thai restaurant. Once we were there, I told him I had gone to the Japanese restaurant the night before by myself.

I have sent an email to the editor of Special Features to one of the major newspapers to see if she can help me get this book published by giving me some names or websites. She is out of the office until May 27, 2013. She never followed up.

Monday, May 20, 2013

Last night I slept fine. In addition, I must say that my legs have stopped hurting.

George and I went to the Art Gallery and the parts I enjoyed the most was a wall sculpture and Emily Carr's paintings.

One thing that I have noticed about our expensive car is that it does not have an electrical plug to plug in cell phones or iPods. This disappoints me considering how much we paid for the car. Now I cannot plug in an iPod.

I am still taking my medication but I do not feel any different. George is still pulling back on giving any kisses and I still feel that we need to see a counselor. In addition, I still feel uncomfortable around him. I do not know when this medication is supposed to kick in but it has not yet. Colours are not bothering me, although I know exactly what they mean.

Today we went to Harry Rosen to buy a grey suit for George to wear at the wedding. We chose a light purple shirt and tie and lavender and white hankie for the pocket. He looks very religious in my mind. (February 23, 2015 I am beginning to dislike the colour grey)

Tuesday, May 21, 2013

I have finished spell checking this document.

This morning I phoned Dr. Brown's office to make an appointment to be fitted with contacts. My appointment is May 30, 2013 at noon. I really hope that they work out for me. I had the best vision when I last wore contacts.

I put a call into Grace today because she has not gotten back to me with an appointment with Dr. Mullard. I have only two days' worth of pills left. I am surprised that she did not get back to me sooner if they feel that I am so out of sorts.

Wednesday, May 22, 2013

I slept well last night but I did wake up at 3:00 a.m. and have to go to the bathroom.

I spent today formatting this document and doing a new resume. I find that I can focus better than long ago.

I finally had to call Grace again to find out when my appointment was. She also said she would phone London Drugs to fill my prescription. London Drugs called me and told me they would have it ready by the end of the day. I had George pick it up. My appointment is June 5, 2013 at 9:30 a.m.

Thursday, May 23, 2013

I slept very well last night. I did not wake up once.

Last night I went to the course I signed up for. It was "Triple Your Reading Speed" by Terry Small through the Duncan School District. This was huge for me. Not only did I go to the course, by myself, which involved learning the way but also, I introduced myself to a few people. I loved learning something new! The funny thing was that it took place in a regular classroom but it was called the "Action Room". I could not help but wonder why they call it that?

I am not sure if the pills are working because I still feel like something wonderful is going to happen. I feel the same way about George; that we need to see a counselor. In addition, I find it strange how Tim never called me to be a Teacher on Call (TOC).

I decided to email Tammy using Donald's Email address to ask about the couch.

Friday, May 24, 2013

Last night I slept well but I did wake up at 2:15 a.m. and because I woke up, I went to the bathroom. I had a harder time getting out of bed today and got up closer to 8:00 a.m.

Tammy got back to me and said she just remembers them going to Segal's in Richmond. She was not much help.

Saturday, May 25, 2013

Last night my computer crashed but it seems fine this morning. The exact same thing happened a couple of years ago. I intend this week to go to Future Shop and buy something to back up my data.

We gave Darcy her presents, a pair of skates and the pendant from me. She was not as excited about the pendant as I would have hoped. Maybe she was hoping for another symbol. (Tuesday, February 24, 2015 I now realize where I went wrong with the symbol. But waiting for them to call is getting hard so I will phone today. I was hoping to have this done before George retired. But he retires this Friday.)

We spent the afternoon by the pool, which is a part of our townhouse complex, and then went to the Keg for dinner.

Sunday, May 26, 2013

Today George and I went to the 10:00 a.m. Mass. I still do not like the change in the responses we have to say.

I am not sure how quickly these drugs are supposed to work but what brought me to Grace is still there. Nothing seems to have changed so I imagine there will be a change in medication. I do not recognize George as my husband and that is the only thing bothering me except I still feel the grandiose thought that something good is going to come out of all of this. However, it has been a long time coming so I think I have to come to grips with the idea that there is no use in hoping.

I took one of my as needed Benztropine (1 mg) tablets tonight for the shakes. I feel that I am moving my right leg too much and it could be an involuntary movement.

Wednesday, May 29, 2013

Yesterday I had to take my computer into Future Shop where I bought it because I got a blue screen twice. The man I deal with, Daryl, and the technicians are always so helpful. I love the service there. I had to buy a new version of Office because George got rid of or misplaced our Office 2010 that Darcy and I used. Now I have Office 2013.

Afterwards George and I went for coffee, we got to talking about my illness, and I finally told him what brought me to contact Grace in the first place. I also told him that I do not think the medication is working because I still do not recognize him as my husband. He took it pretty well.

However, as I was talking to him I was reminded that I had written about the Future Shop back in 2011 and I do not remember reading any of it when I edited this book. I was wrong I just used the Find button and punched in Daryl's name and up it came.

Today I am babysitting Cassie and I took her to buy dog cookies and then to McDonald's. This is the first time I have driven her anywhere!! We stayed at McDonald's until she asked to go home which was about an hour. We got there about 10:40 a.m. It was a great time to get her to eat and stay awake for the ride home. (February 24, 2015 Funny I don't remember taking her to McDonalds on my own, but I do remember taking her to buy dog cookies.)

Thursday, May 30, 2013

Today I connected with Future Shop's online support to have them solve some issues. They did them all only I have to figure out how to use the online backup.

I also went to the eye doctors to see if I can wear contact lenses again. I met with Michelle and she is ordering some in for me to try. I go back on Monday June 10, 2013.

George is still very distant with me and no longer kisses me good-bye or anything. I assume he finds it even more difficult now after what I told him at the coffee shop. I find the change in my medication has only allowed me to sleep. In addition, it has taken away the pains I was experiencing in my legs.

Friday, May 31, 2013

I wish this had never happened to me. Just when I start feeling good about myself I am told that I am ill or having a relapse. I MISS TEACHING! I MISS THE KIDS AND ALL THE WORK THAT KEEP ME BUSY. I am getting older and I fear that I may never have a classroom again. I am feeling down on myself. I never should have agreed to do Learning Assistance that was my downfall. I knew it was the wrong decision but I felt for Carolyn who also wanted back in the classroom and was upset with her constant replacement of me in the classroom. Carolyn was doing Learning Assistance. Basically my principal swapped our positions. If it had been a stranger substituting for me in the class I would never have accepted. Plus George was influencing me but I never would have said yes. I was thinking more of Carolyn.

Tuesday, June 4, 2013

This week George is on holidays. Yesterday we took care of Cassie and today we did various things. We went to Whittle Head for a walk. Basically, we did a lot of walking today.

Elizabeth called to say the form she filled out for the Boys and Girls Club was undeliverable. Therefore, she tried phoning them but no luck, so she left a message. That is all she can do.

Saturday, June 8, 2013

The woman from the Boys and girls club called Elizabeth and they emailed me. I am officially in.

On Wednesday, I met with Dr. Mullard and he has started me on a new drug that I was willing to try. It is called, Saphris. Right now I take 5 mg in the morning and 5 mg at night. I do that until the box he gave me is empty then I take 10 mg at night. I continue to take the Epival. He wanted to try me on this because he noticed that my leg was moving a lot. I had noticed this too. Apparently, Loxapine can make you restless. The other thing he talked about with me is that I might have Capgras Syndrome. If someone had of mentioned this to me a few years ago I might have said yes. (Tuesday, February 24, 2015 Truth be told I was afraid to be honest. I do have it, especially where George is concerned. Plus now I am curious about Darcy because she seems so distant. And I already think there are two Cassie's. She just seems so well behaved and has come along tremendously academically and artistically.)

Tuesday, June 18, 2013

Today I have my orientation at the Boys and Girls Club. I hope they are not all young people working there or I will feel really out of place.

This medication seems to be working very well. I have a pain in my lower abdomen that could be caused by it but I am not sure.

Wednesday, June 19, 2013

The orientation went well. This will be a good way for me to get involved with kids again. It is a semi structured environment so it may work well…. we will see. Today I went shopping with Darcy and bought a pair of jeans and a sundress. The dress will be great for Mexico whenever we go again. I also have some contacts that I am trying out.

I applied for a grade four position at another Catholic School It is downtown somewhere but once I know the route I should be fine. I am going for it anyway. Time will tell whether I get an interview. No sense getting my hopes up.

I like this new medication. The pain in my abdomen went away and I have no side effects!! It is a sublingual, which I like, even though it tastes terrible, I like it. (Monday, March 16, 2020 I do think the staining I began to experience on my lower front teeth were caused by this drug. It disappeared after I was taken off this medication.)

A picture of the Darcy and Jessica at Darcy's beautiful wedding appeared on my desktop after I sent it in to Future Shop for a checkup. Weird. I had wanted a picture of the girls and lo and behold I got one.

I am sure her wedding cost more money than I was able to muster up for her. It had all my colours! She used every cent of the money I had set aside.

Wednesday, June 26, 2013

Today I had my training "Put the Child First" for the Boys and Girls Club. Everyone there was younger than me.

Dear God, I know that I am not a spring chicken anymore but I do have a lot more valuable years that I could offer this school or any school for that matter. I think that I have been out of work for long enough now that I value the position I once had. If I could take back some decisions I made I would, but if you allow me this opportunity, I will be forever grateful. Please Lord please. Amen

Wednesday, October 23, 2013

I did not like volunteering for the Boys and Girls Club. The staff were all in their twenties and not very communicative with me.

I have started being a teacher on call with the Archdiocese near my home.. I finally got the guts when out of the blue I got a call from St. Patrick's the school that Nicky is principal at to substitute for their grade three class on September 10, 2013. I had applied to her school last year for a grade seven position and had explained my situation. I said yes and was very nervous. But everything went well and it felt so good to be in the classroom again! I sent an email to Nicky saying as much.

That one experience caused me to send out emails to all the other schools in my area to be a teacher on call. I got a call from the principal at St. Caprice's where a former colleague of mine now works. (I used to work with him at St. Anne's.) She was pleased to get my email and put me on her list. She asked me to TOC (Teacher on Call) in the morning of October 2, 2013 in Andy's class.

St. Patrick's called me again for October 17 to teach grade 1.

I find it very difficult to be a TOC and figure out what the teacher wants taught. Sometimes they use short hand that I can't figure out.

I asked Tim, the principal at St. Anne's, if I could be on their list and he said yes. I hope this year that he can use me.

Hopefully, this major step back into my career pays off. I would really like my own class.

On a medical note, I am still on Saphris, but only 5 mg once a day and it seems to be working well. I've been on it for months now.

The funny thing about this illness is that when I wasn't on medication it escalated. The base problems like the couch and stuff were real but I began to think my family were imposters and colours and food all had meaning. Those things keep me taking my medication because I know they don't make sense.

2014

Saturday, March 22, 2014

As I said, I know what the colours mean and sometimes it makes me think. I had an appointment with Dr. Mullard the other day and told him that I still think about the couch. He didn't think much of it.

I applied to three positions at St. Fabian. The principal used to be the president of the somewhat union for Catholic School teachers here when I was a representative for my school. There are two one-year positions: grade four and six and one permanent position, grade seven. I feel I could handle any one of them, however, there would be more of a learning curve and challenge to teach grade seven because the curriculum is more difficult, specifically the Math.

I am anxious to travel all that way with late nights and driving in the dark. I definitely would prefer to teach this side of the bridge but I have to get back in.

To reiterate if only I could turn back the clock and remake some of my decisions. I regret saying yes to being a Learning Assistance Teacher. It was the wrong thing to do when my health was so fragile. I knew it was wrong at the time but everyone said that I must check reality with George and when I asked him if I should take it, he said yes. Because George thought I should do it and I knew how Carolyn felt about being in Learning Assistance and always bouncing into my class when I was ill, pressured me into saying yes to the position.

Our financial advisor, Barb, does not think it feasible for me to take a one-year short term because I would earn more on CPP disability up to age 65. However, I am tired of sitting around. Maybe I would feel differently if George were retired but I am beginning to think not. Frankly, I do not think George will be retired for long before he finds some other work.

I am caught between a rock and a hard stone. CPP disability gives me $1,000 a month and I am not allowed to make any more than an additional $800 a month to maintain it. Therefore, it is not really worth it for me to be a teacher on call and strange as it may sound in some way I think the Archdiocese knows this and that is why I am not called that often, because I did a good job when I was called in unlike what George thinks. George thinks I was not called because I did a poor job. I do not believe it!!

Thursday, April 3, 2014

Well I did not get an interview for the positions I applied to which is just as well, it was not my favoured location. A position for an Elementary Educational Consultant opened up with the Archdiocese. It is a two-year contract, which might lead to something else afterwards. Being a consultant is a professional goal of mine. The last time I applied for the position, I had some "lofty" ideas as George says. I thought the consultants could have territories and did not have to go into the office every day and could be contacted via cellphone.

Although my thinking has not changed too much about the need to go into the office every day maybe I will table that idea. After all, they wanted the applications for this position sent by mail, which is surprising. Even though I stress over going to new places I would like to think I could do it with GPS. It would be a challenge I would be willing to take for the prestige of being a consultant. I would be thrilled!!

(Tuesday, February 24, 2015 I recall when I applied to be a consultant with the Archdiocese years ago when Hank Barnett was the superintendent. Back then I was telling them that perhaps they could have territories for their consultants and they could work from home a lot like how George was working as an outside sales person. That way I would not have to travel to the head office every day, but one of the assistant superintendents did not like that idea. He said he would prefer face to face. I think both could have happened. I also said that I was not a coffee and doughnut girl, that I did not want the responsibility for ordering refreshments. I think my thinking was ahead of the time for them…too outside the box. I think my ideas for work are even loftier now with running and getting credit for the idea of an online school for k-12 for both public and private schools across British Columbia (BC). (With continued dreams I now hope my school would go from Junior Kindergarten – Doctorate for the world and at the very least BC)

When I told Grace about the position she thought it might be too big for me but when I read her my cover letter she said I should go for it. In my letter, I told the Superintendent who was the previous assistant superintendent that did not like my ideas before, what my diagnosis is and my regret at leaving my school. The only suggestion that Grace had was not to be so honest with my disclosure. She said I should put mood disorder rather than schizoaffective.

It is precisely this thinking that I want to eliminate. If those that are helping clients with their mental illness do not encourage full disclosure than we have a long way to go.

The position is an eleven month year which is still better than twelve and requires some late days and evenings Something that I'm sure I would get used to, after all, I used to stay at school many times until 5:00 p.m. Now I just have to wait and see.

Jessica is living with us now. She was laid off from her position in Kinter Valley and we went up last Sunday to move her home. She has been nice to me. I was concerned over how it would go but so far so good. I am glad she feels comfortable enough to move back home! Although she does not talk a lot to me.

I planned on taking her income tax forms in because she signed them and they need to go back to the accountant to be filed so she can get her money. I asked her if she wanted to go with me and she actually said she would go with me tomorrow morning. I was pleased but surprised!

Although I do not know how to bring it up with George, I am unhappy with how he is so unaffectionate. He offers no hugs and only pecks me morning and night. One day he is going to want to be sexual and I am not going to want to because he is so stingy with his every day affection.

George bought me a nice jacket for my birthday but gave me a terrible card!

So strange, I found a reference letter for the Master of Educational Technology program that I am interested in through the University of British Columbia with my name filled out. I never did that, the program cost too much but I would love to take it. I am so confused, what is going on? The computer says it was downloaded in 2011 but I swear I never did that. Weird. (Tuesday, February 24, 2015 I am going to have to see if I can find it again on my computer because I didn't delete it.)

We went to dinner at Mongolie Grill for my birthday and the girls spoiled me. They bought me several light blouses that I can take to Mexico. However one of them fell apart. I don't know how many I have left.

We leave for Mexico on April 20th and are going with Tammy and Donald, their daughter and boyfriend, as well as Donald's sister, Nancy, and daughter and a couple of their friends. I hope everything goes well for me and that I am not too quiet.

One thing that I am noticing is that this medication causes me to be void of emotion. I do cry when stressed but I do feel that I am flatter than I should be. (Tuesday, February 24, 2015 Somehow I wonder if it is being flat or just being scared to speak up and not being happy with George)

Saturday, March 29, 2014

I went to a baby shower for our neighbor Elsa and while there I got very emotional. I am not sure whether it was the stress of going to the event, bringing Jessica home or the two glasses of wine. Usually wine does not have this effect. I was so embarrassed.

Sunday, April 13, 2014

Two things really depress me about being on antipsychotic medication. First, it has caused me to gain weight because it has stripped me of my motivation to do things. I have gone from a size 6 to an 8. Second, it has stripped me of my ability to enjoy things the way I used to. I don't laugh anymore. My mood is always the same. None of the comedy shows seem to make me laugh. I think making people laugh by making fun of people in any way is not funny and in poor taste. I used to be so happy, as a child. I had an infectious laugh I was told.

2015

Tuesday, February 3, 2015

We moved again. Now we live in a townhouse in the Diamond Head Complex in North Duncan, BC. The Carrier strata. We have lived in North Duncan since we moved to British Columbia in 1991 except for the brief stay at George's mother's condo.

    First let me tell you that I went off my medication for the months of December 2014 and January 2015. I went off to see if I would lose weight. I went back on my meds for two reasons because I saw that I didn't lose weight and because I didn't want George to keep saying when I disagreed with him on something that it was my psychosis. Also let it be clear, that I fully disclosed to George when I went off my medication and it was he that told me that I not tell my family doctor because I might not get my disability payments. I thought my doctor could've helped me.

    I met with Carl Bartle, the marriage counsellor and consultant today that I arranged for George and I. We talked about all the colours and some of the aspirations I have. I did tell him I was unsure of what my name was and my identity, I also told him that I feel that all that has happened to me was destiny and planned, so he requested that I write down how I feel my life was planned for me, so I will try.

First today I was at the local mall where Save On is and I saw a sign that made it pretty clear to me that there is action against George and that all my beliefs are correct. I am not sick. I have been made to remember with the help of all media and people, memories from my past. There are things from my past that as I recall I never shared with anyone, not even Elizabeth. They knew (and who they is I have no idea) I went to see a palm reader, I went to a stripper club, and a transvestite show with a friend. I hated the stripper club.

People and things I have met recently in my life are connected to people and things in my past. It is as if I have created the world and all that is in it, especially my surrounding area. How can this be remotely possible? Mr. Kaal, my history teacher promising to pass me in history if I promised not to take it again was instrumental in what is going on now, because when I left history, I went to Urban Studies. I feel that I am responsible for decisions being made about urban planning taking place now. I also feel responsible for the standards of various work environments and dictating changes to the Catholic Church.

I no longer crave coffee but my favourite drink now is a mango pineapple smoothie which I first tasted today at McDonalds where I met George for coffee at my suggestion when he suggested we meet somewhere for coffee. It was odd because I tried their mocha and it was awful, so I got some bottled water and I couldn't drink that either so I went to get a mango smoothie and the lady suggested mixing it with pineapple and voila, it was perfect. It was like my taste buds were controlled. I also drink chocolate milk, Simply Orange juice and bottled water!! I crave bottled water here over the tap water. Reminding me of the song by Shania Twain. Although once I was diagnosed, George stopped openly admiring other girls. However, he still always talks about his old girlfriends. I don't want to hear it.

Though orange represented Dr. Argle there was happiness because the colours of the BC Lions were included as all the colours of the other sports teams had.

I do feel that everything I have written about technology being advanced is true they are able to read thoughts, create doubles and mimic voices.

I think beyond the ability of technology to read thoughts that they can dictate taste buds and bodily functions. In many ways it is like the book I read iDoc come to life!

While at Save On I went shopping for some treats for the kids, Darcy, Greg and Cassie and I wanted to be sure I was fair in what I gave them for Valentines.

Tonight I watched the Jimmy Fallon Show and he began making fun of what I was writing and when I thought that they should stop, they did, instead they played a game regarding Darcy (music) and Jessica (caring) and they were even. Then they played another game where there was a target of music and when that was hit Jimmy was doused in water. I'm not clear but I think that one was depicting George. But it could also depict me because music is a desire and I was once dunked in a tank of water at the school I taught at, St. Anne's.

I now feel that the radio and TV are making fun of what I write and if they no longer are inspirations I will have to stop writing. I do not like being made fun of, which is what Jimmy Fallon's show does. I do not like this type of humour!

Saturday, February 14, 2015

Yesterday George had invited Darcy and the kids over and I asked him to invite Jessica too. After coffee George went to pick up Cassie and I met them at home since George and I had taken two cars to McDonalds.

When I got home Cassie was wearing a coloured skirt and a purple and grey sweater which she kept wrapping herself with. It was the colouring book she had that sent a clearer message. It was the picture of a girl holding her tablet with another girl showing her dresses. It reminded me with my dreams of the internet and going shopping.

Oddly enough Brian, my grandson apparently came down with Salmonella poisoning which I don't believe. Plus Darcy has only told these things to her dad which is strange since she's been more communicative with me. I think the case of salmonella may result from the fact that I am salmon overloaded I have salmon and fillet of sole far too often. Like TV that I crave. I crave a variety in my food.

I feel that our choices in the stores are being guided by the choices offered. Carl asked me to choose something that I would like to have and I said lamb chops which have not been in stores. I remember us having pork roast at home and dad having mint jelly which I don't like and when I had lamb chops with George we had mint sauce which I do like. I also miss pork roast where my mom would cook the fat crispy and dad would eat it off my plate.

George came home with my spending money for two weeks and I took a close look at the money. It was made out of paper and had everything that represented what I've been thinking about right down to the queen looking like my aunt. The others were plain and the queen did not look like my aunt. Since paper money rips I thought they should make the plastic money to look like the colourful one.

Jessica did come over and she was wearing all black with a white collar and a red bow. This meant to me that I was right with black and white and she was showing me care.

I think my mom representing blue, stems from the dress she wore at my wedding. What I think odd is at the time she had a dress made that had removable sleeves.

Things to talk to Carl Bartle and Dr. Duran about: I am now under my family physicians care.

1. I asked George to wash the vegetable drawer because I have a hard time getting it out of the fridge and he said yes if I will vacuum the floor. I don't want to vacuum so I said forget it.
2. I asked George to buy me life savers and when I opened it I made the connection that orange is my favourite flavour which stands for health.
3. I think that I am paying you (Carl) 110 dollars because I am giving a 110 percent

4. I also think my name Marie Louise Megan will mean that my third name Megan will become my first name Megan Marie Louise. Who says licenses have to only have two names?
5. I do not think that I am married and am unsure of my surname
6. I made the colour peach represent my sister Louise who supposedly passed away and asked for a sign to show me she was alive and on the CTV news cast they showed two teams playing, one was wearing peach. So I think she is still alive. Which leads me to believe that all the people that I know who have passed away, have not. If Ted, Donald's brother-in-law had passed away his wife would not be able to function as well as she is, the same with a colleague when her husband passed away. Plus my brother in law, Gabe, when my sister Louise passed away. Plus a friend, replaced his wife, a little too quickly for me to believe she is dead. Plus I think Whitney Houston and Winston Reckert are alive. Plus I don't think Donald's mom is dead. I saw no tears,
7. I feel I am trying to fulfill my legacy.
8. Eye Contacts –has brought me friends
9. Technical implants to hear what is said has brought me friends
10. I am not sure what my last name is
11. I feel that I may not be my parents daughter
12. I feel I am helping with the creation of various inventions and urban planning.
13. I feel like my taste buds and bodily functions are controlled plus I can dictate the heat levels in various environments by what I think
14. The news I am presented with seems created and not real. They reported the weather as two degrees this morning on my phone and the news channel but it doesn't feel that cold when I step outside when I check. Plus they show different weather for various areas of Duncan. This does not make sense. They do however bring me colours and actions that represent something I have thought.
15. Overall the colours seem more subtle which is sad and a little confusing and harder for me to read the messages.

16. I would like to talk about my unhappiness with my marriage: money, lack of affection and entertainment.
17. George telling me to give up on my daughter when she stopped talking to me

Sunday, February 15, 2015

Today George and I played pickle ball with Matt and Judy, a couple we just met in the gym. It was good to get some aggression out. At first we were playing with a pickle ball that was yellow and although it represents singing and speaking aloud I felt that I was smashing Darcy and music both things I love. So thankfully Judy suggested switching balls. They had a green ball and that was much better. It felt like taking action!

While resting between games I asked George about the baseball bats we had at Gage Lane and told them about the scary parts of the house.

I also spoke to my brother and was finally strong enough to share certain things with him! He will phone me tomorrow after my meeting with Dr. Duran.

I tried watching the Saturday Night Live special but their humour I did not find funny. It would cater more to George. He seems to laugh at everything!

Monday, February 16, 2015

Yesterday I bought a favourite candy of mine Sweetarts which I craved when I was pregnant with Darcy. Yesterday it tasted great today it was putrid! Some implant is somehow affecting my taste buds as well. Thankfully I now crave healthier choices to drink like orange juice, grapefruit juice, chocolate milk and I will only drink bottled water for that which comes from the tap is awful. I really crave chocolate milk which is what I craved when I was pregnant with Jessica. That is what I noticed with Saphris, it affected the taste of water from the tap.

Now I find my Tide pods, dental floss and makeup pads disappearing.

I feel like my life has been planned for me to give input and think out of the box for technology to discover mistakes in websites and think of new ways to use it. For instance I think they should have everyone register their fingerprints and these are used to withdraw money from machines at stores. Then there would be no need for credit cards, or money. I feel I am made to think of all the ways to revamp the Catholic Church and make it more inviting to Catholics, and marketing of products. For instance I think they should have just hand sanitizers in restrooms which would eliminate the need for towels and sinks. They could have just one sink for various emergencies. All the messages I was receiving from the TV and in the stores made me reflect on my life and I discovered there were many things about my life as a child that do not make sense.

Tuesday, February 17, 2015

I do not get as many messages by colour from the TV anymore. They are muted. The colours now move too fast for me to read. I feel comforted when I go out to the stores where there seems to be more messages for me to read.

Wednesday, February 18, 2015

George chose a car last year without me, a Jetta. He only invited me to choose the colour. Anyhow I've been trying to get the car to play the music I have on my phone and when I went to look in the manual there were incomplete sentences! Which means this car is somehow rigged as well. I want it to play my music. Even my phone won't sync with my computer and give me access to all my music!

I've been thinking a lot about the songs I have written and wondered if they were any good for publication. I always liked the name of one of my songs…Soul Design. Today I was thinking that I don't have much of a singing voice anymore and wondered how record labels choose artists to sing other people's songs and if those creators got credit? Maybe one day I will hear Darcy sing again and Jessica will want to go on mother daughter excursions with Darcy too and alone with me sometimes.

I really think we were never married properly. We never got a marriage license and our parents families were never invited as far as I know. I know my grandmother and aunts and uncles and cousins weren't there.

I am having more difficulty determining the colour messages on the TV because they aren't as bright. When they are solid and bright I can read them.

I do have thoughts of grandeur which I have had before and they give me hope. I think that maybe a grand house filled with native work is in my future. But with the colours fading so do my dreams and hopes. They disappear just as they have before.

Friday, February 20, 2015

I find that the TV is showing me poor taste in all programming. Over exaggerated poor taste in fashion, makeup and violence as depicted in the TV program I watched this morning, Marilyn Dennis. I was surprised because hers is a show I enjoy. Also the TV series I had access to "Justified" I really liked the actor but the rating for the program was poor and there was too much blood, swearing and gunfire.

Last night we went to the Home Show and they seemed to have many new displays and things that I had thought about. It was nice to dream. These were my favourite parts: wooden tables made from trees that had live edges, a wooden plaque of a tree, the many hot tubs with my colour light displays and access to music of your choice as well, the pianos at Tom Lee, a back splash that looked like river rock and Rogers's display of a wireless security system.

Hopes for my day tomorrow: February 21, 2015

Since I gain peace by the TV and music, I hope that they don't spoof on my ideas and continue to let me dream about great designs. I also hope that when I go out of the house that I continue to see the bright colours on people walking on the street and in the stores.

I think a good song that describes me right now is Katy Perry's "Roar".

Saturday, February 21, 2015

Fancy I woke up to the show JuiceBox which is music for kids and Katy Perry's "Roar" was playing! I think all music videos should be made in the way they are presented to kids.

Also Canada AM showed many people in solid black which means that my thinking is correct.

What I find is my mind is resting and I am not creating anymore. I miss it.

Nobody phones me back but my brother.

I plan to try to go to the skating store during the week in case my directions on the phone don't work and I panic and I will have to phone George to give me directions.

Since my plans today did not go well. I think I'll just stay in and work on my journal and review it. I had hoped on going on a flightseeing tour of Victoria and go whale watching. Perhaps it would be nicer in the better weather anyway. What was strange was that Neil the guy I spoke to talked up the excursion and then had to talk to his superiors to see if it was a go. It was not. I think he should have known.

I also thought it was interesting that the counsellor yesterday wrote down my family tree.

I realize that Microsoft and Google have my main colours, red yellow blue and green in their logos. I think they are friends in my journey to the top, although they had these colours long before they meant something to me. It is funny when I chose to have Google as my default search engine because they have no ADS it doesn't happen.

I want so much for my thoughts of grandeur to come to fruition. I have thoughts that I am on a mission to help Pope Francis revitalize the Catholic Church and bring its people back to the church especially the young. There are too many strict rules connected to the church that make a person feel bad about themselves.

Hopes and Desires:

A. That Jessica is close to me again and we can have a sharing relationship that is even better than the one she has with her dad.

B. Catholic Church

   1. No need to sit stand kneel
   2. No need for the readings, just the motivational sermon
   3. No need for the confessional or the sacrament of penance, which can be done in prayer and face to face with the priest if the person feels it necessary. Encourage personal conversations with God
   4. Have more modern music, that is found on the popular Christian Radio station so the kids can relate to it and hear it in the car. A band would be uplifting. Though I felt so good to see the kids I taught recorder to playing in the choir!!
   5. Make it not necessary to be so formal in church where kids have to be quiet.
   6. Have a separate room for Children's Church where they do related crafts. Have their parents pick them up after mass.
   7. Have a separate room where the sermon is piped in for nursing mothers and mothers of young children who would prefer not to be in the general congregation
   8. No demands on regular attendance on Sundays!!!!!!!!!!
   9. Get rid of all the guilt-producing prayers. Hail Mary prays for sinners-not necessary, same with the Our Father just to name two. I am tired of being treated like a sinner when I have not. I want to be Catholic but I can count on one hand the times I went to confession! And yet I taught in Catholic schools where I wanted to be but constantly having to feel like a hypocrite making the children do it and I didn't.
   10. Keep the shaking of hands
   11. Keep the host
   12. Let priests marry

13. Let women be priests
14. I like the vestments but let that be their choice
15. I believe in the right to choose. I had to have a therapeutic abortion and always felt guilty. It is still hard but it was the right thing to do. It was the doctors' suggestions and advice.
16. I believe in individuals being able to die and live with dignity
17. Have Christmas masses or celebrations on the 24th so those making dinner are able to attend.
18. 40 day fast is unnecessary. Lent makes people feel like sinners. Most people are not sinners.
19. Keep the doors open at churches so those who want to pray there can at any time.
20. Priests should give out emails so people can reach out in that way if necessary
21. Allow the study of Religion in my online school

C. New Home

Another thought of grandeur is having a grand home surrounded by paintings of First Nation artwork! Real paintings and colours that reflect me! Also one from Robert Bateman! I dream of a Stone home on all sides that is very modern with some things from my past. A wall with all the family pictures. Built in radio system that gives access to my music and that of my future husbands. An inside pool with access to the outdoors and a retractable roof. The pool would have coloured lights a slide and a diving board. An indoor pool with access to the outside with folding glass doors.

Also I would have a hot tub big enough for family. A beautiful baby Grand piano that had the functionality of some of the other ones I saw at the Home Show the other night, although not too complicated. No glass showers that had to be cleaned, no wood floors. A dining table that fits a lot of people in the natural shape of a tree but round the same with a coffee table. Lots of light!

I've also thought of living on a lake with a dock that attracts no leaches! I'd like a speed boat and recreational equipment. I just want the kids to come frequently and be able to stay. I also want to do cultural things in the city like go to some hockey games, football games, ballets, musicals, symphonies etc. Plus I want a maid, a gardener and chef. I'm afraid of being isolated. Maybe I would live there during the summer and in the city during the winter. I want to be close to amenities. I would love this to be on Lake Muskoka. It is the only lake I have been to, other than in Kinter Valley. I have fond memories there.

I've also thought of living in a huge log home. I just don't know. When George and I were flying to British Columbia one time I remember we talked to a guy who built log homes. I thought we had his card. I thought when we moved here I'd be able to live in one. I don't know how the walls are conducive to hanging things. I don't want it dark and dingy like George's cabin. Maybe a log home on the lake and a stone home in the city. It was my dream not George's. He led me to believe we could live in one as if he was unfamiliar with British Columbia.

We have bought a condo at the Cornerstone. The lack of space for clothes, pictures and storage has me worried. If my dreams came true we would have the entire floor! Plus I would have windows and doors that retract like at a new development in Ladysmith. I am not really interested in a deck that I can only use in nice weather. I think this new development has a great idea!!! I am also tired of living in a home that has beige walls. It is like a hospital. I want to be surrounded by colour, tastefully done. All my colours. The deck here has the railing at eye level when sitting down outside. Very disappointing.

I had a dream of living in a log home like the ones Pioneer Homes of BC make on Timber Kings but I don't like any of the insides on their website.

D. Car

I have thoughts of having a car for myself that is small and very technologically inclined. About the size of a mini cooper in a unique colour! I want it to start and run with my fingerprint. I do not want keys. I also want it to be able to park by itself. I also want it to be decorated with First Nation artwork especially designed for me.

E. Legacy: Online School

I have thoughts of working with Google and Microsoft and starting an online school from JK-Doctorate for both the public and Catholic schools to serve the entire world. It would offer music and linguistics. My aunt thinks I should retire but I want to keep my mind active. I really don't know what this would look like…perhaps three days a week. I know I keep applying for school teaching positions but the truth is I am having a hard time getting up early now.

F. Book

I have dreams of publishing this book and think someone is helping put it together. Who knows maybe it could be made into a movie!!

G. Wedding

I have dreams of having a big colourful wedding like Darcy's with all my colours.to someone who cherishes me and is not afraid to touch me with affection outside of the bedroom. Someone who makes me feel pretty. George is not that someone!

H. Doctorate

I have dreams of getting my PHD and feel people are helping me do that right now

I have thought of ways to rid us of currency and credit cards by using fingerprints. Just register your finger prints and you can enter your house that way too.

I keep thinking that Katy Perry's song "Dark Horse" refers to Jessica's Sandstorm when she says she's coming at you with a perfect storm.

I also hope I have justification and answers where George is concerned and the couch. To know why there were hidden fuse panels at Gage Lane and they didn't bother him.

I am frustrated by not having access to many of the good TV shows that must be out there. Seems I am always watching repeats plus I want a TV Guide that gives it to me a week in advance.

Tomorrow I plan to cancel the super channel package I signed for with Telus. I find I don't like any of the shows on the channels. The only one worth it is channel 421 where I get to see the actor in the show "Justified" but even that show is too full of guns and gore.

I still feel like Katy Perry's song, "Roar" describes how I feel.

I. I also have a dream of having some of my songs published/sung, especially my song called "Souls Design" which I wrote for George on our wedding anniversary. Yellow stands for music and Darcy.

J. I have also thought about having an income property that I/we did not have to manage.

K. I have a dream and a desire to have a family reunion with my relatives, somewhere convenient to my aunt and uncle. Having them meet my family means a lot. I would like my brother, sister and their families relocated here.

L. I would also like to have a lot of money to give away. Heart and stroke is a strong charity for me as well as project hope, helping the babies. Jessica is red and she stood for giving it all away but I don't think I could do that if I came into a lot of money.

M. I would also like to set up my girls with their first homes.

N. I would also like to be on the real Talk Shows and share my story. It has been discouraging to have to use a fictitious name to write this book and change most of the names within it.

Sunday, February 22, 2015

I am so frustrated with the wonky access I have to my computer and the internet and cell phone that I have a service technician coming to work on the TV and my computer. The technician is coming between 3:00 p.m.-5:00 p.m. on Thursday.

I would have expected to hear from George while he has been at the cabin but I haven't. Doesn't really bother me though. I asked him if he would be home to play pickle ball but he said for me to play with another partner. We will see, I just don't want to keep Matt and Judy waiting for us. It would be rude not to show up. I think I will ask for their contact info.

As it turned out I was the only one that showed up. The gym was empty.

Sunday, February 22, 2015

Tonight I talked to my brother, Sam. I have spoken to him more lately than I ever have before. He makes me feel good as does his wife Daisy whom I spoke with yesterday. My brother wanted to make sure that I was taking my medication, which I am. He said it is like taking it for diabetes. I guess it's like taking it for many things.

This time I am glad I didn't have a case worker to tell me to stop from reaching out to my colleagues at school. I did and I am happier for it. Victoria seems more receptive to listening than Carolyn. But I do think that if Carolyn were in my shoes she would eventually reach out to whomever she could. I use to think that I shouldn't speak to people about our private lives but talking only to the psychiatrists and case workers got me nowhere. This afternoon I even talked to Brenda from school. She has a bad cold and it sure did not even sound like her even with a cold! She now has my cell phone number so hopefully when she feels better we can get together.

Tonight we watched the Oscars and they made all my colours easy to read! There was a lot of solid black which means my thinking is correct. There was also a lot of music. There was a lot of red, yellow, Black, black and white, even light blue and solid white, plus some pink and beige. I feel that they are supporting me too by having the colours so simple. I also noticed that the majority of men wore bow ties. The women all wore solid colours.

When one of the songs was played, Glory, I think it was called, it was so powerful. Definitely the best song of the night. It brought a lot of people to tears.

Tomorrow I plan to go to the skating shop using my map GPS on my phone that Victoria set up for me. I pray it works and I don't get lost and can make it back home. In addition, I will pick up some milk for my tea, some more water, and get my pants hemmed at Helga's Dry cleaning.

Well I couldn't get through to the skate shop so until I know their hours I am not going to go maybe George and I can use my phone, I will drive and we can go there this weekend.

I bought my milk and chocolate milk at 7-11 and this time they had black caps instead of any light chocolate milk with blue caps and before that the regular chocolate milk had dark blue caps. Again black means my thinking is correct and the staff were wearing red and black. The only thing I couldn't get is my water.

Every time now that the colours are settling and mixing up and they aren't as vivid on the street anymore and I begin to think maybe it isn't real. I saw my neighbours all coming out of their house all dressed up in my brilliant colours. Brilliant meaning they were very vivid.

George and I have been sleeping in separate bedrooms from before I began to see Carl Bartle. I am sleeping much better. What I found which is strange is that I cannot sleep on the purple or red pillow case without it spiking my hair. However this does not happen with the white pillowcase from Darcy's old room. So I switched out the pillow cases. So now I am sleeping surrounded by my colours.

Monday, February 23, 2015

Today I went to see Dr. Duran about the rash on my hand and got some antibiotic. When I went to the drug store the pharmacist was able to straighten my name out on her machine/computer, which I thought was great!

I also went to Carter's and bought Ben 5 sleepers.

Tomorrow I will go to McDonalds for lunch and try Cowichan Aquatic Centre again for Pickleball.

I hope tomorrow will be a better TV day. I am frustrated with the packages and lack of good programs to watch. I have to rely on my staple shows like Criminal Minds and NCIS and I'm sure I've seen most of them. For years I've been satisfied with watching repeats but not anymore.

It is hard for me to put a date on when my journey began because I do not know the exact date that Darcy fainted. My reminiscing feels like I was destined to take this journey and was meant to do great things. However my eyes were awakened to my distrust of George in 2000 on that date. My colours didn't come into play until after we moved into the house on Wade Avenue and I don't remember the year.

Tuesday, February 24, 2015

Although the media still shows me grey I am meeting with my lawyer to one, hopefully get out of the condominium deal the way it stands now. It is far too small and I want a deck, which is enclosed and has windows that properly open, so it can be used in the winter. Moreover, I would only take the whole floor that is tiles, no wood floors. It seems unreal, no air conditioning, and taking garbage down the elevator. Seems unbelievable, Plus hardly any wall space for pictures and no room for clothes. Two, I want to change my Will.

One of the things I hope to remember to ask my lawyer is whether both parties had to be present to get a marriage license when getting married back in 1984, because I never went as far as my memory serves.

Although George showed me his divorce papers which state 1978, I specifically recall George receiving a call from his ex-wife while we were living in Brampton asking for a divorce. Why would I have a memory like that?

I have watched Cityline ever since I was a little girl ever since Dini Petty used to host. Now it just seems that they are showing the opposite of what I dream about.

Sometimes I wonder the reason behind the nurse asking how Jessica ended up with O- blood was because George had a double and that is how it happened. Now I can't get proof because he has to go through too many hoops to give blood because of his age.

I also wonder where other things went, like the cotton from the cotton plants from down south. Did he throw it out?

Tomorrow I plan to play my guitar and phone the skate shop to see if they are open before I stress trying to find their shop.

Last night I talked George into going to the symphony because it is entitled, "Let it Be" and a tribute to the Beatles. I just hope that this time the seats are one of the best. Because if the site asks if you want them to find the best available that is what they should offer, so far that has not been my experience with Ticketmaster. I don't know the venue well enough to choose my own seats. It is at the Bell Performing Arts Centre and I have never been inside.

Although I am a liberal and believe in the right for a woman to choose whether to have an abortion or not, I do not believe in legalizing marijuana. However, I am unhappy with the Harper governments smear campaign of Justin Trudeau. So I am at a quandary as to how I will vote. Maybe again, I will exercise my right not to vote because I do not believe what I am presented through the news.

One of the other things that I had thought about is that cars could have a heat sensor in their bumpers and around the side of the car to know when people were close by, but from what I overheard on the phone when George was talking to Greg is that they have already invented that.

So many things about my wedding on December 29, 1984 seem so bizarre to me now. I was not present to get a marriage license. My in laws on my mother's side were not there. The relatives on George's side were not there, not one. There was no cake to eat just Christmas cake to put under your pillow. My DJ allowed my sister to upstage my wedding and have her boyfriend place the garter he caught on to her leg.

Wednesday, February 25, 2015

Today I reread my letter written on Mother's Day in 2013 to Father Larry outlining my feelings about the Catholic Church and decided to go ahead and send it. I have nothing to lose. I just felt I had the strength now so if I didn't do it now I never would. Who knows it might bring a friend into my life.

Wednesday, February 25, 2015

Dear Father Larry,

I understand that you are a Vicar now. Congratulations! Although, to be honest I have no idea what a Vicar does or at least that's the information I read but after talking to Father Dennis, you are just at another school. Perhaps though, your role brings you closer to effect change and that is why I am writing you. I have already tried contacting you through the website but alas, I do not think you received it so I will try another method that always served me well when I tried to get my point across to my dad.

Before I begin, I must tell you that in 2005 I was diagnosed schizoaffective; this causes me to be subject to delusions apparently, though I don't believe it. However, I do not feel sick anymore, I feel empowered, which I am sure in the doctor's eyes makes me sicker than ever. Sometimes my illness, that I have a hard time believing, causes me to make decisions that I regret like when I agreed to do Learning Assistance at St. Anne's. If it had not been for that I never would have resigned. I was not happy doing Learning Assistance, I needed the business of the classroom and to be brutally honest I was still trying to get well from being overwhelmed by the colours that are such a big part of my life, and doing something unfamiliar was not wise. However now I have even grander ideas for what I would like to do for the Archdiocese.

Although we never got to know each other well, I did work for you for a very long time and feel comfortable sharing the somewhat shocking things I am about to reveal.

When I was diagnosed, everything was sending me messages and because of it, I never went to Church. However when I was strong enough to go back I was shocked of the changes that had been made. The responses that the congregation now have to say are terrible. This in no way will help to bring Catholics back to the church. I struggle returning myself!! The changes were for the worse!! Because of this faith crisis I struggle with even wearing my Christian jewelry. Something has to be done with the wording. The Catholic faith always treats its people like sinners, and as it says in the Nicene Creed "one baptism for the forgiveness of sin", we are all forgiven so the focus should be more uplifting.

On the topic of sin, I do not believe in the sacrament of penance or having to memorize prayers to confess. I believe that anyone that feels the need to confess should be able to seek out a priest anytime to do so. To be honest, I have gone to confession twice since I got out of grade school. Once with Father Buckley and once with you and they were both almost face to face.

I think that to get more priests to join the faith that we should allow them to marry. My uncle was a good priest and he left to get married. That always saddened me. Also now, perhaps allow women to be ordained as well.

Another thing I am not a fan of is the courses that parents and godparents have to go through to get their children baptised. This is new; I never had to go through a course. I am not sure if this happens anymore but I do not think that when a couple with different faiths are going to get married that one has to convert to Catholicism. I think that as long as one parent/person is Catholic and they choose to marry in a Catholic Church that should be okay. However, I did not go through a marriage course and perhaps that might have helped me with the situation I am in now, I am not sure, because some friends of my daughters went through a marriage course and ended up divorced anyway.

I also do not believe in Pro Life. I believe in Pro Choice. I am a good Catholic (I still believe that!) but when I got pregnant in North Dakota the doctors told me that I had to terminate the pregnancy because otherwise my daughter would suffer. I was not going to pray for a miracle. We moved back home and I had it terminated. So then, I made a deal with God to just let me have two healthy children and he did, before I wanted 12! Of course, when I had my second I wanted more but George rushed out and had a vasectomy. Yes, it has been hard on me but as a mother I could not, let her suffer. The Catholic Church has made me feel guilty.

I believe that females have the right to protect themselves. Of course, I prefer if they do not have sex at a young age but I always told my girls to go on the pill! My advice did not work for Darcy but that was her choice not to take it and she got pregnant.

Perhaps another area that needs addressing is homosexuality. Here too I think the Church needs to be more open. Personally, I do not understand their choice but then I do not understand mental illness either. God did not discriminate against anyone!!!!! There needs to be a change.

Mother's Day seems to be a good day to write to you since I have lost my daughter Darcy to another religion. She is getting married this summer and I always hoped it would be a Catholic wedding. I think Catholic priests should marry couples anywhere they like, not just in the church.

Her church, offers more services to young families where the Catholic Church does not. I was instrumental in starting up the children's liturgy at St. Anne's but stopped when it had to be presented a certain way. It is too staunch and not child oriented. My other daughter Jessica is not interested in religion at all right now. I am praying that I have not lost her too. George comes with me to church but he meditates instead of listens, now he prefers not to come and I struggle too.

I do not believe that all the standing and kneeling is necessary. It is hard on the elderly. Too staunch. Perhaps my being open about my faith makes me a better Catholic, I am not sure.

On the note of listening, words have become very important to me and I must admit that I miss you and Father Buckley. I could understand the both of you. I have nothing against Father Dennis or Father Jim but I cannot get past their dialects so their message is lost on me. (February 25 now Father George Mac is there that I do understand)

Father Dennis and his assistant always makes every Mass sound like a High Mass. He sings everything. There was a time when everyone knew when the High Mass would be and could choose as to whether to attend. I think it unnecessary.

Back in Ontario, I taught First Holy Communion and we did not have to have so many masses that the kids and teachers have to prepare here. I find it just causes unneeded stress on the teacher. The same is true for Confirmation. Have the opportunity for children at that age or older to have baptisms again instead and reaffirm their faith.

I also think that the music should be updated to include bands and use music from Praise 106.5. Music uplifts everyone.

Get rid of the readings and just have the motivational sermon.

Move all Christmas Masses to the day before as to not interfere with the preparing of Christmas dinner. Get rid of fasting and the 40 days of lent. They are not inspirational. God loved us and did not want us to suffer for him. He wanted us to love to celebrate and spread his word.

To be honest as a teacher I usually try to avoid sacramental years here because that coupled with coaching, field trips, science fairs and literacy nights is excessive and too much to ask of a teacher. Plus it is stressful for teachers to have to prepare weekly or monthly masses. They are unnecessary.

The idea behind the Rosary is nice and I cherish the ones I still have but to be honest I taught it for several years and I still can't remember how to say it. I think each one should come with directions and leave it at that. I miss mine that I left at school.

Forget memorizing prayers at school. Instead teach children how to talk to God.

I don't know, Father, I really want to teach in the Catholic or for the Catholic schools again but I too am having a faith crisis!! I feel I have nothing to lose by bearing my soul to you because to date I have not been lucky with my applications to teach with the Archdiocese. I cannot even get short listed. To be frank I want to run an online k-12 school and now want to extend that to both public and private schools.

Part of my delusions believes I was instrumental in creating the idea for having the whole Archdiocese connected via the internet. I feel that someone was reading my work in my Master's program, which I did online. Of course, I keep being told it is all coincidental.

Thank you for taking the time to read this, there is still so much that makes me question my faith. I want to be Catholic but I feel there need to be changes. I really hope that I hear from you soon. I miss you at St. Anne's.

Somehow I had so much hope when Pope Francis came into power for I hoped for changes but I have seen none. I feel like I am on a mission to help him.

I sent this letter to my brother back in 2013 and advised me against sending it but I am on a mission or journey for taking action in my life to bring about change. I have waited for years for things to get better in my life and now feel I have to do it myself. Perhaps you will say to walk away from the Church but I sincerely hope not.

Here are all the ways you can reach me to help me.

Sincerely,
Megan Hall

I have purposely for the sake of this book left out all my contact info. What hurts the most is his not responding. I thought I was a valued human being. Maybe one day my voice will be heard. It is said to children to keep reaching out to adults until someone listens. I have tried to do that. How is it that I worked for close to twenty years at St. Anne's and not one person reached out to me even after I reached out to them? They are Catholic. Is what we preach about caring for others just words? I have a hard time believing this so I prefer to think that there is some undercover sting going on and they are taking action.

I am also a person that believes that expressing and talking things out heals and releases stress.

Last night was the first time since George starting sleeping in the other room that I woke up at 3:00 a.m., then again at 5:00 a.m. and finally got up at 7:30 a.m. The only difference between this time and the past is that I was able to fall back asleep. I hope this isn't a new trend. I was enjoying my solid nights' sleep.

Tonight I told George I wanted to go to Burgoo for dinner which is downtown. We went to the one where we went with Paula, his sister. It is much nicer. Anyhow while there I told him I contacted Barb our financial planner with TD Bank and told her if I couldn't live in my dream home that I would stay in the townhouse. George insists that we have to sell. I pray that my dreams come true.

For dinner I had a babushka borsht because I love borscht except I prefer it with no potato. Anyhow it was comforting because it reminded me of how I used to call Jessica my little babushka! I also had my favourite dish there, their ratatouille. A dish George made only once for Elizabeth when she came to visit in Brampton Ontario.

I will try again to go to the skating shop tomorrow and try to go out of my comfort zone.

Tonight I am noticing that I have to go to the bathroom to go pee every fifteen minutes. No sooner do I go that I feel the need to go again. I hope this doesn't disturb my sleep but if it persists tomorrow I will make a call to my doctor, Dr. Duran.

It is 2:10 a.m. and it seems that my urinary tract is keeping me awake. I constantly feel like I have to go so I'll be seeing the doctor tomorrow. So maybe I won't be getting my skates tomorrow.

Apparently, someone tried to hack my email tonight so I changed my password as they suggested. It was great of google to let me know.

Another thing I recall from my living at the Gage Lane House was how George wanted to try if he could use a condom with me but he wasn't able to. What I didn't understand and still do not understand was why…

We have a meeting with our financial planner on Tuesday, March 3, 2015 and I am really anxious about it. George is insisting that we have to sell the townhouse and downsize. I know there are people looking after my assets but I am still worried.

Thursday, February 26, 2015

For several reasons I do not like to go to George's family cabin. First, I do not own it and have no say about its contents. Second, George and his sister do not claim ownership of it. Maybe because it is not worth much that it does not matter. So in many ways I am just as glad my name is not on it! Finally, I dislike the access to the beach and that it is very rocky and difficult for seniors to access.

When renewing my medication the other day of specific note that they are much easier to pull back. My medication Saphris is a sublingual tablet sealed in an aluminum foil package. I am thankful they are easier to get at now.

About a month or two ago George and I went through all our loose pictures and decided which ones to toss and put the others in photo albums. I tossed some from my drama days in teacher college that I should not have but what I don't understand is that they had already been in a photo album. I also was prompted by George to take the picture of my dad and his sister with their parents out of its frame and put it in the album. I would love a wall with co-ordinated family pictures.

He encouraged me to get rid of my diplomas and yearbooks. I will never be able to replace all those sentiments in those yearbooks. If only I had have had backbone.

I was excited when I saw an infomercial from Keith Urban selling a guitar and 30 DVD's for $300.00, promising to teach you how to play for friends in 30 days. Only you can't access it here in Canada. It seems like a simple systematic process. Seems I can't access it on my computer but I can on my cell phone. However, on the cell phone they don't let you know if it is a secure site or not, so I passed. In the long run it would be better online without the DVD's. In addition he really didn't have a colour that spoke to me. If the black had more colour I would be more interested.

Watching the Marilyn Dennis show I am reminded how they have changed the look of toilets and no longer have the knobs on the side that anchor it to the floor. I don't remember if I have written this or not but when I was first started to distrust George I went into his washroom in the basement and found stuff smudged around the left anchor as you look at the toilet. When Dr. Moran made me tell George everything, George was more concerned with what product I used to clean it, which made me even more suspicious of him.

Recently we had to put Kaiser down. I was not as close to Kaiser although we had her for fifteen years. In 2000 George did his own research, bought the dog before I knew, and only brought me along to pick her up. I was shocked at the poor condition she was in and that George bought her. She was cowering behind a chair and when I took her to our Vets they said she had crystals in her urine and dual ear infections if my memory serves me correctly. Jessica was begging for a dog. Therefore, Jessica and I took her to training classes at Pet Smart.

Although she was not my favourite. She was my quiet companion while I struggled to the surface of whatever you want to call this journey.

I understand that Darcy was allergic but maybe there was a pill or something she could have taken. That way Barclay would not have had to spend the rest of her days outside! Then we could have gotten another boxer.

I sure am glad I have TELUS coming over here because nothing is working. The TV or the internet. Somehow, I feel it is deliberate. The technician was great! He gave me a direct line for help in the future. This makes me very happy because getting through the automated system on the phone is frustrating.

Seems strange to me that George does not know where the tribute for his mom is. He has never watched it since receiving it and watching it at Tammy's house.

I am beginning to lose the wind in my sails. Am I a fool to seek out an annulment or divorce? Darcy would probably hate me. But, I have to believe there is a life and more affection for me. I was surprised he was willing to go to the symphony but then he added this comes out of our entertainment allowance. (Then there is all the mistrust issues).

Friday, February 27, 2015

I do have a bladder infection so after I saw Carl Bartle today at 11:15 a.m., I went to Dr. Duran's office thinking that the clinic beside his office was open but alas it was closed just like Dr. Duran's because he doesn't work Fridays. I went home and looked up clinics nearby and found one, The Lions Road Medical Centre with the Pharma City drugstore right next door, and called. Low and behold they were open and I got seen right away!! It was fantastic!! I saw a Dr. Venter, she was so nice she said they would send my sample off. I had suggested they give me a container so that I could give them a sample. They will call me if they need to change the medication. She gave me 100 mg of Macrobid to fight off the infection and CMPD Phenazo which is an anaesthetic to help with the discomfort. That is so handy that they send off my urine sample. She said they would get back to me if they had to change the medication. When I went to the drugstore next door they had everything ready. It was super!!!!

I went home and immediately took both. It is 2:20 p.m. and the anaesthetic is working great. Like she said it masks the symptom so she only gave me three days' worth. I am so thankful she did that. I also have aches in my left hand. I imagine it will take care of that too!

Mr. Bartle reminded me that I stopped playing my guitars because I didn't have them. In fact I don't remember ever taking them from my parents place. Somebody has been messing with my things and my life.

I am reminded by Dr. Phil which I watched today that my makeup brushes from the modelling school are missing. I only have two, as is the painters pallet with eyeshadows attached.

When we first moved to British Columbiawe stayed in George's mothers' condo. The girls were not used to staying in the same room so they were a little more excited at night time. Upon leaving Ontario we were told that Darcy had bowel problems and speech problems. One night in the condo Darcy went to the bathroom and George would not let Darcy out of the bathroom until she went. We argued and he stormed out.

As much as I like Ellen DeGeneres, I don't like the sense of humour shown. Maybe she isn't a host that would do me well. I prefer the seriousness of Oprah's talk Show. The Meredith Vieira show is more my speed. Although just yesterday May 15, 2015 Ellen did something really sweet. She reunited a student with a favourite teacher!

Leonard Nemoy died today. This reminds me of one of my grade school friends, Angela. She wouldn't let me be her friend unless I watched Star Trek. I came to love the show.

I feel like my life with George has been friends with benefits. I had most of my fun when my parents would come to visit. Even when I had my hysterectomy in 2000 and my sister, Louise, had come to take care of the girls I begged George to stay but he went off to help his sister find a place for his mom. He always put his mom before me.

George had his send off from Black Bell Trucking tonight and got drunk. He had the audacity when he said he was putting his pyjamas on to come downstairs nude expecting sex. I told him to put his clothes back on and expressed how I was not happy with him or my life with him. I told him that I had expressed myself years ago and didn't want to go through it again. I absolutely hate having sex when someone has to get drunk to do it. I have no interest in sex right now. Another reason I was repulsed is because he had no sympathy for the extremely painful urinary tract infection he knew I had.

Saturday, February 28, 2015

Last night at about 4:00 a.m. I passed out and hit my head on the nightstand. George helped me back into bed and brought me some cereal because I thought maybe I hadn't eaten enough for the medication. Then this morning George vacuumed the house while I washed my hair and proceeded to get sick in the sink. George didn't know. He was so incensed that I wouldn't have sex that he left to go to Tammy's. It will just make it that much easier for me to leave the house myself on Monday to go to the jewellery shop.

The wax mold for Darcy's pendant is ready for me to look at. The process is so different from the last time. Last time when I bought the High 5 pendant for Darcy and the infinity symbols for Jessica they showed me the unpolished version but no wax mold.

Saturday, February 28, 2015

Today I lay down all day on the couch because I had a headache.

Tonight I watched Shania Twain but she didn't sing "Water" I was thinking she or Katy Perry would be good to sing my song.

I don't know if I've written about this or not but the "Happy" song that was Cassie's favourite reminded me of my kimono which is called a Happy Coat that dad brought back from Japan or China. He said that was what they were called where he bought it. It was powder blue and beautiful. I don't know where it went. I never would have gotten rid of it. I loved it. It was hand stitched and everything. I wanted another one so when Jessica went to China with Miki I asked her to look for one.

Sunday, March 1, 2015

When I was in University Mandy came to visit and I gave her a laundry basket with some clothes to take back home, unbeknownst to me then she had scoffed it. Until one day I saw her walk downstairs in it. Dad was always disappointed that she had treated hers so badly and had given it away. Anyway I got it back that day! Until it mysteriously disappeared.

Just like my happy coat disappearing the bottom sheet disappeared off Darcy's old bed, after his cousin and his wife stayed at our place at Diamond Head while we were on vacation. We now have towels I never bought and that George says he doesn't know or keep track. Please forgive me Lord but I sure do not trust him!!!

Towels caused me a problem at Gage Lane too. A mysterious blue towel showed up and George did not know where it came from when asked. I washed it and hung it up for him to use but he refused. There were other towels too so I took an inventory of our towels and threw out most and bought new ones.

Tomorrow I plan to pick up my pants from Helga's Drycleaners and drop off some dry cleaning. I also plan to go to the jewellers and check out the mold for the pendant for Darcy. I pray it goes well. I have no idea how it should look.

Thank heavens for NCIS. It seems to be on for me when there is no other crime show on for me to watch. I really like it especially when I can focus on it. I tend to prefer crime shows where they get the bad person. In my Master's program online I don't know how it came up, but I said that my favourite show was CSI. That was because they research DNA and detailed things and that is what I felt I needed in my life and it seems I still do.

I was asked if I ever thought of suicide. I said no but the truth is, I have. I began to think it might be easier to be like my sister, Louise, and be rid of all that surrounds me…Because it seems nobody believes me…even though I feel the media and everything supports me. I don't want to be in a loveless hopeless marriage.

I think Darcy gave me the pink pendant because it's my favourite colour but more importantly I think she gave me the Family pendant because in my mind she is for family and Jessica is not. She spoils me. I think Jessica gave me the heart (which has gone missing) because she loves me, it stands for caring and wants me to pursue love. I also think that she is playing out my book here. I say Jessica is not for family therefore she is not. I say that Darcy is and therefore she is. However these portraits I have of them stem from before I was diagnosed.

I remember when I was teaching and the students were seated in two separate groups in front of me and I felt then there was a tug between family and love. I choose love because love and family are synonymous. Somehow I think that it is what I've written here is what keeps Jessica from me. I believed George's understanding of LOVE was to just include him and me.

George lets me have the bigger couch to lie on when watching TV but that is not enough.

All the records that Jessica has, come from me and our friend Randy, George only brought a few.

On a side note this computer should correct my spelling and lack of grammatical marks like my cell phone does.

I am so scared about crossing the border because when I was young Dad would always tell us to be quiet and let him do the talking. Maybe he was scared too. So I hope it becomes easier to travel.

Here are the places I have lived.
- † My family home in Sunshine Park in Tinsel Town
- † My apartment in Tinsel Town

After Marriage

† North Dakota. I'd bet my bottom dollar this was rent to own, though George always argues with me over this. Purchased from Reed Development PO box 241936
† A rented town house at Treble
† Our first house in Brampton Ontario, from January 1988 - July 18 1991
† Sandra and Buck's condo
† Rented house in North Duncan-Moved out April 29 1992
† House I picked out of the newspaper on Saber Road and in North Duncan, British Columbia but it was late at night so I couldn't even see the backyard. Lived here for 10 years.
† Gage Lane Avenue in North Duncan, British Columbia. I felt it was like a book with a untold story June 26, 2002 - August 2005
† Wade Avenue Drive, British Columbia. I did not want to move and was promised to be mortgage free but wasn't. Plus I was surrounded by disturbing colours. We lived here for seven years.
† Presently Diamond Head, British Columbia

The sewing machine I used in North Dakota to create some dresses while taking lessons with a neighbour, Patricia, was from George's grandma. However, he did not have it in his townhome when I met him. I didn't have it at Treble or Brampton where I had to make Darcy's comforter and curtains by hand. It appeared again on Saber Road but it burned up and I made Jessica's red curtains for Jessica by hand. She could never get the room dark enough.

The Sound of Music is a wonderful musical and I remember playing some of the songs but I don't know where they are. Maybe I could meet Julie Andrews too. She played in Mary Poppins and that was the first movie I ever went to see where my dad had my older brother, Sam and sister, Louise take my sister, Mandy and I. It was magical!!!

What happened to the bassinette I had for the girls? I had two one on legs and one that you carried, that had green bedding. The bassinet we had was much like the one Paula loaned us.

Wednesday, March 4, 2015

Yesterday morning George and I went to see Barb our financial advisor. She laid it out on the line and said that if we split we would only have $250,000 each. It was an awful meeting,

Afterwards we picked up some food at McDonalds that I could barely eat but the smoothie was great, mango pineapple. Then I had George take me to the clinic about my headache. We are waiting to see if it's the Macrobid I was on. From how I feel I think that was it. Yes, I am allergic to Macrobid.

Later we picked up Cassie from school and George dropped me off at home while he took her to ballet. I asked him to pick up sparkling water on his way home.

While I was at home my brother called and he said I should not make any rash decisions right now about divorcing George because he felt I wasn't myself. I agreed I would see a psychiatrist again and Sam said that he would talk to George about me doing that, about us continuing to see a marriage councillor, me cancelling my appointment to see the lawyer re the condo, and him putting off selling the townhouse.

When George came home he stormed out again not telling me where he was going, I made the mistake of asking Darcy if he was there. She sent me a scathing and hurtful text saying I was the reason she was struggling as a mother and parent and that whom I've become lately has put stress on her. Anyhow I think what she said is bogus!! If she thought it was easier on her to have to drive me everywhere because I couldn't function on my own she is the one who is nuts. I will continue to be an ear for her. She said a lot of things that were untrue. It still seems surreal that communication has stopped between us. But since she wants to limit conversation to once a week if that so be it. She can reach out to me.

I got the phone number for Randy, a family friend, from his daughter, Amy and texted him last night. I gave him George's number and maybe we will get together.

Today I plan to tell George that I don't want him inviting the kids over for dinner until Darcy feels better. It would just be too awkward for everybody.

Darcy must be having her own troubles. She is just not herself.

Wednesday, March 4, 2015

Today George had coffee with Darcy and she told him what she told me. My brother called tonight as promised and thinks she is being stupid and insensitive. So do I. She has given me a bigger blow than Jessica has. It will be hard for me to forgive her accusations.

Tonight George went indoor golfing so I went for a pedicure and manicure.

I told George I didn't want the kids over for dinner until I let him know except Jessica but he said he didn't want to anyway.

Saturday, March 7, 2015

Thankfully Darcy is talking to me again! She sent me a lovely message, saying I was her best friend. Actually I have Darcy and her family coming over tomorrow to celebrate Greg's birthday with ice cream cake. I am so grateful for her being there for me.

I did think I would go to the cabin with George this weekend but he didn't want me to come. He was taking Jessica and didn't want me along. I think George was hoping that I would file for divorce, at least it seems that way. I don't know what kind of miracles marriage counsellors can do but we are not happy and George is doing nothing to help the situation. I feel it can't be saved.

I have joined a women's group and have decided to go for a walk and coffee chat every Monday and Thursday morning. We meet at 9:00 a.m. in the morning, walk for an hour and then chat. Sounds perfect. I hope I make some friends. May 16, 2015, actually I find 9:00 a.m. too early to go for a walk, especially when I have to leave at 8:30 a.m. to get there. I only like the coffee and chat.

I think George will be surprised when he sees me leave that early in the morning. I'm going to do to him what he does to me and say I'm doing something like, "I'm going for a walk" which takes little time and then stay away for hours. The only thing is I probably won't get the satisfaction of seeing him at home when I return.

I have also signed up for guitar lessons at Long and McQuade. I go for my first one on Monday at 2:00 p.m.

Seems to me that if my mental health was suffering this past while and I must admit thinking people are alive is pretty bizarre, I don't think that it was compassionate of George to leave me every other weekend to fend for myself. As my sister Mandy also agrees with me, he is showing to the girls in this day and age of how not to care for a mentally ill person.

I have to stop making excuses for Jessica not talking to me. She has not communicated with me for over a decade now. This is more than a passing phase. She is done very little if anything to support me. I worry about seeing Wellbutrin and Abilify in her dresser drawer, it tells me she suffers from depression. She has not spoken of it and I dare not bring it up. I let George know so he could somehow broach the subject with her but he would rather not.

Sunday, March 8, 2015

Judging by what I am being advised by my brother and sister, they do not trust George either. I will keep what they advise to myself for now. It is so nice to be able to talk to them.

I made a simple request of George's sister, Paula, telling her we were seeking advice from a marriage councillor and if she knew of any places I could take cooking classes. Unfortunately, she felt the need to forward the email to George. I guess she is not a sister after all. I will not attempt to communicate with her again. In the end, she is no great resource for anyone after having three failed relationships. George did respond to her that we will be separating and hoped I wouldn't be bitter or angry.

This medication takes all the colours from me which is sad. I also find that it does not give me the courage to go out and do things as much. It is a struggle for me to get out of the door. When I have the colours I just go. Once again my hopes have been shattered.

Tuesday, March 10, 2015

I saw Dr. Jake and Diana, a caseworker, at Duncan Mental Health and they said that I am too healthy to be seen by them, that I will be referred back to my family doctor, Dr. Duran. Dr. Jake did say that I would have to be on the medication for two years then at that time talk to Dr. Duran about tapering me off. Dr. Jake also took Carl Bartle' contact information. So in January 2017 I plan to see Dr. Duran about tapering me off this drug. Maybe sooner.

I am capable of much clearer thinking when I am off the medication.

I also talked to my lawyer today and I have an appointment for Thursday afternoon. I am so happy that I don't have to wait until next week. Plus it looks like she, my lawyer, can handle everything.

Yesterday George invited me to lunch at Blue Angel Cafe. While we were there he went on and on about what he did with Jessica on the weekend. When I told my brother about it, he wasn't impressed either. It was as if he didn't know that it was him that would not allow me to also spend time at the cabin with Jessica.

Saturday, May 16, 2015

Although my gut was the one encouraging me to get together with my lawyer. I finally cancelled. Also, George is no longer thinking of separation. We are not touching yet and the main reasons I went to Carl Bartle still exist…no affection. I am waiting for George to start touching me.

One might say he withdraws because he knows how I feel about him but this lack of affection started before I became sick. My mind just awakened to what I was missing.

If George is my husband then there needs to be affection. But I still have my doubts. I still have Capgras Syndrome where he is concerned.

I still see Carl to deal with my distrust issues regarding the couch. I next see him in June.

My birthday passed with no Jessica. She phoned to apologise to George for not making their golf game which they planned for the same day (which

I thought was wrotten) but did not call me. In addition, I got no word from her on Mother's Day...absolutely nothing. I just hope she doesn't make me feel worse by making a big deal over her dad, like she has in the past.

I can't believe that she hates me that much. There must be a reason. I have to believe in my delusions that she is secretly working undercover somehow and soon maybe in two-three years she will come back to me. I say only two-three years because that is when my psychiatrist says that I can have Dr. Duran, my family doctor wean me over my anti-psychotic medication. Then maybe this journey will be over and maybe I will be rich in many ways!!!! (Jessica will be close to me and I will be pill free)

One of these days I plan to come right out and ask her.

It has been ten years since I was diagnosed I pray that I am left with more than reality when this is all over. I want my dreams to come true!!!

Duncan Mental Health, Dr. Jake sent me a Care Plan and it opened my eyes to how confused they are about my delusions. They say I believe I work for Google and have an online school. That is not true, that is a wish or dream of mine. Plus, they have it wrong I also thought of working with Bill Gates and Apple to help me get my online school off the ground.

Saturday, May 30, 2015

I have applied to yet another long term grade four position. This time it is at Queen of All Saints. I have not heard anything. My thoughts are divided. Sometimes I think it is my age and how much they would have to pay me as opposed to those coming out of college. But, I also think that I don't get called or contacted because they have something better in store for me, I just have to wait for two to three years when I begin tapering off my drug. I keep thinking that I just have to be patient and all my dreams will come true and George will be shocked and awed that he didn't believe me.

I did come right out and ask Jessica why she doesn't respond to my texts etc. but I made the mistake of premising it with "you probably don't want to talk about this" and of course that is exactly what she said.

Monday, June 15, 2015

A few weeks ago when I got my hair done with foils at Colour Me Crazy. Angela, my hairdresser had another lady there at the same time, her name was Candy. We struck up a conversation and seemed to really get along so I asked if we could exchange contact information. We exchanged phone numbers and email addresses. A couple of weeks later when George and I returned from LA, I emailed her. She responded and said it would be nice if we got together for coffee so I took her up on it and gathered the courage to call and arrange a date. I am meeting her at Timmy`s across the street from Colour Me Crazy on Wednesday at 10:00 a.m. This is huge for me. I have been so afraid to do things for myself because of how George might react. I bet my bottom dollar that he will not be home when I return but it would be nice if for a change he was.

Today is Friday and George's weekend at the cabin so this is where I am. George made a tuna sandwich with some frozen stale bread which I didn't care for because the bread was stale so I only ate one square. He was offended and took it personally so he decided we would not go grocery shopping afterwards because now he wasn't hungry. He always gets his way. He thinks he is punishing me but he is acting childish. The only thing that will happen is that the choices at the store will be gone because everyone will have bought up the stuff…so be it. Heaven forbid I bring it up, he will then say that I should do the shopping by myself.

Josh Groban's song, "You Are Loved - Don't Give Up" gives me hope. I feel so overpowered by George sometimes. I wish I were more independent. I keep hoping that in two years when I will approach Dr. Duran about going off my medication that some of my dreams will come true.

After George mowed the lawn he felt better and we went shopping like nothing had happened. I was glad.

Darcy, Greg and the kids are coming down tonight. That's great! Yikes Darcy just called the cabin and she has lost Cassie's passport, plus she doesn't have one for Brian. I hope they make it across the border!!!!

Sunday, June 7, 2015

Amazingly enough, the kids made it across the border!! And low and behold Greg found Darcy's old purse in the car and found the passports right where I thought they might be.

It is a whirlwind when they come to the cabin, but I love it!! Cassie and I played several games that she made up.

Brian was sick again which made things harder for Darcy. In order for them to all sleep at the cabin Cassie and Greg slept in their tent and Darcy and Brian had the backroom.

When George and I had dinner with Jessica at the Boathouse at Kits Beach near her new apartment, she said I overthink things. She may be right, I also question things. I have a picture on my computer of Jessica drinking Champaign on my desktop that appeared at the same time the picture of her and Darcy appeared; after I took it in to Daryl to get my pointer on this laptop fixed.

My computer was doing wonky things like giving me the French accents while I was at the cabin but now it's not, it is back to normal. I plan on typing the brand of my computer into google and seeing if I can get a guide in how to use and access the French part so I can use accents for my name and my uncle's.

Tuesday, June 9, 2015

Today George and I went to check out a couch and chairs for Jessica at Accents in Madewell Square. The couch was a durable light gray fabric. I liked that it was grey but I wasn't too partial to the material. It was a sectional. The chair was cute and blue and white. George did not like the chair but I thought it was cute but I didn't see how it was going to coordinate with the couch. George doesn't like chairs but I do.

I am thinking that instead of a sectional in the condo we might be able to do a couch and chair. A pretty lazy boy chair. Maybe Tammy's friend Melena will have some ideas. We are using her to decorate our place. George promised me.

The interesting part of the day was the furniture store being close to the Microsoft Store. I spent the better part of the afternoon there talking to them about the new Surface 3. They even helped me get a new outlook email so I could upload my pictures to Onedrive which is Microsofts icloud. They uploaded all my pictures and told me how to access them. The Surface 3 is cool but the keyboard does not come in the colours I like. Oh well, I may take blue which stands for the internet or black which means my thinking is correct. As time passes though I don't think my thinking regarding Darcy not being married is correct though. I think she must be and that my grandchildren must be my grandchildren.

I really went into the store to find out if this HP was capable to hold the new Windows 10 that is coming out. Then the manager came over and talked to us about the Surface 3. I think I will wait until Windows 10 comes out before I buy it though so it will already be on the computer.

Wednesday, June 10, 2015

This morning I met with Candy at Tim Horton's. We spent two hours gabbing. I did tell her about my diagnosis and was quite myself. I figure if I can't confide in her then we won't be close.

I phoned Elizabeth today too while George was golfing. She has been my rock through my journey. I also phoned Judy but she wasn't home. I hope she's not upset with me because we went to Tinsel Town and never saw her.

Friday, June 12, 2015

I revisited this list in 2017 and 2018 and my needs and wants blurred where I felt I needed everything, but always at the top of the list was the desire of a fuller relationship with Jessica. All the rest are hopes, dreams and desires.

NEEDS and WANTS	NEEDS and WANTS
1. Jessica to talk to me and share her life with me. I need us to be close and for her to want to hug me and text and call me and do things together. I want to hear her call me "Mama" again.	1. I would prefer a stone house with an indoor pool and hot tub where my maid would do the cleaning and a beautiful garden. The pool would have a slide and diving board and have accordion glass doors with access to an outside Pool and a hot tub. A house decorated with all my colours beautifully done by a designer. No beige/tan. The house would have a baby grand piano and I would have someone come in to give me lessons. I would also have someone come to the house to give me guitar lessons.
2. Affection in my life. A new man in my life willing to touch me and make me feel pretty…it might be someone from my past like Andrew or Derek. April 21, 2018 I now know the new man in my life is Gary Barlow. He sought me out on You Tube! Though we cannot physically touch each other yet, we do so through our thoughts and I believe it will become real!!	
	2. A shower with no glass doors that plays your own music if you want
3. To get married in a beautiful Catholic church and for us to say our own vows	3. To get my doctorate in Technology which I think will be given to me
4. For him to want to dance and go to musical and dramatic shows. For him to want to go to concerts and sporting events. Maybe we can have special seat tickets. To go cross-country skiing, downhill skiing and ice skating etc.	4. A speed boat at the cottage so the kids can go waterskiing and I can go fishing and try waterskiing again too.
	5. To publish all of my songs
	6. To publish this book about my journey with colours and have it made into a movie and musical. Darcy and I love musicals.
5. For him to make me happy about celebrating birthdays and Christmas again	
6. To publish this book and made into a movie and musical.	7. To have my story told on W5 and 60 minutes
7. A revitalized Catholic Church	8. To be a part of talk shows to share my story and forms of abuse

MY COLOUR-CODED LIFE

NEEDS and WANTS	NEEDS and WANTS
8. Friends close by that I can do things with. Elizabeth on the mainland with all her wishes realized. To have my family, extended family and friends close by where they all have mortgage free places and careers offered them if they want. Move back to Ontario! Where I live now does not make sense. But how with the girls so settled here?	9. To meet Oprah and share my story
	10. (Although they may all already know, I would like the opportunity to share it in person)
	11. To have a Roy Henry Vickers original painting.
	12. To have a Robert Bateman original painting
9. A beautiful winterized private cabin (log cabin) with plenty of rooms for family reunions on a recreational lake like Muskoka that I can hand down to the girls. It would have a large round dining room table made out of a tree or perhaps something more durable, not glass. I haven't seen a table I like yet. Something that is mine that has a dock with no leeches and plenty of recreational toys – waterskiing, canoeing, paddleboat. It should have a sandy shore so babies can walk in the water.	13. To have another Bruno Coté painting
	14. Maybe some by some artists I am not familiar with
	15. To have a button blanket with a button for every student I taught
	16. Music lessons at home, guitar, singing and piano and guitar
	17. Another pure bread female Boxer. Barclay already had her name so hopefully the new one will have a cool name too.
10. A shed to hold all sorts of water equipment!	18. To work for Google, Apple and Microsoft on getting an online JK-doctorate school for the world that I would be the creator of (get credit for-my legacy)and be allowed to work at to keep me busy
11. To have the park in Brampton renamed and dedicated to me and my daughters. I did it so they would have a safe place to play. Darcy had hurt herself on the slide.	

NEEDS and WANTS	NEEDS and WANTS
12. To work for Google, Apple and Microsoft on getting an online K-doctorate school for the world that would be non-denominational up and running that I would be the creator of (get credit for-my legacy) and be allowed to work at to keep me busy if I wish. I want it to offer the study of any language and offer the study of music, with no limits on how many languages or instruments. The school would be both synchronous and asynchronous with a definite face to face component, so those working asynchronously would feel connected to a human being. It would make using Dad's estate for my masters worthwhile. 13. To see Louise and my parents and all those who have passed again (the real ones) 14. For justice to be served regarding George and for him to go to prison for life for playing me as a fool. For his crimes. For him to believe me. And for all the kids to be there too. 15. For my dad to go to prison for his crimes if he is guilty of anything. 16. To have my places filled with my music. To have a guitar, ukulele, singing and piano teacher come in to teach me at home and online	19. I would want my log cabin to have a carving of a totem the first nations had applied to me like an eagle with 3 eaglets. One to represent our daughter in heaven, Poppy! Perhaps even a totem pole especially designed for me representing the animal they think I depict. What I've been through must be something like a Spirit Quest. 20. I would like the cottage to be more like a home with a beautiful kitchen and with plenty of colourful native work by Roy Henry Vickers…originals and Bern Will Brown and others I don't know yet. A log home that is uplifting on the inside perhaps on Lake Muskoka. 21. Income property that someone else manages 22. A home on a warm ocean. Not the pacific coast 23. A techy sports car with First nation painting on the side. It must automatically play my favourite music when I drive. It automatically connects to my phone and plays my music. A car George did not choose but one that is economical and chosen for me. Maybe electric

MY COLOUR-CODED LIFE

NEEDS and WANTS	NEEDS and WANTS

17. To meet all the musicians and actors who have helped me so much. Maybe a big party that lasts more than a day so all the musicians can play!!
 	
18. To see everyone in my life that I believe are not dead. I want George to be witness to that!!
    Mom, Louise, Dad, Linda, my aunts and uncles, George's mom and dad, Donald's mom, Ted, my Aunt Laura, Uncle Jacob, Uncle Lester, Darren is a colleagues husband, and, Elizabeth's mom, dad, and brother, Judy's mom and dad, Whitney Houston, Robin Williams, Dr. Brown. Elvis Presley, Winston Reckert, George Denver, Princess Diana. Jim who is George's old friend his other dead friend, John, him too. And my first friend here…Kay
    To see Declan, Georges' friend, I do not believe he lives on the street.
    There has to be dancing!! It would be sweet to have a live band with strings and many of the musicians I only have seen on You Tube.
 	
19. To have nice clothes. To learn to have faith in my own choices
 	
20. To meet the Royalty and Lady Diana whom I do not think died.
	24. My own jet to take my girls and future husband and sisters and brother and mom everywhere.
	
	25. For a husband to want to touch me outside of the bedroom, even French kiss. Someone who makes me feel pretty.
	
	26. To have an unrestricted passport for every one close to me
	
	27. A maid, cook , a gardener, chauffeur, a hairdresser
	
	28. The Catholic Church to change
	
	29. My diplomas framed and hung again. I worked hard for them and dad was so proud.
	
	30. Photo albums made into skinny books like Darcy has made
	
	31. My yearbooks back
	
	32. All homemade videos accessed by my computer and on DVD
	
	33. A stone house in Rosedale or Moore Park where I used to live. Preferably my old house where everything was updated and the stonework was inspected. The house has been torn down so this will never happen ☹
	
	34. To know what happened to the beautiful butterfly broach I gave to my mom which was a gift to me.

I would like to think that dreams come true as I listen to Josh Groban singing "Over the Rainbow" from The Wizard of Oz.

I visit Roy Henry Vickers art gallery on the internet but I do not see anything that moves me which surprises me. I would love to meet him and have him make a huge painting for me. Maybe he could even carve something for me that represents my vision and determination for my future log home built by Pioneer Homes.

Sunday, June 14, 2015

I found the Catholic Mass online and was pleased they had it online. I was disappointed that the music wasn't more inspirational. The sermon was good though. I also went to church and ran into Anne a former colleague. We sat together. Seeing her was the most uplifting part of the experience. The sermon was good. I walked away with his analogy of the dandelion thriving among the cement and those struggling with crisis like myself. I feel like I am like that dandelion he spoke about. I am finding my own help out of this quagmire I am in.

I also listened to a speech last night by Roy Henry Vickers which gave me insight into his life and disappointments. Though he did not make it into the RCMP, he became a renowned artist!!! Maybe I can leave my mark too!

I keep hoping that since the condo will be finished next year that somehow miraculously we will find that we have the 34th floor with all the bells and whistles one could imagine, like a built in stereo system. I am so anxious about it. I will be let down if it's just the regular 750 square feet. If it is I will know that none of my dreams will come true.

We went to look at purchasing the condo beside it but it was too much for us to afford. Both condos on either side were still available…I can only dream that my dream comes true.

I wrote the Archbishop and someone from his office responded saying he read it and will pray for me. Basically, I just re-sent my letter to Father Larry. That does it, I do not want prayers!! I want someone from the Catholic

Church to talk to me. Maybe I do not need religion in my life at all!! I will just talk to God!

Thursday, June 18, 2015

George finally agreed to let me get the Surface 3 from Microsoft. I don't need it, I just want it. It will be something new for me to play with and something smaller to take places. I am going to wait until Windows 10 is out. The lady said it would be about 10 days for the stores so it should be anytime now.

I tried to contact Daryl, our computer expert at Future Shop. But with the change to Best Buy, he no longer works in the computer industry. I went to Best Buy yesterday and it was definitely not as warm or special without the special consideration I used to get from Daryl. I was treated much better at the Microsoft Store, plus they wear all my colours.

I must admit I am a little scared to replace this old computer. I am so used to it.

Friday, June 19, 2015

Today George and I went to see Carl. I got my points out but I don't know how much it is helping. We didn't talk about the upcoming birthday celebration that Paula is arranging at the cabin though. I did talk to George about it at the cabin today though. I told him that I told his sister my point of view two years ago and she never responded. He said he talked to her then about it but I told him that I doubt very much that he did. I think my idea of celebrating everybody's birthdays is not outrageous. George said he does not care one way or the other whether I go or not and I have said that I will not go and that is how I feel. I am tired of Paula getting her way all the time!!!!! It's like my feelings do not matter! Sometimes I wonder why I try with this marriage. Maybe if I am lucky nobody will want to celebrate either.

Darcy has said that since Paula has chosen Labour Day weekend for the party at the cabin that she won't be going because Greg is going camping that weekend. Anyway, I don't know what to do. I really don't want to go but I don't want to be by myself all weekend either.

I talked to George about my visiting my girlfriend Judy. She invited me last year and when George and I went to Tinsel Town he wouldn't take me to see her because he doesn't like her husband. I told her about it and I am hoping it hasn't cost me my friendship with her. I emailed her today asking her if I could visit her this summer. Before she had offered to take me to visit my family. I am not sure she is still willing but I have asked. Now I wait for her response.

Darcy leaves with her family on July 18-25. They have to take the red eye but I hope I fair better than that. After all, Aeroplan said they would help me.

I feel so let down by the Catholic Church. I am not sure what I will do. I will probably keep going online. It is shorter and although I don't run into people I know it was more enjoyable because I didn't have to stand and kneel.

Ever since Carl brought up the idea that I could run a tutor business out of my own home, I have been thinking about it. George seems all for it but I am hesitant because I fear I wouldn't be any good at helping the kids with their problems. I would not be able to offer the parents any guarantees. I like the idea of having my own business. I would like to have an email that was for my business that the kids could contact me with. It may be the beginning of doing things online, who knows?

Friday, June 26, 2015

I am sad. Jessica has invited George to a baseball game tomorrow and likely George will take her out to dinner first. I guess she is inviting him because she missed Father's Day. Anyhow, she always does something special for him and absolutely nothing for or with me. I am sad. I don't know where to go for help. Carl is of no help. The problem is all Jessica, she has not matured and I don't know how long it will take.

She is thinking of coming back here Saturday night and making blueberry jam with her dad in the morning. She will probably not initiate any conversation with me. She never does. She makes having her around so awkward.

A few years ago I spoke to Jessica about publishing this book and she was all for it. Lately I've been thinking about submitting an article to Chatelaine magazine. Why? To help other people and maybe help others understand that mental health and drug addiction are not married together.

Saturday, June 27, 2015

I tried calling Judy again today but I got her answering machine again. I hope she is away and I haven't lost her friendship. I am concerned.

Thursday, July 2, 2015

Hurray!! Judy emailed me and we are still friends!! She had problems with her email but I still wonder why she didn't phone me after I left her a message.

Apparently her phone was out of order too.

Monday, October 5, 2015

I am looking forward to 2017 when I will taper off my medication. I was able to figure things out so much better when I was off it. I did things like change my password on my bank account and put a picture on my Gmail. Right now I don't even know how to do those things. Plus I am anxious to lose weight and I think that will help tremendously.

George and I are still seeing Carl and finally we are dealing with the affection issue. Carl has suggested that I have a face to face for about 15-20 minutes with Jessica and tell her how I feel. He suggested we go through George to set this up. I love the idea.

Strangely on my phone she is the only contact I have with a picture and I didn't do it. Plus the last time I took my laptop in to get serviced pictures appeared on my desktop that I didn't put there. Strange.

I still have all my needs and wants. And my instincts could not be so far off. In fact why did George hush me in Carl's office when I brought up the drug issue? Carl thinks it's because George is scared that Carl would report it but he wouldn't because everything is confidential, whereas I would hope he would be honour bound to.

I still feel that come 2017 everything will be revealed and my patience throughout all that is happening to me will be revealed. Does this illness affect instincts too??

Saturday, October 24, 2015

Last weekend was Thanksgiving and on Saturday George and I met Jessica for coffee to check out some antique shops. Carl had suggested that I talk to Jessica face to face about my feelings. While out for coffee I tried to express myself. She responded by saying that she wasn't ready to repair the relationship and that I push too much and to not push. Frankly, I have been timid and have given her a lot of space. But now I know I have done everything I can.

On Thanksgiving she poured me wine and seemed nice but I think it's just an act for the extended family. Her character seems very much like my sister Mandy.

George brought up this journal I am writing the other day and told me he would sue my ass if I published it without changing the names.

Today I have made a coffee date with a neighbour while George goes golfing. I hope I can carry a normal conversation. She belongs to the Women's group that I am joining on Thursday. They do many activities but I am just interested in Thursday morning coffee.

Friday, October 30, 2015

I went for coffee and joined the Women's Group.

I am always on the phone looking at the Archdiocese's website and checking for teaching vacancies but rarely do any pop up that are this side of the Alex Fraser Bridge. Although, I probably will have no luck if I can muster the guts I am going to call to make an appointment to see the new principal at St. Anne's. I plan on being honest and hope it leads somewhere.

In many ways I feel that the school and church let me down. No one came or phoned to see how I was doing even after I reached out to them. Maybe there is a reason for this. I would like to think that they are not scared by me. But for a Catholic school and parish, I am surprised at how they did not reach out!

Saturday, December 26, 2015

Well my suspicions have subsided and I guess with that comes the realization that none of my grandiose dreams will come true. Everything must have been in my head.

Come 2017 I do intend to try to go off my medication because I strongly feel it is responsible for my weight gain. Perhaps with the guidance of my doctor things will go better for me. Anyway that is a year away and I must try to do what I can to feel good about my body until then. I eat well but am admittedly sedentary. I have little energy or motivation to work out which I do once a week.

MEGAN JACKSON HALL

2016

Wednesday, March 23, 2016

While out for coffee with George at Starbucks the other day he got really mad and swore at me when I didn't agree with him on where a certain event took place.

I was a 100 percent sure that he had asked his mom about her contact so he could invest in Starbuck stock at Saber Road. He was adamant that it was her condo.

George spent the night down at the cabin and hasn't contacted me. He seems upset that I have discovered music on You Tube and am transfixed. The music seems to be making me stronger. It seems like it is giving me my life.

I am not in agreement with our Wills that he dragged me to make several years ago.

If we had more money I am not sure that I would stay married. I would live by myself in the condo.

I may be having a relapse but I don't believe so.

I went out and bought a wireless headset and I can't return them. The direction for setting them up don't make sense so if I can't do it, I hope Greg can help me.

I am not happy in my marriage. When George exploded in Starbuck he asked if I was taking my medication. I am. He doesn't touch or want any disagreements. He exploded because I did not agree with a memory he had. I believe it happened differently. It was about his investing in Starbucks and talking to Sandra's advisor. We really can't afford to separate. The smallest things upset him and no one sees it. He always says, when I disagree with him that I must be off my meds.

I do not have Capgras syndrome because I no longer believe he is a double however I do not recognize him as my husband. Thinking back to that picture Paula showed me really confuses me.

Inventions or Creations

1. I think that we could rid ourselves of keys for cars and homes by registering handprints to open them. In the case of cars being repaired, car shops would have a universal access to all cars and everyone working at a car shop would have to go through a criminal record check.

2. I think we could rid ourselves of many of the sinks in our public washrooms by using motion-censored hand sanitizers. Have a variety of different scents of hand sanitizers in different colours at kid level. Everybody would love this. Have only a few sinks and automated hand dryers only, at levels toddlers can reach too, this goes for the sinks as well. They just have to make them so that they are quieter because they scare the children. The best ones are the ones that you immerse both hands. By offering these would save the paper mess.

3. I think we could rid ourselves of currency, credit cards, and passports by registering our fingerprints at our banks. Every place you purchase something would have a fingerprint reader where you

choose which account you want it to come from based on your fingerprint. When infants are born their prints would be taken for a central registry.

4. I think we could rid ourselves of lineups at the grocery store by having everybody register at their grocery stores giving their bank information. In the stores there would be many scanners and people could scan and pack everything as they shop. These scanners would be located on the shelves where the cost for the goods are displayed. Even produce can be packaged for scanning with stickers if need be. In the bar code there would be something that would cause bells and whistles to go off at the door if something wasn't scanned. However there would be packers to help those that don't want to do it themselves, like me sometimes, ha-ha.

5. I have a dream of being responsible for creating with the tech giants the creation of an Online JK-doctorate School that is worldwide. It would be asynchronous, which is taking it at a time convenient to the student. However, the teacher would record an introduction of themselves and post some lectures so the students feel connected to an actual person. These lectures would be made in written form for those that need to reread material to understand. It would also be offered synchronously. There would be no need for transcripts. There would be no tests or essays. The students would be able to progress by subject at their own pace. They may be at grade 6 in one subject and 8 in another. The curriculum would be the same across the world in both my online school and on the ground school across the world. Students may also be able to take online subjects at a ground school if desired. Students would be able to take as many languages as they like, they would be able to study any instrument both in my online school and in a ground school.

6. At the movie theatres they should monitor which the favourite flavour packets are used and supply those out of their machines… then I would have some.

7. I also think they should make antique fashion home phones that act like cell phones. They would have built in contacts no need for an extra message machine. I have always wanted an old phone, now I want it mixed with the modern times.

Thursday, March 31, 2016

Today I went to my family doctor and complained about my 40 pound weight gain. I now weigh 154 pounds. He is changing my medication to 5 mg Abilify. So until the 7th of April I take half a pill of Abilify along with the 5 mg Saphris I am on. On the 8th I will be transitioned to the new medication. He is also giving me injections of B12 to help with energy and weight loss!!!

Wednesday, April 6, 2016

The only thing I've noticed so far since transitioning to the new medication is the disruption to my sleep pattern. I wake up several times and get up a lot earlier.

I phoned Sam today and told him that I thought it wise that we talk more frequently with the change in medication so he can let me know if he thinks I'm losing it. I thought it wise to get another opinion than just George because he only likes me as a "yes" girl…someone who agrees all the time.

I must admit, life, when the medication is working is boring. The reality that dreams don't come true is disappointing. When I first found the music videos on YouTube I felt hopeful which made me stronger. Music is therapy for me but now they aren't as exciting. I like the songs that have a message like Roar by Katy Perry and Hero by Mariah Carey and When You Believe by Mariah Carey and Whitney Houston. They make me feel anything is possible but then reality sets in and I am disappointed again.

Wednesday, April 13, 2016

I am back to taking Saphris because I had side effects with the Abilify. I had nausea light headedness and insomnia. However the doctor did say that after I take the Saphris for two weeks and stop having side effects that we can taper off the medication entirely and see if I still need it. It will be scary for me but wouldn't it be wonderful if it is not a lifetime thing. I pray all goes well.

Wednesday, April 27, 2016

Well on Monday I started taking half a tablet of Saphris. I have to do that for 3 weeks and see how it goes. Then they will do every other day for a period of time. So far so good. I pray things go well.

Dr. Duran also put me on half a tablet per day of Metformin 500 mg to help me lose weight. It is supposed to be an anti-aging drug that they use for diabetic patients that has a side effect of losing weight. I weigh 153 pounds. I hope it works.

I realize now that I have been ill. Nothing was real. I realize that all the dreams this illness allowed me to have are all pipe dreams. Reality is too boring for any of it to come to fruition.

Wednesday, September 14, 2016

I was wrong, all my dreams will come true! At least I want to believe that. I have spent a month at Oak Castle hospital under the care of Dr. Markle. I am now on 10 mg of Olanzapine and it's the best drug so far. They transferred me from Serenity Memorial to Oak Castle by ambulance. The odd thing about the trip that it did not trigger any memory of that trip to the hospital with Darcy, so many years ago. It was like I had never been in an ambulance before.

I am seeking a divorce from George and have an appointment with the lawyer on Wednesday September 21, 2016. Although everything I believe are grandiose I feel the one thing that is certain that I need to move away from George. He is too inconsistent for me. I also have an appointment with a new financial advisor with the bank. I have a new planner because Sam thought it wise considering George and I are separated.

The odd thing is back in July on the 12th it was George who walked out and said he had contacted the lawyer and the financial planner. That is why I contacted the lawyer. He was the first one to talk to her so I am confused that she didn't take him on but instead said I had contacted her and he had to find his own lawyer.

I do recall thinking and writing before, somewhere in this book that her full name represented places and people that were significant to me so she is my lawyer not George's. Maybe this is why she took me on instead of George.

On September 20, 2016 I see Dr. Jake at Duncan Mental Health at the odd hour of 8:30 a.m. in the morning.

Monday, September 19, 2016

Everything is rigged. I'm not sure I can trust what I have anymore. I went into Jessica's memory box I made and realized that the journal, baby book, I wrote look like my writing but the content is wrong and someone has been in my jewelry box and added notes from Jessica that had gone missing and added some keys.

Saturday, September 24, 2016

I went to see Dr. Jake and he said I had a good memory and in fact we had met. Well I did meet a Dr. Jake but it wasn't him because the last one I thought was handsome. Not to say Dr. Jake is not handsome.

I had to prove my competence to everyone so Dr. Jake arranged for a person to come to my apartment and assess my surroundings and my fridge. The man said to me that now I have proved them all wrong.

The lawyer was pleased that I had put a stop on the 1500 dollars George wanted to withdraw from the sale of our townhouse. There's no need to withdraw it and place it into a joint account when we will be opening separate accounts.

I met my financial advisor and he seems nice. I am confused because he did everything under the name Megan Louise Marie which I believe my name is, after all my father had my SIN card to read Megan Louise, but Barb had changed all documents to read Marie Louise Megan. Although my lawyer gave me a strange look I believe that someone duplicated my birth certificate to read Marie Louise Megan Jackson so I would correct all my documents to read the same to protect my identity.

I do feel that my dreams will come true soon, but at the same time I am guarded because I'm getting impatient and I don't want to be let down yet again.

It's like I'm living in a dual world. One where I pretend everyone is as they say they are and one where they aren't as they say and are working to give me my dreams.

Friday, September 30, 2016

Unfortunately my music is not as inspiring as it was. I keep hoping they will show me more music videos to inspire me. The more I take this medication the more reluctant I am to go outside.

I find that I need sunshine and this place has very little. We are living in a run-down rental apartment building. I am struggling figuring out where to go to get outside. It was the same with George though, he couldn't think of where we could go either when he lived here.

Thanksgiving is coming up and I'm not invited to Paula's because George and I are separated so I sent a message to Darcy that although I know she will be going to her in laws I hoped we would be able to get together.

Thursday, October 6, 2016

Yesterday I went shopping and bought myself a cool coat and boots. While I was at the mall George called and said his lawyer called him to say that my lawyer had called his lawyer saying that I thought he was buying me out of the condo. I told him no, if I couldn't have my dream home I intended to buy him out of the condo. I haven't heard from my lawyer so I guess that's how it's going to be.

George said he doesn't think I can afford to buy him out.

From everything I see on TV and the stores I feel my dreams will come true. I feel that many of the musicians I listen to on my phone and IPad and the actors on HGTV are my friends.

An example of the store supporting me is this. Today I went into the dollar store to buy wrapping paper and 98 percent of it was in solid colours, red, yellow, dark and light blue. I didn't want a solid colour plus I didn't want to choose.

If I have to limit my dreams I would take the whole floor of the condo building decorated like a dream and a cottage on the lake I described filled with music and paintings.

Maybe I will also meet Morgan Freeman who will know my entire story and he will be able to tell me what he thinks of me.

I checked the mail today and Jessica and I received an invitation for a bridal party for Wendy. I was all ready to say yes but Jessica thinks I should not go considering George and I are separated…so I sent my apologies.

As each day passes I think maybe my dreams won't come true but there is all this tangible proof in this apartment of documents I never had before. Plus why would the church and people at school leave me to my own devices. Why has no one reached out? There must be a reason. Just like my girls. Thanksgiving is coming up and I haven't heard a word from either one of them about it. Considering they were so concerned with me living on my own, why haven't either one of them phoned to see how I am doing?

This temporary apartment that George and I rented before the condo was completed is dreary. One of the big reasons George was anxious to be out of.

Sunday, October 9, 2016

If it wasn't for Elizabeth, my friend, whom I can always count on I think I would go bonkers. I totally lost it today when she called because she totally gets it. She herself is shocked that no one but Sam is calling to see how I am doing and even he doesn't phone often. I am feeling like I never should have agreed to move to British Columbia!

There is an opening to teach grade three at St. Anne's that appeared today. I applied but I'm sure I won't be shortlisted. It's not my dream but it would challenge my mind. It would mean a lot to me if they called though. At least it would mean that they care. On the other hand maybe I'm a problem they don't want to take a risk on.

Tuesday, November 1, 2016

I have been on 10 mg of Olanzapine since I've been in the hospital (Friday, August 12, 2016) I got myself out Tuesday September 13, 2016 by recommending I be referred to Duncan Mental Health.

The doctor in the hospital wanted to talk to my family so Jessica and Darcy came. Jessica thought I should live at some halfway house and Darcy thought I should live in a senior's residence.

The medication over the years had sedated me so much that all they saw while I was living with George was someone totally reliant on her husband. It's no wonder they thought that I couldn't function on my own.

The more I take the medication the more I am challenged to believe my dreams will come true. However, there have been some strange things happening that still make me feel like something is happening.

For instance, I noticed that I was unable to access my other mailboxes on my IPad and when I mentioned this to my ladies group I came home and low and behold I could. When I did I checked my Junk mail and trash to see if I had something from the lawyer. There was nothing but I did find my resume and cover letter sent to St. Anne's in the trash. I have no idea how they got there.

It sounds strange but I still feel special and that my gut is right. Somehow I feel I just have to be patient and I will be living in a much happier place with a happier life.

While in the hospital Mandy called me to say that Mom had died on Saturday, September 3, 2016. My brother had asked everyone not to tell me. I was angry at my brother and thankful to Mandy. Just because I was in the hospital is not reason not to tell me. Because they didn't I was robbed of grieving properly for my mom by attending her funeral. It has been hard to forgive my brother for that. My health team said they would definitely have let me travel and go. I know he thought he was doing the right thing but it hurt deeply.

My new financial planner, Roland, makes me feel that things will work out. I hate the idea of using my RRSP's already because I so want to leave a legacy for my girls. I so want to own a place. I hope if George and I don't get back together that I am able to buy him out of the condo.

I would like him to **want** to get back together with me. I'm the one that suggested coffee last time it would be nice if he asked me. At the same time my gut tells me he won't. Let's be clear I do not want to be together with him..

Sunday November 20, 2016

George has made it pretty clear that he wants a break. Although I hate being alone, I also do not know whether he should be in my life. It is as if he aged and I never saw it. He doesn't look like how he would age according to the picture Paula showed us. I am still so confused where he is concerned and it certainly isn't fair to him. I know I miss his companionship. But why can I look at everyone else and I see them. I see them as they should age but George is different. It doesn't make sense to me so how would it make sense to him?

I don't feel special anymore though. One thing that I am thankful for is that the TV is giving me good shows to watch on the weekend.

Some days and weeks are better than others. Some days I am able to face the world and socialize and others I make excuses as to why I shouldn't.

I so wish this illness or whatever never had happened to me. I feel so lonely. I think Christmas will have a big impact on me. I think if I don't see Jessica make an effort or care to see me that I just might start considering suicide more. I am so tired of being the one to reach out. I know Darcy is busy and she has been an angel but it would mean so much more if she would arrange a time for us to get together instead of me.

I really need more help than I've received from my immediate family.

My brother has done his best although he turned me down for escaping to his place for Christmas. My sister has not been very supportive and very hard to reach. She is fine to talk to when the timing suits her. She has to be the one to phone which I don't understand. She never used to be so hard to reach.

Sunday, December 4, 2016

I should not believe in all that I believe and maybe not dream but believe. I think my dreams will come true and that for some reason my demise right now is temporary. When I am with Sherry, the community worker, Don and Dr. Jake and in the community I feel it is all in my head, but when I listen to music and watch videos it makes me feel special and that my dreams will come true. But if I am honest about this they are more than likely going to increase my medication and I am so afraid of losing control of my physical body that I am now regaining. This medication has allowed me to be flexible again. And I don't want to have a medicated affect.

I have received the first draft of the separation agreement and I doubt its validity because it has so many errors.

Monday, December 12, 2016

Dear God,

I've been praying to you every night about my situation and I have added Darcy because of her marital problems. She is distant now and doesn't converse with me through text as much as before. Is it because of me? I think talking to you is giving me the strength to carry on, but I need a sign that things will get better and that I won't stay alone.

I still think something strange is going on because why do we have my baptismal certificate dated 2007? George had no idea why we had it and I never asked for it. It is things like this that mess with me. Please don't forget my family God. George is right, ours is not a healthy relationship while I still mistrust him. However, him living with Jessica and his seeing his sister Paula most days is not helping our situation.

Also why does this computer fix the word "don't "when I don't put the apostrophe in but not the words "I've or I'll"?

Friday, December 16, 2016

I have such good news. On December 5 I texted Jessica not expecting a reply. I wrote that it was just a message to say I love her and that if I weren't so afraid to go downtown, I would offer to do so much more with her.

SHE RESPONDED!! She said she loved me and no worries at all. I of course was elated and had to respond telling her that she had just made me cry and though she doesn't like hugs from me, I was sending a big one anyway. That ended our conversation.

A few days later she emailed me on behalf of her and Darcy saying they thought we could get together the three of us and celebrate a late Christmas and early birthday for Jessica on December 28 or 29. I responded saying I thought the 29th was good because that is George and my anniversary and I will want to be busy. I also said that I didn't want to be alone on Christmas day and that I didn't know if Darcy's invitation to spend it with her and her in-laws still stood. Darcy confirmed that I was definitely invited.

Today I went to the constituency office for the liberal MP for North Duncan. I asked how I could help being a spokesperson to dispel the stigma of individuals diagnosed with more scary mental illnesses. I spoke with the manager of the office, who is supposed to get back to me next week.

2017

Sunday, January 8, 2017

The office manager never contacted me and so I wonder if she was just pacifying me by saying she would call. Coincidentally, there are more commercials with the Bell let's talk team on the TV trying to dispel the stigma of mental illnesses. They have commercials now based on mental illness but I find them condescending and offensive. One has a girl talking about her mom and it looks like she is about to laugh and doesn't believe what she is saying.

 I have a meeting with Al on the 18th of February, to discuss what I can afford to move into. Thinking of this I went to see about a one bedroom at the Diamond Head condo building which won't be built until the fall of 2018. It was a nice ground floor (which I prefer) and cost 339,900 plus taxes. If I can't afford to buy George out of the condo we invested in than maybe this is a viable solution, unless Al's real estate guy can find a nice cheaper one that isn't too old etc.

Thursday, February 16, 2017

I am still on 10 mg of Olanzapine. I also take tecta and Mometasone spray for Nasopharangeal reflux.

I am working with Al's friend Nolan to sell the two bedroom and secure a one bedroom in the same building. The Cornerstone. The one bedroom is 314,000 dollars plus GST which is more in keeping with what Al says I can afford. I decided I didn't want the one at Diamond Head because I don't want to wait until 2018 for it to be built.

The bank didn't seem to be able to give a bridge loan for us but Al, my financial planner asked Nolan to reach out to his mortgage broker. He did and says Karen believes she can do it. So, I have to call her tomorrow and apparently George will call as well.

I had a great conversation with my best friend Elizabeth who seems to understand that my delusions seem to grow out of a seed of fact that doesn't make sense!! She gets it totally. For example I thought Sandra, George's mom's burial was disrespectful. She was driven through the border in the back of George's pick-up truck. I was so appalled then, that I had my brother-in- law drive my daughters and me. I refused to go in the truck. As well, I was involved in the arrangements at the funeral parlour with George and Paula, his older sister. But why was I there and not his younger sister Tammy? These things did not make sense to me so then I believed she could not possibly have died. Why did he leave his mother's PowerPoint with me and never look at it? Inconsistencies based on fact became a delusion! The same was true with other loved ones that died. No one ever shed a tear. No one mourned. Plus the PowerPoint made by George's niece, Kendra, showed pictures of Paula's wedding and our wedding but not Tammy's which led me to think she may not even be his sister. Also, the CD made for my sister had no pictures of myself. It simply did not make sense. (March 1, 2018 Although, I let others convince me it was in my head, but I believe they are alive!!)

Today is Thursday, my busy full day. I now regularly go to coffee and meet with the ladies group and Danielle now comes which is great. I met her at one of the dinners with the ladies and she wanted to exchange contact info. I was so pleased! We've taken turn phoning each other and I think I might phone her Saturday to see if she is free.

I found the courage to phone a number on a flyer by the Newcomers Group that I held onto for six years. Until now I did not have the courage. I felt so alone for so long so I went to the coffee meetings.

I recognized a dad of one of my former students today in the mall. We caught up on each other's kids and I filled him in on my health and marriage or lack thereof. He told me that Paula, his wife and the principal who hired me quilt with some other ladies every Tuesday, so I have made it my goal to visit Tuesday morning. I told him that I thought that my school and the parish had let me down when I needed them the most. He admitted that it didn't speak highly of the Church and parish.

Elizabeth feels I need to keep writing hence my entry today. She also feels that I have a message that needs to get out. Regarding this book, she feels that I should talk to a lawyer to see if George would have grounds to sue me on.

I received the revised version of the separation agreement and basically the parts I understand makes sense.

You know something my community worker Sherry said to day doesn't make sense. I told her I think I'm waiting for a tax form from the bank regarding my savings account. She asked me if I was referring to the one with 12,000 dollars in it. How did she know how much I had in my account?? I never told her. I didn't ask her how she knew that though. That's a pattern with me. When there is something I don't understand I don't ask for an explanation because I think they'll just cover up by saying I told them.

Friday, February 17, 2017

Well its 2:00 a.m. and I can't sleep. Just like two weeks ago. I am so wrought up about the condo and having a place of my own fully paid for. I don't like not sleeping because I fear I won't be able to think clearly.

I don't know if I have mentioned it or not. But long ago I said that once the Cornerstone is completed and I see what I get to live in will be the result of whether dreams come true or not. For I said that if I had to downsize into a condo I wanted the entire floor. If I don't get it, it will confirm that wishes and dreams really don't come true.

George and I have been separated for 7 months. It sure doesn't feel that long. I worry about how much the legal fees will be.

I have noticed a glitch with my emails. Whenever I forward an email from Diana, my lawyer, to my brother I can't then respond to Diana's email without my brothers comments being present so I have to create a new email to respond to her. It's annoying. Apple have really messed up their system.

Sunday, February 26, 2017

We have listed the two bedroom condo and I have purchased a one bedroom in the same building. As I have said before what reality shows me when it's time to move in will be my sign that indeed dreams come true or they don't.

George has asked that we get together to "talk". I could've said no but decided I would agree. My stomach is turning upside down for tomorrow's dinner with him. We are supposed to walk the pier in Whittle Head first. Hopefully I can remain strong!! I don't want to discuss the agreement.

Last time I saw Dr. Jake, he was thinking of switching my medication because this one is known for adding weight. He also thinks it may not be right because I still do not recognize George. I've been doing so much better on this medication so I'm a bit leery of changing it but I want to lose weight!!

Tuesday, February 28, 2017

Well George and I got together and he blew me out of the water. Not in a million years would I have guessed what he had to say. We went to Whittle Head for coffee at our favourite spot and no sooner did we get settled when he told me why he wanted to meet. He told me, with tears in his eyes that he was sorry for how he treated me. That basically I was in need and he bailed. These were not his words verbatim. But essentially that he had withdrawn from our relationship. We also walked the pier and had dinner at the Boathouse.

I was honest with him about my feelings and expectations. He is wanting to get back together and I told him that I couldn't go back to the way it was. I told him he left me because of my illness and I couldn't do more to help that. On the other hand I expected him to change, for the reasons I left him were the hurtful things he would say and the lack of affection. I told him he caused me to hate being intimate with him. I was very honest, just as I was with my needs to him back in 2005.

Stay tuned, for I need to process this. When I left his car he said we would be in touch.

Now I have a one-bedroom condo to think about which he said we could rent out.

Thursday, March 2, 2017

I asked George to contact the realtor and cancel the sale of the two bedroom condo. He told Nolan, the realtor, we were getting back together. This rushed matters for me.

On Mandy's advice, I asked him to arrange a dinner with the girls so we could tell them together that we were getting back together. I also suggested that we bring our rings and put them back on each other's hands. He arranged this dinner for this Saturday at The Keg. It comes fast for me and I hope I have done the right thing. I think George was missing our life more than I was. I just wanted to show the girls that you work on a marriage when it gets rocky that is why I decided to get together with him again.

Friday, March 24, 2017

As if on cue when he told the girls the news he cried again.

The unthinkable happened. The day after we told the girls George texted me at 11:00 pm and said he thought we should separate. I was shocked but he said that he talked to Paula and that explained everything!! He should have spoken with Tammy who is far more stable and hasn't been separated and divorced three times!!!! He talked to the wrong sister.

He wanted to be married but continue with the family as if we were separated. He didn't want to see the grand kids or our daughters with me on a regular basis he preferred to see them on his own. I understand occasionally but a happy marriage includes seeing the family together on a regular basis. To me his thinking is thwarted!

As far as I'm concerned he should've talked to whomever he needed to before he approached me.

I have no idea what the girls think of their dad now but he sure showed his true colours. I hope it affects their relationship with him.

What strikes me as odd was the girls' reaction when we told them we were getting back together. They were both upset.

Darcy is separating from Greg and now needs help with picking up Cassie and taking her to dance so I offered to do it Monday, Tuesday and every other Friday. She was going to ask her dad for Thursday since I can't do it. She asked and he said no and didn't offer to do any other day. So much for him helping out!!

Today, Nolan, the realtor arranged for George and I to meet the mortgage broker Karen because George forgot everything he agreed to regarding securing a line of credit for the two bedroom.

They suggested we go to the bank that is now George's. I hope we have no problem because everybody seems to think George works. Now I wait for George to set up the appointment.

Sunday, April 9, 2017

All went well at the bank although it is not solidified yet. I am feeling down feeling that reality will win and that dreams are just what they are, dreams. I would by some miracle end up with the entire floor of the building or at least the two bedroom we bought. The closer we get to see our condo on the 25th of April, the more I get sad because my wishes will not come to fruition. I'd like to believe that my not hearing about the one bedroom yet is somehow a sign that miracles happen.

Sunday, April 16, 2017

Well it is solidified we are approved for $200,000 which is a relief.

I still have no idea when I can see the one bedroom yet.

Darcy and Greg have sold her house and have to be moved by April 29.

It seems she has found a place to live in West Saramin thank heavens!! It will be a two bedroom basement suite.

For Easter my friend Danielle invited me over to her house for dinner on Saturday plus I spent the day with Darcy on Saturday and Sunday. Monday I will have dinner with her and give them their Easter presents. Don't know when I'll be able to see Jessica.

Tuesday, May 2, 2017

I haven't seen Jessica yet but she is responding to most texts!! Alleluia!!!

I have been helping Darcy with her move. Her new place is in such a nice neighbourhood in West Saramin and the kids sleeping together is working out, thanks heavens!!

Darcy is coping with her stress extremely well and admittedly so am I, according to all my family and health professionals.

I see the one bedroom this Friday. Since only three people are allowed in the unit I have asked Nolan, my realtor, and Ellie, an interior decorator I have hired. She seems friendly and her voice makes me think she's around my age.

I hope everything works out with the lawyer. She doesn't seem to give me much advice. I have to rely on my brother.

Friday, October 13, 2017

My brother feels my lawyer is doing a great job on my behalf. I have copied him on all conversations so that is how he knows. My brother has been a great support to me.

Today I met with a girl from the Coastal Society who went over how I feel about different aspects of my life and helped narrow down some goals that I have. The goals I have focussed on for now is, first, family, specifically my relationship with Jessica. Second, going on more excursions. I also asked her if they could help me publish this book.

I feel quite happy with my surroundings. I found a furniture refinishing company and phoned them up. The guy came over today and picked up my mother's end table and was able to pick out the colour I wanted right away. I chose magenta!! He gave me a price of $100.00 to do it whereas, if I had my decorator do it she would charge me $150.00 an hour!! Plus she has never done it before.

I am lucky that I met my friend Danielle. She has introduced me to several of her friends and has invited me to various places. I was going to Zumba on Mondays at the senior's centre, now one of Danielle's friends, Penny, goes there too. It's great! It gives me more incentive to attend the class. Plus we usually go out for coffee afterwards.

Danielle likes to entertain and has invited me to several dinner parties. She also takes me on excursions downtown. Surviving this marital breakdown would me much more difficult if I didn't have these new friendships.

I decided that I would utilize all the support that Duncan Mental Health unit has to offer. Seems because I am on my own I get more support. I could've used it while I was living with my husband. At that time I only had a psychiatrist and caseworker. Now I also have a community support worker. She meets with me once a week and the focus can be anything I want it to be. Right now we meet for coffee. I think since she can't join me at the She's Fit gym, I will have her join me at the Rec Centre and see how that works out.

I have come a long way in my journey and it took me taking the first steps to join The North Duncan Newcomers and Friends Group to gain friendships and acceptance. It is through this group that I met Danielle and subsequently her friends. I had to help myself.

Honestly, I think some medications are better than others in helping individuals to want to socialize. The medication I am on now, 10mg of Olanzapine has helped me, but it has caused me to gain weight. I have gained thirty pounds since I have been put on it. I will once again bring up this issue with my psychiatrist. Although it helps me socialize this medication still makes me fearful of driving new places or going to the airport. I do not feel like the leader I used to be. I am close but not quite there.

I have come a long way from that woman who could not eat, dress or sit on the furniture, from not being able to read, play guitar, listen to music, listen to sermons, use the computer or talk on the phone. I was aware that I was receiving messages which caused me to withdraw and I was paranoid that things did not appear as they should. I felt my mind was being read and I was determining everything around me. I felt people I phoned or who phoned me were not really them. I am grateful for those who listened and offered their support. You know who you are for I have thanked you in person.

Look at me now, I am living in a beautiful brand new condo mortgage free. I am as high as I can go without paying penthouse prices.

I was led to believe while living with my husband that I could not afford to live on my own, but according to my planner, I am doing fine. It is so refreshing to go shopping for things when I want or need to.

My living space may not have ended up the whole floor space of the building, but my condo is uplifting. My dream may not have come true of having the whole floor. This may just mean that I have to work harder at getting this book published so that maybe this dream will come true. Well, one can dream.

Friday, November 3, 2017

I am feeling so good about my future. I have made friends and have an active life now. I go to Zumba every Monday with a friend I met through Danielle whose name is Penny. Penny and I sometimes go for walks.

Danielle invites me to dinners which she hosts at least once a month and she also invited me to go to the West end with her.

Now there is a coffee group starting in my hi-rise starting November 17th every Friday morning. Maybe I'll meet more friends.

I received an updated separation agreement and went over it with my brother. It is getting closer to being finalized. I stress over how much this is going to cost me.

Friday, November 17, 2017

Today I went to the coffee group in my new building and met a few nice ladies. I exchanged phone numbers with a couple of them and joined a walking group.

Now I know what other people say when they retire that they are so busy they don't know how they fit in work. My weeks are so busy now!!!

I saw my psychiatrist, Dr. Jake, on Tuesday and he has reduced my medication to 7.5mg Olanzapine instead of 10mg. He agrees that gaining thirty pounds since first taking it in the hospital is too much. He says the medication has this side effect. He wants to put me on a new medication but he is away for the month of December and we decided we would reduce the medication instead and see if I lose weight. He doubts it.

Tuesday, November 21, 2017

The separation agreement between my husband and myself is almost completed and as it draws closer it seems more unreal that after 31 years we got separated.

This separation would have been a lot more difficult had I not had all the friends that I have made. Plus the decision to hire an interior decorator helped me be happy in my space. I made most of the colour decisions, she merely drove me, which I am thankful for.

Last year for Christmas I had suggested we all celebrate together but George and Jessica did not think it was a good idea. This year however, it looks like we will all be celebrating together at Darcy's for brunch on Christmas.

Since they will be celebrating dinner with the Hall clan, I have been invited to my friends for dinner. At least I will have somewhere to go. It is awfully sweet of my friend to do this for every one of her friends who have no family to share Christmas dinner with.

Sometimes it is hard for me to reflect back to September 2016 when I was coming out of the hospital and both my girls did not have faith that I could take care of myself. I felt ganged upon by my family, but I survived and showed them!! I wonder if they reflect back to their beliefs at the time and think how wrong they were.

Saturday, December 2, 2017

I believe this book and my journey will soon be revealed. I think in many ways that I was right and that those around me were not yet ready for me and my intuitive insight. My medication has been reduced and with that my vision of what I read in the music videos and TV seem to be acting upon what I think. I am not afraid and it makes me feel strong.

I reviewed the flash drive of the pictures from my past that I am giving to George, Darcy and Jessica for Christmas, and discovered that many of the pictures were never taken. Also looking upon their faces, I could decipher in many pictures that it was not them. I will let George decipher for himself what he feels is real. I don't like looking at pictures because I question who is who which is absurd.

I am again believing in dreams coming true. Maybe all of mine will. When looking at those pictures it was like watching the credits at the end of a movie.

I can't get my hopes up and continue to live each day as if maybe they do.

2018

Sunday, January 7, 2018

Well my separation agreement is signed. I was the last to sign on January 2. Now this condo is all mine!! He however, received all the profits from the sale of the condo we had first invested in in the same building.

I see my psychiatrist on the 16th and I am anxious for that meeting. He is supposed to put me on a new medication that shouldn't cause weight gain and is known to increase motivation!!

I have gained quite a bit of weight since I have been on this medication, Olanzapine. I now weigh 164 pounds!! The most I have ever weighed. And it is affecting my health. I do not want to rejoin Weight Watchers until I see how this new medication works.

I meet with George Tuesday morning at the Tim Hortons near my place on Tuesday January 9, 2018 to receive my alimony cheques for the year.

Thursday, January 18, 2018

My meeting with George went well. I had to take care of Cassie, so she was with us.

I had my meeting with Dr. Jake on Tuesday and he is waiting until Tuesday when my caseworker Kay is in attendance. He asked me to make sure my family was on board with switching my medication to Rexulti.

I texted my brother and both girls and they are on board with the change. According to my brother it is a newer drug and sounds good. Dr. Jake feels the drug I am on now, Olanzapine is not healthy to stay on long term.

I met with Julia today and she suggested that I ask the girls if they mind me publishing my book and offer them the opportunity to read it first. I thought that was a great idea. However, I have decided not to.

Tuesday, January 30, 2018

I have started transitioning to the new medication, Rexulti. I started on the 26th. Here's the regiment to move over to the new medication:

> For 4 days take 1/2 of a 2mg tablet of Rexulti plus 7.5 mg of Olanzapine
> For 3 days Take 2mg tablet Rexulti plus 7.5 mg of Olanzapine
> For 7 days take 4mg Rexulti plus 2.5mg Olanzapine
> Only take 4mg Rexulti

I meet with my psychiatrist on February 1st to check on how the new drug is working.

Tuesday, February 13, 2018

I have been only on the new medication 4mg Rexulti since February 9. So far so good although, I have not lost weight.

Thursday, February 15, 2018

I mentioned to my caseworker that Duncan Mental Health should have dietitians for their clients because all anti-psychotic drugs cause weight gain. This weight gain then causes depression and physical health problems. She thought it was a good idea. So, I went further, I wrote the Prime Minister, Justin Trudeau. His office forwarded my email to the Minister of Health for Canada who responded very quickly with a very thoughtful email and the contact information for the Honourable Health Minister of BC, Adrian Dix and the Honourable Minister of Mental Health and Addictions Judy Darcy.

I wrote them today and copied the Minister of Health of Canada. I hope to hear from them soon.

I have decided to divorce George and will be setting up the appointment tomorrow.

Thursday, March 1, 2018

I have made my Will, but upon reading it I know it is not real. I know they say you should not sign something without reading it first but my lawyer who was acting as a real lawyer summed up each page and I trusted her.

I have also filed for divorce on February 20[th, 2018] and that part of my life, I hope is real. George used and abused me in many different ways over the years and I need it to be over.

Although maybe this started out as a game, the powers that be discovered things far more sinister going on. Perhaps George still thinks this is a game but I do not.

I am now having my medication brought to me every night at my condo. It is allowing me to think clearly and oddly enough my beliefs in everything have become stronger!!!!. My dreams will come true! My only concern is when. How much longer do I have to wait?

I have come to learn that my and my daughter's lives have not been our own and I am not entirely sure whether all the dreams are mine or have been implanted in me by someone else, could be God or the FBI and CSIS.

I want the dreams of my daughters, sisters, brother and all those involved in this journey to have their dreams to come true too!!

I believe that my dad sold my sisters and I each for a million dollars and that I am undergoing this fight for all of us. I believe that I was implanted with a GPS and tech devices at birth, so my life would be protected. I believe that this has been a Sting to bring down my father and George and they have been following them all my life. I believe that I will be able to go to court and give testimony! Perhaps my intuition and gut were right. Answers will come.

I feel I have an iDoc implanted in me controlling my emotions. And when that fateful day arrives they will allow me the strength to face my persecutors.

I believe that the two daughters who have been in my life are doppelgangers.

I think Jessica has been farther away from me because hers is not as similar as Darcy's. I have not been able to discern any difference with Darcy.

I also believe my grandchildren are not mine. Plus I see differences in how they both behave. I think each either have a twin or a doppleganger.

I don't think I am mentally sick at all!!

My favourite colour has become magenta. A blend of purple and pink.

I have started to think of past relationships thinking that someone is searching for me. The media will show me:

- † *Solid Black meant my thinking was correct.*
- † Solid Brown if it's the real George Hall
- † Light Grey with blue if it is Preston, a grade school friend
- † Light Grey with green if its Liam, a university boyfriend
- † Grey with pink if it is Derek, a high school crush
- † Solid light grey with no other colour if it is someone else coming for me like Andrew, a high school boyfriend or add blue if it's Frank, a grade school friend
- † The signs on Madame Secretary showed Grey, White and blue which leads me to think its Paddy or Frank with the rest of the world.

MY COLOUR-CODED LIFE

† *Red and grey came to stand for my high school because these are their colours (Monday September 19, 2016- they are supporting me and I will see them all again.)*

† *Green and black was love, which probably stems from the beaded bookmark Jessica made me that I still have! I love my girls and believe that someone is waiting for me and getting to know me. (April 23, 2018 I will have someone in my life again. I believe this person to be Gary Barlow.)*

† *Red and black in one piece of clothing or combined in patterns stands for First Nation People. I see Jessica and the First Nations standing together when I see red tops and black pants or red and black items like the chairs in The Voice. They are watching over me and taking action as well to guide me through this journey.*

† *Solid Light Blue represented Mrs. Hall who was also standing with my mother. Soon her colour represented her entire family excluding George.*

† *Blue and white in combination in one piece of clothing means friends who support me. I started by my thinking that George was sending me a message that he wanted to be only friends because he was not sexually attracted to me, but he has robbed me of half my life and I definitely do not want to be friends. Well, I do want to be amicable for the girls.*

† *Solid brown meant that the real George whose identity was stolen is coming for me. Nevertheless, I do not believe that anymore. 2018- This colour I created a few years ago. When I see solid brown on the artists or actors it does lead me to think that maybe he is coming and if so, I can believe in my dad again. Maybe if I see or don't see brown, I will have my answer. April 2, 2018-Today watching Bryan Inc. on HGTV Bryan was wearing a brown winter coat. Today I was thinking about my gut and my gut tells me that George's identity was stolen. My gut tells me the picture Paula showed me of my husband when he was younger was the real George that no one in my family ever met. I have doubts about the George I married. I was attracted to the guy I met in the hospital and the guy in the picture, not the men whom I was living with.*

- *Orange- March 29, 2018 I started this colour a few years ago to represent my psychiatrist who did not want to be involved so I made it my health. Later I made it my favourite flavour of candy. Later, I needed a colour for my brother and sister, Mandy and so I made orange their color.*
- *Peach is a colour I added for the stores and the media to prove to me that my older sister, Louise is alive. March 1, 2018, Peach is back in my life now so I now believe she is alive!!*
- *Coral I added this year (2018) with the help of the media to represent my niece Carol whom I wrote a song about saying no colour could match the one of hers. I hope she likes it. Coral you can see in pretty oceans and just as they kiss you under water, she kissed me while I was drowning by not judging me with things I had to say. She was the one I dragged out back of Gage Lane and showed her a misplaced evergreen branch. There were no evergreen bushes or trees around. Where did he drag it from?*
- *Solid White I added later to mean the whole world was supporting me and later it also represents Leon coming for me. It looks like it's happening.*
- *Purple was school/religion, they wanted me to have a miraculous cure. 2018- I feel that the Archdiocese here and back home have reached out to protect me and that I was never sick at all. They have used the musicians around the world and the media to reach out to me through my colours and lyrics. Purple used to stand for Catholic Church wanting me to have a miracle cure. I believed if I thought of this colour I did not have to choose between my family members. This colour now represents my first daughter that I believed Gary Barlow named Poppy. . She was terminated just under four months or otherwise she would have suffered tremendously and may still have died. I had no choice!! His daughter with this name was stillborn.*
- *Solid White is the background of the Canadian flag and it means that the whole world is standing with Canada and me.*
- *Red and white means that Jessica and the whole of Canada and the world are with me.*

Phillip Phillips' song's lyrics says "I'm going to make this place your home". I believe someone will do that too, only I don't know where. This community where I live now does not make sense. Tinsel Town made sense. I just want to be in an area that makes sense surrounded by my real family and all my friends. I want the girls who have been such a big part of my life like Darcy and Jess to always be a part of my life.

Upon looking at different parts of this book. It appears part of it has been rewritten by someone else. It is too challenging for me to reread this and make sense of things I think were different than what is written.

I can't find the part where I want a big bash with the musicians that have made me stronger. One of them Bon Jovi!

I feel through some of the music that George is trying to reach me and wants me back. But these love songs leave me flat and cold regarding him. He stole my life. We did nothing for fun! I feel robbed of my life. I believe my time will be coming soon.

When I met him he was not frightened when I told him that I wanted a dozen children. But after our second he was quick to get fixed. It's as if he knew the pact I had made with God to give me at least two healthy children after we lost our first.

Now I feel that the Halls' are not George's family and have been helping me all along.

I also am dreaming bigger now. I dream that I will have a clothing line shared with my daughters. I analyze clothes now and decide whether it would be appropriate for various age groups. Perhaps even my own search engine. The world will know our story and our colours will be everywhere. They will not forget us!!

I watch the media and find that they are all friends from around the world. However, I also realize that this is likely only shown to me on my TV. The concerts I see seem to have overly large crowds to be realistic. But then I think what if they were real? Realistically, perhaps they are just camera tricks. I'm so afraid to believe that my time is coming.

It makes it very real when I saw my psychiatrist the other day and he said I was doing very well but my beliefs and dreams are still very vivid and stronger than ever!!

Friday, March 9, 2018

I met with Julia yesterday, my community support worker and she made me feel that my thoughts were okay to have. It's like everybody believes me now!!

Like the new lyrics of "The Bridge over Troubled Water" saying that my dreams are on their way. That's right I feel the lyrics are meant for me.

It is hard for me to believe because these thoughts of grandeur have come and gone before, but this time it's different. I can see them coming true on my iPad, and iPhone and TV and with my health professionals believing me. I just don't know when they will come true. The anticipation is hard.

If I have not said it, I want my online school to be worldwide from JK-doctorate

Covering every discipline. It would allow the study of music, linguistics, law, doctor and so much more. There would only be evaluation on work completed. There would be no tests, or essays. It would be asynchronous or synchronous. If asynchronous there would be face to face portions so the students feel connected to their instructor.

Friday, March 16, 2018

I have asked the television to show me brown to prove that the real George, the one I met in the Keg is coming for me. The TV has shown me an abundance of brown in performers' eyes.

Also my gut used to say that he had brown eyes, like Louise. I never understood why her eyes were brown.

Now if they continue to show me brown it will prove that he is a good man, if not then I will know that I was bought.

The TV has just showed me a solid brown shirt on a singer named Matt on the X Factor show so I have my answer!!! But the medication won't allow me to feel that joy that is trapped inside, so only tears rush out!!

However the man whom I lived with, as my dad, created this whole spin of Tim Horton's and he had his home more modern than I see today, Plus he was able to afford to go on so many trips on one salary. My gut tells me he was into something elicit. So I am not sure how to ask the media if my dad was an honest man. I understood from the media before that my dad sold me for money. How do I confirm this?

They have confirmed that my thinking creates what I see. I think because God is watching over me I will ask them to show me someone in solid purple to show that my gut is correct that my dad was dishonest. If I don't see it then I will know that he is an honest man looking out for me.

12:14 p.m. The TV has shown me a solid purple shirt on the X Factor with black trim that shows that my thinking is correct, that the man I met long ago in the Keg is innocent. Maybe they will sing a song now that shows that my dad was evil and cruel to use me like Collabro's song "Stars"; seeing him too behind bars.

I pray I read the signs correctly and I gave them enough time to read my entry.

I believe everything will come to me. I just do not know when.

I think that this may be wrapped up in a show which they've disguised as a game where the producers came across the complications of my life and it became a sting operation too or vice versa. So, if this is true, I want those Georges that did me wrong to spend their life in prison because that part was real life!! I married the wrong man, so I want a huge happy wedding with the man whom was meant to be in my life and I feel the powers that are behind all this know whom that is. Well maybe an intimate wedding.

I believe my girls have been doppelgangers' too and I really am not sure whom I've reared. I told this to George when I met him to do our income taxes. I told him everything including that I did not believe he was a Hall. I also believe Tammy and Donald are not related to the family. I gave him yet another chance to come clean.

I want my life's story to be documented on W5 and 60 Minutes and to be interviewed by other talk shows that are interested in my story. (Sept 8, 2019 - In this search of my mind that betrayed me and cost me my career and marriage, I feel was a blessing and caused my mind to awaken.)

The X Factor alternates between three or four judges, I have not figured out why.

I wonder how my sister Mandy and I drifted as she got older. We were so close when we spent our summers together at the cottage. We had names for every chipmunk that we used to feed. How did it happen? I knew I stopped liking her with the way she treated my mom and she always got away with it, as well with how she tormented Louise. I blame dad.

I barely have a memory of Louise during that time…only that she had difficulty learning how to waterski. All dad could do was the dog paddle and mom loved the breast stroke. I learned the side stroke and breast stroke by watching her. It was Sam that taught us how to waterski. I think he learned by the some neighbours he visited all the time and Jack Fitz Morris, the man we rented the cottage from.

Mandy turned around though, she was awesome with caring for mom while she was in a care home. She is good at taking charge of a situation.

Although sometimes I feel this book is going to be written as a biography rather than an autobiography it allows me to vent my frustrations by writing it down. Writing has always helped me to express myself. I used to hide it under the heading Math so that George could not find it on my computer but now I know it is protected. It will be my story and will hopefully help others. Maybe not so much a biography but edited by a ghostwriter that I know nothing about.

Those that will write my book has followed me my entire life, so there is nothing I can write that they don't already know, just like God, all knowing and I seeing.

Sunday, March 18, 2018

There are not enough swear words to express my hatred toward my dad and George!! Besides learning through the media and perhaps my overactive imagination, that they both molested their children (Sam, my brother and both my daughters) they each robbed my mother and I of having loving relationships. Plus I found out today that George might be the cause that I had to have a hysterectomy due to dysplasia cells. I believe this because I was married to George for 16 years when I had been diagnosed. He used to brag about how he slept with girls a lot and a female friend of his told him he should wear a condom…but he was never able to with me. However, these type of cells may lay dormant for much longer.

For some reason he even tried to use one with me while living on Gage Lane. I did not understand why at the time and didn't ask. He was not able to use it. I was insecure at the time and not in a good head space. I thought he was doing it to practice on me so he could use one with someone else.

I only wish that Dr. Bersi had talked me into going with the other doctor for my hysterectomy so I didn't have a scar across my stomach which makes yet another roll of fat.

I pray my dad and my husband rot in prison in the worst one there is. No fancy meals, no courses to take, no TV, no music, no visitors allowed, solitary confinement and no chance for parole!! Which unfortunately will be a short time considering how old they are. God forgive me I hate them if it is true!!!

Tuesday, March 20, 2018

Today I saw Dr. Jake, my psychiatrist and told him what I feel about my dad and my ex-husband. He thinks that I may be misinterpreting. That is possible but I have asked three times to the media to show me signs and they confirm my gut feeling. The fact that he said this makes me wonder, is there something for me to interpret off the TV and my music?

I knew about Jessica, and it explains that even as her doppelganger lived with us, she would have sleepovers with her friends. George came across an entry into her book where she tracked her food and wrote her activities. He showed it to me and it said that she loved me more than anyone knew but that she had to leave to protect herself and she loved me infinity x infinity, infinity x. (Jessica started using this phrase with me when she was young.) I used to think it was because of me that she left but now I see that it was so George would not hurt her.

With Darcy, it explains why she stopped singing as a little girl. And she seemed so distant. She, I had few clues.

Which leads me to wonder how long I've been rearing doppelgangers whom I love.

What worries me is that my dad had my brother's room sound proofed under the guise it was for him studying. I remember when my brother left and I would sleep in his bed why there was a punched hole beside it, even back then I thought of this. Here goes my mind again.

But I asked the psychologist regarding Jessica being molested years ago, so why did the psychologist not tell me the truth?

This medication I am on doesn't allow me to feel any emotion but mild crying. It is frustrating.

Dr. Jake, said perhaps the Rexulti is not working, but now I feel no matter what medication I am put on this communication with the media will not go away.

It seems my life is everything I began thinking when I started this book. I had thought it was a sting, a game, a movie etc. I think it is all those things. I believe I don't have to worry anymore. Justice will prevail and all my dreams are coming true at the very latest Christmas and as early as my birthday.

All the signs point to Frank being the man from my past who is going to be my hero who is working to make my dreams come true and will be knocking on my door. I don't have to seek him out. He will come to me. Twice now they've shown me solid grey with blue!! We never even fooled around way back in the day. He was always super nice though. Now Phillip Phillips' song "Home" makes sense.

Actually they keep showing me grey and black which means that it would be Andrew, which would make far more sense. All these years I felt I had made a mistake in marrying George. My brother keeps saying that George is George. Well maybe to him but not to me. How would he really be certain he was the man I met? However, all the signs have revealed that the real George is not my hero. It is Andrew. I wish the TV would inundate me with the colour so I could have a clear answer.

One thing you must understand is that it has been very difficult to live with a man that I do not recognize as my husband for a good twenty years. Trying to believe everyone that says he is my husband therefore expecting him to act towards me like a husband I expect would. Even going so far as to initiate intimacy with him.

If I haven't made it clear there is more than tan I want eliminated from existence. I also want burgundy gone from everything. Plus black and white combined in a solid piece of clothing. Why? Because tan has been a nightmare for me and burgundy reminds me of the George's couches and my bridesmaid dresses. Black and white is because of George's character.

However, black garments with white trim or vice versa are okay.

If I haven't said it before I told George at the H&R Block in front of our tax lady for the past few years that I believe he is not a Hall and that I believed his parents weren't dead, although I am not certain about his dad because I was not there.

Thursday, March 22, 2018

It feels that the messages I am receiving from the TV and YouTube are settling down but I still am receiving black and coloured lights when asking to verify on the sexual molestation of my brother and daughters by their dads. I have asked for them to verify again by showing me someone wearing a piece of black clothing with red, yellow and orange stripes. THEY HAVE SHOWN ME A JACKET WITH FULL ON **ORANGE.** Now I need verification for my daughters. Again I see red, yellow and orange lights. Okay now I see on America's Got Talent the judge wearing a bright **red dress** and they all have **yellow mugs**. As I watch a wedding celebration there are several red dresses and plenty of yellow singing.

My gut also verifies this now that my mind is awake.

With George there were problems with our sexual life. He had to be intoxicated to have sex with me most of the time and this started with the night of our honeymoon. Why didn't I see the signs?? Why was I not strong enough to leave him earlier I am now 61, he robbed me of half my life? As Collabro sing "Stars" I want to find him and his partners in crime safe behind bars in prison!!

I can't wait to face him in court!! I know that I will have the strength to face them all!!!!!! I believe God won't forsake me this time. I really feel that this time it won't matter what medication they put me on. My media friends will not leave me. It's like Bon Jovi sings, "It's my life and it's now or never" The only thing though up until now I have not done it MY WAY as Frank Sinatra sings!

I'm finding it harder and harder to find music I can listen to which is frustrating me. It's as if all the lyrics from the songs are from George's point of view, wanting another chance. Instead if they must play love songs they could be more from Andrew's point of view. Something to give me hope for the future.

Whatever I have been a part of must have been going on my entire life. They know everything about me. I feel that I have been tracked since birth in order to catch my father and George. According to what I've been taught I was bought and sold for one million dollars. This may be true for my sisters.

Now it seems they are giving me songs of hope from Gary in mind. God I pray it is him!! The signs I read before all point to him showing up at Christmas time. He is coming to whisk me away. I do not know how it will happen, I just know it will.

One thing that does make me feel like dreams are coming true when I see lyrics with the performances and sometimes in different languages, though I need English.

The more I look at the colours and want answers for whom my new lover and husband will be, the more I get confused. If it is Andrew, I need to be inundated with solid Black or Grey or Blue. Grey with pink if it's Derek. I would choose black and green but that won't isolate the person.

Friday, March 23, 2018

Ellen DeGeneres showed a man with a grey suit and pink tie. He had not had a prom just like Derek. Maybe, it is Derek coming for me? I will need more proof. Wow, Ellen just provided me more proof.

With my brother and his wife coming in June during his birthday and his daughters only affirms the fact that they are doppelgangers. Plus he has been incommunicado for over a week now. Things will happen when he comes.

I also feel my sister, Gabe and Carol and Aunt Dorothy are doppelgangers too. My Aunt by voice.

I should've added Connor to my list of possible old boyfriends. It's funny when we had the grade school reunion Mandy had said he was a snob now. How would she know? Perhaps whom I met was a doppelganger too. He was my first heart throb, but I have no idea what colour to assign to him. I have seen grey with pink today to verify it was Derek. Maybe if I see more than one individual person wearing green and black with no other colour in a TV show and a musical video I watch tonight (March 23) which means love, it will be Connor. Perhaps the media will have more than one individual wearing one of these combinations while I continue to watch.

- † *Solid brown with brown eyes for the real George who was not my husband- I was his mark and doppelgangers followed.*
- † *Solid grey no other colour for Andrew –friend-*
- † *Solid white for Leon (boyfriend)*
- † *Grey with blue for Paddy -friend*
- † *Grey with green for Liam(boyfriend)*
- † *Grey with pink if it is Derek–high school crush*
- † *Grey and red if it is Connor-grade school crush*
- † *Grey and purple for Tommy -friend*
- † *Grey with yellow for Darren - friend-*

Somehow watching Ellen today seeing the guy never having his prom really makes me think it is Derek. Rekindling an old relationship with Derek would be exciting. I even joined the powder puff football team to be near him. I had waited and waited for Derek to ask me to our school formal. He finally did One minute after I said yes to another boy. My sister thought I should have made some excuse to the other boy and gone with Derek. But I could never do something like that. I thought I would at least get a dance in with Derek but he never went to the formal. I was crushed!

Rekindling my relationship with Liam would be great but scary because he slapped me in the face so I'm not sure if I would be going from the flame into the fire again. Madame Secretary showed me several army men wearing grey and green. So, I am thinking the media is just trying to confuse me. I just know the people in charge of this journey won't let me down. Happiness and a better life is within reach. I just have to be patient and participate in this journey as best I can until June when my brother and Daisy come or the latest Christmas. Seems I will once again have an uneventful birthday. But patience is often a virtue which I believe I possess. So I just have to tell myself to hang on, be strong, and do my best to make sense out of that which doesn't.

I look forward to the day when I see my real daughters, my sisters and brother and mom again!! Dad I will see in court.

A message just passed the screen on TV saying "I am not the only one for you but you are the only one for me". It makes me feel bad.

I am not dying inside. I feel exhilarated trying to figure the mysteries around me. I haven't felt this energized since I took my Masters online. Feeling connected to people who care. Music back in my life has been so exhilarating!! I just cannot get enough.

One reason why I think it might be Frank is that Skyhawk high school where the girls went have their team named Griffins. It might be Tommy because of the cough medicine named Buckley's.

I have seen all brown with a white shirt. All the music just teaches me that he is consumed with himself. I could care less.

The person from my past that makes more sense is Andrew, Leon, or Liam because I actually went out with them. Leon always treated me with respect and was Catholic as was Andrew. Andrew was nice to me too until he went out with my sister after me. As I said, although, I think of Liam, I just do not want any physical abuse and that would be possible. I have no idea if he is religious.

I had another boyfriend, Tom, but he chased me across his bed in his dorm room at York University when I did not want to put out and I had to race home. It reminds me of when George chased me across the bed when I did not recognize him. I was scared.

For me I have always thought it would be wonderful to have a second chance with a boy from my past.

Two of the judges on the show Britain's Got Talent I am watching are wearing complete white. It is the clearest indication I have seen over every other sign I have seen. Therefore it must be Leon!! There were actually three judges including Simon Cowell, with a solid white shirt. The cross he gave me has been yet another item that has gone missing, but I have the earrings still.

Upon reading this for my final edit (November 13, 2019) I see Whitney Houston dressed in all white singing, "I Didn't Know My Own Strength". As I look at her I still would like to think that the musicians are all helping me, but more importantly the song's lyrics really ring true to the journey I have endured. However, all white could also mean that the whole world is on my side.

Sunday, March 25, 2018

I once again looked at past photographs and I have seen the photographic tricks that have taken place. There are pictures with clothes on me that I know I have never worn. And pictures with George and I with no glasses and then with him wearing blue rimmed ones which I know he never had. In fact I believe he never wore glasses when I met him!

I believe my Action Research for my Masters ended up being ACTION research into my life and giving them access to our computer/s.

I have seen my doppelganger and have recognized George's too. I have been taught that I was sold for 1 million dollars and they were trying to scam me and they put a spin on this activity by setting George up with doppelgangers too.

I believe that the medications I have been on have caused me to be quiet through the years so he would not know anything about my past and led him to believe he would be famous. But these dreams were mine!!

Sometimes I feel like God has caused tech wizards to lead me to each decision I have made and are making, but if that is true, is my idea of an online school my idea? I pray it is. But what should it be called? And will that Catholic Church really change? Will all my other dreams come true?

I have been exposed to many more people dressed in all white that leads me to believe that Leon and the whole world is helping me create my legacy and help me take action against my dad and my husband.

I believe that I have tried to be as good a person as I possibly could be and that it looks like my dreams will come true. It looks like I will see Leon again.

I believe that the stars helping me have been all three of my daughters!!

The song "We are the World" states Jesus made bread out of stone, George's nickname. I believe this song is for George. I have no interest in seeing George become different. He is led to believe in giving to charity because that is what Jessica represented in my colourful life. He believes red means "love" because I got angry at him for giving me "yellow roses" which by roses means friendship. He then gave me red roses.

He neglects Darcy and chose to move further away. Unless he knew she was not our daughter. I do remember him talking to her on the phone at Wade Avenue asking her if she talked with her people.

He took music out of my life. He made me sell my stereo and everything that was mine. I feel blessed with all the music that has entered my life again though it is very difficult to decipher which songs were designed for me and those for George.

I am not interested in George even if he was going through what I was going through. Everything was wrong from day one of our marriage. I am only interested if the person I met so long ago in the Keg is not the man I married. But what I have learned is that Leon is coming into my life again. I want my happy ever after story.

Dr. Jake said I only had to have the nurse bring my medication every night until the end of March but he has planned to see me April 5, 2018. My medication has it hand written that there is only the 4 mg of Rexulti. The other pill looks different than before. I believe it is a sleeping pill or placebo.

Every time I see solid white I think of Leon and the world. But we were just kids. It's probably not realistic to think it would be him. But even in my apartment I am surrounded by grey and white. He was so kind to me. He bought me opal earrings and a beautiful gold cross with a chain. My other gold cross and silver heart from Jessica went missing.

But YouTube has recommended a video to watch with Barbara Streisand and Barry Gibb (a strange combo) entitled 'What Kind of Fool" and they are dressed in white. The lyrics from my iPhone appear to be as if George were singing. Why would they recommend that for me?? When they sang it was different. I have moved on, George is the one who is "sorry" now.

One day I will see my real daughters and brother and sisters again in person, as well as every person who has apparently died. George will have karma happen to him.

My head and heart wants Andrew. I would have liked to have spent more time with him. I was so torn when I left him behind. When we reconnected he was a separated Catholic high school teacher who was not able to remarry and continue teaching due to the rules of the Catholic Church. I also would love it to be Derek.

Wow! I chose a comforter that Daisy agreed was great. It is grey and purple with a white background which indicates Tommy. Our neighbour at Port Angeles where the cabin is, is named Tommy. However I never dated Tommy or Frank. Our neighbour was just a mental connection to my past.

As the title of the book "Second Chance" by James Patterson that Jess bought me with her own money, I will have a second chance at a happy life. She never had her own money for we never gave an allowance. Plus she signed it "from" not "love". But she did sign it with her infinity phrase which touched me. I have kept this book.

I've been looking at pictures on my computer that those in control of this computer have led me to see. There are pictures of everyone, even of people I did not take and they are close ups. However, there is no picture of my sister, Louise.

I'm watching Celine Dion and her dancers. She's wearing solid white and each of her dancers are wearing white with one of my colours. It must mean Leon and the world will bring my dreams to fruition.

Darren was yet another boyfriend from high school who broke up with me because I would not put out. I had invited him to dinner and Daisy said he was a keeper. Unfortunately we did not see eye to eye. He must not have cared for me if that was all he was interested in. He would always meet me in the park though when I would call and try to change his mind. If I assigned him a colour it would be Grey with yellow.

I can only hope that my dream of someone special comes true.

I'm so confused. Although they show me so much white it is hard to understand. How could it be Leon? If not Leon than the rest of the world is helping me.

Maybe it is someone completely new that will enter my life when this mountain has been climbed. Someone that will come to me on purpose, not by chance.

I can't help but continue to think about Andrew, but I know nothing about him. But faith in what is happening to me will bring him back in my life. He will fly here and take me home to Tinsel Town where all our dreams will come true.

I could care less if George has been going through the same life I have. I made a mistake in marrying him and even if he lost me after that month we spent together. It was wrong too. I am almost free. Come June this divorce will be official!!

I am so looking forward to seeing him go to court and face all of us!!! Andrew or Derek will be there to give me support.

Monday, March 26, 2018

Today I had my music lessons. I told my guitar teacher today that he was very good at what he does. My singing teacher is also very good. I am making progress with both.

On my way home the coolest thing happened. Instead of just listening to my downloaded music I was able to listen to YouTube through my car radio!! Fantastic!! This opens up a whole new world for me!! It just doesn't let me turn my cellphone off and put it back in my purse so I don't forget it like the downloaded music will.

Robbie Williams is wearing complete black tonight so my thinking about the dead people alive must be correct including Lady Diana. Unfortunately, I can't hear his song. I really like Gary Barlow and Robbie Williams, especially their group, Take That. Often they are yelling at George for his behaviour or making fun of him. Tonight they are angry at him.

Tuesday, March 27, 2018

Trying to do what's right in this mixed up world of mine, I tried signing in to pay my Teacher dues for this year so that I maintain my teacher status but I was unable to. Seems someone has changed my log on.

Frankly I don't believe in having to pay dues to maintain our status as teachers or any other profession that might be expected to do the same.

Perhaps it will be taken out of my hands. I believe the powers that be are controlling this and protecting me.

Just like the courts will know if the same people are divorcing, they let the Supreme Court know!

Tuesday, March 27, 2018

Weeding through the music on my devices is getting harder and harder. On my iPad it was as if someone else was saving songs that I hadn't which confirms that George or my doppelganger is using my name to save music too.

I am tired of it all. Most of the songs seem like they are from George trying to get me to lie about my feelings and emotions, but I cannot. If it means I lose all my dreams and my trust in the unknown is not to be, so be it. It would be worse for me to be in my marriage again. But if my gut serves me right then my time IS coming and I do get a chance at a happier life.

There are times when I do not think I am even a Jackson and maybe that was made up too. The way I feel, I no longer want my father's name. I will take on the name of my new husband and if the girls want he will adopt them too and it will be done automatically, no lengthy paperwork!!!

I keep seeing an overwhelming amount of solid white!! So it must be Leon coming for me. No other sign is as great as solid white which stands for Leon and the world helping me with my legacy. I am not interested in ruling the world. It must seem that way when my wish for a worldwide online school and for the Catholic Church to change which involves millions of people.

The song "Memories' by Barbara Streisand suggests that I may not have had a choice in the choices I made and I think this is right. I was under the care of the medical profession and given medication to control my impulses and capacity to think and act for myself. This only accounts for the time since 2005 and it feels like this has been going on since my birth or at least grade school.

I fear this divorce is not real. I sent my lawyer an email and she sent an automated out of the office message until April 3, 2018 and she had a lower case "I" instead of a capital. Errors like that have no place coming from a lawyer.

I have just read my creations and inventions and realize that the scanners in grocery stores are created around here now. As well as automated soap dispensers. They haven't started with the hand sanitizers though but I really think they should. Are these my inventions? I also think I am responsible for all the variety of colours for everything from soap to paper to clothing and more. However, the grocery store line ups for the self-serve scanners at Superstore are too long so I have thought that scanners throughout the aisles could be implemented where people scan as they shop.

The following is a song I wrote for George and now I feel that the song is coming true. Now that my world has spun and I am making something of myself he needs me. But too much time has passed. He may need me in some way right now but I am not willing to spend any more wasted time on trying to mend the great divide between us. He treated me like no person should be treated.

Even if he was instructed or made the choice of not being able to say "I love you" to me, it does not matter. He had no idea of how to express love in other ways. I often felt he was not attracted to me and told him so.

Wednesday, March 28, 2018

As I look back on old photographs. I realize I had taken most of them for granted. Either no one had a camera at the time to take the picture or there was no one extra at the time able to take the photo. The photos look more like for a movie. Most of the individuals I believe to be doppelgangers.

The pictures of my parents together smiling just are not real. They were not a happy couple but they put on a good front. This is but one of many examples. Another was the 40th anniversary party I hosted for my parents, my mother did not take individual photos of those I invited nor did she give them to me. It's like she's naming people who are part of a movie. Probably my future movie.

This song was written and performed for George on our 18th Anniversary when I was so unhappy. I tried my best to express what I needed in so many ways. I think the name of this song is the best part. Maybe one day my songs will be recorded.

I had always wondered who had written the last verse to this song when I was mentally able to revisit it, now I know. If I am wrong, then I know positively that his spirit guided the words. I dedicate this last verse to the new love of my life, Gary Barlow!!!!!

Soul's Design

CHORUS

```
   G              Em    Am
There's a song down deep in my heart
   G                  Am
Wreaking havoc with my mind
   G                  Am
Telling me girl you better take your time
                   G
And listen to your soul's design
```

Verse:
```
   C                 D
When I slow down to a trickle
       G        Em
And I listen to that song
   C
There's one thing that always seems to come
   D     G                    Em C G
Along and that's our love seems very wrong
```

```
   C              D
```
Verse:
Passion flared on weekend nights
```
       G            Em
Needs to lend itself to the sun
```

```
C                    D
For I've awakened to a brand new light
       G            Em
and fear you want to run
```

(CHORUS)

MY COLOUR-CODED LIFE

```
Verse:    C                D
So I've stopped down by the ocean side
          G           Em
Freezing hormones deep inside
   C                 D
Waiting for that light in your eye
     G             Em
To show itself in the daytime sun
          C           D
Shouting out "dream girl #1"
       G                Em
You make me strong, you make me long
       C              D
For the fire that burns within you girl
        G            Em
Stokes my fire. I need you too.
         C              D
So listen to your souls design
         G             Em
Let it burn and let it shine
C                              D
For I am with you till the end of time
G                  Em
We're together you and I
```

(CHORUS)

I also wrote a song for my niece Carol years ago. It was the first time I wrote about colours interesting enough. I will copy it and insert it into this book for her. I have written several songs. One back in Teacher's College that one of my professors wanted to keep after I submitted it for an assignment. I wouldn't let him have it because I was afraid I would not get credit for its creation. It was entitled "Teacher Teacher."

This was written for my niece in 1976. It was my graduating year from high school and the year she was born. Her parents had a speedy wedding because my sister became pregnant. There was talk of ending her pregnancy. It touched me. I do, though, believe in choice after the tragedy I went through.

Carol

Dm　　　　　　G　　Em　　　　　　C
White is the colour of winter in the cold
Dm　　　　　　G　　C　　　　　　Em
Green is the colour of spring in the warm
Dm　G　　　Em　　C　　Dm　　G　　　Em　　C
Now all you unborn babes, start to laugh, start to play
Dm　G　　　Em　　　　　　C
No colour can match the one of yours
Dm　G　　　C　　　Em
No colour is as beautiful as yours
Dm　　　　　　G　　Em　　　C
Don't you cry, don't you fret
Dm　　　　　　G　　　　Em　　　　　　　　C
You're my babe and you're worth the bet
Dm　　　　　　G　　　　Em　　　　　C
They won't hurt you, they won't get near
Dm　　　　　　G　　　　Em　　　　　C
You're too precious, you're too dear
Dm　G Em　　C
Oh babe don't you cry
Dm　　　　　　　G　　　　Em　　C
You're going to make it to the sky
Dm　　　　　G　　　　Em　　　C
Make that mountain, meet that top.

Thursday, March 29, 2018

Let me review some facts and what messages I am being taught:

1. I drove home today from Carftsman Collision and thought back to living with George in the city we met. We had Carol stay overnight and we played "Pass the Coke – a can of coke" where each took a turn taking a drink. Ever since I have been married to George he has never drank pop, so why did he have some? He says he doesn't like it. This leads me to believe that perhaps his identity was stolen and I did not marry him. This would explain the song that says "I should have followed you home"
2. I was sold for 1 million dollars from my dad to my husband.
3. However using my head when I asked the media to show me solid brown to reveal the real George whom I thought I didn't marry, they did not, instead they showed me solid grey for Andrew. I want to believe in Andrew.
4. The BCAA magazine which I received, which is the first we have ever received had an ad about the true grey having a base of brown. I disagree. Black and white makes grey!! And I like it with more black!!
5. I have asked for proof again about :
    † Being sold for 1 million dollars by asking for a specific colour to be shown and it was confirmed
    † My brother and daughters being sexually abused by their dad and it was confirmed

While watching Lionel Richie he showed me that it is Leon who is coming for me!! I am ecstatic. I have no idea what happened to us. He always treated me with respect and for not really being involved he lavished me with jewelry. He gave me opal earrings which I still have and a cross on a chain but the cross is gone now. Somehow, I think if I had said it was missing out loud it would have reappeared, just like my spider in the box.

Imagine George buying me a hair pin from Kendra that was a massive spider!! It ends up he was the poisonous spider in my life.

It seems I have so much to be thankful for now, for as I use my phone it has come to life with Musician names and actors and so much more. It shows me videos of these artists but not performance videos. Maybe they will come in time.

I feel that action is going on regarding George. I thought that as I reached out to express myself over and over again that there was no one listening or caring, but I see now that everyone was listening and caring and that Jessica and Darcy truly love me and are my heroes.

> † *Monday, April 2, 2018 -Today watching Bryan Inc. on HGTV Bryan was wearing a brown winter coat. Today I was thinking about my gut and my gut tells me that George's identity was stolen. My gut tells me the picture Paula showed me of my husband when he was younger was the real George that no one in my family ever met. The George I married is the one with the black and white character. I was attracted to the guy I met in the hospital and the guy in the Paula's picture, not the men whom I married, so I am still seeking a divorce. This proves to always trust your gut!!*
>
> † *I even forget if we introduced ourselves and if his name really was George. I may not have known what his last name was. I gave him mine on the napkin but he would've had no reason to share his.*
>
> † *So if this is true then maybe I can trust my dad again. Because I had said if I saw brown that is what it would show. However, he was controlling financially with my mom and could afford things that don't make sense on his income. I know he received money from my grandparents to fix the house. However, he got the most advanced there was possible. I haven't seen since. They even had a built in stereo system which was never used. This does not explain how he was able to afford to fly everywhere. Mmmm I am back to thinking he was in cahoots with my husband and it was he that sold me for 1 million dollars.*

> *My gut tells me my dad was dishonest. Does being schizoaffective not allow you to trust your gut?*
> † *Although I asked my brother today why there was a punch by his bed and he said because he banged it with his elbow and it was only plaster. I do not believe him because I tried punching that wall and I could not. It would have taken tremendous force and I was in first year university at the time. However, it may have been a weaker spot in the wall.*

Yesterday, Easter, the girls agreed to celebrate with me and chose to eat at Blue Angel Café near where Darcy lives. I had to figure out how to get there. I made it though and Darcy showed me how to get Spotify and my GPS to work.

The dinner went well but it was confirmed that they were not aware of things that happened in their lifetime. Darcy seemed unaware that she had gone with Jessica to see Hilary Duff. I had expressed that I was worried and should have gone in with them because it was hard to find them afterward. Darcy said they had the family cell phone. We never had one. Only George had one. Jessica was not aware that she had a sister that passed away. Just served to prove that they are doppelgangers, but I care for them nonetheless. They are my heroes as well as my real daughters!!!

I am still looking forward to seeing George eat his thoughts about me I want to see him in court!! And by my side will be the person I met whom I don't even remember his name way back in the Keg. I cannot even remember the year.

So this is a message to him while tears well up.

> *Soon I feel we will see each other and that attraction I felt for you that one night will be there again!! For I have no attraction to the man I have lived with for over 30 years. I am so sorry to have taken so long to trust my gut. I knew something was wrong. As I understand it the powers that be have used this time to put together my dream of having an online school put together, for they now have an online dictionary and soon it will show each word in different languages too and many more developments! While I have been medicated they have been busy on my dreams which are also yours, I hope! They are*

also doing something miraculous with all the music of which I am addicted. They are also listing all movies and TV series, as well as actors on my phone. It really is quite remarkable. Ours will be the story of a lifetime. Perhaps we can be the poster couple for The Keg!

I no longer want to live in Duncan, if you do not mind. I would prefer to have a house where I used to live in Ontario or maybe somewhere else, and a beautiful log home on a beautiful lake. I would also like a place on a warm blue ocean.

Will you please adopt my girls? We want no attachment to the nightmare we have lived with. As well, I would like to make sure that the girls who have been acting as my daughters are taken care of and all their dreams realized, that includes, Cassie, her twin and Brian and his twin or their doppelgangers. Plus I would like all the friends I have made here that have helped me to be taken care of.

May we please visit Montreal so my girls may meet my side of the family? We have so much to learn about each other. I do not know anything about you. I just remember watching you as you walked away. Unfortunately we cannot have that full dozen children I spoke about.

I have been living for so long with a man, but have always felt so all alone. I also think this marriage was not legal. You have to know that my experience with sex has affected me and that will be a huge barrier to overcome!!!!

Everyone on the TV and the musicians seem to be amused. Only the performer for "You Ain't Seen Nothing Yet", Bachman and Turner seems to portray some of the emotion I am feeling.

His eyes were not yours.

I do not know why the powers that be led me away from my gut feeling but how can you blame me. I have felt this about you for so long and told it was all in my head. Now we will be together soon and from what I hear it will be Christmas. It feels yet like an eternity. Nine more months!! But if my gut is wrong, which I do not think it is, and you are one in the same (either the man I stayed with for a month or the man I married) then I want nothing to do with you.

Wednesday, April 4, 2018

Yesterday was my 61st birthday and Darcy was nice enough to ask if I had dinner plans. Since I did not I suggested we go to the Keg in Whittle Head. One I had never gone to with George. Her boyfriend Royce bought me a very touching card that made me cry, as well as a $50 gift card to The Keg!! Plus he gave me some type of scratch cards. It was nice to celebrate with someone. If she had not asked I would not have gone out. I am very tired of arranging my own celebrations!!

I have to admit that my mind has drifted to Connor today. Back in 1999-2000 when dad paid for all of us to be together and celebrate the new millennium we went to church for the first time all together at Christmas. We were in the front row.

A few rows behind and on the opposite side of the church sat Connor with his family. I so much wanted to connect with him at the time. My heart did flip flops! I just saw him and the crowd he was with. I didn't focus on exactly who was with him. I only saw him, so I did not see if he was married.

Again when I spoke with him at my grade school's reunion I didn't want to leave but his wife and kids were there. She came up and made herself known. I would have done the same thing.

Somehow I am thinking that maybe the reason why there have been so many pool tables everywhere I go is to make the connection of when Connor in our youth took advantage of me on his family's pool table after getting me plastered on screwdrivers, while Tucker Morrison and another looked on. Who wouldn't want to get together with their first "love".

I was looking to see obituaries for my family online and they were there but they made no sense. And George knew nothing about his dad. He made him sound like an irresponsible drunk, but he was a well-respected individual with many accomplishments. But then maybe George pegged him correctly for he showed some of the traits he described his dad had. I only met him a couple of times. I will never know.

As far as Sandra is concerned they said that the celebration would take place at Tammy's following but there was no one but family there. She had many friends and not one was around. Plus the Power Point Kendra made showed the weddings of Paula and George but not Tammy. I thought this was odd. Plus why was I invited to the arrangements for her funeral when Tammy was not there. I felt how her corpse was taken to the gravesite was disrespectful. She was taken in the back of George's pick up, claiming she would finally get her ride in his truck. This played on my brain because she often went for rides with him in his truck. He even brought a step stool for her. I asked Donald if he would take the girls and I to the gravesite. He did.

Uncle Ronald: When I tried to look up my dad's, it led me to my mother. In one posting they had a picture of the portrait that had been done of her, but the write up had a mistake too. It led me to my Uncle's (Aunt Dorothy's husband) but it did not have his complete name and the picture did not look like him. He helped me love guitar. I have a fond memory of him making organ pipes out of Christmas paper tubes.

My **Uncle Jacob** made sure that I got my lobster at dinner when my dad denied it to me at a dinner at Ruby Foo's

My **Aunt Laura** is whom I wrote to about all my boy issues and she always wrote back. I sure wish she could advise me now. .

Uncle Lester I rarely saw. I do not remember seeing him at Christmas but he would come and vacation with us. He changed every one of our neighbours idea of what a priest was like.

I do not believe any of these special people in my life are dead. I do not know when, but I will see them again.

I am probably repeating myself, but I will see Sandra and Bucky too. I do hope George has to face them in court as well.

I am just hoping the media and YouTube will show me the colours for who is trying to reach me through these songs I keep hearing.

All brown stands for the man I met in The Keg that one night, but the songs I hear from Mike Bolton makes it sound like you are the man I married…so I will think of Connor.

To have somebody who cares about me where we can enjoy each other without him having to be drunk to do so would be a dream. I have grown to hate travelling because it meant I would have to have unpleasant sex. I also hated every family celebration for the same reason.

Tonight listening to Philip Phillips perform "Home", he was actually expressing anger which made me feel better. It made me believe in his song. He makes me realize that I don't have to worry about figuring it all out. The powers that be have it all under control. I will just try to find music for me and do my best to interpret it all in my favour. Today I asked Linda, Darcy's friend to help me plan a surprise birthday party for Darcy who will be turning thirty, but she is due then, so she suggested I contact Royce. Darcy may not be my daughter and Linda may not be the student I taught but they are the only representation I have. Who knows maybe Darcy is older? Anyhow, I contacted Royce and he is going to take care of it and get back to me. Yippee!

I wonder if the nearby pub I used to frequent with Elizabeth a lot still exists. I also wonder if the local hang out still exists near my old high school.

So as I watch Sting who is Gordon Matthew Thomas Sumner tonight, he and everyone he introduces is wearing solid black. This may mean that Connor may once again be in my life forever. How often does someone end up with their first twinkle in their eye? Even Lionel Richie is wearing all black.

Today I see Dr. Jake and later Julia. I am looking forward to it. Julia, if I haven't said so is my current community support worker. I hope she isn't so focussed in spending only an hour. I can tell when she has had enough. I wish there was not a time limit when a client is meeting someone to speak with. She is very nice though and has been very helpful. However, they have many clients.

My goal is to be pill free and for someone to say, you are cured!!! Lately I feel I was never schizoaffective. I think it was a made up name to cause enough data to be collected about George and my dad. I imagine real efforts to catch criminal could take decades.

Thursday, April 5, 2018

This morning while watching David Foster and Java Jazz my mind drifts to James, in high school whom I have no colour for. I only have a saxophone for him. He and I used to have great fun dancing. We even entered a dance contest. But so many of the boys of my past I have no idea why we stopped seeing each other.

On David's show Eric Benet is wearing Purple and Grey which stands for Tommy singing 'I swear". Tommy and I only petted. I remember Andrew and I petting at the skating rink, so so many years ago. I came out of the clubhouse where Elizabeth was waiting for me and she made fun that my jacket was buttoned up incorrectly.

They have not shown me red and grey which also represents my high school, so maybe it is more likely Tommy. The suit Eric is wearing is very nice, a beautiful shade of purple with grey lapels. And if it is Tommy he can wear those colours at our wedding.

The signs for Tommy have been The Griffins for some team at Skyhawk High School where the girls went, our neighbour at the cabin, Tommy and the Tony Awards.

Mitch Bolton's song with the lyrics, "you don't know me and watched you walk away with some lucky guy" reminds me of Connor watching me leave the church. But his lyrics, "You don't know me", in the same song which is sung by Michael Bublé could mean Connor, any of my old boyfriends or someone I really have never met. Every time I think I have figured out who is singing me love songs other than George, I am confused

Friday, April 6, 2018

I am excited!! I have reached out to an event planner to host a 30th birthday party for Darcy. She turns 30 on Friday, May 25, 2018. It has been 27 years since we moved here and she has never (maybe one) had a party with George's family so I think it is about time. I want to have music so I am hoping at the very least to have a DJ.

Darcy has never complained or asked why she never celebrated with the family but over time it began to bother me. So since George does not take the initiative, I will.

Today as I put the date, my computer would not do it automatically for me. Sometimes it has a mind of its own.

Her boyfriend Royce was suggesting Olive Garden, but I want a bigger party and music. He is helping with her friend list though.

I want to invite some family friends as well.

I remember a few of her friends like Jesse and Calinda. She has so many friends…I just do not know them all!!

I would like to have all our relatives too! Not so sure about Mandy though because she has not been very nice to Darcy. It is one thing to treat me badly but my daughter that is something else.

> † *So now I have it clear while watching YouTube. Joe who was wearing brown and George Michael, sang "Don't Let the Sun Go Down on Me". I now understand that Brown is bad. So, that means that it will be someone from my past or someone I have never met that knows me better than I know myself that will come and be the man of my dreams!!*

Tonight my computer lost connection to the internet but now it is on my own private network. I am not sure if it was like that before or not. Why it asked me to connect automatically is beyond me because I thought my computer already did that.

Although, I feel my every word written and spoken and thought is being read, I am determined not to let that stop me from doing what I want.

Dear God, as time passes my need for vindication grows. I do not believe in confession. I do not believe all sins are absolved or there would be no hell. Frankly, I do not ever remember going to confession growing up.

I need to know what my daughters' confirmation names are. Mine is Catherine. I didn't study to choose it, I just picked the name of a friend whom I liked.

Today while on the elevator a family entered with a brindle boxer whose name was Lacy. She brought me to tears. Maybe with a name like that it is a sign that it is Leon who will re-enter my life.

So many boys who were so nice.

I have feelings that I have not felt in a very long time. I believe that Gary Barlow is the man that will sweep me off my feet!! I listened to one of his songs and it implied that he was the man that knows me better than I know myself, just like what I wrote.

I know that his songs have been love songs to me. My stomach is doing flip flops!!

What a wonderful world it would be to be surrounded by his music. Maybe I will have love forever, just like a forever home for my girls and me!! Let my homes be filled with music!! Please do not, God, let this be misread.

Darn this medication does not allow me to feel the complete emotions I should feel, therefore, my words are not as expressive as they should be!!

Gary seems to know me better than I know myself. There is nothing for him to learn yet there is such a mountain for me.

I know nothing about the act of love. I have resented it for so long and I find it messy and unpleasant. So Gary, I yearn more for affection! Sweep me off my feet!

What a wonderful twist of fate that my story will end with the best romance a girl could hope for.

I'm falling hard for you, but I must also use logic, I knew little of George and look where it got me. Please forgive me if I'm scared. I so do not want to be naïve this time around.

So if you hear me or read this, my virtual knight in shining armour/amour, please somehow let me know how you feel and please, if the message is in a song let you sing it.

When will you make this into something real? Quando? Quando?

Sunday, April 8, 2018

I have a rush all over my body when I think of you now. I am moving from focussing on the past to dreaming about the future.

Mariah Carey's song "Hero" was one of the songs I clung to, to help me out of the quagmire I was in. Gary is now my Hero going forward!! I do believe this!!

Once I was able to listen to music again, it has been my saving grace. It was my art therapy.

I have hired an event planner to arrange a bash for both my girls on Darcy's birthday. I plan to make it big!

† *All the Hall clan, including George*
† *My family and extended family*

- † Montreal
- † Tinsel Town
- † Alberta
- † Ottawa
- † New York
- † I want both girls grade school friends and the parents that wish to come and their teachers
- † I want both girls high school friends and parents and teachers
- † Family friends –
- † Darcy's friends
- † Cassie and all her friends
- † Brian and his friends
- † All my friends from high school
- † Gary Barlow

Wednesday, April 11, 2018

Today there was an emergency meeting for the building and at the meeting I found my voice. I am a part of taking action against the developer. In fact I would say I was quite the instigator!

It seems in this journey of mine while watching Gary and his friends perform that I must flip my way of thinking. They had asked what kind of revenge I wanted toward George and I said whatever kind of hell would be worse. So they have created all sorts of videos to drive George bonkers, so that he will have to walk a mile in my shoes. However for him, there will be no happy ending. There will be no handsome prince to rescue him.

Yes, I also feel like Snow White who was put to sleep by her wicked husband and it was the kiss of her prince charming that brought life back into her body!!

In the videos Gary and Robbie are trying to make George fall for them. However, I had no idea that George would even watch music videos. I guess he is now interested in music.

This slant toward George that I am watching is yet another mountain I must climb and figure out. The fact is, Gary knows George as well as he knows me, and knows what will play on his head.

To hear the same songs I interpreted for me as being written for George is a hard pill to swallow.

However, all this being said, I am much stronger now and have courage that I can weather this storm too as long as Gary continues to talk to me, only for me!!

In my song I had said that I was freezing hormones, well I think they were frozen well before that because I have never felt this way even as a teenager. So as much as I think George was cold as Ice toward me. I was frigid, but I tried to ignore how I felt and build a relationship that I believed was wrong. I tried to entice him in every way I knew how even though I had absolutely no sexual feelings toward him!

I told Liz, how I felt about Gary and she is afraid I will be disappointed and hurt. I believe I will not!

Part of my sweet revenge would be George recognizing Gary but at the girls' party, Gary is with me!!!

It gets harder and harder to believe Gary is real when he is not tangible!! I do not want to make a fool of myself.

I battle between believing it is all real and thinking Megan you better be wary. You may not be able to trust everything you see. I worry I may not be interpreting the messages properly. I do get insecure at times.

Today I met with the event planner and I have decided to blow the wad. So I will be approaching their schools and hopefully getting contact information. Please pray it works. The kids are older now…it has been a long time…

MY COLOUR-CODED LIFE

Tuesday, April 10, 2018

Today I was thinking of what I could name the Online School I dream of and this is what I came up with. Tell me what you think Gary? This is a name I admire.

M-Make
I-Internet
C-Classes   *JK-Doctorate starting at age 4!!*
H-Help   *Access for the entire world in all different*
È-Express   *languages covering all disciplines.*
L-Love
For
E-Education

Friday, April 13, 2018

I am deflated. I contacted all my girls' schools and not one has records dating that far back. And if there were emojis on this computer which I think they should have on all computers, it would be one showing a sad face!!

Perhaps there is reason I am being blocked. There may be someone already planning this and it is out of my hands and everyone I care about will be there and perhaps we give thanks to a new life!! The best Thanksgiving party ever!! And my new boyfriend, Gary, will be there to give me my first kiss (heart)

So before I was having to pick out phrases which led to different singers and musicians. Now I am having to listen to some songs that lead to misleading musicians, singers and songwriters to George. I think the idea is for him to get as overwhelmed as I was and to end up in the hospital... from there...Court!!

I had asked Jessica if she wanted to get together with me for coffee, lunch or dinner after I tried to pin Darcy down for a meal. I wanted to make up to Darcy for missing out meeting her for lunch at her school.

Hopefully we will be getting together Sunday. Jessica got back to me saying she and Darcy would arrange something. She also said she would be at my meeting with Dr. Jake on Tuesday to support me. She even knew when it was, which does not surprise me. I am rather curious as to how it will go now.

Tuesday, April 10, 2018

As time passes I wonder if my thoughts are my own. I worry that my creative mind has not been my own. It will be crushing to know that I may not be as inventive as I thought. My sister Mandy says I am ahead of my time, am I? Perhaps I have lived in a bubble and I have not seen how truly advanced life is. I pray I have been inventive and these ideas are mine!

I was frustrated the other day with Word Art and the highlighting because they did not offer me the multicolour choice! They have never had one for highlighting but I think they should.

Watching HGTV disposing of toilets reminds me that toilets are more haunting to me for more reasons than my distrust of George.

Now I will share what cuts to the core and crushes me every time I wake up. When I was first pregnant in North Dakota I had to go to have an ultrasound and I had to go by myself. While there, they made me wait in the office after they took it. I had to wait so long I felt that things were not good. They came out and told me that I had to go somewhere else for another one to be sure of what they found. Again, though scared, I had to go by myself. They told me our baby had a brain disorder of which I forget the name and that if I gave birth she would suffer. There are no words to express how I felt. I came home and told George and one of George's bosses.

His office and neighbours had thrown me a baby shower, way too soon.

I wanted to go back home and have the support of my family, even though George had been transferred to Knox Valley.

I had to find someone to give me a genetic termination before sixteen weeks. I adored my family doctor Sam Merston, but I was ashamed, so did not reach out to him at that time.

MY COLOUR-CODED LIFE

When I was in the hospital I had an amniocentesis. George slept in the room with me. I was so drugged I could barely stand, yet I had to walk myself to the bathroom and place the hat on the toilet so the baby would be delivered in that. George never helped me to the washroom. I forgot to place the hat the last time and my baby was born in the toilet.

The nurse was furious with me. She rescued my baby from the toilet and placed her on the counter. Yes, she was a girl. There is definitely a human being at that time of life.

I had asked George if he wanted to see her, but he said, no. No support, no love, no goodbye from her dad! I can understand his not wanting to.

After we got home, George went back to work and I had to grieve on my own. All I remember of the support was my dad hugging me and sitting on the bed beside me while I cried saying that I wanted my baby back! Yet, I know I did the right thing.

I had to use Kotex napkins at the time and for convenience I kept them in the bathroom, which was pink, but my sister, Mandy, yelled at me and said I should not leave them there. She never offered any support!

I had to grieve somehow, so I wrote the hospital, and expressed how hurt I was with how the nurse had treated me.

Also, years later there was an opportunity for people to write poetry and have it published in a book so I did. I tried to share it with a colleague Brenda, but she was too busy. Again, crushed.

I had made a deal with God that although I had wanted a dozen children, after several miscarriages afterwards, I would be grateful for two healthy children and that is just what I got!!

Here is My Poem I wrote for my daughters and got published in the National Library of Poetry:

Daughter of the Night

*So many stars within the sky
Twinkling right before my eye.
To dream, to touch, to hope about
To listen to my child shout,
and answer all my thoughts out loud.*

*Light my life, my little star
The twinkle's in my child's eye
A star? A star? Up above?
A star? A star? I can hug?
Twinkle, daughters of the day,
guiding gently our precious way.
I thank the gifts I have out loud
and thank the path you've paved for us
My sweet, sweet daughter of the night.*

I had only shared with Darcy about her older sister much later in life, when she was pregnant. She thought that I was going to name the unborn baby Cassie, so she named her daughter that. Cassie was going to be Darcy's name but my sister, Mandy, said that she was going to use that name. The truth was MY baby never had a name.

I have never told Jessica. I brought it up for the first time with her when she, Darcy and I had dinner the last time at our favourite Japanese restaurant. She said it must have been difficult, she may never know just how hard it was.

But even when I told Darcy, I never told her the crushing parts.

When I share my life with Gary, we will find a colourful name for her. And frame my poem!!

They have made a thumbs up emoji why not one to represent infinity? These are the symbols I created for my daughter's 25th. I wanted their necklaces to be individualized. I want to use these symbols interchangeably. Why can't I? I am so glad the symbol I struggled with for Darcy has come alive to rate movies and music videos on You Tube I am presented with!!! Is it like this for the world? If not it should be!! They both need to shine! You will not have me choose one over the other. Make the infinite emoji please.

Tuesday, April 10, 2018

Well Gary hurt me today. While watching the videos I watched one where he surprised a woman in a wedding dress at her wedding and nearly held her face in his hands. This was too real for me and I in no way felt like I was wearing that dress. He knows me. He should have known I would feel hurt and jealous.

In another video he had a girl named Megan at the piano to which he sang to. That was fine, but then he had her come around to him and she kissed him.

I simply do not need to be hurt anymore. I have gone through enough. If he didn't mean it he will have to find another way to reach me for as he says "he never gives up!"

Today, I had lunch with Darcy and Royce and unloaded on them much of which I had only written about and shared with the psychiatrist. However, this I have not shared with the psychiatrist or written down. I only told Darcy.

While I was pregnant with Darcy while living in Brampton, George's sister Tammy and her husband Donald came out to visit. While at work Tammy got busy baking cookies and I found her scraping paint *off* the window with a razor blade that had been all taped up on the other side so it was easy to hold. She had found it in George's tool box. He never used it in front of me, so I think he used it for drugs.

I had bought him an electric razor and instead of replacing it when needed he used a razor with replaceable blades. I would like to see the world rid of razor blades!!!!

Also, while they were visiting I went into false labour and the hospital was an hour away. For some reason George would not come home so Donald unfamiliar with the extensive highways in Tinsel Town had to take me to the hospital.

I am certain that Gary really does love me. He will cherish my soul and mesh it with his own after it was discarded by my husband.

I went out with my girlfriend Penny to dinner and to Riverdance. While at dinner my eyes flew to the grilled cheese, it stated that it had jalapeno jack cheese with 4 exclamation marks. I had recently thought how I like this cheese and I tend to write texts with Exclamation marks. It was the only thing on the menu with this marking. I knew it was meant for me.

While watching Riverdance the lead dancers were wearing green and black representing Gary and I.

Tuesday, April 17, 2018

Here is proof George does not make sense to me. He fell off a ladder and as a result a few of his spinal disc fused which caused his right arm to be permanently bent so he could not straighten it above his arm. This happened while living at Saber Road. When we moved to Gage Lane and afterward his arm was fine. Mmmmm?

He fell while washing the second story windows. It was Darcy that called 911. However, the trajectory of his supposed fall never made sense to me. He barely had a scratch. Jess put a mitten under his head. They were both recognized by the city as heroes.

When living at Gage Lane I found things that disturbed me. So when Carol was visiting I asked Darcy, Jessica, and Carol to look at the crawlspace with me. I showed them what bothered me. I had found a large pile of dirt in the far end of the crawlspace, with no way for it to have naturally gotten there. Also he had set up completely one of the spare girls' beds in the crawlspace. I thought that odd. In addition I found three bats, one red one that was teeny for a toddler, a black plastic one and a yellow spongy one with a black handle. The girls had not been taught to play baseball at that age.

I always felt he had another family because of this and because when we played bowling or anything it was like he did it all the time. He would always win. Also, I would notice that half of everything like dishes and things would go missing. The very first thing that went missing was Darcy's black hoody that said princess on the front in red letters. My parents gave us a set of twelve piece silver set of cutlery, I'm certain. Yet four of the knives went missing and some of the other pieces too.

When living at Saber Road when I began to distrust my husband I checked out his bathroom and found a lot of smudgy brown stuff around the bolt of the toilet. Also, some white powder in his drawer with an extra-long toothpick. I've never seen one that long. Stupidly I tasted it. I wouldn't have known what it was anyway.

When I brought the pills, from his truck to Dr. Moran which I believe was hash and told him what I found in the bathroom, he said I needed to tell George. So, I did. I was high and all George said was not to worry that he had talked people down before. Also, he was more concerned with the type of cleaner I used on it. I tried everything. He seemed that he wanted to know so that he could still use it. I also found this stuff smudged to the top of a shelf in the laundry cupboard. I don't remember what he did when we got home.

When I was in grade school, my grade school friend Tucker asked me and a few other friends to have our picture taken for an organization called CODA. Which is an organization against drugs!! We did, Connor, George, Frank, Alison and myself.

Even back then I was against drug abuse!!

Living on Saber Road I would have several yeast infections. Perhaps twice a month, but once we left that house they stopped.

Also, I began to get terrible migraines after I had Darcy. They only stopped once I was diagnosed and under major health care for my mental health!!! I swear I was being drugged. I use to think it was in the coffee because he always made it.

When the Olympics were on here in Vancouver in 2010, George did not want to see anything and I wanted to see everything. I was glued to the TV. Anyhow at that time Jessica was very distant to me, no birthday wishes, no happy mother's day no conversation….so I missed her. Paula asked George if we would like to see the opening ceremony for those that are disabled.

He asked me and I jumped at the chance to see something. While there everything turned Red and I started to cry because you see red (caring) was my colour for Jessica. I wrote to her at University which I often did and told her I saw her everywhere.

Now I see Darcy everywhere here where I live. In my world she is yellow (Music). She is by me every day!!

Every power tool George has I bought for him.

When buying new couches he started to insist we buy leather but I wanted cloth.

Once George understood my dreams and knew some of my colours he would make me decide where we were going for coffee, or dinner, even though at the time making those decisions were difficult for me. My father represented Tim Horton's and George represented Starbuck's. He did not does not have Alzheimer's but he would not know which wine we liked or small things he should have.

When it came to gift-giving he always copied me and gave me things I had given him. When I gave him a cup with the girls' picture, ditto. I gave him a collage of family pictures of which I thought were real, ditto. I gave him a cashmere sweater, ditto. Once sweaters entered the picture that's all I ever got.

For Christmas, I didn't want to surprise him anymore. I had lost all interest in celebrations so I agreed to just go shopping for something. I would have liked a ring or something but we bought each other shoes!! He was so proud of those shoes.

With the girls growing up before my mental break down I used to throw parties for the girls with their classmates, but George never suggested we invite his family once the girls were in grade school. Why not? For the short time while in Ontario we always celebrated with my family the girls' birthday and Thanksgiving. It is like he was putting on a show with my family and his true colours came out when we moved here.

Ever since George has been out of my life I have been very healthy!!

I also don't understand why he would have his grandmother's sewing machine and button box in North Dakota when he did not have it in Tuckerville when I lived with him for a month. Also why did he have a family tree? His father never gave it to him, that I remember. He did not have it when we rented at Angels Corner or Saber Road.

As I told Jessica today at the psychiatrist's office he used to insist I keep all my old cotton shirts for rags but he never used them. He would also buy cotton rags. So I suggest they stop making cotton rags! He had explained to the girls that you can take certain drugs on bits of cotton. He may be doing just that. I have no proof.

One day I pray he will know my name and the girls, and wish as Adele sings from "Rolling in the Deep" that he had never met me.

On the Brighter side:

Now I am strengthened by a wonderful man that found me. His name is Gary Barlow and I believe I am in love with a phantom. Making love through thoughts, music and actions depicted through other actors. He seems only able to reach me through love songs there is no actual conversation, but I hear and see him come alive on HGTV where sometimes I feel I am being questioned or queried on what I like in fixtures and colours for a new home and places to live.

I feel I am being asked to dream bigger. I feel he knows me better than I do know myself in that regard. I thought my dreams and inventive thoughts were big. My mind keeps coming up with ideas to invent or improve on something, but for myself? I will try to dream bigger.

As much as I believe he loves me too, it is so difficult because I so do not want to be hurt, in that he never makes this real. I want to play music with him. I want him to teach me how to play the piano and sing with him. I want someone to come to our house so I can continue to play my guitar. I want to go downhill skiing with him, cross country skiing side by side. I want to bathe with him in a warm sea. I want to jump in a lake and wash each other's hair. I want to go waterskiing and boating to various places. I want him to not be afraid to hold and touch me. Bring love and happiness to the Daytime sun. I need and want Gary in my life permanently.

I need to get to know him as well as he knows me. Perhaps the network can think of some creative ways for me to do just that.

Tuesday, April 17, 2018

Here is the song I wrote last night to outline my mental health journey:

One Life's Journey

D
There's a place
G
Deep in my mind
D
Trying to escape
G
Life gone wrong
D
What I thought
G
Was 18 years
D   G
Ended up 32
D   G

Chorus:
Reaching out to clouds
C   G
Walking in a fog
D   G
Hoping someone somewhere
C   D
Could hear my cry for help
D   G
Not knowing at the time
D   G
That my hell was my help

MY COLOUR-CODED LIFE

```
D                    G
Swimming all alone
D                    G
Drowning in the water
```

CHORUS
```
D                    G
Being my own hero
D                    G
Through my choice of music
                              D
Till it lift me higher
D                    G
And my hero took over
```

CHORUS
```
D                    G
Now it has led me
D                    G
To a brand new story
D
One of love and
G          D
A soul protected
```

Jessica suffered from Rye neck when she was in her teens and given some pain medication. I think it was OxyContin. She was so high and loopy on it that she played in a box of Styrofoam peanuts. Her dad kept taking her medication so I had to hide it from him.

When Jessica came home from Malaysia she gave all her medication to him. He started using it all.

The last time Jessica was given Tylenol 3 was when she had her wisdom teeth out and she only took a couple. The last time I used Tylenol 3 was when I threw my back out.

I did not know where this medication went but years later I found HUGE bottles made out with Jessica's name on it from our dentist and one for me with the physician from the hospital when I threw out my back. I get small bottles of 30 pills for years now so I estimate 100 or more pills were in each bottle.

I spoke with Dr. Rob, our dentist, about what he prescribes when he takes wisdom teeth out and how much. He merely said it would no longer be good and to get rid of it.

Since I thought George was selling the pills, I took the Malaysian pills and the Tylenol pills to London Drugs. George never asked where it went. How could he?

George told me he was allowed to dispense medication at London Drugs when he was a young man. He packaged the medication.

When we first moved here I went to Dr. Moran to get help for George's drinking and he told me to get the book Co-Dependent no More. I did. I guess there was no family help for Al-Anon at the time.

While living at Gage Lane I was so worried about what George was up to that I searched the whole house. In the pool room I found George had some screening material in a long role. Attached to the plastic were about 50 scanning labels!!

I also found plastic grocery bags under the stairs in the kitchen, which could be accessed from the basement. I was certain he was trafficking something because he used to spend hours outside. It was such a perfect house for it, so private.

What spooked me was that at the very end of the property at the back, George cleared a pathway to the public stairs at the side of the property. We never used it. I was certain he was using it for illicit purposes.

When I was first married George and I were living at a hotel until we found a place to live. George had been living there for quite a while. When we went to pay they cut up his American Express card. That was the last credit card that was ever in his name until we split up. He's always been on mine.

He got rid of everything that belonged to me. He made me sell my car which my sister bought. He got rid of my bike, couch, record player, and said that my Chevy cavalier here was hit by a truck that jack knifed on 64th Avenue. I do not believe it. DO you?

I have a nephew who grew up to be a firefighter. He is my favourite on George's side of the family! At every celebration at Paula's he was picked on and verbally abused for years until he was a strapping firefighter by his older cousin. When Jim had no one to pick on he made Darcy his next target!

George did nothing to stop it though I asked him for years and years to say or do something. Even when the target was his daughter. As much as he controlled me he was a scared little boy when it came to protecting anyone or standing up to anyone in his family.

One thing that George never thought was odd was that Jessica did not like chocolate growing up, only candy. Yet it was her that brought Nutella into the family. She ate it!! Just one thing that indicated to me that she was a doppelganger.

When I look at Cassie and Brian, I love them to bits but I do not believe they are my true grandchildren. I also believe that they each have twins, just judging by their characters and Cassie's school pictures.

I need help coming up with a colour for Gary, the new love of my life. Nope he will be Green and black!!!!

Above the false ceiling in the basement I found an empty pack of cigarettes and a fuse panel above the false ceiling!!! When I showed George he told me to leave the cigarette package and not to bother with the fuse panel.

I also found an empty shell of a pen in the vacuum hole. Plus a beautiful pen that the Wagner family gave me was all pulled apart in my purse!!!

What I do not understand about the cabin that George and his sister own is that our children, nor I, ever saw low tide or the beach until they were adults!!

He knew how much I wanted to go to a cabin on a lake but he would not help me find one. He said to my brother that he did not like partnering with his sister on the cabin and was going to give it up and try for a cottage on a lake but when we got back he got even more enamoured with the cabin.

Every year when asked if he owns property in the States, he always says NO.

I did inform the Prime Minister, Justin Trudeau about this.

Wednesday, April 18, 2018

While living at Gage Lane George hired an electrician. But the things he fixed didn't make sense. He fixed the coloured lights in the ceiling but did not put any covers on the electrical sockets. Things I thought he should fix, weren't and George never fixed them.

At one time George was obsessed with nail clippers and insisted we use clippers that had an R on it. I guess from Revlon. He bought some for all of us. I do not have mine anymore.

When I was snooping into George's things I found in one of his personal papers or book, I do not remember. Anyway the name CHRIS stood out because he had never mentioned anyone with that name. I thought it odd, so I phoned the number and it was a male. I hung up.

George said we enjoyed it at Maui and that he floated, which he did most of the time. What is odd is the fact while living at Saber Road I was unable to teach him how to float, he only sank. He could sit at the bottom of the pool.

North Dakota brought some problems for me mentally later.

One day in North Dakota, George asked me to go to a certain jeweller in town and ask for a jewellers rouge. What they gave me was huge. It was at least 6" and cylindrical. For the number of times he cleaned our rings, it dwindled drastically the last time I saw it.

Also in North Dakota George and I took a drive to visit a man on the second floor of some building. The only reason we were there was for this man to show us how easy it is to forge someone's signature. All you have to do is turn it upside down!!

I found George's signature never changed with emotion or stress. It always looked the same. It was eerie!! This is why I would like to rid the world of cheques and signatures!!

We made some friends who lived across the street in North Dakota. They invited us to a party. Phoebe and Jason lived on a big farm and raised quarter horses. George went in the pool and apparently George asked him how he made his money. Jason told George that he invested in something called Futures.

Upon entering Gage Lane for the first time I was stunned and haunted. George grabbed one of my breasts while standing at the bottom of the staircase and said "so these are little Sarah's"!! He had never ever called them that. He called them grapefruits!!

Afterward I was haunted by anyone named Sarah!!

What was worse was one night George stimulated me for sex in much the same way a man might do to another. He had never done that before. I felt strange and actually felt like I wanted like a man would. Jessica walked in on us that night at Gage Lane!!!!

In his drawer at Gage Lane he had two bow ties a red and blue one. He never had those before. He also had a hookah pipe.

George was given one duty to take over that my brother passed down to him at my wedding. I am an arachnophobic!! He let me down big time!! North Dakota had spiders as big as coffee cups and one day after George left for work there was one in our bathroom!! Our dressing room was adjacent so I couldn't wash up or get dressed. I phoned George to come and get it but he would not until he came home for lunch. His work was very close. I sweat watching that spider for four hours until he came back to the house!!

When we separated in 2016, he seemed not to be interested in taking gifts given to him. Some of these gifts I had given to him but I was just as pleased he did not want them, or more likely, remembered they were gifts to him.

He used to tell Darcy that we always had fruit on the table for whenever they were hungry. Excuse me, we never did!!!!

If I were granted one wish it would be that I could spend the rest of my life with Gary Barlow in a real home!!

I envision a few things in my future. My name changing to Megan Marie Barlow. I would also have my email changed where my surname is Barlow.

More Creative Dreams

I think that all kitchens should be outfitted with a computer screen that can be updated when new technology becomes available, so that parents can colour code the activities for their children to replace a paper calendar.

Also there should be a world-wide white pages translated to each areas language. You should be able to say any person's name into your phone and anyone with that name would show up. That way friends trying to find friends could. Females would be required to use both maiden and married names.

I think those making outer garments should make long winter vests so women or men could wear bulky sweaters.

I would like to have a TV Network that brings live music into homes everywhere with lyrics on the screen so everyone can sing along and understand the story!! Every Sunday night would include a show like Ed Sullivan's!! This network would be named MGB (Megan Gary Barlow)

Wednesday, April 18, 2018

Some of the songs that helped me swim to the surface is Josh Groban's song "You Raise Me UP". Another was by Kelly Clarkson, "Stronger" and her song, "Invincible". It is important to mention that I first listened to Josh Groban once I was strong enough to listen to music, and it was he whom I clung to. I first heard him on the CD that my niece made for my deceased sister. He helped me stay close to her. His songs brought me strength.

The very first song I religiously listened to is "If We Dare to Hope" by Bobby Fisher. I had gone to my first teacher's conference with the Archdiocese in 1991. It was the first time I had heard a choir and I felt like I finally belonged to something much bigger than myself. I felt like I had a huge family oddly enough. I bought that CD.

The next song was On Eagle's Wings which I first heard by the 11:30 a.m. choir at my church. I always related that song to my father whom had no music at his funeral.

Many of the songs I now hear on You Tube have had the lyrics changed to either support me and reflect my life and take George to task. They support me by both sending me love songs for Gary and vengeful songs expressing how I do feel towards George. Robbie Williams, I love to watch because he expresses repulsion for George!! He sings a song by Frank Sinatra, "My Way" rewritten to represent George's personality "My Way or the Highway"!!

How in heavens name do I thank all these "angels" My real angels though are all my daughters!! They are all helping me!!

When we lived in North Dakota I bought George a Diston hand saw. I never saw it again. I bought all his electric tools too as I said before.

I had put in my book that people should take action for someone rather than just pray or hug. Little did I know that I was really missing that in my life until 2005. George NEVER initiated a hug with me or the girls!! He just would group hug. Darcy and I would often ask for a hug which he never denied but Jessica never did ask for one from her dad!!

Since we were moving to George's part of the country, I was surprised how George behaved. He made me think that it was dangerous because he insisted on installing an alarm through Brinks. He created the access code. Also, he had Canadian Springs installed into the house. Why when we lived at other houses he thought the water was fine and made fun of me when I couldn't drink it. (I probably couldn't drink it because my medication was altering my taste buds.) He even had bought fluoride tablets at Saber Road saying our dentist Dr. Rob had recommended for the girls. I do not think they ever took them!! What were they really for??

At Gage Lane Jessica came down with some illness that we thought might have come from the water, even her school, Skyhawk was having problems. George had someone come in to inspect the water. Why no Canadian Springs? What do you think??

My Masters online was the most fun I had in my life and I was so stimulated and aired a lot of my problems. I was asked what my favourite drink was and I said water because of Shania Twain's song, "Water".

George, when we were out at a bar, during the time we lived at Gage Lane, he looked over my shoulder and googled some girl behind me. But much worse than this he did the same while we were in CHURCH!! He scanned a girl sitting in front from top to bottom. We then found things in the missal to express ourselves to each other!! I was no longer jealous of his actions because I did not love him anymore. I felt disrespected!!

George set up the TV, Phone and our first computer service at Saber Road. But with all the other houses, he had me do it. The same was true with the alarm services after we left Saber Road he had me set the access codes.

George always insisted we use our home bank even if we used the machine to withdraw money. That is why when I opened my own account I went to the other TD on the street. When in Tinsel Town I opened both girls' accounts. I do not know what happened to their money??

It was also my idea to make sure we had enough money for retirement. So when I received dad's money Bennett, my first financial planner reached out and even came to the house and had my RRSP transferred from my old School Board in Ontario to the TD branch we used.

When I received the money from my dad's estate, I put some into the girls RESP and asked George if he wanted some in an RRSP. He said no because he did not believe in them. So that is why for our 18th anniversary I had a ring made for him. And I am positive it had two Stars in the Saphire ring to represent both girls. Maybe I am wrong however the one I see him wear does not.

With dad's estate I also bought our green leather couches and the coloured set. In addition, I bought our patio set and a curio cabinet to hold all my china dolls. Also, at that time once we moved to Gage Lane George suggested I look into the University of Phoenix to take get my graduate degree online which he knew I wanted to do but he insisted I use my dad's estate money to pay for it.

It always hurt that I was never able to put it into practice and reap the financial benefits from it because my mental illness got in the way.

One day on our way to the bank when I was really broken and barely hanging on, instead of supporting me or calming me he said, "Aren't you at least going to put lipstick on?" I was hurt. Jessica was the one that said I look pretty without makeup on. Darcy, once said she wished she had skin like mine than she wouldn't wear foundation which she calls cover up. Their dad never told any of us we looked nice unless we asked how we looked.

He would always have me enter contests online and buy lottery tickets. I do not believe in the lottery! I entered one contest for a home to win which was difficult for me. They wanted those entering the contest to express what "HOME" meant to them. It was difficult because I haven't lived in a home for so long. So for me, it represents being surrounded by my favourite colours that make me feel warm. I never want to forget my colours and still feel and want to be surrounded by my colours. But I want my future to be the pulse of a heart with a soul being its guiding force. Where there is love, laughter and music and fun!!

George blazed a trail by the stairs while living at Gage Lane. No one ever used it, so what was it for? My mind wanders as to reasons why. He also blazed a trail to the railroad tracks at Wade Avenue. Paula would use to walk her dog Moka (whom I named). I went to walk with her. George never did.

What Makes a Good Parent?

Simple really, always think of how you want to be remembered once your children have grown up and long after God has called you home!!

What might this look and sound like:

- † *Hugs*
- † *Kisses*
- † *The ability to apologize to your spouse and children when you feel you were wrong or were impatient. They will respect you for how you were able to do that*
- † *Respect your spouse and be open with affection…they will learn how to love and treat another*
- † *Always be a role model in their lives*
- † *Cook the meals together*
- † *Share responsibilities for finding activities for the kids and watch them together*

- † *Play all sorts of games both inside and out (George would do something once and if it did not go well, he would not go or do it again. Examples of this was the girls getting hurt at the PNE. They got hurt so he never wanted to go again. We have gone once.*
- † *We bought rollerblades for Darcy and George and she went out once. She got hurt. They never went again. Jessica gave him grief at a fun putting game (I cannot the proper name- oh mini golf), we never went to another one.*
- † *Plan fun excursions for the family together.*
- † *Play games both inside and outside together.*
- † *Rent boats so you can go learn water sports or just go somewhere*
- † *Willing to discuss problems rather than ranting and leaving the house. Children will not respect that*
- † *Always use proper language, no swearing, around your children and never compare them negatively to their siblings*
- † *Be transparent with the finances. It was me that was worried about our budget. I did not understand where the money was going. I was working so hard. I do not want to be on a budget anymore, although I think it is a wise idea. But set it up together with your bank…they are the ones who know what you can afford.*
- † *Dance with your children from the day that they're born!!*
- † *Expose them to cultural activities not just trips to the park or a walk*
- † *Be sure to tell your children how proud you are of them and even of the accomplishments of your spouse*
- † *Remember all that glitters is not GOLD! Your personality is what glitters to your spouse and children. Words can be said but can be empty if the actions are not there to support it!!*

More Creative Ideas

1. Knitting: there should be an online shop where you can search for what you want to order and it will come in a package with all you need in any colours you want. They should also have scarfs and sweaters pre-packaged where you can choose any colour. The store would also offer videos in how to read and follow the directions and how to do a variety of stitches. The sweaters would have no need to be blocked and if so they demonstrate how to do it or even better, offer to do it for free with purchase!!
2. Jamming station: Much like you can play games with friends over the internet you should be able to play instruments or sing with others. Also you should be able to jam or sing with symphonies and bands as well.
3. You should be able to say out loud into your phone or tablet or computer "Download such and such song" and it will automatically be done.
4. To rid the use of plastic bags and cloth bags which are becoming another problem, I suggest:

a. *Having online shopping only, both grocery and clothing and shoes.*
   i. *Grocery: have them deliver the groceries to your door, help you unpack them and they take back the container they brought them in. (Tuesday, December 17, 2019- Save On is now doing this) There should be no minimum purchase amount.*
   ii. *Clothing: Have a tailor take the whole families measurements periodically. Have them registered in a main registry that will automatically appear at any store you wish to buy from. This could possibly be done at the local Dry Cleaners.*
   iii. *Shoes: There would be a local store where the family can go to have moulds taken of their feet which again are sent to the main registry and available at any store you wish to shop at. No more sore feet!!*

Remember the letter that I sent to my parish priest and the Archbishop:

My Archbishop only offered me prayers and the parish priest never responded. Perhaps as Paul Anka says I did not act like a Christian who knelt at church! In many ways I feel more of a Catholic than Catholics that do!!

Earlier in my book I had thought I was working for the Pope to bring Catholics back home to the church. Well in my rebellious ways I guess I am doing just that. However, I am tired of going into a church and being let down by seeing or hearing no changes. So, the next time I enter a church will be with Gary Barlow and then only if changes are made!!

The best part of Church for me is the music and the sermon!!

George would always criticize individuals on the street and both girls as well behind their backs. It made me wonder where I stood. Darcy and I are nearly the same size and he would call her overweight etc. It did not do anything for my self-confidence.

When my brother stopped me from divorcing George before he walked out on me, I said ok but I wanted us to see a marriage counselor. It was agreed so I just found one off the internet, Carl Bartle. It was not very effective. I would write notes on the computer to help me remember what I wanted to discuss. Although I was very careful for George not to see these notes. He somehow came across one of my notes, so he got angry, where I complained that George only pecked me on the lips when he came home. Instead of trying to do better he withdrew even more and did nothing!!

As part of the burgundy chesterfield set the chair had an even stranger thing. Not only did it have the mattresses with hidden zippers, it had the name Taylor written on the foam of the chair cushion.

George was always talking about past jobs. It seems to me that he had more jobs than one person could have. Just a couple were working in a mine and working at a tire store which I only found out about the year before we separated. How funny that he knew nothing about tires.

In 2011 I went to the Open Door Agency which is an organization that finds work for those with disabilities. Believing at the time that I was disabled I went. I wanted to do something constructive and I was burnt out from teaching. Since I had no alternate career path, the lady suggested I go through an evaluation. So, I did. Right after the lady suggested this, I received the news that my sister, Louise had died. I was hysterical!! This agency kept calling insisting I come in and go through the testing. I had no time to grieve. I had to go through it constantly thinking about her. I thought I did very well on the test which included facial recognition. The lady who did the analyzing of the tests said I was not very bright considering I had a Master's and that I was not good for anything than what I was familiar with!!!!! I think it was at that moment I had reached rock bottom. There was not much further I could go!!!

I have had it with the demands of the Catholic teachers here where I live. They see how much blood they can draw from you and stretch you like an elastic band until you snap!! They require you to coach, even if you know nothing about a sport. Also, you must take them on field trips and I had to give 45 minutes of homework. Well, I used to give none on Friday. I hate coaching, I do not believe in homework or report cards, so I guess that makes me a poor teacher. My vision of school has the children learning what they are passionate about and what they are curious about. High school students should learn skill sets as well as their passions. I would have loved to learn how to sew, and type and learn about finance. My online school will offer all these things it will only be completed work and positive comments given with emojis on every piece of work with no essays or tests!! Nothing to memorize only to forget!! I remember nothing of those courses I took in the States and nothing from those I took through the Open Learning Agency. I want education fun again.

I want education to be again where parents respected their child's teachers and did not feel that they had to oversee everything.

However, I do believe in Unions for all schools. One union for both Catholic schools and public schools. In fact, I would have been an active member!! I was happy when the public school teachers went on strike that meant the Catholic schools had to follow suit or they would not have parents or teachers attracted to their schools.

Catholic Schools also require you have a parish letter proving how active you are in the church. What a crock that is!! A catholic is a Christian. Going to church every Sunday does not in any way prove that individual is a respected or type of teacher you want in your school. It is only a piece of paper. I chose not to go through it this time. I told them if they want me they can ask me. I think this letter should be abolished from all Catholic School Boards.

As far as the students are concerned, when in a Catholic or public school, receiving sacraments should be a happy and joyous occasion!! Yes, it should be allowed to public school students without PREP classes. You do not need religion classes to be a Catholic. Did not Jesus say, "Let the Children Come" I think God's minions have misinterpreted God's intentions. God does not turn people away. He does not care about their sexual orientation or whether they go to public school. Honestly, anyone going to Church right now faithfully are saying that you agree that we turn people and children away and make them bleed (PREP) to prove they are worthy. If I had my way, Catholics would boycott the church until humane changes were made!! Do not go to church, talk to God, until changes are made. I have made my personal strike against the church. Perhaps more will join my cause!!

I believe in baptism at birth and reaffirmed if the child so wishes at a later date when they are aware of their faith. I believe in communion, with a chocolate mint host ha-ha!! I mean it!! However, that would not be wise because some do not like mint and some cannot have chocolate. But where communion is concerned I do not believe in all the prepatory masses; that suck both the enjoyment and excitement for the celebration. I also believe in Confirmation, however, this is where I think they can reaffirm their baptism!! Again let them have fun. No research on saints for their chosen name. Let them choose a mentor or someone's name that they admire. No extra prep masses either!!

Where marriage is concerned I do not believe you should have to be Catholic to get married in a Catholic Church. Honestly, would God turn down anybody!!! I am Catholic and because my priest had not seen me in years while at University he refused to let me get married in my church!!!!!!!!!!! Perhaps a blessing, for now I will marry a man who really loves me and in any church I wish even though I haven't gone in years. This time around I am not certain which Church I want to be married in, my old church has left a negative taste in my mouth. They would have to reach out to me and apologize!!!! Maybe like the majority of couples now I will not marry in a church.

I do not believe in obligatory marriage courses before getting married in the Catholic Church! I know some who have gone through it and it did not work. However, it can be offered and those who chose to, may. They must be transparent in what it covers prior to those enlisting in it. If I knew what it covers I might be better informed and it may have helped me, we will never know?

In my future I want my new name to be Megan Marie Jackson until Gary asks me to marry him!!

The other day I got out my hammer and smashed all the china dolls George gave me. The only one I wish I had was the miniature Royale Daulton figurine Jessica bought me. It is missing. I remember George packing it and I told him it was so small I was afraid it would go missing but he assured me it would be fine. I should have insisted I take it.

I'm the one that went with my parents to pick out our china pattern. Later I brought George to the store to see which one he liked. He chose the same one I picked like he knew which one I liked.

Personally, in my future I want new dishes and they do not need to be china. I'd like to have something not made yet. I'd like a set of my grandma's Limoges' plates in a set of Corelle dishes. Those dishes were meant for me according to my mother but they rightfully went to my Aunt. However, they are china. Corelle are light, would be colourful, safe for around a pool and not breakable should a toddler drop one.

Over the years I am sure I have dreamt however, I only remember one. This was, my dad saying to me, Bring George Home!! He was passed away but he shouted it and he woke me up with a start. The only way I want to bring him home is to, as Collabro sing, "See him safe behind bars". And by this I do not mean the bars in a piece of music, or a ballet bar!!

With "the game" I have been a part of figuring out songs and films hidden with songs, is so intelligently done. What I find awesome is that they use thumbs up or down to evaluate it. Thumbs up was the symbol I gave to Darcy and also represents my idea of thumb prints to open and sign for everything. Perhaps even better than that is all finger tips!!

After I met George I sent him a song on a tape that I wrote and knit him a sweater!!! I do not have the song in my repertoire and he never kept it or the sweater!! He merely said I scared him off with the song and that the arms were too big on the sweater!! Wouldn't you keep a song written and recorded for you??

When George left me he asked if he could have the trunk, I said yes because it came from his side of the family. However, he said he was going to put his records in it. That means he took back all the records from Jessica because he had no records and only brought a few into the marriage. They were mine and a friend of ours!!Of course I just may have forgotten. If George brought any there were few.

Keith Urban sings a song with the lyrics "you shouldn't have treated me this way" makes me think of Jessica singing it to her dad. After I thought that, Michael Jackson's song, "Beat it "played!! Jessica and I were telling George to "take off"!

Yet More Creative Ideas and Dreams

1. I had always wanted to have a dude ranch for children and teens. Much like that on Neon Rider. I had always admired that show and wanted to meet Winston Reckert!! George said he knew him!! He also told Darcy he knew David Foster and Sam Feldman. He was full of you know what!!

    Years ago when I was jogging in Tuckerville, George said he would jog with me once I could do ten minutes. I reached that but he never jogged with me or alone!! Always broken promises and actions. Anyhow back to the dude ranch. I envision children of all ages being able to stay there when they are having problems. It would have more than horses though. For children may bond with a different sort of animal. The ranch would give the parents the opportunity to always come back once the child heals, so the child never mourns the loss of the animal they have grown attached to.

    This ranch would also have music where there would be instruments of all sorts. The children could pick the instrument of their choice. There would be a music teacher on site. This singer would be *a song writer, to help the children learn how to express themselves, much like talking to God in a song. All songs written are about one of God's children...they all have meaning.*

It used to bother me how when I was more interested in the lyrics of a song George would get mad at me and tell me to only listen to the beat. If the lyrics were not important there would be no songs!

At the ranch there would be more than one psychologist on hand but one psychiatrist. Although I have had a very pill ridden life, I do not believe in pills to solve a problem. I believe in talking!!! Should there be doctors that possess both these roles would be ideal. There would be a place like this available in every major city across the world!! We need to take care of our young. All my daughter had was a tape and bubbles to blow with no follow up!! This is for her!!!

I simply love listening to Robbie Williams song for us that is called "Come Undone" It has swearing but it makes me feel like he is yelling at George and saying also that if Gary hurt me his revenge would be so sweet because the musicians care for my girls and I too!! I know these songs are made for us and would not be for the public!! He is too respectable!! No Matter what they say about Robbie and the band. I believe Robbie and Gary are like best friends!!!

2. *Since I see strings and wind instruments a part of every school until they have graduated from University, I envision a Royale Conservatory available in every community to accommodate students after graduation or for further instruction!!*

I want my online school connected to all actual schools so kids can take some classes either way or both. For instance, music lessons. They can learn both online and in a school. They will never feel isolated.

Gary is more of a quiet revenge with Take That "Love Love" I love that song!!

I also love his love songs. I just would like one I can keep looking at and listening to that is just for me with no hidden songs. One I can keep looking at for strength in that it will come true!!

3. I also would like to have invented a tech toy for Toddlers that has cartoons with morals to learn for toddlers and appropriate music from the Wesley Disney movies!! Brian would love it. So would grade school students.

1. I would like to see Major Record labels open up their doors to those who are trying to enter the industry. Each major industry would have a link on their website where artists could upload their music. As well, they would open the door to a local studio in most major cities where an individual could record music that would be sent out to all labels. Thereby eliminating such shows as American Idol and The X Factor where most hearts are broken. Those shows would be reworked to offer individuals to showcase their talent like Ed Sullivan did.
2. I also think all major cities should have a dinner theatre available to attend like Stage West in Ontario. They would offer plays, musicals and symphonies and bands. It would also have a large dance floor!!!
3. When asked to dream bigger: I would also like to have a fashion line. One that is filled with colour. For both men and women from toddler to seniors.
4. I have contacted the media in the hopes I can share my story. I am so ready and not afraid. As long as I do not come across slanderous or abusive and my daughters will be forever proud of their mom!!

Saturday, April 21, 2018

One thing George used to brag about, was all the mischief he was involved in as a teenager that he never got caught for.

I think they should bring back the show by Mark Kistler where he teaches children how to sketch in 3D. Something I am sure I am not alone in wanting to do. This type of class will be a part of my school.

Oddly enough I feel that Kelly Clarkson's song "Piece by Piece" fits our (my girls and I) lives perfectly. I feel that Gary has picked us up piece by piece from an unloved childhood (for the girls) and marriage. I feel he is putting me together like a puzzle. Maybe he is taking us from rags to riches and for me the story of Snow White and Cinderella combined. Only I had only a wicked husband!!

They say nothing is impossible but honestly if I didn't have this wonderful help how on earth would I have been able to succeed in getting my dream of an online school become reality. I would not have known how to contact the tech giants on my own. (Friday, March 20, 2020- I find this an interesting paragraph for I only figured out how and who to contact on Tuesday and sent them an outline of my dream for an online school.)

I think somehow we have to make reaching dreams become easier for children to reach.

I thank God every day now that Gary is in my life and may be instrumental in making all my dreams come true!! I know he has taken some of my feelings in this book and created a song, "Dying Inside". It sure expresses how I felt. I no longer feel like I am dying inside due to all the music and performances you have sent my way!!

† Maybe I will dream since encouraged to dream bigger. I would have my own and Gary's recording studio where no age were turned away. We would send the recordings to all major record labels. This studio would be available in all major cities.

I do not know where the letters are that George wrote to me but what is disturbing is that he had all of mine and threw them in my face expecting me to reread them, I suppose!! I think my doppelganger has them!!

† I have now added the colour Coral to represent my niece Carol whom I wrote in her song, no colour is as beautiful as hers. Hope she likes it …the media helped me think of it.
† Also I watched an interview on Gary where he said he had children, which were shown, and that he had a stillborn child. I find this too

coincidental and they did not show his wife. In his bio he is married to Dawn French. I know this not to be true by other videos.

† I had asked for him to come up with a name for my stillborn in my thoughts and in this book. In his interview he apparently had Poppy for the name of his stillborn. I however, think this is a name for mine. I LOVE it!! It is the symbol for Remembrance Day…always to be remembered and never forgotten!!!! Poppy Marie Barlow she will be!!!!

† Although, we did not conceive of her together, I have felt more compassion from Gary through what I hear from him and other artists and how Simon reacts to the performers as if they are speaking to me. They seem to care for her more than her dad ever did.

I have an ultrasound picture of her which I was never given. At least I do not remember and the year is wrong, although the date seems appropriate. It says May 13, 1986 but we did not live in North Dakota that long, I do not think. I assume the people who gave me this picture have a real one for me that we can frame!! She'd be in her 30's now.

He never grieved over her. I cannot fathom how he thought she was a boy when we spoke of her later!! It cut me to the core. Perhaps George never knew his doppelganger was given misinformation!!

When Darcy was pregnant with Cassie, Jessica gave Darcy a large framed picture saying that said, "COURAGE". As I rocked Cassie in her bedroom, in the same chair that I rocked my girls in, at our house, I looked at it and felt as much as it was for Darcy, it was for me!! George had removed the arm rests on the chair which had frayed but he never replaced them which made rocking Cassie harder!!

During the time that we were helping raise Cassie, George never walked her or tried to soothe her when she was a baby. If there'd been music, I would've walked her to do it. Oddly enough it was running water that soothed her…music might have done it too…it helped my girls when they were babies.

At the risk of repeating myself, what I thought was hurtful was when he had Cassie repaint the gnomes from Sandra's (Paula's) garden at the cabin.

I thought it was hurtful to her because he repainted them so they would look perfect!!

Most restaurants I go to have paper napkins which remind me of several things:

- † We never used to use napkins, only paper towel. But then George insisted we have them
- † It reminds me of the napkin in Tuckerville that I wrote my information with an eyebrow pencil, on a napkin in the bar at some Keg in Tuckerville before I flew back home the next morning. I gave it to the man I met there. Wanting him to write before I would give my phone number. George's story is that he crumpled it on his dresser and forgot about it. The man I met would not have done that. (What is interesting is several years later when we were in Tuckerville and I asked him to take me to the one we met at and he could not remember.)
- † I think there has been such an emphasis on girl's eyebrows of late because of this
- † It also reminds me of all the notes I wrote every day in the girls' lunches mostly on paper towel. I remember Jessica keeping them.
- † It reminds me of my dad. He only wanted to go to restaurants where they have cloth napkins. So George took us to the most expensive restaurant in the city. I forget the name. We could've gone to The Keg for they are the only restaurant around here with cloth napkins. I like cloth too. My dad always had the habit of making a fold on his napkin when he had finished a meal!!
- † Perhaps you can take drugs with paper towel and napkins. Perhaps we rid ourselves of these items and clothes made of cotton.

I feel that maybe it was Gary I met so long ago, especially when he is singing that song with Agnetha Faltskog. He is almost bursting with excitement!!!! It is as if Gary has searched high and low for me and is defending my honour!! Could this be right?

I am so happy now, I have a name for my daughter!!

From that visit to my psychiatrists Jessica suggested that instead of me posting to Facebook that I write to her, so I have been sending her copies of my entries into this book. Also, at that visit Dr. Jake put me back on Olanzapine because I did not seem to be doing very well on the Rexulti.

Jessica said in one of her texts that she was glad that I was writing music again, but she never knew I wrote songs, unless George or Darcy told her. She has never heard me play. I gave the tape that George helped me tape record of all my songs in Brampton to Darcy for some reason for safe keeping. Maybe because even then I was afraid it would go missing.

What is disheartening now is that the new song I wrote I can't remember the melody.

I had a history teacher, who said, "If you promise not to take History the following year, he would pass me." From that time I was not much of a History fan until I was introduced to learning about the First Nations!!

I also had a math teacher, who treated me poorly. After a year of being at the top of the class in grade 9 taking Algebra, which I loved. (She sat you according to grade which was not good) but I studied hard to stay out front competing with Carl Leiderman, the boy behind me, my friend. In grade 10 I chose a seat upfront in my math teacher's class. However every time he reamed out the girls for wearing halter tops he would leave notes on my desk saying things like of course this does not pertain to you or you look lovely in your red dress. The dress was my mother's. I would've worn a halter top too if I could've fit one. They did not make it my size. That will not be the case with my fashion line. All sizes will be available. Although I do not think those tops should be worn to school.

My first real boyfriend was when I was in grade 13. He was in first year at York University. One night he wanted to be intimate and I did not want to, he chased me over the bed getting ready to grab me. His reaction was scary. Much like George did when I thought he wasn't my husband while living on Wade Avenue.

Because of this he had me go to the hospital again. They admitted me for sure because of him. But they made me sign commitment papers. I want him to feel this pain and fear.

When going out with a boy, Lonnie, his brother was going somewhere with us. I went with his brother in the truck and we met Lonnie there.

While waiting for Lonnie to arrive I felt trapped because I did not know where to go. His brother forced me to give him head after he MADE me laugh. When I told Lonnie he said it was my fault and his brother said it was because I had a funny laugh. Back then the police were known to not always believe females and it was difficult and I was too ashamed to tell my parents. I might have told George.

I never reported the brother. Kept it to myself. I did report George to my psychiatrist and I spoke of the other incidences to the nurses at my last hospital visit, but no one has offered counselling or help in any way.

At Lonnie's apartment building while in the elevator I was molested again. While in the elevator there was a man, and when I remarked how silly I was for hitting the wrong floor as he left he grabbed my breast and said it was because I had big boobs!!

I am grateful there are cameras in our elevators here in my building. **I think they should be in every elevator everywhere.** Lonnie helped me report this incident.

When I first moved here (British Columbia), I had to take two history courses to be able to become a permanent school teacher here. I had to do this while teaching full time, raising two girls and coaching or helping coach volleyball with a parent!! I took these courses through the Open Learning Agency which was an antiquated way of online work through the mail. The history courses I took in the States for my Masters were not accepted because they were not Canadian, basically those courses went totally unrecognized in Canada. Mr. Kaal and his lack of encouragement came to bite me.

I do not want anyone to go through what I went through so I think once you have a degree in anything from anywhere it should be accepted EVERYWHERE, especially within the same country!!

What has me wondering was that while I was living with George I had so many ailments that I do not have anymore….massive migraines that lasted 3 days. Colds, yeast infections and bladder infections!!

What was so unforgiving was the way he behaved toward me when he returned from his retirement party. He was SO drunk. He went upstairs and came downstairs stark naked, as per usual when he was drunk, and wanted me to perform. Now you must realize that we were not getting along, he already was repulsing me and we were seeing a marriage councillor. If this was not bad enough he knew I had a bladder infection, one of the worst I have ever had. I told him that he had to be kidding and to go back upstairs and put some clothes on.

He always wanted me to massage him but I let him think it was the cream I disliked, well it was the cream plus I just did not want my skin to touch his. So he always seemed to have plenty of surgical gloves on hand for me to use, sometimes blue, sometimes black. Seems he had a new box before we could possibly have gone through one. What on earth did he need them for? I never ever saw him use them? Tell me what was he up to? Probably a lot more than I asked help with!! Plus those old t-shirts of mine and his were never lying around in the garage…where were they? Plus once we went to some shop and he was looking for 100% cotton rags. I never saw them afterwards. When I went to him to ask for one, he had none. Yes, the more I reflect…rid the world of this item….nothing made of 100% cotton or cotton blend if it applies, no more, napkins and paper towel. Now, what to do about toilet paper, where he insisted on buying 3 ply. He said it was for when he blew his nose. He NEVER used toilet paper to blow his nose, he used Kleenex.

Speaking of Kleenex, my dad used to have man size Kleenex that I have never seen again. This is odd because he used handkerchiefs. I do not recall seeing them being used. I just remember seeing them in the basement where he hung out…nowhere else.

I cherished the pretty handkerchiefs I received from a good friend, Charlotte. They came in a beautiful pink pouch. I have started using them.

Yes, I think it is time to go back to using handkerchiefs, not made of cotton.

Tomorrow I see Darcy, I wonder if Jessica has forwarded my entries to this book to her. I hope she no longer worries for me…and is Okay with me writing too!! I am a little anxious about our brunch.

In the performances that Robbie Williams directed toward George provides me with satisfaction, even though I'm sure that it is not for the public's eyes. He sometimes wears an undershirt, which is now referred to as a wife beater. He shows many tattoos to look tough, but I believe these are for show. Funny Gary and Robbie's boyband is called "Take That" for I interpret it as here George, "take that" perhaps better, "Take This" Anyhow I am curious as to how they really came up with their name. Maybe it refers to all the things George was taking for his other family. Did he have one?

Sometimes I feel like Curious George, so many unanswered questions I have of my past. It seems my mind works so hard to make sense out of real events that do not make sense.

Remembering back on shoes. George did not polish his or my shoes on Saber Road or before, he only started, once we lived on Gage Lane.

Robbie's song, "Me and My Monkey" has the lyric, " I've been following you a long time Baby, and now your monkey is going to die" I interpret this to mean that Gary has been following me a long time and now George is going to die".

When I think of God I often think DOG! My beautiful puppy was hurt and I hurt thinking about it. Darcy came down with allergies so they say. Why did they not offer allergy medication? Was there none then? George placed my Barclay who was a boxer, in a dogloo outside. I have not seen one since. He also built her a wooden home over it and put a heater in there.

I never knew what happened to her toys from North Dakota. I also don't know what happened to the clothes I made which I would like to see as part of my clothing line! The one shoulder dress could also come with quality built in strapless bras for those of us who are well endowed!!

But I think dogs are pack animals and now she only had her pack when we came outside. Why did we do this to her? Was I in control then? I believe though once she could not use her legs anymore that she had a broken spirit.

Ronan Keating's song titled "Life is a Rollercoaster" and I interpret this to mean he wants to know if I like rollercoasters. I have only been on one with George's cousin where he tricked me in saying it was nothing. It was petrifying!! I felt like it was a straight drop down and it was in the dark!! Is Gary fond of rollercoasters? I'd love to go to the fair. Every year I have wanted to go.

Even when we lived in Ontario we never went to Wonderland. I have never been. So in over 30 years I have been once…pretty sad I think. Not something I would do alone though.

MY COLOUR-CODED LIFE

Dear Poppy,

Mom here! Just want you to know that your new dad and I love you very much!! I know you would have been a wonderful big sister. Seems like I am allowed to grieve over you once again, now that your dad, Gary, has named you. You are now in your thirties and it is about time you had a name. I am having a big party for your sisters soon and we will celebrate you too my sweet little one!!

Funny I know what it is like to not quite have a name too!

I did not know how to grieve over you so I wrote you a poem combined with your sisters and had it published. I know had you been around maybe you would have all played together even as teenagers.

So in my colour-coded life I need one for you too!! I am running out of colours maybe your dad will help with that too.

Maybe that's it. God gave you to me and took you away so your colour will be purple!!! It is perfect!!!

Forgive me for ending your life, it was a difficult decision but we agreed with the doctors' advice! I was told you would suffer, which would have made me suffer too to watch!!

There's been so many times I have thought of you. But I had no way to express it without your name. Your name now is so unique, and sounds so British, I absolutely love it. I really hope you do!!

So as my dad had done you are really #1, Darcy #2 and Jessica #3

I do not think your sisters would be bothered. Jessica did not know until this year about you. I preferred to keep the pain away from them for as long as I could. I did tell them to go on the pill though and if an accident happened we would help.

Yes, I went against the church and told them to take the pill. So that is another area that the church should adjust in. I also was on the pill as soon as I decided to consider having sex. I was 21 and decided it was time. Although I do not ever remember having sex with anyone, though I know I did, especially with Andrew.

I meet #2 tomorrow for brunch. I will tell her you now have a name!!

Forever Love, Mom &Dad

So now that the term I thought Gary was using for me, "Baby" was just another song which leads to a video I do not even care for by Justin Bieber. How I will know when he is trying to reach me is not known yet. He has to reach out. For it was a blow to discover.

I guess I made a mistake his bio says that he is married to Dawn Andrews. But when I look at all the pictures of him with her. It does not look like him. I am getting insecure again…I need reassurance!!

Justin Bieber does have a song with the Lyrics that go something like this, "my mom doesn't like you and she likes everyone". I do like this song! I do feel it relates to me for I haven't met anyone yet that I dislike except George.

Yes even my beautiful picnic basket went missing. I took `it once in Ontario to George's place of work with the girls. I believe I had both girls. It disappeared after that.

At Gage Lane he had the briefcase I had bought and had engraved for him but it disappeared too afterwards. In the garage I had run across some papers/hand written notes on Blue Angel Cafe. It looked like he was up to something with the restaurant. I can't remember what it said.

(Sunday, January 12, 2020 - Upon doing my final edit for this book I do not see where I have written about green broken safety glass I found stuffed into the pocket my computer case. It was a substantial amount, at least a whole windows worth. I had not used it for some time and discovered it. I thought maybe that George had borrowed it and had it in his truck when it was stolen while taking Darcy to the medical clinic. We were living on Gage Lane at the time. I discovered it while living at Diamond Head. It is my only explanation for the glass being there. However his truck windows were not this colour. I asked George and he thought nothing of it (per usual), but said he had not used my computer case and just to throw it out.)

As I listen to an interview James Corden has with Gary. Gary says he was the responsible one, so was I growing up, although I was very much into being a party girl. When Elizabeth and I went out to bars. She would have me make sure she did not bring any one home. The same was true when Amy was along too.

My girls never had dance parties but my parents allowed me to have them as much as I wanted but I always insisted they be home. Even though

I always had a bouncer at my parties. When my sister and I attempted to have one together it was disaster. The boys actually got into the turkey my mother had in the fridge. This was when I left with my friend Preston. This was when he complimented the colour of my hair that I told him I did not like because it was commonly referred to as dirty blonde. He said it was Sandy! I have always been touched by that.

One thing I have noticed with some of the songs presented to me, they use slang. Instead of saying, love isn't here anymore, they say love ain't here anymore.

George's sister one time brought a pink lipstick to Tammy's asking who wears pink. I said I did and she gave me a Lancôme lipstick called Champagne. It has been my favourite. However they stopped carrying it at London Drugs and I am too lazy to drive all the way to The Bay to get it. I tried to match it with another. The positive thing about my new lipstick is that it does not leave marks on my cup.

As I want a real fireplace I recall in North Dakota that they cut, delivered and stacked wood for 100 dollars. I thought that was great!

I have gone on vacations with George's sister and family but I wanted another one with the girls and with my family. I have a feeling that may come true too. HGTV keeps showing me different places to live so maybe I need to broaden my thoughts and think of where else in the warm climates I would also like to own?

When I see the colours on HGTV for instance Fixer Upper. Seeing the colours makes me feel that this is real.

HGTV has always been my savior and it still is!! It started with Holmes on Homes. Although they always seem to choose the opposite to what I am thinking or envisioning.

† I would also like Gary to go on a camping trip with Elizabeth and some friends so that I can pay her back for the one I couldn't finish with her back in the day!!

Although I am a jewelry girl and like giving it to my daughters. The only necklace that Gary would need to give me is one that is a symbol that represents me to him. I would never take it off!! No need for another one. I tend to like yellow gold! I am a ring girl and earring girl.

If one were to draw a soul what would it look like? If that could be discovered I would have matching ones made for both of us…never ever to come off!!

Now my keyboard on my iPhone only displays a question mark on every letter and symbol I press. I do not quite know why? In fact all my emojis are now questions marks as well. This has me disturbed!! Why have they done this? It is only on my phone.

While Gary and his two friends performed songs for me tonight! Yes they were to me tonight on my iPhone. I came to the discovery that since I have been given an alias when I moved to British Columbia that I am being protected. I first noticed it through the Ministry of Education here in the documents they gave me, that I have not sold any of our houses including the one in Brampton!! The house in Brampton he sold himself through a company called PEARTREE. I signed nothing. At least I do not remember clearly.

The boy band I am watching took turns being lead singer which I think is how it should be. Because they all want solo parts. At least that is how I would feel if I were part of a singing group.

Little did I know that I have been protected this whole time?

Listening to Bruce Springsteen and Sam Moore sing "Hold on I'm Coming", tells me to hold on, Gary is coming. Bruce is angry and is singing with anger in his voice that Gary has not expressed because he has a role to play I guess. But this song says he is a soul man and Gary is my soul man… right from our song that I created.

Another song by Bruce Springsteen and Billy Joel and friends "Your Love Keeps Lifting me Higher and Higher" is sung with feeling from Gary!!

I wish I could access the new songs Gary and his friends performed on my iPhone, on the TV.

Maybe I can get on a horse again. I have only been once and then it laydown while I was still on it. It freaked me out. But I have often thought about having the experience. I would love to go on a picnic while going somewhere on a horse. Is that even possible when you are on a horse? You probably can't carry a basket.

One day George surprised me by bringing a blanket to a nearby beach to watch the sunset…but he did not hug me or anything. So what could've been romantic, only half met its mark.

You know I have said it before and I wonder how performers feel. I have to know, but isn't it hard to take your family on the road to perform everywhere or worse leave them behind? Can't you just perform in your own city and have it broadcast all over the world so families across the world could tune in. Also, eliminate the need of interpretive videos just provide videos of the performance on stage or the studio.

This would satisfy the desire of being on stage and reaching millions more!!

Funny when l met the man in the Keg years ago I do not recall what he drank. I barely remember his face. I just know he was handsome. When living with George for that month I do not even recall us ordering any alcohol or drinking it at his condo that summer.

In Ontario he would drink beer at my dad's but that was it. How come he drank so much when living at Saber Road? Then it was mostly bud light. Then at Gage Lane it switched to red wine and sometimes white… the same with the townhouse.

I do not like the machines and the expectations on tipping. I believe the owners of the establishment should pay their employees well enough that they do not need it. I often do not feel like tipping but feel obliged to. I mean it, most establishments do not get tips why should the service industry?

Personally what happened to me definitely affected me but it was closer to PTSD!! Post-Traumatic Stress Disorder!!!!!!!!!!!!!!!!!!!!!!!!!!!!!! Now that people are willing to listen to me, and my daughter is definitely communicating and supporting my writing, I feel healed. But it is still difficult for me to remember what I have written in this book and what I have not. Which makes it harder for those making this into my biography, a movie and a musical and perhaps even a Disney animated movie!! And of course it will incorporate the part where we lived happily ever after. Everyone loves a sad story turning happy.

I now have the first need listed in my life now, which was Jessica, so Gary must come next because he is second on my Needs and Wants list!!

My computer gave me a picture of a field filled with Poppies. **If that is not a sign I do not know what is. Gary approves!!**

"Yesterday" by the Beatles with Paul McCartney supports George. I do not believe my troubles are here to stay!! I prefer "I Saw her Standing There"

If my girls do not mind having a real dad like Gary, I want the adoption to be automatic…no paperwork. :
Poppy Marie Barlow
Darcy Marie Barlow
Jessica Marie Barlow
And me Megan Marie Barlow.

I stay up all night so I can dance in my mind all day and night!!

When evaluating Oliver Twist, I did like the film but I think it could be better. No one gets physically hurt and all the thieving boys find homes and Fagan goes to jail as well as his accomplice.

Even Annie, though I liked the story I was sad for those that were left behind. Starbucks should have worked to find homes for all those girls in the show and why were there only girls?

Listening to Donna Summer with Seal "Unbreak my Heart" I feel that it is directed toward George. It said that the nights are so unkind. For me though the nights are filled with those singers trying to keep my spirits up!!

I do not think what is happening to me is a miracle from God. Even though I had thought that the condiment Miracle Whip meant that the Archdiocese wanted me to have a miracle. This is man-made!! Though what is happening to me is miraculous!! It is still so wild that this is happening to me!!

I think I've done with crying except when I think of Poppy.

I am getting anxious about Darcy's party because no one has responded yet except Paula. She said she was going to Iceland with her son. That one I do not believe. I believe she will be there. I hope she is!!

I want the opportunity to thank them for helping me.

I really enjoy listening to Peter Cetera. He sings with body language meant for George but lyrics meant for me as well. They are love songs through Peter from Gary. Except the first one which sounds like it is from

George, maybe not though. It is the first line where it states that he heard her say even lovers need a time away which confuses me. The second and third ones from Gary!! Maybe they all are because he says baby in the first one too!! The third one is from Karate Kid apparently, though this music was not part of the show.

Jessica was my karate kid. It was me that signed her up. It was me that took her to class. George came to watch her evaluations. He destroyed her wish to continue on because he wanted her to spar and bought her red equipment. I never knew what happened to that equipment. I so wished for her that she received her black belt!! So I kept all her belts.

One of my mother's friend's daughter had her black belt and when Jessica expressed interest I was excited.

It was me that took them to swimming classes. It was me that had them re-evaluated if I thought the instructors were wrong. It was me that hoped they would be a life guard as a possible job to fall back on growing up and to be able to be safe around water. It was me that signed them up for all their activities. It was me that held their hair back when they got sick. It was me that gave them their medication. It was me that filled their prescriptions and most often took them to see the doctor.

It was me that found a contact through a colleague for Jessica to go into acting, Colleen's Talent. It was me taking her to auditions until they started to be during the day during the week. He made it always sound like I had nothing to do with it.

I was livid inside when George had Jessica spend her $17,000 from her commercial on a car!! She could have invested her money and bought a car later in life. I wept watching from the window as it was leaving the house for good. Then later he bought a car for Darcy for her birthday and told me later!! I had to tell him it was unfair!!

He did come to the ballet recitals with me when we lived at Saber Road

For Darcy's performances he would offer to build castles and work backstage but he never saw her perform in those. The only one he saw was Joseph's Technicolour Dream Coat where she was the baker. It was nice of him to help though.

He reminds me a lot of my sister Mandy's character growing up. Acting one way with family but shine in front of a crowd or people. Always the nice guy.

He always bragged that it was him taking Jessica to baseball games but I was right there too!! I could be wrong but I think she joined because of what I had written in my book or in my online class about baseball. I remember, a colleague at school, saying parents were vicious at the games. So I think she joined to find out. The parents may not have been that way but the coach was mean. Her name was Meaghan. When I thought she was unkind to the team I told her, whereas George said nothing.

Even with her cheerleading I was at every game and worked the concession while George did the line thing. I was there too.

Why are there no boy and girl teams? Why are all sports gender specific?

He always complained I was so quiet, but when I did speak he did not like what I had to say…so as much as he was bragging about himself and all his many jobs and past girlfriends I clammed up. Honestly, what wife wants to keep hearing about past girlfriends? Even for this game or whatever I am involved in I did not care to know or hear him brag! It was so unattractive.

In fact it wasn't until 2016 that I learned of the job with London Drugs dispensing medication, as I told you, and having a tire shop. Is this true? He also said he worked in a mine and was part owner of a business with a friend in Kinter Valley. He also worked with a guy cleaning fish tanks and knew all about fish. He did not know how to clean our girls' fish tank or keep the fish alive. Also he was a chimney sweep but he never swept our chimney.

Richard Marx's song with JC Chasez, "This I promise you" is from Gary too. His song "Right Here Waiting for You" is not. I can't listen to the lyrics, they bother me.

Sunday, April 22, 2018

Margarine here is like soft butter in a tub. Margarine back home is like bright yellow plastic!!

Maybe it is just me but don't singers have to spend a lot of time doing interpretive videos? Would they not just prefer to do their performance and have it made into a video? Videos like performing on stage or the process of making the song for the video in the studio is a positive option.

I wrote in my online class about, "Paying it Forward", just like the movie of a boy with an idea. The sad part, the boy dies before he sees the impact he has made. This movie should be remade to have a happier ending. When I see the crowds at the venues all the singer songwriters perform at, I often wonder if I have done just that, but what have I done except to have a dream of an Online School. How would I have made a difference? All I want to do is leave my mark and have a legacy to leave my kids. Have them say,"My mom did that!!"

I sometimes feel that the musicians are touring and playing to raise money for my online school.

When I reflect on the Park in Brampton that I fought to have remade for the kids, which I never got to finish. George never helped my movement or cause. Why not? Why did we have to move in the middle of my project? What was the rush, he had no job prospects? Sometimes I wonder if this is why all the new parks here are colourful.

When we revisited the park several years later I was hurt that the park was not named after me.

Sometimes in this journey I am asked to evaluate movies. No matter the genre, even horror films. I believe they should make them child friendly so that the whole family can watch them. The same is true with TV series programs. No more rating of films to exclude those who are offended by foul language or violence…just abolish it!!

Over the years I have been immersed in this offensive and gory detail that I have become desensitized to it, which I feel is sad. It is not me nor does it express my values!!

As much as I want George to go to prison. I do not believe in executions. Executions are an easy way out! I want him to suffer with life imprisonment!! That is the same with all major offenders. As long as prison life is not made to be comfortable. He isolated me and took me away from all my friends, family, and accomplishments. I want him in isolation!!

As part of this journey I am on I have felt that I had the role of St. Bernadette and Mary.

In addition to my letter to my priest and the Archbishop let me try to reiterate my wishes for change:

1. Abolish the Rosary! I have taught the Rosary to students for years but I still do not know how to use it properly.
2. No more prayers taught to memorize, teach our children to talk to God. Those that pray the Rosary and religiously go to Mass may be the one we need to fear the most! Prayer and Mass do not necessarily make a good Catholic! A good Catholic challenges and questions. Maybe I am more of a Catholic truly trying to bring Catholics home to the Church!
3. Abolish the kneeling and standing
4. Abolish the first and second reading
5. Only have the sermons, they are most inspiring
6. Having upbeat inspiring music is a must. Personally, I went to the Pingle choir because at one time they were the best and I felt fuzzy in my heart knowing those boys playing the recorder that I had taught them. However after my breakdown when I kept trying to go back the music was no longer inspiring.
7. I believe that the priests should not wear robes or wear white collars. They need to look approachable.
8. I want a life like the TV program BLUE BLOODS. A family meal every Saturday or Sunday with a simple thanks for the fact of being together!! Not necessarily for the food but the people.
9. Open the door and allow women to be preachers as well. If we make changes more Caucasians too may choose this field. Yes Caucasians, some of the priests at my church are from the Philippines and I have a hard time sometimes understanding the sermon.
10. As I said before, change the host to a circular colourful perhaps chocolate mint or something that is easily taken by all. Make it joyous!

11. Do not bring back the wine and do not use juice. It would be difficult to find one that everyone likes
12. No more confession to a priest or anyone
13. No sacrament of first confession
14. Keep Baptism and reaffirm this again for Confirmation if the child wishes. Let them have fun choosing a name. My kids never got to choose a name. At least I do not know what they are. No more studying saints to choose. Let them choose a name of someone they admire. No more masses to prepare them or journals to prove they attended mass.
15. Everyone allowed to be married in the Church even if they do not attend the Church. NO One turned away, even if they are of the same sex.
16. No more collection of money from the congregation. The Archdiocese would be responsible for paying them!!
17. No more masses that the school children have to prepare, which only stresses both the children and the teachers.
18. It could also be made possible that children are offered the opportunity to give the sermon…let the children lead the way!!

As Robbie in his song expresses there is a very big hole in my soul regarding the Catholic Church and love!

I thirst to enter a church and celebrate again, but it suffocates me now and as I have said before the next time I enter a church it will be with Gary.

I would also like to see preachers able to be married…no more celibacy.

Regarding Face to Face schools and Sporting Events they should sing not only O Canada but God Save the Queen! It brings back a sense of pride!! As far as I recall history we are a part of the United Kingdom.

Since I enjoyed smashing the figurines George gave me. I would like to collect them from places Gary and I visit.

One thing that I have noticed, my cutlery which we bought at the townhouse has been in 3 different dishwashers and look the same as when they were bought. Just verifies to me that something weird was going on with the others. The old knifes would get black marks on them, like oval circles.

George planted grass out back with chicken wire at Gage Lane so the raccoons would not dig it up. Once I was in the top floor of the house and I could hear our dog Kaiser crying. She had got caught in the wire and I had to rescue her. The door was closed and there was no way out, so I think she had gone out with George and he pretended to come in the other way. The girls were at school and I thought I was alone.

When George put Kaiser down, I was surprised. He came home and immediately threw everything out. Although she was not my favourite pup. I am the one who brushed her when she was young and she was my companion during the tough times quietly lying there. I needed to grieve so I kept her little squeaker for a few months. I had to dig it out of the garbage!

When she was gone I could swear I heard her bark coming from some nearby house.

I am elated!! I suggested that Gary and I have a network named MGB. He has come back with BMG! I absolutely love it because now I feel protected from him on both sides!!! At the risk of repeating myself I would like us to have our own recording studio where we were known to help others break into the industry. We were the connection to the major record labels. How awesome would that be!!

He does expose me to videos where he speaks of having children and being married. He may have children but I definitely do not believe he is married!!! In fact, I do not think he has children either!

I think these videos are made to confuse George. Since they are making videos that are geared to sending messages to him.

I do wish they would not show these videos to me for it makes me scared and insecure.

Another individual I do not think has passed away is Princess Diana.

Dreaming Bigger:

- † It would be cool to have our own jet with a pilot to take us anywhere we want.
- † To have a float plane to take us on excursions.
- † Meeting Royalty and having tea with Gary and the girls and my family. I am sure they would be as thrilled as myself. Meeting the

Queen, Princess Diana and Prince Phillip and their sons. I do not believe the scandal that was reported about Princess Diana and Prince Phillip.
- † No more taxes to report or pay forever for myself and my entire family and friends.
- † Having my family and friends all be trusted travellers and no border questions or limitation as to how long we can stay in a certain place.

Monday, April 23, 2018

I have just discovered Sam Moore and Bruce Springsteen singing "Hold On, I'm Coming!!" Which may be named "Soul Man!" It gives me tremendous HOPE that Gary is on his way!! I love it!! The passion with which Bruce sings it uplifts me.

Sir Paul McCartney "I saw her standing there" is a fast love song telling me he won't dance with another!! These songs plus "Twist and Shout "now help me cope!!

I will listen to "Dancing in the Dark" again by Bruce Springsteen and "Born in the USA" which I wish the lyrics were more suited to Poppy. Maybe he will rewrite it again someday for me and her. I love the music to Dancing the Dark but not the lyrics!!

Dancing in the Dark was written for George because that was the only time he seemed to want to "dance," in bed. In no way was it dancing…that is too polite!!

Roy Orbison's song, "Pretty Woman" sung by Bruce Springsteen and John Fogerty is another hopeful song. The music does not drown out the lyrics!! It sounds like a love song to me from Gary!!

"No Time" sung by John Lennon, Burton Cummings, Joe Walsh and Dave Edmonds expresses my feelings toward George. It is as if through them I am singing to him!! Through Gary and all his friends in the music industry I have found myself a pair of wings!!

I am left with wondering still when this all began for me. When was Bluetooth a part of my body? Was it maybe embedded when I was born? Did it all happen in 2005 when I began my Masters and this journal or when I had my best to be forgotten hysterectomy or eye surgery! Perhaps they see what I see through my glasses that would explain why my eye doctor says I cannot wear contacts. This seems fishy and my gut tells me this is temporary and I just might get the transition contacts I think they should have the technology to do!

It was my mother who bought me my contacts back in the day when you kept one pair until they gave out!!

It was when my parents came out to visit that I got pretty clothes. They always took me shopping!! Well dad took me once. But I remember exactly what they bought me. Mom always sent pretty clothes to the girls too. They were awesome. I kept them but I do not know where they went!!

Darcy struggles financially right now so I help her when I can, just passing down on her what was bestowed on me!!

This reminds me during that summer I spent with George how he made me feel bad over the glasses I had just bought and said they were not nice!! Thinking back he was always cutting down my choices!! Man why did I wait so long?

Right now I feel so liberated…not constantly under his critical eye. Little did I realize, how I just wasn't myself. Now that I have found the music again I can stay up as late as I want!!

For a guy who said to me that summer that he had no habits and took a different way home all the time, he was very regimented and full of routines!!

Burton Cummings and Randy Bachman sing a song, "These Eyes." It is written and sung to me as if George is singing to me explaining how hurt he feels now and regrets his decisions. Their song, "She's come undone", makes me angry and sad for one of the lines says "she's lost a son" which speaks to George thinking Poppy was a boy!!! He was so insensitive. He never grieves over anyone. How can that be? I know people grieve in different ways but he chose no way!

Honestly, here is another song using slang, "You Ain't Seen Nothing Yet" They really should only use proper English. It should read "You Haven't Seen Anything Yet!!" This is a song send to George.

George said if it were not for him that I would be living on the East side with the homeless!! Did he actually think that my family would forsake me? How hurtful can a person be? I so love the revenge I am led to believe is happening toward him. He took music out of my life. I want music taken out of his life entirely!!

As Gary says in his song, he wiped my past. Then the government helped me by giving me an alias!! So, this happened when I moved here. So this protection must have started before I moved here in 1991!!

I so want my girls to know my side of the family including my mother's family!!! As well as my Uncle Chuck and Aunt Ellen!

I am curious as to whether Gary still performs? Everything I see is dated so long ago.

The lyric in my song "Let us be there when the sun emanates from within." that I wrote in a song that I also wrote to George on our 18th anniversary. I feel has been rewritten for me. The windows to my soul are slowly letting the sun in through the thought of Gary and Jessica now back in my life. Honestly the sun won't be fully shining until Gary takes me in his arms!! Tonight I will include my song "Windows to my Soul" in here too!!

Now instead of thinking of Neverland, I will think of Somewhereland. Places where Gary, the girls and I thrive. How will our first encounter go? Will he give me a bear hug? Will he grab my face and kiss me? Will we be prim and proper, hoping for more? Will we meet in a crowd first or on our own?

I had originally included pictures of family and musicians but the lawyer advised against it. I had even wanted to include a URL for one of Gary's songs but there may have been copyright issues. I wanted to include one for the Queen's 90th birthday which he arranged!! It is called "Something about this Night" for his musical "Finding Neverland" The other is for a musical which I know he is working on to reflect the story of my life and the girls. The musical is called "The Calendar Girls". I think it is based on the calendar I sent my mom of the girls which were not a part of her possessions that were returned to me.

This song was written to George on our 18th anniversary but rewritten for me. Where it said, "for Dear we cleared away the mist". Lyrics I never used because I was DEAR, therefore the lyric in the song refers to me. But now my original lyrics are back. So that means within the last few weeks someone has entered this condo of mine and switched the lyrics again. These lyrics are the same as what I originally wrote.

Perhaps like the HGTV show I saw today where the lyrics of a song had been etched to hang in their house. It is quite possible they are doing this for Gary and me!!!!! The lyrics are the same but the intended target now is me!

I no longer wish to see sunbeams emanate from within George! I am SO done. He cared very little for the music which I also gave him a tape of. He cares little for music or sentiment!! Now as I think of the second line to me it represents both Gary and I giving thanks for each other!

This song I want Gary to put to music if mine does not make sense. I know the melody but when I try to play the music it does not make sense to me anymore. I do not understand this because it made sense when I wrote it.

Windows to the Soul

Chorus:
G   D   Em
We're on a never ending ride
C   D   G
How I thank the Lord you're by my side.

Verse 1:
C   D   C
Looking into the windows of your soul
G   D   C
Tells me everything I need to know
G
Let me be there
D   C   D   C   G
When raindrops well up and when sunbeams emanate from within

Chorus:

MY COLOUR-CODED LIFE

```
G         D              Em
We're on a never ending ride
C            D              G
How I thank the Lord you're by my side.
```

Verse 2:
```
C                      D         C
When you look into the Windows of my soul
G           D      C
Can you see that I love you so?
G       D          C
Let our windows open wide
```

```
G           D         C
To the LOVE that's deep down inside.
G            D     C       G
Let us be there when raindrops well up
D              C         G
And when sunbeams emanate from within
```

Chorus:
We're on a never ending ride
How I thank the Lord you're by my side.
```
G            D     C       G
Let us be there when raindrops well up
         D            C        G
And when sunbeams emanate from within.
```

Chorus:
We're on a never ending ride
How I thank the Lord you're by my side.

Gary states in one of his songs that, "Every wish is a command in this place of Neverland". I think he is referring to my wish. If I were granted one wish, it would be spending the rest of my life with him.

When we first moved here George said he was going to take me to the best hamburger joint. He took me to Blue Angel Cafe. Sorry my best hamburger was in Las Vegas where they are not overwhelmed with this ridiculous mad cow disease. I had a medium rear burger and it was awesome!! I am not afraid to try new things and I knew they would not serve what would cause you harm!! Frankly I think this mad cow disease has something to do with George's ridiculous story that he was chased up a tree by a cow near the cabin!!

"Take on Me" by Aha, is another powerful song that I enjoy. I feel it is like Gary saying, "Take on Me" which I think is happening already!! Just listening to the song again, it is not what I thought. In fact it is depressing and talks about one leaving in a day or two. I am not fond of the new lyrics. But the title is very effective.

I listened to Westlife sing one of Robbie's Williams' songs and they appeared just as upset!!

So many things bother me about George and the dogs we owned. He is the one that taught me with dogs you never, no matter how small they are, pick them up for it only encourages them to jump. He allowed everyone to pick Kaiser up, which yes caused her to jump up until she got old.

It was Jessica who had wanted another dog, which was fine but George picked and bought the dog without me. He took me along to pick her up and as I have said before she was very ill. It appeared to me he had no idea how to pick out a dog but he had raised Alaskan Malamutes and helped me train Barclay.

When it came to training classes, it was me that went with Jessica. He had nothing to do with training our dog, Kaiser. In fact he spoiled her. Quite the opposite to how Barclay was treated and trained. I spent my days training Barclay then George did the same when he came home.

Again, it was me that took Kaiser in those early years to the Vets!!

When it came to breeding Barclay, our first dog, which he had done with his Alaskan Malamutes, he had no clue how to help me deal with Barclay when she went into heat. He took her to the vets and said she would not come out of heat so he had her spayed. I do not believe him. Frankly there is probably no such thing!!! This happened while we were living on Treble in Ontario. Poor Barclay! SO sad!

George was sure I would be able to work in the States, so I agreed to move. It turned out not to be the case. I had just started my career too! So I found other things to entertain me. I started my Masters and took and completed my three most dreaded courses first.

I fully realize that as the song goes, "Every Breath You Take" implies that Gary is watching everything George does, says and sees, while protecting me, but I have to tune it out when I am with others so I can keep my life on the ground.

Judging by George's behaviour around me he thinks he is a part of some movie too. He so many times acted like a fool around me.

When I think of the song SHINE, I cannot help think about George shining shoes. He did not do this while I stayed with him that summer or anywhere. He became obsessed with it at Gage Lane and the townhouse. He did not even have these polishes before.

Monday, April 23, 2018

Every time I hear a song I hear Darcy reaching out to me!! I tell her doppelganger always how much I care. Do my daughters hear me?

Even when I saw my desktop with poppies I do not only think of Poppy but Jessica and Action!! Both girls are filling me with action in my life through Gary!!

I am curious if FACEBOOK could be created for families so parents do not have to worry about their children. I want to have a life with no secrets and separate lives within the sham of a marriage.

Also, I believe in family cell phones, so that if one person is busy the call can be answered by anyone in the family. I do not like how cell phones work. I would like them to work as a HOME PHONE. Then you could also speak to someone even though you may not be the intended target for the call. Home phones were friendlier.

I do not understand, if George had been a chimney sweep he changed our fireplaces to gas without considering how I felt. He even had to have the one for the basement custom made. He may have asked me but it does not make sense to me!! I do not like gas fireplaces.

I believe the song of Peter Cetera that the real George is the hero I am looking for and he is fighting for my honour.

It still does not make sense why George was so upset when I preferred to wear the watch from Venice and kept saying it looked poor, when he supposedly was with me when I chose it!!!. Sometimes watches that have clasps stop working and the watch gets too small. With a strap you can adjust it with weight gained or lost and is relatively cheap to change a strap to another colour. I love my watch from Venice it is colourful. I hope my next watch is as colourful. It was the most colourful pretty thing I could find and afford made out of Murano glass.

Murano reminds me of one of my students. A student I taught in my first school, in Ontario. She wrote me for years but after I went to her house after graduation the letters stopped. I never threw out her letters. Another item mysteriously gone.

Perhaps seeing me after meeting her at graduation at her home which she had invited me to, I had let her down in some way. I used to have a picture of her for so long but unfortunately when I downsized it went. Perhaps I can have the picture again!! However she is always in my heart. Receiving those letters made me feel that maybe I had touched one heart.

It was cool because I had kept in touch with my grade three teacher for a long time, as well. I wonder if my teacher still has the scarf I knit for her that my mom stayed up all night to finish for me?

Most of the LOVE songs shown to me where there is a male and female are Gary and I singing to each other… not just him to me!!

So many things missing, Darcy's tricycle…Jessica never had one she hung onto her sister for a ride around the cul-de-sac. Where did it go? Where did their bikes go, that they never rode? George had a bike at that time why did he not ride with them? He made me get rid of mine when we were living in Brampton, Ontario. Why?

Regarding mail through the post, which I call Snail Mail. I think it would be safe and nice to continue. No matter how techy this world gets, which I love, it is so nice to receive something that is not a flyer or a bill through the mail!! For this reason, I would send letters to my Uncle and Jessica!! Plus you can put something in an envelope or package that you cannot through email.

When Jessica would send postcards from her trip to Malaysia, I saved them. She never knew how to spell my name.

Mail would be safe to sign if you wanted to handwrite. We should get rid of Cheques and the need to sign important documents!!!

I tend to prefer to type my letters off the computer and then sign and add my name after it has been printed and add a PS.

I guess I believe in Choice!!

Tuesday, April 24, 2018

- ✓ I have just had another idea I had from watching Will Smith on the Graham Norton Show through YouTube. I think instead of having concerts aired only into the homes they could be aired in grand theatres around the world. Each theatre would have dinner provided with waiters and waitresses. Not just popcorn!! So these theatres would offer both major movies and concerts!! Families could have dinner out too and watch Wesley Disney films. So either a romantic night or family friendly!!
- ✓ Even as I try to watch these late night shows I am not a fan even if Gary is being interviewed. They are always making fun of someone! So far the only talk Shows I can watch are Oprah, when she was on, Cityline which I have watched since a young girl, and Marilyn Dennis and Dr. Phil. 60 minutes and W5 I really respected because they usually spoke of true stories! Those two talk shows I would feel honoured to tell my story!!
- ✓ My brother always watched Saturday Night Live which I never saw. These other night shows are trash! I feel the same with America's Funniest Home Videos. They cater to people who like to make fun of someone or watching someone or an animal get hurt. George had no sense of humour because he laughed at everything. Perhaps I do not have a sense of humour because I am picky with what I find humorous!! But when I do find something funny, it really makes me

laugh. Over the years, being married, it was my mother who made me laugh. Man, I miss her!
- ✓ I do firmly believe that musicians would prefer to do their art as I have previously described and have quality family life! I think this idea would help musicians spend more time with their family.

Someone, somewhere has all my things, but I care not for the letters George wrote to me. If I possessed them I would probably burn them like I smashed the figurines he gave me. There are things here I want to burn but I have no way of safely doing that.

I absolutely love Gary's song, "Something about This Night!" He seems so happy and is glowing!! I think it is my favourite but I adore all the songs. When he sings a "Million Love Songs" I feel it is for me, though I do not like how he invites someone on stage to sing to.

I only sometimes wonder about that first night in the Keg! The face is hazy, the voice forgotten, but I am positive it was not whom I married.

I thought of Gary today as I bought Darcy's birthday gift and the choice to reset my ring. I wondered whether he would have encouraged me to follow my instincts and feelings or just say it is too expensive.

I have bought an emerald ring for her which is being engraved. Emerald is her birth stone!! These are the things that last forever. Being engraved with LOVE MOM 2018. She will never forget when or who gave it to her and with it hopefully a celebration that will touch her heart and soul!! Always connected to the ring!!

For Jessica's birthday I will get a ring with either a garnet (which is her birthstone) or a ruby, whichever looks nicer, both are red. With diamonds on either side. This would be similar to Darcy's. The significance of having the diamonds on either side is that they are being supported by my love, for my birthstone is diamond. I would like to have it engraved and to incorporate the infinity symbol somehow, with her birthdate and mom on it. I chose the infinity symbol MOM 2020.

When the girls were getting confirmed I wanted rings engraved, but my downfall was taking George with me and not having enough money according to him, or my own account. We bought cheap rings that broke. He did not offer to have them replaced when the jeweller could not fix them. I had wanted a ring with their initial on the top and an engraving on the inside.

- † It would not be difficult to rid ourselves of licence cards, health cards or passports. Police would have a reader where people who have been stopped would have to offer a hand print. Since you have to give your hand print to get your passport already this technology already exists. I firmly believe this technology is what will save the world from criminal activity. If you have nothing to hide it should not bother you. The bonus is no more cards.

- † Regarding promotional cards…they can be done through a website where you can click on the ones you want to join. No more promotional cards!! Men, no more wallets!! Women no more wallets, Just something small to carry collapsible brushes and a lipstick!!! How wonderful would that be? Frankly I might even offer my lipstick and brush to be carried in my husband's pocket, if I am wearing a dress with no pockets. Though I think they should make all dresses with DEEP pockets!! No more shallow pockets for women!! If I end up with a fashion line everything will have DEEP pockets. No one will ever tell me again to get my hands out of my pockets!!!!!!!!!!!!!!!!!!!!!!!!!!!!! Never did I tell him to unfold his arms, which he said was for his sore shoulders. Bunk!! He was protecting himself, just like I was!! I am pretty good with Body language too!!

I previously wrote, it is said by many that I should let go of things that are or were real incidents and move on. However, I look at the present and still so certain with what I see make it so difficult to let go. Am I caught in a game? Yes! I am locating songs within songs, editing and recalling names of people I know!! Am I caught in an undercover sting? Yes! The girls have made it clear now that they are helping me and the music makes it clear that this is so too!! Am I part of some sick reality show? Yes!! I may be sick, but I know for a fact they can see everything I see or write, hear everything I think or say. They have also tapped my phone because I can hear the echo of my own voice many times on the phone!! Am I merely ill with thoughts that are my own? No! Gary and all his friends, the musicians, those in Hollywood and my daughters all are helping me. It just took them time to gain the evidence they needed. They were not ready for me. On the other hand, did I agree to be a subject in research where no one would know during one of my discussions in my Master's Degree? I vaguely remember something like this. Yes!! They have used medication to keep me quiet while they gathered information on George!! For this meant he would have no information on me, since even before I was medicated I had never shared my entire past. He really knew nothing about me!!

Interesting how this last paragraph turns out green and black (when my entries were colour-coded)!! Gary's been taking care of me all along!! Right along with my girls and my dad!! In fact, all the colours are helping and taking action…I love them all!! I hope to receive messages to clear my thoughts about my dad.

When listening to Gary and Dawn French perform. I love her part!! It depicts how I feel but would never say!! The song is called, "Fairytale of New York" on Text Santa. I think having a way for children to text Santa would be great because communicating with him could be all year long and they would have a wonderful way to express to him more than just for presents. I would suggest it be counsellors on the other end, just in case something pops up and help is needed. What a wonderful suggestion was made to me through this video or perhaps they are reminding me of something I had already written!!

Just like I thought before when I gave George and the girls flash drives of all the pictures, at Christmas, it would be interesting if he could decipher between which were actual pictures and those that were not!!

I understand now why he had no pictures of his past. He took nothing. He said they got everything. When he left me he took hardly anything.

I rewrote "I Want You to Want Me" by Cheap Trick for George on our 18th. I gave a total of three songs that year, two of which I wrote!! No one can say I did not try!! (Sunday, January 12, 2020 - I have not included the song I rewrote for fear of copyright laws. I contacted FriesenPress, whom I have decided to self-publish with, but they were not able to advise me and suggested I contact a copyright lawyer. I did but he could not advise me until I retained him.) I decided not to retain him for I feared what the cost would be.

I hope with every fibre of my body that my new home is filled with all my colours!! I never want to forget what I went through. I want my life filled with music and dance!! Seems like Gary's life is filled with these things.

Sometimes I wonder if Gary and my family are proud of me! I stated in my dad's song that our memories had just begun. Is this true? That was 18 years ago. I guess this has to speed up if I am to see him while he is still alive 2018 minus 1912 equals 106 years old. This reminds me of when George told me that Jessica told him that he should know that some people are living into their 200's now! I believe my dad is one of those people!! As is Mr. Pierre Elliot Trudeau who died the same year! Man, I miss him!

So this journey cannot go on forever if I am to see my father and my mother alive, as well as everyone we've been led to believe to have died over the years. I want to rub my husbands' face in the fact that he did not believe in me!! I want him to face everyone and he will be shocked and they will know how he showed no grieving for them!

When it came to my father's death why did he not want to go with me and then phone to see if I wanted him and the girls there?? I said yes and they came.

My psychiatrist says that I am doing fine. But I replied, "How can this be, I believe dead people are alive!"

Wednesday, April 25, 2018

Dreaming Bigger: In addition to my Needs and Wants list:

1. For myself and extended family to have houses of their choice near me and to not have to pay mortgages
2. For my extended family, friends and myself not to never have to pay for any utility bills, including phones
3. To have my family and friends never have to work again unless they wanted to
4. I have already wished for musical instruments in my life: piano, folk guitar, maybe even an electric one, banjo and ukulele. How

would I ever be able to learn all of them? For my family to have instruments of their choice in their homes.
5. To have music teachers come to us. To have Gary teach me piano.

When I watch Gary singing with ladies in red from his musical Finding Neverland. I feel it is like he is singing to me. I am the lady in red, reminiscent of the red dress George had bought me. Never to buy another.

Yet George would read the song and the video as Jessica being the lady in red.

Sunflower used to be a happy flower for me when we grew them at Saber Road and they reached above the deck. I took a picture of the girls standing on the porch and the sunflower was above them! However at the cabin Paula used to grow them and when she had a picture taken of the family George grabbed me and I was on the other side of the flower away from the family. When I saw the picture, it hurt! I no longer like sunflowers!! I am like the outcast in the picture!!

Just like the time when Sandra did not think at Christmas that I should get a necklace from Paula's border. She said, "Why does she get one, she is not family?" George never defended me. It hurt, and never to be forgotten!! The saying "sticks and stones may break my bones but names will never hurt me" bears no truth!!!!!

Every time going to the cabin and going to the bedroom, Paula had the picture on the dresser…it just rubbed it in how I did not fit in!!

So, even though people are waiting for the sunshine to emanate from within me and they use the sunflower as a symbol, I prefer a Shasta Daisy, Buttercups and Daffodils, Even a red and yellow rose plant!!

Every time I hear "Could it be Magic"sung and performed by Gary Barlow and Robbie Williams with Barry Manilow. This is Barry Manilow's song. It states, "Come into my arms". I can't help but always think of the hugs that my girls' kindergarten teacher had the students do and give at an assembly. Darcy gave it to her grade 7 buddy and Jessica gave it to her sister. It crushed me!! I felt like an awful mom. I wonder where the hug Jessica gave Darcy went? I never saw it after that day!!

George never came to any of the assemblies while he was off work. However, he went on all the field trips! Everyone admired how well he led the kids on the trip to the beach. Of course a big show for everyone watching. I never got to go on any field trip. I was the bread winner! I felt like I could not take a day off! I needed those days for I got sick so often!

One reason I believe my dad is not dead is the scarf story between us. He and I near Christmas had gone shopping, as we often did at the Eaton's Mall, and he fell in love with a burgundy cashmere scarf. I, a few days later, went to buy it for him but it was gone and there was not another I could buy.

At Christmas, I gave him something else and told him how I went to buy it but it was gone. He much later told me, he had bought it but knowing that I had wanted to spend my money on it, he did not want to wear it anymore. I guess it might have choked him with remorse or something. He had said to me he never had the heart to wear it again. It was not part of his affects. I deliberately looked in his dresser for it, but only found my song and cassette on his dresser which I took…and his black wallet I bought for him and then gave to George. Maybe the scarf was in his locker either at The Granite Club or The Board of Trade Country Club.

I asked my brother if it was among his affects, but he said, no.

Which has me thinking since I never formally withdrew my membership from The Granite Club, maybe I am still a member, though I have not paid any dues.

So I would wish that I was still a member and that Gary and the girls would be members too and that we would never have to pay dues!! We would be honourary members ….everything would be free to join or partake in.

When I hear Boyzone and Gary singing about a Hurricane stuck in the back of her throat, it reminds me of how George always would have me set up the internet Wi-Fi everywhere we lived except at Saber Road. I had Hurricane, Crazy2, and finally I made it Mickey!!

He is also the one that set me up with TD Easyweb at Saber Road. He set the password and everything. I did not have to do anything. He also chose my first cell phone and my number which I still have. I hope in the future to have a new number perhaps using the acronym of my favourite name: MICHÈLE-642-4353!! I only got a cell phone because Mandy had spoken to Sam to have him talk to George about it. I probably never would have gotten one otherwise.

If I didn't feel so protected now, I would be panicking!!

YOU

(The song I wrote to George and sang on our wedding day. My brother, dad and Rick were concerned about me doing this)

Verse 1
```
C             D
Feelings run so deep
C          D
Feelings run away 'till they're
G         C          D
Caught by the magic of you 'till they
G         C          D
See the smile in your eyes. Now my
      C                    D
Chorus: Feelings have a place to stay
         G        C        D    G
My feelings feel so safe (with you)
```

Verse 2:
```
C          D
Talking is so nice
C          D
Listening is so right and when
G              C        D
Sharing is the power that we hold than I
G              C
Know we have a treasure 'till we're old
C                         D
Chorus: Feelings have a place to stay
   G       C       D   G
My feelings feel so safe (with you)
```

Verse 3
```
C                            D
```

MY COLOUR-CODED LIFE

Understanding is what you are
C   D   G
To me or friends a far. Now I want
Everyone here to know, just how proud
That you're my 'bro"
           C   D
Chorus: Feelings have a place to stay
      G   C   D   G
        My feelings feel so safe (with you)

Verse 4.

People are so different

Games have different rules

But for DEAR we cleared away the mist

From the very first day our eyes first kissed.
         C   D
Chorus: Feelings have a place to stay
      G   C   D   G
My feelings feel so safe (with you)

Verse 5:

All the feelings deep inside

I could not bury or try to hide

Feelings are what life thrives upon

And feelings are what you chose me on.

He also originally set me up with Aeroplan, even though it was my card. I was so worried then that I said my birthday was April 4th, which I recently corrected.

Even though Gary's song says, "haven't we heard it all", Seems there is always something more to share.

Hearing Boyzone sing, "Better" now is like Gary singing to me that he is happy with what I have just shared.

Gary and Take That have taken sentiments I have expressed in this book and turned them into real musical hits. I can only believe that this is all real and maybe I will have a fairy-tale ending to my life.

I desperately want to change my email to rid myself of the Hall name. I want it done automatically for me where everyone was notified even me as to what that would be. I am afraid if I figured out how to do it I might not be able to let all the utilities and contacts know.

This is the song I wrote to the man I thought I was marrying: It appears it was rewritten for me. For it uses the phrase, "But for DEAR we cleared away the mist," which I would not have written. I realize the lyrics have been altered

My girls have never heard this song. They were there when I sang him the songs on our 18th. This one I played at our wedding. It is now titled, "YOU" The sentiments in it are now intended for Gary and he has cleared away my mist and is fighting for my honour!!

Before George and I were married my feelings felt safe with him as outlined in my song to him on our wedding day. However during our first year of marriage I was given reason to be jealous.

On our drive south he had me review applications for his new secretary. I chose one whose name was Sandy. She ended up being a mature women that I felt was qualified. George hired then fired her. He hired a much younger, taller beautiful women whom I felt he flirted with.

When I expressed my jealousy, at home during lunch one day, He slammed his fist on our glass table and said he demanded complete trust! I was so scared. I should have said that trust is earned, not a given. I should have known then that something was wrong.

As I now have been copying my entries to this book to Jessica. As much as she may not have known me before, for I never shared about my past. She will know me now!!

Maybe the knitting website I spoke about can be mine. Gary will help me!

Listening to Paul McCartney singing, "Here There and Everywhere" is a message from Gary to me (heart and soul).

I just listened to Gary or his doppelganger, Mark and Howard interviewed where they say they are going on tour this year and if this is true, then I believe I will be going with them, for I do not believe Gary will not come for me!! I had asked if they were still performing and I guess I have my answer. He looks different to me than how he looks in the piano medley.

I really wonder how well I do with facial recognition. I do not want to be tested anymore. The evaluation, I spoke of earlier, had said I was stupid and not reflective of someone with a Master's Degree. Whereas, I think my girls get their intelligence from me, perhaps even their empathy and sensitive natures.

I so wish he could be here for Darcy's birthday!!

Thursday, April 26, 2018

I think I have figured out what a SOUL SYMBOL could look like. A circle within another circle with Hands coming from the outer circle gripping onto the inner circle or better the hands coming together within the inner circle. Maybe if Gary wears jewelry he would wear one too and it would be a complete reminder of our SOUL journey!! I hope he wears jewelry. This could be the only necklace that we would ever need. Connected from the heart to the soul. I envision it surrounded with all my colours.

When I went to the jewellers I chose to have my Great Aunt's ring changed to white gold from yellow gold. I like all my rings to match in colour of gold…Since I had a yellow band for my wedding ring with George, I want it completely different in my future. I also plan to trade in my wedding band and pinky ring for store credit. My only problem is that

I really dislike buying my own jewelry. We will see. I changed it to white gold because it sets off the diamonds more.

The more I am involved in this "game" the more it seems they knew me when I was a child. They even know what shows I preferred as a child. Perhaps this book of mine goes much farther back then I imagined. Perhaps it is my life story. Perhaps even I will be surprised when I see it in print?

George's iPad is really mine as well as the one I have. The iPad came with my iPhone and he took it over for work.

Goal: To be PILL FREE!!

Here comes my insecurity again. I watched an interview where they have said that Gary was expecting another child. I do not believe it. As with most of the news I have been presented over the years I do not believe.

It is so hard to believe and now trying to find more messages from him either on You Tube or HGTV is becoming more difficult. I am so scared to be crushed!! Listening to his ballad and love songs give me hope as does listening to Bruce Springsteen and Same Moore sing "HOLD ON, I'm COMING".

Tonight is harder to find the music to help me. I need them to present the music for me!! I must admit his song with Agnetha Faltskog, "I Should Have Followed You Home" has me confused. I believe it to mean that the man I met in The Keg that summer should have followed me home because I flew out the next morning. I believe something happened to that man and he's been trying to find me. Sometimes I think that the Archdiocese found him and he is learning all about me.

They wouldn't manipulate the colours to reinforce me if it was false. I do not believe they would lift my spirits just to crush me.

Since I do not believe that George is a true Hall and in the future will be paying dearly for his transgressions, I would like to help the Hall's for helping me by having their cabin expanded for them. Maybe we can all be friends in the future where their characters are more reflective of whom they really are. I will never forget how kind Donald was when I first met the family at the cabin.

Take That's song ,"Love Love" is directed toward George, telling him to teach his heart to talk, directly coming from my wish that Catholic Church teach children to talk to God rather than learn prayers.

Everything I see and hear on YouTube seems to be directly coming from what I think and what I write in this book. It has to be real.

Thursday, April 26, 2018

Upon reading my supposed Uncle Lester's obituary it is from Legacy.com. I take that to mean that I am leaving my mark and leaving a Legacy and that I have left my mark!! But it would all mean nothing unless I can share it with Gary!!

When I tried looking up the obituary for my dad it took me directly to my mother's supposed one. I did write my father's while in Connecticut where he supposedly died but I do not know what my brother did with it. I never saw it in the newspaper.

I chose the keepsake card and the one I now possess is not the one I chose for him!!

What I do not understand is that the night Louise supposedly died, Carol called to break the news, and, she spoke like it was any other day. My sister is not dead!!

So as Barry Gibb and Michael Jackson sing, "what is my life if I don't believe there is someone to watch me follow my dreams?" They sing, "That is all in the game. It is all in your name".

I still believe with Gary at the hub, that he is helping my girls fulfill my dreams!! I believe my dreams were expanded to include all singers, songwriters, those in Hollywood and newscasters as well.

Like for their dad, my girls with Gary are my heroes too!! When my husband fell off the ladder, I was only aware of one picture being taken and that was at the front door of our home…The pictures we have, had to be taken without my knowledge and George never told me they came to take more, nor did the girls.

It was me that reached out to the media when George had his supposed tragedies!!

I have just got news that my divorce is final May 24th 2018!! I will be legally free to remarry!!!
So much for me to celebrate on Darcy's Birthday (May 25)…so glad I can walk to the celebration at the Keg. I can cheer myself. Since George will be there I will have to be discreet!

I feel while living with George that I had a bit of Stockholm Syndrome. Although my feelings for George were dead 18 years ago. I did everything I could to make it work and I feared that I could not survive on my own. Look at me now! I live in a beautiful condo which I own and several friends!! With only better things to come with Gary!!

My girls are intelligent!! Even though I tried to keep them out of my desperate situation. They must have realized something was wrong with our family life. I am sure they realized that our marriage was all wrong. Even more so because they are instilling themselves into our lives to gain information.

I will never forget how Jessica's eyes focussed on her dad while she was playing with Cassie at the cabin. He was being disrespectful to me regarding getting dinner ready. I was grateful someone witnessed how he treats me.

Gary's song, "Face to Face" is written for me!!

Boyzone's song, "What becomes of the Broken Hearted" is made for George.

> *April 26, 2018* What if by chance the person I met at The Keg was not George at all, but Gary. In any case my heart and soul is Gary's. We have a romance that no one can deny!! I have faith he will make it real.

After I wrote this, Ronan Keating came on and he is so excited and happy!!!

He is singing "Life is a Rollercoaster" You know it very possible that it could have been Gary because I do not recall him even introducing himself to me that night at the Keg. He left so soon after we met. Why he left so early I may never know. If I am wrong again, my feelings are for Gary!! From what I see and hear, he feels exactly the same. So that means Gary is brown and green and black, as well as the combination **of green and black**!!

My head is spinning!! If this is true how did they find him? How did he find me? I hope in my future that I can one day sing a duet with Gary!! Have our Soul song permanently etched as I said before hanging on the wall of our home.

I want that fairy-tale ending that Cinderella had.

I feel that I am supposed to examine all sorts of destinations in the world that I would like to go to and where I would like to have a family vacation, or honeymoon. I have felt so negative about travelling because of my experiences, that this is very difficult and it was always my chore to make the arrangements and use my money. We went travelling and deep inside, I just wanted to be home.

I really like, Adam Lambert when he sings, "Mad World". It really speaks to me!! I also like when he sings with Queen and sings, We Will Rock you and We are the Champions!

When One Republic sings, "I lived" and the lyrics say, "with every broken bone, I swear I lived," makes me believe that Poppy is alive!! But this cannot be, for when I wrote the hospital to ream them out for how I was treated by the nurse, surely they would have told me!! My God is there a possibility? Her body did not seem broken though.

- † I know I would like to take a float plane and travel around here or wherever they go.
- † Go to an all-inclusive with the family. It must have excursions! Anywhere but Mexico and Cuba…those places will take me awhile to get over.
- † Go to and stay at Disneyland, and bring Cassie and Brian, their siblings and ALL my daughters!!
- † Places to go with Gary, Hmmm, I am curious about Sweden, Switzerland, Holland, Iceland, Arctic, England. Maybe take a year and travel the world in our own jet!! But I really want to go on the Rocky Mountaineer and see Canada, visit my friends in various parts of the country first. It is more important to me to have a happy home with a boxer pup. I travelled without trusting but depending on George.

I also like the boyband, Westlife (Shane Filan, Nicki Byrne, Kian Egan, Markus Feehily. Their song, "Hit You with the Real Thing" feels like it is meant for George but I feel like I am a part of hitting him with the real thing too!! I love it when they look right in the camera and sometimes point to it making me feel certain they are singing directly to me.

I want to meet all the members of Take That, that sing with Gary; Robbie Williams, Mark Owen and Howard Donald. Their music has meant so much to me!!

Reading back in this book, it is certain, that someone has taken control of it, which I am thankful for!! Someone was able to write the Pros and Cons much better than I could. They know me better than I do myself.

Here is another CON: If I do not have my fairy-tale ending with Gary Barlow!!

He sought me out like Sir Elton John sang; he was waiting in a line of Green and Blues!! Seeing all he has done for me and all his friends singing for him, how do you ever thank someone for doing so much? I have never been sought after, I have only been used.

Gary has not physically touched me yet, but I already feel more loved then I ever have before.

He just sang a song, where he said, "let me start by saying, I love you." I just know he was singing to me. I believe I love him more. A man so respected has to be someone I can trust with my feelings and my soul!!

I feel I was robbed of half my life!! Perhaps my biggest mistake was not having my mother meet George before we were engaged. She may have had some insight. Only dad, Sam and Daisy did. It seems he fooled them too!! So when boys ask for permission to marry someone's daughter, I strongly suggest that you ask the mother too!!

So since my parents are probably too old to walk me down the aisle, I will choose my brother.

Also, why is it the dad is chosen to walk their daughter down the aisle? Moms suffer to have their little girl, I think they should also give their daughter away.

According to Coldplay's song, "Viva la Vida" it is about a king losing his kingdom and based on revolutionaries and guerrillas. It speaks of the Catholic Church. I am not scared or feel any regret in saying that I feel I am definitely a revolutionary regarding the Catholic Church!! As I have said this before there is no point going to a church where you do not believe in most of their practices!! I believe I am a better Catholic than those that attend church on a regular basis for I know from casual conversations that most are unhappy, especially the children, once they have a choice to attend or not.

When I first met George he introduced me to coffee and I introduced him to tea. Over time coffee was all we drank but when it was difficult for me to choose where to go for coffee because dad represented Tim Horton's and George Starbuck's, George still made me always choose where we were going to go. Thankfully now I have stopped drinking coffee at home and am drinking tea!!! Somewhat moving back to whom I was before I met him.

I love Take That's song, "KIDZ". It speaks to the problem when the kids come out. I think it refers to the problem George will face when all our daughters come out and all their friends!!

Was Michael Jackson's song Annie, which was changed to Smooth Criminal, truly depict George? I strongly feel it does! I believe he was involved with fraud along with other things, I will be enlightened on. I have no proof. I had a well-paying position and I wonder where all my money went. I see other people with incomes like mine and they own boats and go on trips. Why did we only go once the girls were much older? Where did my money go?

I also really like Michael Jackson's song, "Beat it!"

Seems I really like Boybands!! Ronan Keating, Stephen Gately, Shane Lynch, Keith Duffy, Mikey Graham of Boyzone also speak directly to me When they and Westlife sing their eyes really twinkle, just as if Gary was singing to me. They are all really good at singing with intention and making me believe they are singing to me.

I believe they sing a beautiful song to me and when I input the title of their song into Google it is input all messed up. I think it is for what George will see when he looks something up. I believe they show me the real people and beautiful songs now.

Our neighbour, a friend I made at the townhouse, invited us to the Jazz Festival downtown but George did not want to go. I have only heard Jazz at high school. If he did not like it why did he like the saxophone player in Las Vegas where we bought a CD of the performer?

As Kelly Clarkson sings, in her song, "Stronger" my life began when he left. However, her lyric, "just me, myself and I" doesn't fit me. Once I found my music, hers being one of them, I did it with the help of the singers who sang inspirational songs!!

It all started with "On Eagle's Wings" and "Dare to Hope"

Saturday, April 28, 2018

Luther Vandross and Mariah Carey singing, "Endless Love" is Gary and I singing to each other!!

Seems now that which I input into Google is correct and not messed up.

- † Seems to me I should be able to get Siri to play an artist without them being in my playlist
- † Plus when I write a letter in word I should be able to choose which language I want it translated into so the document is then written in that language.

I also believe that Boyzone's "Here Comes the Boys" reflects all the boys that have born witness to what has gone on in our life. So it will be all the girls and all the boys.

You know I am so glad to be free of George shaping my world. One day while living at Diamond Head, a few years before we separated, I bought not the prettiest dress but it was all I could find. It was grey with white horizontal stripes. Anyhow I wore it one day and George quickly cut me down saying how impractical it was. Instead of standing my ground, I changed.

Adele's song, "Rolling in the Deep" where she sings, "you're gonna wish you never had met me" really fits my inner feelings toward George. I have even created a playlist on YouTube specifically for songs directed to him to help me vent my feelings.

Here is a brand new song trying to express my present feelings to Gary.

Painted Lady

Verse:
```
     D              C
Please do not toy with me
         D              Am
My soul cannot take it you see
D                C
My dreams perhaps too steep
         D              Am
To ever really see complete
```

Chorus:
```
         D                  C
I would give them all you see
         D                      Am
Unless you were here to share with me
```
Verse:
```
         D              C
I am feeling happy now
D                    Am
Hoping that we touch real soon
D                    C
So bring on all the colours
         D              Am
Both in song and TV
```

Chorus:
```
D                        C
I would give them all you see
         D                          Am
Unless you were here to share with me
```
Verse:
```
         D              C
My life without you
```

```
   D              Am
Would be so less vibrant
   D              C
For I am your painted lady
   D                    Am
And you are the keeper of my soul!!
```

Is it possible that I did not recognize the man I met so long ago in The Keg? Could I really have not been that good at recognizing the facial differences? Did the person who took his identity really fool all of us?

I want so much it to have been Gary!! I am so attracted to him!! And if it is not, then the man I met, "should have followed me home," for my heart belongs to Gary now!!

Funny though, I do not see the twinkle in Gary's eyes as I do in those performing in Westlife for him. I keep waiting for that twinkle. I saw it once in one of his performances with all the clowns, where he looked directly in the camera for quite some time.

Perhaps he will take me to his special place he calls Neverland!! I find it interesting how he does not sing with his beautiful accent.

I am so blessed to have had Darcy stay by my side throughout my struggle. She helped me shop when I could not do so by myself. I kept my true feelings from her though for a long time though for she did not want to hear it. I am so thankful now that they have ears and are willing to listen. The fact that Jessica is now willing to accept daily copies of what I write in this book is awesome. Unless, they come to bite me later. She has been so appreciative of receiving them so I am believing that I can trust her with my emotions!!

It seems the phrases from songs I input into Google is back to being messed up, for reasons I have explained before.

I just looked up Sandra's obituary and it does not make sense. It states she passed away in her home which I know was not true. She passed away in her nursing home according to George. Plus it states that her name was spelled oddly because of the loss of her father and her mother renaming her, however this is the proper way to spell the name!! Just proves to me she is alive somewhere.

I feel so blessed, but I feel so robbed!! You know if it was not for me, Jessica and her friends would never have been able to enjoy going water-skiing in Kinter Valley. I had to talk George into it.

If it was not for Jack and Mandy the girls and I would never have had a ride on the ocean!! How is it possible that you live in such a place that has a variety of things to do and he never wanted to do anything that cost money? Where did all my hard earned money go? Why? Why were we so strapped for money that I could not shop for anything but now I am okay?

For someone who bragged about how he went skiing every day in Sanchester City, why did we never take the kids skiing? Even when they learnt snowboarding we never went. He only started going when Jessica was in University. We only went once while living here with Kay and Randy and that was it and that was back in the 90's. Back in '84 while living in North Dakota, we went skiing with his boss, Wesley, and his friends. We never went again.

How is it he went skiing with Jessica and yet needed her help to buckle his boots but was able to go on a skiing holiday on his own recently?

There are so many things I want to try and enjoy with Gary, but I am not getting any younger I am afraid that I will not be able to keep up with him!! I have tried to get a personal trainer for that would be the only way I would be motivated. I have been blocked to finding one in this area. Maybe I will try at my gym that I have not gone to all winter because I can't get motivated. I do not want someone to give me a routine and that's it. I want someone to be there every time I go.

George, when it came to shopping for Jessica's camera, I wanted him to purchase one that was not so big and easier to handle, but no, he had to buy a more substantial one that she would have to lug around. We paid so much for it and the bag, that it was my idea to split the gift up between her present for Christmas and her birthday. She reamed her dad out but it was my idea. It was me she needed to direct her anger.

I feel very strongly that so many were hoping and waiting for this sever between George and I. It is I that needs to apologize to Gary for having taken so long. I should've been stronger and lift my head higher. The only thing that makes me feel better about my sad marriage is that I can easily say that I gave it everything.

So Gary, Darcy and Jessica please accept my apologies for not getting my act in gear. I should've been able to fight the affects the medication was having on me!! Although when I was stronger before I was talked out of it by Sam!!

I regret that it was George walking out instead of me kicking him out!!

One thing that still bothers me is the dispute George and I would have over our house in North Dakota. I was there when we chose it and I will swear up and down that it was a rent to own home, whereas George insists it was not. If I am mistaken then why was there no realtor or sign on our lawn? He never told me if it was sold or what we made on it!!

Just one more reason to make me swear that I married some sort of con man…and maybe this is why the whole music world seems to have opened up to me, for it started during my first year of marriage.

I sometimes feel the music industry is making money for my online school dream. The crowds they sing to are immense and all the audience are standing.

When we were living at Gage Lane he took all the cheque books from North Dakota and burned them in the fire.

I am not quite sure whom Pink is referring to when she wonders why we fall in love so easy even when it is not right in her song, 'Try'. Perhaps me, perhaps George? I am not going to let her burst my bubble.

I am the one who thought there was a division between love and family. But I will not choose, for they are one. When you have a family you love them all and you do not play favourites or make one feel inferior. In my mind, George interpreted the "love" part of my psychosis to mean just him and me.

I now have a pair of pink pants, something George would not approve of. A while ago I bought some and he said they were for young girls, I should have kept them, but I returned them. The same goes with my yellow shoes. I was at the store having difficulty picking a colour when a lady suggested the yellow ones, so I bought them. George made fun of them and said they were too loud. I stopped wearing them and bought black ones.

I felt he was doing this because he was not wanting to support Darcy, remember she is yellow. Later he bought red shoes, so I mentioned to him that they too were a bright colour for him. He said he had no choice. Red is Jessica, so I felt he preferred to support Jessica.

Robbie Williams whom I believe is one of Gary's best friends no matter what is said. He would not get so emotional over this journey I am a part of if he really did not care for Gary.

There is a picture of Robbie Williams with two thumbs up which directly relates to Darcy and the symbol I have for her!! It just happens to be the symbols used to evaluate the music and movies too!!

Sunday, April 29, 2018

In sending this to Jessica the picture did not send likely for legal reasons. So I took it out. But I will put it here for those helping to write this book to decide what can and cannot be published. (November 16, 2019 - My lawyer said to take out all the pictures.)

So I have gone onto my saved music for Mickey and I have discovered music I did not, would not save!! So who is saving music on my site, George or my doppelganger? I know he apparently has a Rock n Roll TV!!

I again am feeling shaky regarding the music. I am needing something new from Gary. Plus, I have very little to choose from on the TV, Even HGTV is letting me down. There isn't enough variety in their shows.

I hope Gary that you understand that I do not want you to be mine just to make my husband jealous!! I want us to date, I understand maybe it is too soon to say that I love you without having met you face to face. However, I do feel this connection!! You are my soul man!!

It is crazy to have this infatuation with a grown man by a grown woman. It is like being a teenager again.

In my meeting with Jessica and my psychiatrist, it was decided that instead of posting on Facebook that I send what I want to Jessica, which is what I have been doing. Also, it was decided that the Rexulti was not working for me.

Right now for the past two weeks I have been on 10mg of Olanzapine and 2.5 of Rexulti. I really dislike the Olanzapine. It makes me very lethargic and tired. It gives me dry mouth as well. It seems that it is more difficult to find music for me. Perhaps because I want new performances to watch that are made by Gary for me.

CAR:

I sometimes I feel and think that with all the car ads I experience that I am supposed to see what I would like. Well, I just haven't seen a car I like. The one that Gary rode in "Something about this Night" comes very close. Maybe a car that is older made newer. I was always told that Chevy's stopped making nice cars after the year of my birth. As far as I know those cars appreciate. I want a car that appreciates both me and my pocket book and is unique.

- † So, an old car that has the colours of my daughters on it through decals of Indigenous art. It has to be able to play my music without me turning on my cell phone.
- † No key entry, no key fob entry…palm print entry only, so that any finger used can open it too.
- † Can park itself
- † Avoids accidents
- † Insurance free
- † My own license plate that Gary picks out
- † GPS intelligent
- † A very techy car
- † Perhaps electric
- † Also it would be nice to have a chauffeur for Gary and I
- † A car for all my daughters of their choice…palm print entry

Although everyone seems to want to make sure my dreams come true, I also want the dreams of those close to me fulfilled. Gary is working hard to fulfill my dreams, but are my dreams his? In one of his songs with Dawn French, he says this year will be the year where all our dreams come true. I have put my faith on this lyric!

George did not put his faith in my dreams and scoffed at me. My health team are encouraging me to meet my dream of getting this book published.

So, if I must choose amongst my dreams, I will try. These are in order:

MY COLOUR-CODED LIFE

6. To have the Pope drastically revamp the Church

1. Getting to know Jessica
2. To own a knitting shop
3. To have my story to be published and a sequel of my life with Gary or someone special. For this story/book to be made into a movie and musical. Making this into a book just may come true for my health team is helping me bring it to reality.
4. My legacy of an online school for the world: MICHÈLE (Make Internet Classes Express Love for Education)
5. Record my songs
6. Being with Gary forever after. I am sure he would not be afraid to touch me, nor would he isolate me from friends and family
7. To have it automatic that Gary can adopt the girls
8. Log home big enough for the girls' families to summer together once I leave this earth and for it to always remain in the family
    a. For it to have a totem pole
    b. Carved front door
    c. Be right on the water like Muskoka Lake in Bracebridge
    d. Surrounded by indigenous art
    e. Filled with instruments and music
    f. Gary to teach me piano and someone to come in to teach me other instruments. No idea how we'll find the time
        i. Piano
        ii. Guitar
        iii. Banjo
        iv. Ukulele
        v. Sing
    f. A big round table to have family feasts
    g. A chef, a gardener, a maid, a personal trainer for Gary, my family and I
    h. All kinds of boats and water equipment like waterskiis etc.
    i. Plus winter equipment like snowmobile for two
    j. To have a pure bred Boxer pup
    k. Enter with palm print or any digit on the hand

9. If possible inherit my parent's house and have it updated… and made of pretty stone. If not a house in the area.
    a. Again filled with music and instruments
    b. Filled with indigenous art
    c. A wall filled with family photographs with plenty of room for photographs of our future life with Gary
    d. Plenty of room for kids to play
    e. A chef, gardener, maid, personal trainer
    f. Palm print entry or any digit
10. An extended family vacation where I have never been before
11. To have our own float plane and jet
12. To have a techy car with indigenous decals. A car that appreciates with time
13. To have our families mortgages and all utilities and cell phones free for life
    a. To have Gary and I to have a family cell phone
14. To have a network GMB as described previously
15. To have a recording studio with Gary: Perhaps named GMB Studios…those interested can upload there performance to us, or come in face to face.
16. To have a huge party reuniting my friends and family where all sorts of musicians and singer songwriters attend to perform.
17. My legacy to rid the world of coins, credit cards of any sort and cheques!!
18. To have border free travel hassle when travelling for us and our extended families and friends
19. To have free Medicare for life for our families and friends
20. To have a dude ranch for troubled kids
21. To have a clothing line from baby to senior

Monday, April 30, 2018

With my feet firmly on the ground, as Gary sings, I have decided that I no longer want to be remembered by my daughters or Gary as someone that was out for revenge. For I do not think that their father would have the strength to go through what I went through for as long as I did. So, let it be enough for him to have to face all his daughters and supposed family, plus all those who had supposedly died, in court. Let it be enough that he should have believed in me and have to see what does become of me.

But as Mariah Carey sings, "Then a hero comes along with the strength to carry on", if Gary and my girls think otherwise then they can carry on. Maybe this will bring me closer to a real life with Gary!! To interpret this another way, I have found the strength to be my own hero.

This in no way means that I forgive George!! I likely never will. As Keith Urban sings, "'he' never should have treated me this way"!! It is just more important for me to move onto a happier life than to seek revenge for an unhappy one. Knowing that his future is behind bars is revenge enough for me.

Going through what I went through was hell and I wore it like a crown in the end. I wore my supposed disability with honour in the end, believing it was true. Now knowing it was not and only suffering from PTSD, I know that their father could not survive it. The doctors have not confirmed I have PTSD, it is just my feeling.

Here are just a few of my new friends, Yes Gary will be my future husband and my best friend, the keeper of my soul!! There are far too many friends to include in this book!! Stevie Wonder, Whitney Houston, Diana Ross, Luther Vandross, Elton John, Elvis Presley, John Denver, Kelly Clarkson, Mariah Carey, Josh Groban, Keith Urban, Bon Jovi, Beyoncé, …

Hopefully Jessica will be able to see the pictures. The pictures say they may be copyrighted but they do not say for sure.

The group "Take That", which includes: Gary Barlow, Howard Donald, Robbie Williams, Mark Owen, Jason Orange and the group Westlife which includes, Kian Egan, Shane Filan, Markus Feehily, Nicky Byrne have really uplifted me. I never knew how much I enjoy boy bands.

I feel like my whole life has been leading up to this point. Only I am not at the peak of the mountain yet. I will be at the peak when Gary takes my hand in his.

As much as music and dance was taken from me for years I feel it filling my life with Gary!! I envision us learning how to do ballroom dancing together in our own dancing studio which is part of our new residence. I believe I will be going to several concerts. And for concerts to come alive in our home!!

How do I Envision My Future:

I believe Gary will fill my void of affection. The same is true for my girls. He will give what they always had to ask for…a hug!! This goes way before I ever called for action over a hug.

I see weekly family dinners, a lot like the TV show Blue Bloods, where there is fun with music. The girls will dance with their significant others if they wish and future babies will dance on our feet!!

We will have fun with a new Boxer pup!! With any luck we can breed her.

Some of the activities I would like to do and try again:

- † Waterskiing
- † Downhill skiing
- † Cross country skiing
- † Squash
- † Horseback riding

I would like to see some sports events. I prefer to be there than watch TV

I see Gary sweeping me off my feet and feel like he is working hard to surprise me!! He needs Forever Love from me and I need a Forever Life with him which encompasses Forever Love

I see dinners with friends at home and out.

I wish for Gary to teach me how to play the piano and to have someone come in to teach me music lessons

I envision being able to jam with Gary and his friends

I believe in being able to help write future songs with Gary

I envision playing backgammon with him and board games with the kids

I picture doing a duet with Gary. I am not sure if he still performs but if so I picture being there with him. Perhaps our song can be made into a duet!!

I believe all my dreams will come true!! I pride myself on being intuitive and it lead me to believe that I will have a life with Gary!! It also leads me to believe that all my creations and ideas are being worked on now.

It would be my wish that he assist in helping me direct my online school. He can manage the music side of things.

There is so much more:

We can travel alone and with the family to far off places in our own plane.

Wouldn't it be the ultimate love story if it was Gary that I met so long ago and he has spent all this time fighting for my honour and justice!! But if it is not than that is over too…as I once said before…the real George should have followed me home!! Did he orchestrate this fraud or was his identity stolen?

Tuesday, May 1, 2018

Today I saw Dr. Jake and Kay and now I will have only 10 mg of Olanzapine. How I will view it? I am glad that I am only on one pill, but I will think of it as a placebo!! He seems to think I will never be pill free and that that is unrealistic…I do not!! However, I do not ever intentionally not take my medication!! There was only once when my husband talked me out of taking it and not tell anyone because he did not want me to stop getting disability payments.

Watching One Love Manchester, Take That and Robbie reaffirmed my thought that they were good friends!! How Robbie, sings, he says words I cannot. He is singing to and about George most of the time!! He hurts when he sings. His song about Angels is like me not forsaking Gary when he arrives!! It is also to George who may be according to the music be focussing too much on religion.

Their song, 'The Flood'" speaks to the many years when I did not have my music and led to deal with my mental health assuming I would never be happy. It speaks to the forces that be, catching up to me in knowing what I believed to be the truth.

Where George was concerned in our marriage he only showed me superficial love!! I may not have physical love yet, but I have more love through the music I hear than I have ever felt. Plus You Tube allows me to see so many live performances!!

Knowing that this is real do I get credit for inspiring my Archdiocese in creating their online system? I know full well I am responsible for it...it was not just timing or coincidental!! It is only missing email contacts from the priests to the public which should be made available.

It takes all my strength to be honest with Dr. Jake but I am not giving up with what I believe in this time out of fear, like I have done before. Thank You God for sending singers into my life who with their music have given me the strength to believe in myself again!!

Growing up the only cause that existed was the Salvation Army and Remembrance Day where you bought a poppy. Why so many more causes? Seems like there is a cause for everything!!

Interesting how George was never satisfied with our mattresses and I was never there for the old one to be taken away. Oh oh, thinking about mattresses again! Not sure if Jessica has ever heard of the mattress nightmare so I will tell it yet again.

When my parents complained of having a hard time getting out of our couches (burgundy) I thought about having them fixed but I noticed they were fine so I looked inside once we moved to Gage Lane. They were stuffed with old blue and white striped mattress with hidden zippered pockets inside. It totally freaked me out so I showed my sisters!! What the heck were they for but for something elicit?! I have no idea but my mind wanders and is troubled by it. He travelled with those couches everywhere!! The chair inside had the name TAYLOR inside it in black felt in huge letters!!

It still hurts that George would criticize our daughters behind their back and everyone on the street. It cut to the core when going to the bank he criticized me for not wearing lipstick!! It was only Jessica that said I looked pretty without makeup. It's a sad day when your husband cuts down your self-esteem!! Honest to God I feel I must have suffered from some sort of Stockholm Syndrome!! Isn't it interesting that this problem is named after a place in the world!! It must have been the medication that made me feel so dependent. Even my girls never got to see how my real personality is. I am a leader not a follower when given the chance. As you may have gathered I am an action oriented person! I hope they understand why I needed to publish this journal and are proud of me and not upset with me.

One day soon, he will see that I am a force to be reckoned with through the help of my daughters and Gary!! Even St. Anne's has been helping with the STING against George!! In fact they may have started it for I leaned on my colleague's!!

All my closed doors while reaching for understanding and friendship from people I knew at school and church only opened another window! I sought out other ways to find friends. It takes strength to not give up on myself. As Kelly Clarkson sings, beat down on me like a waterfall for I am stronger than I knew. It goes something like that!! So, I guess one of my strengths is having inner strength!!

But I am so curious and haven't figured out how Gary sought me out? How long has he been waiting for me? When exactly did he enter my world and I was so blind to see?

Watching Lady Gaga tonight makes me truly believe that the whole music industry and all the presidents are behind me and are taking action for me and are here to help me. It is a show for those suffering from some catastrophe I do not believe in. I think I am the catastrophe that they are raising funds for. It might be that they are also behind my legacy of an online school.

I feel that Darcy's Senior High were behind me with their very special production of a popular musical of which Darcy was a part. She has such a beautiful voice. She also played the lead role in Skyhawk's production of another special musical. She was awesome! But again George worked in the background and offered to help backstage. It was a co-worker of mine that also went to see her and it was us that gave her flowers after her performance. I was so happy and proud of her. He did watch her production at her Senior High.

We hosted the cast party for her junior high school musical and even had the constable from the school attend. It was quite a party!

George and I also had another adults only party while living on Gage Lane. It was so much fun for me because one of Jessica's friend's dad played DJ.

We had all our records at this house and I often went downstairs and danced alone. I was so happy when I danced.

We got T-shirts with the name of the production written on them. I saved mine to frame for her in the future and that is exactly what I did. I had no pictures to add unfortunately.

At the time I gave her this for a Christmas present, I gave Jessica her diploma framed. I was so thankful that my dad did that for me and I regret that I let George press me to take them out of their frames. I worked hard for them and was proud of them.

Darcy sometimes sings in the car and I think back to when I encouraged her to try out for Canadian Idol.

I was so proud of her that when I hosted my school's Christmas party that I had her sing.

There was a time when the superintendent showed up with others from the superintendent's office at one of our school's events. I couldn't help think it was because of something I had shared in my online courses.

Wednesday, May 2, 2018

Jessica has made a reply to one of my entries today saying that she and Darcy are not helping in a "Sting" against their dad and that they love him very much. I do not believe this or there would not be doppelgangers for me to be aware of. I do believe my original daughters have been protected from what is going on. I feel there has been two Jessica doppelgangers and one Darcy.

I totally understand what it feels like to love a dad but totally disrespect how they treat their mom. If my father has done wrong I do want him to pay!!

I know Jessica's role in this "show" has been to stick by her dad and put me on the back burner for all these years. But I kept the faith and knew there must have been a reason and now she is back in my life and learning all about me. I never gave up on her even though her dad thought I should. He did nothing to try to bridge the gap and keep our family together as a unit!!

(Speaking of "Unit", while attending one of my school's function, George complimented a colleague on what she was wearing. He did not remember the name "Dress" so he said "Nice Unit". True to form he compliments others but not me.)

This total disregard for family could stem from my book and illusion that there was some divide between family and Love. I felt that Jessica was against family and only for love and charity (Care) and Darcy was for family and music. I believe that George was siding with Jessica because of this.

He always said he spoke to her, but, he always did it in private where I wanted him to do it in front of me. I do not believe he did talk to her.

The way Jessica spoils her dad in various ways also must have its reason, if only to lead him to believe that she is on his side. There must be a reason that she recognizes special events for him and I am always hurt.

(Sunday, January 19, 2020-Also to note while living on Wade Avenue, when I wanted to put candles around the living room he insisted on a certain type of candle that performs well in TV shows. This confused me because we were not part of a show.)

A memory from the past that I was sure I had expressed is how God is looking after me. While teaching one year at the beginning of my teaching at St. Anne's, when I got to work I was called into the office. Taking the suggestion of a co-worker since I was working late that I burn a candle and relax. I took her up on her suggestion. Stupidly I had my little candles in yogurt containers on the prayer table. You can foresee what happened. I left for home with the candle burning. Everything in and around the prayer table burned, smoldered, but the Bible. The parish priest and my principal made me feel so good. They knew I already felt so bad and very stupid! So, that is why I think all candles should come in glass containers.)

There must be some reason why I punch in to see my father's obituary that I wrote, that it only takes me to my mother's when I click on the link for my dad.

But since Jessica has responded in this way, saying they are not part of a STING, I think I will stop copying her on my entries... Nope, I will stand my ground!! I cannot take away that he is their father but respect is nothing they can feel when he has disrespected me so many times.

Jessica's response felt like the text I received from Darcy years ago when she blamed the troubles of her marriage on me. I did not believe that either and forgave her.

Honestly, I feel that I am in competition with the original George somewhere. Having all these songs hidden amongst songs, must be for some reason. When in the car with my family I used to look in the opposite direction feeling my family were going the other way.

Dr. Jake asked me how I felt about Jessica's problem when she was four, I stand by my maternal and protective ground here too. Something happened to her and it was more than just copying her dad in being OCD. Why was her scream in the middle of the night so blood curdling while sitting on the toilet just trying to get dry, and why just once? Why no follow-up with her psychologist?

Royce let me know that he and Darcy were around for me to talk to, which is something Darcy was never before prepared to do.

Darcy said to me when I took her to lunch and said that I thought she was a doppelganger, that she thought she had the same cheekbones. She admitted to me she was not the original by saying that.

I do belief in Take That's song, "Kidz".

If Gary has been with me and waited for me all this time then as one of his songs goes, "She is holding my heart in her hand". There was a possibility that it might have gone totally differently had I not fallen so hard for him.

The ladies at my building coffee group created a list of everyone so we would have contact information. I phoned one of the ladies the other day and asked if she wanted to go out to Timmy's for coffee. So we did yesterday. So hopefully we can do it again!!

I am once again reaching out to make friends which was difficult for me to do while on Saphris and being married.

I'm so excited, I invited Penny to go to a Joseph Ribkoff trunk show at my new favourite store on Friday!!

MY COLOUR-CODED LIFE

I have a vague memory of George and myself sitting by the fireplace at Gage Lane and Jessica coming out and saying surely you recognize me over him, and she pointed at George. At the time I had no idea what she was referring to. I kept thinking that my instincts were wrong. Not anymore!!

Dear Gary,

Perhaps in your Neverland, the second star on the right that you take me to, can be Poppy's star? I am feeling rather deflated and forgotten today.

Thank you for the new video, Take That: These Days Tour. It gives me hope and gave me a glimpse into you and your friends!! I am trying as your new song suggests, to have a lot of Patience!!

I realize that I do not really have to participate in this music game but I do in the hope that I will hear more from you!! In case no one has ever said it before you have lovely hands that are very unique and come alive when you sing!!

I just love listening to Peter Cetera as he sings "the Glory of Love" where he says "I am the man that will fight for your honour and be the hero you're dreaming of". I cannot help believe that you are singing to me through Peter!!

Sometimes I think Robbie is working with you in being my heroes, because he is so emotional. It truly makes me feel someone truly cares, for the situation in which he is singing under normal circumstances would not bring tears!!

He is now wearing a purple jacket, so I take this as a sign that you agree that the star we go to will be Poppy's. I also love his song, "You're the Inspiration".

It is gratifying to hear Howard in Take That sing, "saved from disappointment for so long" which I feel refers to George. Everything seems to go his way all the time!! It is he that could have a super relationship with Jessica!! He has never got into trouble for his criminal behaviour as a youth and goes so far as brag about his drug use. It is gratifying because my life has been filled with disappointment for so long that my turn is coming.

It is not coincidental that your friends dress up in my colours. These are MY dreams and you are bringing them to life.

Until our eyes meet and with the hope of a Forever Love,
Mickey

Thursday, May 3, 2018

I do not think that I have fully shared the story of Poppy for my girls. If I have then those editing this book can mesh it together. When I was pregnant George's office threw us a party at our place for the baby. It was well before 12 weeks.

When it was time for me to have my first ultrasound in the United States, I had to go by myself. While there I had to wait for quite a while in the waiting room for the result. I knew something was wrong because I had to wait so long. They came out and said that I would have to go for a more in depth ultrasound.

I was worried, naturally. Although George was the manager of the warehouse, I had to go to this ultrasound by myself as well. I was terrified. They told me that I would have to terminate the baby or she would suffer terribly and there was no guarantee she would survive.

When I came home George's boss was visiting. He was there when I shared the result with George. I told George I wanted to go home (Tinsel Town, Ontario) even though George was going to be transferred to Knox Valley. I had to have the termination before 16 weeks.

We came home and I had to search for someone who would carry out the genetic termination. I should've sought out my family physician Dr. Sam Merston, but for some reason I was embarrassed and did not.

When the date came George was given a cot to stay with me. They injected me with some sort of saline solution into my uterus through my abdomen. I was told to always put the hat on the toilet whenever I had to go to the washroom. I was given such powerful drugs that I became very loopy. I had to make it to the washroom each time by myself even though I could barely walk! The last time I went I forgot to put the hat and (my) baby was born into the toilet. The nurse came and gave me heck for forgetting the hat. She scooped (my) daughter out of the toilet and lay her on the counter.

I asked George if he wanted to see her but he chose not to…that is fine… what is not is what follows.

When we came home he immediately went back to work and did not grieve with me, my dad did that. Years later even though I had written the poem, to grieve for her, years after Darcy and Jessica were born, which was published he seemed unaware of the poem and referred to her as a boy. I kept thinking that he was a doppelganger and given false information, otherwise how could he have not known!!!

This is why I refer to Poppy as (my) daughter and not (ours) because he did not acknowledge her birth, help me when I needed him both during and after, and not remembering that we lost a girl!!!

I am in possession of an ultrasound picture of her that I was never given!! At least I do not remember. I was probably in shock.

False Information given to George's doppelganger:
    The gender of our baby
    The name he referred to my breasts
    Not understanding what Cabriolet meant
    Not knowing the nicknames he had for our private parts
    Not knowing about Jessica's need for a psychologist

Things he cannot do that he could do the summer I spent with him before we were married:
    Like the same music
    Clean his teeth with a toothpick from the inside of his mouth
    Willing to share a baseball steak at The Keg
    Drink pop
    Not be interested in alcohol
    Feel confident with my driving

I could care less if he is somewhere going through what I am … I am so done with all the George's in my life!!

I have been led to believe that I was bought and sold for one million dollars!! The powers that be knowing what was going to happen have protected me.

I know full well that I can communicate with the TV. They see what I see and hear what I hear anywhere I am. They are also privy to what I write in this book!! I also think this is true for George!! I try desperately when I am out and about to forget about this whereas when I was out with George before I was aware of this happening, he was acting like a fool on stage.

Where my dad is concerned, I feel that he knew one day I would be going on this journey and therefore filled my life with memories of the two of us. In fact, I feel he spoiled me over any of my siblings. Whereas, my mother had no clue. This might explain when I input the information into Google to see the obit I wrote for my dad, that it takes me to my mom!!

When I think back to the person I met, that person would not have aged as George did!! I was attracted to that person, I have not been with the real George for at least 18 years!!

I remember I would look at George and try to see if I could see some mask that he was wearing which they sometimes do in movies.

He would say and do cruel things:
- † If I disagreed with him, he would say, you must be off your meds
- † If it wasn't for me you would be living on the East side
- † When I was in the hospital and given day passes, he said I had to be nice or he did not have to take me home

I believe I was admitted the second time in 2005 to protect me from George. George wanted sex from me and I did not see him as my husband. *His reaction was scary.* No we did not have sex! I was taken to the hospital soon after that.

My friends think that he is a narcissist with schizophrenic tendencies!!! The internet offers a definition which I do not think is the proper definition for schizophrenia!! This term used to be used to define someone with multiple personalities. This describes him more if there truly is no doppelgangers. However, I believe there were /are doppelgangers!!

Did he really think my family or my daughters would not care for me? He was so cruel to me!!

Even knowing making decisions on where to go for coffee was difficult for me, he would always insist on me deciding. I had to make the decision on everything, coffee places, dinner places, TV choices, presents, celebrations of all kinds!!

I wonder how he functions now.

I am so much happier being by myself than with George and as Kelly Clarkson sings, "the bed feels warmer". But one day soon my whole life will be warmer!!

Once Jessica, you helped name the bed and breakfast I had wanted at Gage Lane as "Megan's Point of View". George had a disagreement with me because the municipality put certain restrictions as to how many people we could have at one time and I wanted to follow the guidelines and your dad did not, so there went my thought of a bed and breakfast.

Now, I am giving my point of view regarding my life!!

Today, I met with Julia, my community support worker, and told her how I felt sad with the winds out of my sail. It could have stemmed from your email where you said you loved your dad and that I rarely ever hear that or actions from you showing that…until now!

I told her I needed more music to uplift me because everything has been so repetitive and I rely so heavily on it!! The music is my lifeline!! Tonight they have blessed me with plenty of new music

You know I have also felt that the girls high schools as well as my own have been involved in this journey with me, as well as George's trucking companies especially Black Bell Trucking!! They are all supporting me

I also told Julia, that I get confused when songs have the word "Baby" in it. I feel sometimes they're for me and sometimes for George and it bothers me. I believe now they are making it clear for me. When "Baby" is used it is definitely from Gary!!

I have just asked my brother if he would like to receive the excerpts I send to Jessica and he said "Sure"!! Not sure how interesting the rest of my entries will be. Hopefully my entries will not dry up.

Not sure if Darcy would like them too. According to Royce she currently is pretty stressed so I do not want to add to it.

Tonight listening to Paul McCartney sing, "Hey Jude" there were many other famous singers like, Sir Elton John, Sting, and Phil Collins and others playing with him!!

Friday, May 4, 2018

Funny how now I am alone in my condo that my extremities do not get cold anymore. Also, I do not need to put on the heat. It is automatically set to where it is comfortable for me.

Just as Justin Bieber sings, my mother doesn't like you and she likes everyone", explains how I feel toward George. I seem to be able to forgive other people but George. Although I had been out of love and mistrusted him since the year 2000. I kept trying to make it work and listened to everyone but my own gut!!

Why if Robbie Williams is an international superstar, have I never heard of him or Take That on the radio here??

I have decided to follow through on doing something I have always wanted to do. I am going to contact a local flying club and look into what is involved in learning how to fly and if the cost is reasonable I will do it!!

There used to be a sign along a local highway here that we always passed thinking how much I wanted to do it. So now is the time!!

Gary's song "SING" with the Commonwealth Band is a testament to what he did for me. He travelled far to have this song created for me urging me to voice my thoughts!!

I knew something was wrong with my marriage when everyone was saying the man I was living with was my husband, yet, when I was in the hospital the second time in 2005 and there was a beaten man that I played ping pong with reminded me more of the man I met so long ago in the Keg. I wanted to continue with him, then George arrived and I just knew he was not whom I met those many years ago. It was not a sexual connection but a visual one with this other man.

But I now am more inclined to think of Gary in my life. He and all his friends have done so much for me. However, it may not have been him I met in The Keg because I do not recall an English accent. Surely I would have remembered that because it is like music to my ears. But like I said before the face is a blur and the memory of the voice lost.

When we first moved to British Columbia in July 1991, it rained the whole month. The first thing your dad said we needed to do was buy rain gear because we had to get used to it living here. However, living in the townhouse

I wanted us to buy rain hiking shoes, so we would have appropriate gear to walk the beaches in the rain or go hiking. So we bought them but when it came time to use them George only wanted to go out in the sunny weather!! How is this a man that grew up in British Columbia??

I phoned the flight school and got the low down on the cost and the process!! I will sign up after I have paid off this month's Visa, which will be after the 10th. Should my life turn around before I complete, which I believe it will, then maybe in Tinsel Town there will be a place where I can transfer my hours!!

I honestly think they should not allow cell phones at their concerts. I am only interested in seeing that which is filmed professionally!!

Perhaps they allow cell phones because the cell phone giants are sponsoring these productions. I still do not like the cell phone uploads. The sound is off and the hand is usually not steady.

I went to the trunk show with my friend Penny and was totally disappointed. Most of the new fashions were for the fall instead of the summer. Something that happened while we were there rubbed us the wrong way. Penny liked a coat, so we went to admire it and before we could try it on she whisked it away to show another customer. So she never got to try it on!!

I was thinking I might be responsible for my medication being delivered to me. I remember thinking or writing that if medication was delivered there would no longer be a need for pill bottles which can then be used by dealers for distributing prescription medication illegally.

Being part of this process there are just a few snags to work out!! But I do like the special packaging because it cannot be reused!!

Maybe I said it before but I will say it again. The last time I used Tylenol 3's was when the doctor at emergency prescribed them to me when I threw my back out by putting Cassie down when she was around two years old. The last time Jessica had used Tylenol 3's was when she had her wisdom teeth out. Several years later while we were living in the townhouse I found large pill bottles made out to Jessica and I. Each bottle held at least 500 pills of Tylenol 3. Now I know what a container of 30 pills hold and it is tiny. These bottles were huge. Not one I had ever had prescribed to me!! I said before maybe it was 100 pills but upon thinking it as closer to 500.

Since I was too afraid to approach George on why he had them I asked our dentist if he prescribed Tylenol 3 for the extraction of wisdom teeth and how many. He did not tell me but told me to get rid of them. I also asked Jessica if she wanted them and she did not reply. So knowing it could not be for a good reason that he had them, I took them to London Drugs.

What is odd is where in the world he had been hiding these pill bottles before I found them. Also he did not ask me where they went. He just kept acting normal.

One thing I learned is that George could lie with a straight face. You could not tell when he was lying. I learned this because I caught him in a lie. One day when Jessica was returning from a trip she had messaged him about him coming to the airport to pick her up. His cell phone was on the island in the kitchen and he was upstairs so I could read what was displayed. I asked him later if he had heard from her and hoped I could go and pick her up as well. He said he had not heard from her. Although he had looked at his phone.

That day he was working at Kendra's and phoned me later that he was going to stay late and then pick Jessica up. A straight up lie.

Now you tell me what he was doing with about 1000 Tylenol 3's? Would you not also think it was for the purpose of distribution?

Now remember one of the jobs he bragged about was working for London Drugs and being responsible for filling prescriptions. How in the world would he have been allowed to do this without training?

Also, when I went into that drawer and found another drug I did question him on previously, he blew up at me and accused me of snooping. How is it snooping if that is also the drawer we keep Tylenol and Advil.

In my future whenever Gary and I have a problem he will sing whatever song I want to make me feel better according to his song, "Want You Back for Good"!!

Another inconsistency in my life is that when Darcy's hearing was tested she could not hear the low tones so George always said he had to speak higher for her. But he never did and she seems to have no problem with male voices!!

When I became so paranoid of our big house on Gage Lane and thinking it would be a perfect drug house I searched it. I've said it before but here it is again because it bothers me so:

I found a hidden false fuse panel above the false ceiling and an empty cigarette package. When I showed George he told me to leave the cigarette package there and not to worry about the panel. It was odd I thought to leave the package there. This did not help me trust him.

Also from the basement you could see under the stairs in the kitchen. Under these stairs there were plastic grocery bags. This, with the pathway George made to the stairs out back and all the hours he spent out back by himself, I thought George was dealing drugs. It would be easy for others to access our back yard and meet with him. I was so paranoid.

I found a cylindrical package of screening material in the pool house with about 20 scanning codes attached to it. What would they be for?

I found a pen without its insides inside the socket for the built in vacuum cleaner.

When looking behind the chair by the fireplace into what should have been a heat vent I saw dirt under the kitchen. I thought that was odd because we were well above the ground.

One day I came home from work and went into our bedroom and was totally freaked out. There were about 5000 lady bugs everywhere. On the walls, ceiling …everywhere. I called George and I never watched him but he got rid of all of them…not one smudge on the wall. Now you tell me why they came once and never again? You tell me what they would have been used for?

What was also coincidental was that there was a sign at the end of our street that said, maintained by "Lady Bug Productions"!!

I had thought that our neighbours' house was a drug house so I contacted the mayor and she sent a private investigator to look and talk with me.

Jessica knew back then what I thought about George because I had discussed it with her. She said to me that she was okay if we divorced. I have the picture of the discussion with her in her bedroom in my mind. She was at her closet and I was sitting on her bed.

This was when she printed off the Feng Shui material on LOVE in a house!! That was in 2002 when I wrote 3 songs to George outlining what I needed from him. He merely threw my songs back in my face.

It wasn't until 2005 that I faced George and told him what I thought about his preferences. Now all the signs I have been given just reinforces this fact.

When I told him he just had a poker face, he was neither upset nor anything. He just listened. Over the years nothing changed!!

I should have been smarter and figured it out much sooner.

Saturday, May 5, 2018

George made me feel that we could barely scrape by on the joint RRSP's however, my financial planner says I will be just fine and to live and have fun.

I cannot help but think of Bruce Springsteen's song. "Born in the USA". I always related it to my daughter that was conceived there. The lyrics were all wrong and now with this game they are even more disheartening. Maybe one day there will be a song for Poppy who was conceived in the USA.

Alan Parson's Project Album with, "Eye in the Sky" played a big part of that summer we spent together in Tuckerville. Back then he had no qualms over my driving. He let me drive his car everywhere. When he visited me in Tinsel Town he admired my driving. Later he was just full of criticisms!!

Jon Bon Jovi's song, "You Give Love a Bad Name" is one I would send to George.

Here are my beliefs:

- ✓ I believe I lived with more than one man that claimed to be George
- ✓ I believe that George is part of the same music game I am part of, otherwise why is there one? They put messed up info when I input the info into Google. I believe it is being sent to George. When I input a phrase from a song sometimes it is the wrong

artist displayed and some of the lyrics seem like they are meant for George and some seem they are from George to me. The ones from George are crude. (I want a You Tube that only sends me tasteful performances.)

- ✓ I believe there is a reason that Jessica took all our records. There is also a reason for her not having any of the albums given to her when we went to her apartment…they were all new. Doppelgangers! George ended up with them I guess, because he wanted his grandmother's trunk for all the albums that Jessica gave to him. Just so you know most of those albums are mine and a family friend's. George did not bring any albums into the marriage. I could never find the one's he played in Tuckerville when we met.
- ✓ I believe there must be a reason why George took the music out of our life and gave Jessica our only turntable. Also that the only radio we had only would play one station!!
- ✓ I believe that George thinks he is part of some TV show
- ✓ I believe that my thoughts are read, that people can see and hear what I say and do no matter where I am
- ✓ I believe that most often the synonyms I am given for certain words are incorrect
- ✓ I believe my dreams are happening now.
- ✓ I believe that my online school is being worked on now and that the musicians are raising money for it.
- ✓ I believe Jessica is working with the powers to be on the online school and Darcy is working on the music end of things. Poppy is like a guiding light just like in my poem. There had to be a reason why I was in my Google account years ago that it asked me if I trusted Jessica.
- ✓ I believe Gary is helping them be my heroes as well as him
- ✓ I believe I have 3 heroes, Gary, Darcy and Jessica
- ✓ I believe there will be a big bash with all my friends that I have known, and my family with all the musicians!!
- ✓ I believe Gary is not just in my head, I believe I will have my forever after with him in real life

- ✓ I believe he is working on a log home for me on Muskoka Lake big enough for my girls to have their families and friends stay there together
- ✓ I believe he is going to take me back home and I will have a stone home in Sunshine Park or Raleigh
- ✓ I believe there have been two Jessica's in addition to the original whom I have not seen in a while and one Darcy doppelganger and the original I have not seen for a long time either.

They have all become my daughters but I have not seen the originals for a long time.

- † I also believe that all the people that have supposedly passed away have not!! I have never stopped believing this. I pacify others who think this not realistic but this time I am standing my ground!! I cannot answer as to where they are now….but there are too many things that do not make sense surrounding their deaths, especially my sister!!
    - † Carol on the night of her mother's death was the one to inform me. This was odd. She also expressed no emotion. This was odd. The CD had pictures of everyone but me. This was odd. The pictures chosen for her memorabilia did not look like her. This was odd. Carol included her present boyfriend, Todd, whom she hadn't known long and I felt this was just another sign she is alive. Her keepsake pictures did not even look like her which made me think she was alive.

My only bothering thought is knowing when (QUANDO QUANDO) Gary will come to sweep me off my feet!! For when he comes my biggest need will be fulfilled!!

Sunday, May 6, 2018

I am not liking being on my original medication of Olanzapine at 10 mg. I am feeling down and could cry at any moment. So, I think I will phone Kay, my caseworker. It could be because I am more immersed in thinking that my thoughts of Gary are just that. I am so guarded of my feelings. Although I say I believe in that we will be together but honestly I am scared of hurting my own feelings. I so want it to be real. All the signs point to it to be true. I so need Gary to reach out with more music for me because I fear I am fading in believing my own instincts!!

Even his music for his musical Finding Neverland do not seem to be scores that would be for a musical of that sort. They seem more to fit the story of my life with Gary!!

It seems timely that as I watch Westlife tonight they sing "My Love" to a girl from Stockholm, Sweden. I had spoken of Stockholm Syndrome. They gave her cut flowers and I had spoken to my friend today about my thoughts of cut flowers. I had also in a thought how I would like to go to Sweden.

I like to think his song SING is meant for me! It speaks of finding your voice and not giving up and standing your ground even when it gets hard to do so.

Westlife is performing new material tonight!!! Singing UPTOWN GIRL, I've had my backstreet boy now I want my uptown man!!!

As my brother and daughter read this it is important for them to know how I realize that feeling this strongly in someone I only see through YouTube and HGTV…Sometimes through other TV shows as well, seems so unrealistic. If I were them I would worry about me too unless they knew something more than I am aware of. But my life is full of hope now, something I never had before!!

Monday, May 7, 2018

Tonight I have been given a lot more to watch on YouTube, especially from Keith Urban. In one of his songs he started to cry. I could not help but wonder what I was thinking to make him cry. Yes, I still believe my thoughts are read. In fact other musicians are playing different music too!!

It is so hard to believe in something when no one can see what I see.

The musicians keep saying that I have not seen anything yet. They also imply that I will not have to wait much longer for my dreams to be realized.

Tonight a priest Father Ray Kelly sang "Everybody Hurts" on a clip from X Factor. It touched me to the core just telling me to hold on. Coming from a priest made it so special to me. You have to know the song to really understand how I really needed to hear it tonight. Just as it finished Jessica emailed me asking how I was doing. I'm falling apart!! I am losing my faith that I will have a happy ever after with Gary.

I know he can hear me and see what I see but can he see me? If he can then I do not understand why he has singled me out. How would someone like me fit in his life?

Every time I feel my life is like someone keeping me from catching my breath while in the water, like George pushing my head under the water, I picture that picture Jessica gave Darcy saying COURAGE!! There is so much to look forward to.

Most times I feel like I am floating on the surface…it will be Gary that will help me out onto the ground.

There must be a reason that Gary has used exact phrases from my book and made them into songs that he sings!! Actually I cannot find those phrases, so maybe I only thought them.

But the performers sing songs about the soul and that is Gary's and my connection!! I only want to hear that word in a song meant for me.

Tonight playing the lyric game I said the lyric "OUT" into Google expecting a definition and it came up with a magazine for Gay and Lesbians as the first choice, then Outlook, then the magazine again!!

Knowing what I do not know about what the true act of lovemaking should be like, I urge schools to make it mandatory that students have sex education!!

Tuesday, May 8, 2018

I did talk to Kay today and she encouraged me to continue with listening to the music because I get enjoyment from it and "you never know". I find it difficult to watch because I am definitely not getting the same response from it.

I am almost afraid to listen and watch in case I will get hurt. By her saying, "you never know", gives me hope!!

What I do not understand is this medication is the same I was given in the hospital and I was glued to the music. Right now I do not feel the same drive. Perhaps because Gary will not become real. Although, I have to say that I still feel that it will happen.

Wednesday, May 9, 2018

Although my excitement for the music has waned because I seem to have lost interest in most things, with this new medication, I feel Gary is reaching out to me by offering new music that expresses how he feels. My gut tells me that he will be in my future and I am sticking to that!!

I feel the songs that truly expresses how I feel right now is:
Rachel Platten's, *"Fight Song"*!!
Keith Urban's, *"The Fighter"*
Peter Cetera, *"Glory of Love"*
Gary Barlow's, *"Million Love Songs"*
Gary Barlow's, *"Rule the World"*
Gary Barlow, *"Sing"*
Robbie Williams, *"Love My Life"*
Phillip Phillip's. *"Home"*
JLS, *"You Light Up My Life"*
Westlife, *"Flying Without Wings"*
Beyoncé, *"Listen"*
Katy Perry's, *"Roar"*
Katy Perry's *"Part of Me"*

Kelly Clarkson, *"Stronger"*
Christina Aguilera- *"Fighter"*
Kesha, *"Praying"*

As I watch the music the more I am engrossed in it. Seems like the same old feeling is coming back!! Yippee!!

What now, if I am on the medication they thought would take away my thoughts of You Tube and my creations away? My mind may not be as active but I feel they can't take away what I believe!!

I still believe in all the things I believed in before. Gary and I will be together!!

It is interesting how they started to do more duets after I had written that. I would like to do a duet with Gary!!

Jessica once again is not making Mother's Day and not wanting to see me on another day. It has been about a decade since she has celebrated with me and for many of those years I did not even get a text. I know she is reluctant to see me on her own. There must be a reason she is unwilling to celebrate mother's day with me. I still have faith that one day it will happen!!

In hoping to give a family birthday party for Darcy which she has never had, both her aunts and families have said they are not coming. I have yet to hear from her cousin Kendra and pseudo Uncle Ben. I will follow up next week.

When Gary speaks of the fog lifting and having a voice again. I feel that now I am being heard by those around me even those that oversee this book. However, my physical voice for singing I still feel I do not have yet!

His song "SING" is definitely for me!! When I first heard the young girl she said 'Sang". I thought it should be "sung" and afterwards it was sung with the word "sung"!!!

I feel his songs and that of Take That, are meant for me except "Jump". When he refers to giving back what was frozen, this refers to my song to George where I said I was freezing hormones by the Oceanside while I reflected. Since they awakened those feelings when I met Gary, I asked for them to have them remain frozen until I saw Gary in real life and they have done that for me through the medication!! Olanzapine does not allow me to feel sexual urges whereas Rexulti did.

MY COLOUR-CODED LIFE

I must tell you that it has been years since I introduced my colour coded life in this book. Grandiose thought or not I believe all the colours available today everywhere are because of me from soaps to clothes!!

When Gary chooses a girl from the audience to sing his love song to in one of his performances, she is wearing a red dress. The first time I saw this I said to myself wow it is me, Lady in Red, and then he said Lady in Red!!! It brings me back to how George should have made me feel better about the dress he bought me. I want to be that lady in red and through this performance I was. One day in the future it will really be me!!

I just discovered that his album 12 months and 11 days was released by BMG and RCA, which means that BMG already exists, but when googled it is in Miami which does not make sense. Since I have come to understand he already has a recording studio, I wonder what the "M" stands for. Perhaps in the future it will stand for me. No worries for me!!!! I just looked it up on ITunes and the album does not exist!!!!

You know there must be a reason that not one of the teachers I taught with ever reach out to me. Perhaps they do not know my cell number, but Brenda does. She said she would phone and never did. I will try again and phone Brenda and see if she will meet for coffee. I mean I was not a bad teacher socially. I have felt so isolated from people that knew me before and seemed to truly care at the time.

I do not feel I want to teach face to face anymore though. I truly believe in my online school but have no way of knowing how to involve myself in helping to make that happen with the powers that be that are putting it in motion.

I believe that Gary believes in this school as much as I do and since Apple is sponsoring many of the concerts they might be raising the funds for it. There are so many people at these concerts. Many more than I have ever witnessed.

When Gary asked if it is anyone's first time seeing a symphony; that would be me. I just cannot get enough!! I have not seen one since high school.

Robbie's part in this journey seems difficult and maybe it is my fault. I had asked Gary to not be the one to attract George but for it to be Robbie.

There is a possibility it was out of my hands. It is just that he gets so emotional. Why doesn't Gary or the others get emotional?

Thursday, May 10, 2018

Honestly, I also think the movie DREAMGIRLS came out after I wrote the song I wrote to George on our 18th called Soul's Design. I think I am the reason for the movie!! When looking up when it aired, it aired in 2006 and I wrote my song in 2002. The synopsis rudely only lists Jennifer Hudson's last name rather than her full name. As a test to my knowledge of her proper name, I presume. I am constantly being tested in this manner.

There has to be a reason that Gary fills my YouTube!! I can save tunes but I am given so much more. No matter what I choose he appears a few songs away, never far away. In his own way I find him to be the one to reach out which I love!!

I am still editing and name matching. You Tube and Google have me trying to remember all the students I taught and friends and family from my youth.

Why if what I found smudged around the bolt of George's toilet was normal do I not see it on toilets since? In fact I will go one step further and make a recommendation that they cease making toilets that are bolted to the floor with removable caps. I thought and think it was hash.

The result of me tasting it was the same reaction I had when one of my friends unbeknownst to me laced a marijuana joint with hash. I became quite paranoid and had to leave the party.

Yes, I tried marijuana in the comfort of my friend's house under the supervision of her mom. It is pretty harmless and only had the effects of laughing gas for me. It made me laugh! However, you should not drive under its influence and it is not good for your health and likely has the same effect on your lungs as cigarettes.

Perhaps my trying the substance surrounding the bolt on the toilet and the powder in the drawer is really what has caused my psychosis?

MY COLOUR-CODED LIFE

Friday, May 11, 2018

Dear Louise,

Today I want to dedicate my entry to you!! Although I do not think you are dead, I have no other way to speak to you, albeit a one way conversation. Since your colour is peach to represent you being alive I am using that colour to write this letter to you. The computer does not offer a good option though.

I want you to know how sorry I am that we did not visit with you more often. I always was led to believe that we did not have the money but I have come to understand if I had lived on my own with the kids we would have had much more money.

I am not sure how it happened but I should never have handed over the keeping of the books over to George when we were living in Treble. Back then he was not much into budgeting, he did not even know how to balance a chequebook. In fact he did not get into budgeting and RRSP's until I reached out to a financial planner so we would have enough money to retire on.

He is funny because he was never interested in RRSP's. He never planned for the future until I worried about it!

In fact having girls, it was me that put aside money for each girl to help with their weddings. I had asked Donald how much he spent on his daughters and thought it reasonable.

I have to share with you that I have fallen for a man, Gary Barlow, whom is from the United Kingdom!! He is working hard to make all my dreams come true!! In fact, I think my dreams have become his and he has made them even bigger!!

I believe that in the future I will live in a beautiful log home on Lake Muskoka with Gary!! Our home will be filled with music and friends!! If I have my way you will live close by too!! Since he is from the UK, I imagine we will spilt our time and visit there too, which is exciting!! I know what it is like to be away from friends and family and wouldn't want him to face the same loss!

Knowing that he is such an accomplished man I am sure we can figure it out and travelling will not be an issue!! I think Louise that I will be like

Cinderella and Snow White all rolled into one, although I did not have wicked sisters!!

Honestly, I truly feel that my life will go from ordinary to extra-ordinary!! I wish to take you with me because I know you would love it!!

Miss you,
Big Hugs,
Your Sis

Saturday, May 12, 2018

It is odd, ever since I have written with more questions some song lyrics are filled with misplaced question marks. Also when I went to put today's date the auto fill wanted to input the 11th instead the 12th.

Also what is odd, it was not until I mentioned it might be nice if my story was made into a musical, that I was faced with musicals that Gary has written scores for.

As I listen to Kevin Rogers and Lionel Ritchie sing it brings tears to my eyes. Their song will not show up in Google but for me in YouTube. I know that they are singing for me, from Gary!! They are the songs, "Lady" and "She believes in Me"!!

Lionel Richie and Tim McGraw sing, "Sail On" and one of the lyrics Lionel sings says, "I'll be giving back your name and I won't be back to stay" speaks to exactly what I will be doing to George.

One of Gary's songs tonight "Forever Love" I believe is also directed to me saying he needs "Forever Love". I need the same. Maybe he phrases it "Forever Love" because I sign to my friends, "Forever Friends"

Tuesday, May 15, 2018

I was so thrilled although Heartbroken that Jessica did not surprise me with her appearance on Mother's Day, she did text me and hoped I had a good one, which was why I was thrilled!! That was huge for several years she did not even do that!!

There is a card she wrote me the last time she celebrated with me at Wade Avenue that I was touched by. I kept it but it went missing.

Darcy gave me a beautiful card that made me tear up. Her cards are always so thoughtful and she always adds something of herself that means even more!! She even surprised me by paying for the meal!! That is a first and it meant so much to me!! Even though she waited to make the reservations we got the best seat in the house!!

As Kay suggested I kept watching You Tube, and it has lifted my spirits!! I now believe that my life will turn around. Although I should not because of this medication, I believe that my thoughts are still read.

I believe that You Tube is reaching out to me still, especially Gary through a variety of new singers and familiar singers with new performances. I told my girlfriend Penny today at lunch that although I was trying to avoid him because of my feelings getting hurt he was everywhere and popping up on YouTube but tonight it appears he is keeping his distance. However, I do not want him to be too distant, that would crush me.

As Peter Cetera sings it feels like heaven watching over me!!

I meet with Kay tomorrow and I am not going to be afraid to stand my ground regarding my beliefs.

So many broken promises George made. He said he knew David Foster, Sam Feldman and Winston Rekert. I think he spun stories just as he accused his father of doing.

I am so disappointed that Darcy's party will have only her immediate family and maybe a couple of her friends if Royce is able to reach them. At least her dad and Jessica will be a surprise!!

Gary refers to me as "baby" and most of the love songs tonight have it!! Air Supply is playing and I had one of their albums. It was filled with love songs.

For the longest time I could not and would not listen to love songs when I was healing. They always reminded me of George and I wanted nothing to do with them. But over time as I have mentioned I felt someone was trying to reach me. Now that I discovered it was Gary reaching out to me I realize that most love songs now are rewritten and are from him to me.

Gary's songs with Take That seem more about the journey I have been on and am in and about my dreams. If I understand some of the lyrics they lead me to believe that George has made my dreams his own and can't play this musical game, if that is what it is, without me. That in fact he has built his world around my dreams. Their song "Pray" seems to make fun at George's yoga and the idea that the more he was expected to show his affection the more he stayed away. If that is true then who came in his stead?

"More than Words" by Extreme talks about not needing to say I love you if the actions were there. That was what I was trying to get George to understand. He could have been the first to say "I Love You" (Which he never was) and it would not have meant anything because his actions were not there. I was afraid to touch him and he never touched me. The only time we touched was when he wanted his back or shoulders massaged. I began to hate and resent it because I knew that if I asked for one I would have to reciprocate. It got to the point I could not stand to touch him because I did not respect him as a man or a person.

Wednesday, May 16, 2018

As this medication sets in I find that I find I do not write as much. I also find that I can distance myself from the You Tube and watch movies on Netflix. I am watching the Notebook tonight. I seem to distance myself partly because I do not want to get hurt by my feelings for Gary.

I met with Kay today and she suggested that I try something more tangible like signing up with a dating site. I must admit that this romance through songs has to become real soon. I am in agreement. I will wait until my divorce is final on the 24th.

As I have always said it seems so improbable that Gary would really be interested in me but it seems so probable when I am watching and listening to the tunes.

His songs and that of the group he sings with really doesn't have many love songs but he gets his message across with the other singers. Whatever is going on with these songs just seems so real.

If we are really meant to be he will seek me out

Thursday, May 24, 2018

Seems like YouTube has opened up for me. I am able to watch concerts I have not been privy to see before.

Yesterday I signed up with Dr. Bernstein to lose weight. I currently weight 161 Pounds. I should be between 115-125 pounds. It is a strict diet no wonder they have success. Hopefully I will survive it.

Through the coffee group in the building I got the names of some men that wash windows and build pullouts for the cupboards. I hired them to do my windows today. Just in time for Sam and Daisy's visit in June.

Now instead of my medication being delivered each night they now deliver it every Friday morning. So I am back on 10 mg of Olanzapine.

From what I've been able to deduce Rexulti had me feeling very happy, involved, fixated on YouTube and especially fascinated with Gary Barlow.

When I watch and listen to the You Tube it still makes me believe he and I are possible but when I am not watching reality abounds and I feel foolish for believing in such things.

Today is a big day. George and I are divorced! When I met with Julia today I was weepy. I think I am sad because I wasted so many years being unhappy.

She suggested that one of my dreams was to publish my book, so she is going to help me with that.

Sunday, September 9, 2018

I now have the actual certificate and the actual date of divorce is **May 25th**, which is Darcy's birthday, and it happens to be her 30th. It sure does not look like anything like the one George had with his previous wife.

I have been mourning what could have been with George. (The date I have entered this information does not make sense for I celebrated my divorce on her birthday and had received the certificate prior to the 25th.

Just one more example of someone trying to make sense out of my entries and helping me write this book)

Coming off of Rexulti has opened my eyes that I definitely think better on Olanzapine. This is true according to those on my medical team and family as well. I can see why they would think that. However I cannot interpret or think as creatively. Right now I am on 10mg of Olanzapine.

Before I end this book you must realize how I lost confidence in myself in making decisions. I should have realized it before I was married but I didn't realize what was happening. When I first stayed with George when we were courting I had bought a new pair of glasses that were unique. When George saw them he was quick to say he did not like them. One time I bought a pair of pink pants when I went shopping with Darcy and he was quick to say that they looked ridiculous on me, so I returned them. I went shopping for shoes and it was so difficult for me to choose what colour to get that another customer told me the yellow ones looked good, so I bought them. When I got home George said they were too bright, so I bought a black pair. I felt he was putting Darcy down. When we were going to Mexico I had bought two pretty one piece bathing suits in pink and purple. George said they were awful and I needed new ones. So we went shopping on his suggestion. They did not have any that I liked and while I was trying some on they were blue and white striped tankinis; George did not seem interested in choosing suits at all. I was so confused. We bought two suits that I disliked.

He'd tell me we had to watch our money, yet when I need a coat he was willing to pay $500 on one for me. We bought the coat and I did not even like it.

I am ending this book now with the hopes of starting a sequel should this one be published, but before I do, I want to give you one last song. This is the song I wrote for my dad and gave him as a present for his 88th birthday. My purpose was to thank him for everything he did for me and for driving me to my guitar lessons.

I had also thanked my mother for teaching me knitting by making her an Intarsia blanket, which I now have and use to keep her close. Although the colour yellow seems much brighter than I remember being able to find at the time. I taught myself this way of knitting. Unfortunately, my brain has difficulty reading and understanding patterns now.

Although my last mental journey while on Rexulti caused me to think and have doubts about my father and his relationship with my brother. I think I was just exaggerating things. They had a strong and happy bond. I loved my parents.

This book has helped me express myself and I am determined to get my story out. I pray that those who know my story will still stand by me and that my family will support me even though parts may be difficult to read.

It is my wish that this book helps destigmatize those afflicted with a mental illness. It happens to those who hold white collar positions too. The newscasts and the television shows need to show that it is not just those addicted to drugs that have mental health issues. We are inundated with negative viewpoints of mental health and those with no homes and on drugs are the ones televised, especially by the newscasts. Then they change their tune on mental health day (Bell Let's Talk Day). Also on this day (Bell Let's Talk Day) they need to interview people with the more scary types of mental illness, like those who are Schizophrenic or Schizoaffective.

Right now well-educated individuals believe that those suffering from Schizophrenia have multiple personalities. The definition for Schizophrenia from Google is as follows:

> **A long-term mental disorder of a type involving a breakdown in the relation between thought, emotion, and behaviour, leading to faulty perception, inappropriate actions and feelings, withdrawal from reality and personal relationships into fantasy and delusion, and a sense of mental fragmentation.**
> **Schizoaffective combines these, or some of these symptoms with depression or a mood disorder.**

In my case I had, still experience, thoughts of grandeur, believed in imposters, perceived things perhaps incorrectly and only at my worst would I withdraw from socializing. I did not suffer from inappropriate actions or hallucinations.

I suggest that there be more communication between the psychiatrist, case worker and community support worker. When asked, they currently do not have team meetings because of privacy issues. I think they should. I shared so much important information to my community support worker but it went nowhere.

It is important that Fraser Health and all health authorities separate the link between mental health services and those for drug addiction. The locations for help with these matters should be separated. Is it no wonder then that my husband said, "If it was not for him I would find myself living in the East side with the homeless." He has been misinformed by what he sees in the news and perhaps had ulterior motives for saying such a thing. For those of you not familiar with the area referred to as the East side, these are the slums of where I live.

I have rejoined Weight Watchers since I am a life time member. I was successful before so hopefully it works. I joined in August and so far as of October 24, 2018, I have lost 2 pounds.

Most anti-psychotic drugs cause weight gain so it is my wish to see weight programs a part of the mental health help. In BC, Fraser Health mental health programs offer psychiatrists, case workers, community support workers and clubhouses where they offer physical activities one can join, but they do not include dieticians who could monitor a client's weight should they wish. I believe if they did most clients would not go off their medications as often.

For me these clubhouses and the activities they offer were difficult for me to participate because I am higher functioning and it actually made me feel worse about myself by attending.

I also feel that clients have access to help and activities with their caseworkers and health team on the weekend as well. Right now there is only the CRISIS line available on the weekends. I feel this isn't enough for everyone. It's very name implies that you should be in crisis but you may just need to talk.

My brother believes that I have found the medication that helps me most….Olanzapine. I am not so sure. I am on 10 mg currently and the goal is to lower the dose gradually and see what I can handle. Unless they discover a new drug.

MY COLOUR-CODED LIFE

Through the Years

```
         G      Em  C
Chorus: Through the years
                   Am
        There are memories
                   Dm       G
        That touches the very soul
        D6 (?)   Am     C              G
        Gluing us together more than you can know
```

Verse 1
```
C              Dm      G                Am
One looks back upon a life and sees what they've done wrong
C              Dm           G        Am
Now sit back and listen to how you've touched my heart.
C              Dm          G           Am
Barley sticks and markets and shopping Saturday morning
C              Dm          G           Am
Open arms and guiding talks and driving me when needed.
```

Chorus:
Verse 2
Smiles and laughter and tickles at night
Followed by water and ridding monsters that fright.
Education, graduation, struggles we did share
Diploma presentation, pride you did bear!

Chorus:
Verse 3
The Cabot Trail, P.E.I, New York City TWICE!
Florida, Muskoka, water skiing fun
Planning and paying for my perfect wedding day

Chorus:
Verse 4
Christmas reunions, Vancouver visits, Steveston and Whistler
Vancouver Island, Tofino all we have enjoyed.
The girls enjoy your leg games and chasing little ways
Teaching them to ride the bike you proudly saw them receive.

Chorus:
Verse 5
I love you Dad for oh so many moments.
Including this guitar and the lessons you paid for
All I have to give to you is who I have become
Happy 88th Dad
Our memories have just begun!

(August 29, 2019)
    I have decided to insert my entry for my second book because I feel it finishes this book. I think it wiser to start the second book, if there is one, after this book is published.

Friday, October 12, 2018

As I watch Gary Barlow interviewed on YouTube about his book and his mental health, I am embarrassed by how I let my mind believe that a miracle might happen, that I would spend the rest of my life with him. One day he and his wife Dawn might read my book and I just pray they will not be hurt by it. I pray they will not be hurt that I chose and still choose my unborn daughter to be remembered as Poppy.

    This all brings me to tears tonight. While I watch him perform I want so much to have it be true but reality is it will likely never happen. But I cannot help but wonder why he does not wear a wedding band.

    If I were to be struck by cancer and given a wish, it would be to meet Gary and have him put music to my song and for Beyoncé to sing my songs. If there was another wish it would be to have a big party arranged by Gary so I could see all my friends from grade school, high school and college. Maybe Beyoncé would be able to get the emotion out that I am feeling through her voice. Her whole body is used when she sings "Listen".

While I was solely on Rexulti I felt so intuitive. His words in Gary's song, "Back for good" state that you can tell him what song to sing and he will sing it. It seems so directed to me. However, I figure this isn't true. It is the magic of singers to make you feel that it is directed to you.

I must say that having my community support worker, Julia, meet with me every week really helps. She is my anchor and has helped tremendously. She and my caseworker, Kay make me feel that my book will be published. We have taken steps for it to happen. I have gone through it and changed most names. I do not like that I have had to change the names in my book though because how do my other hopes of being interviewed by some of the talk show hosts like Ellen, Marilyn Dennis and Oprah. I only say Oprah last because she does not have a talk show anymore sadly. Also, I would like to be on City line, W5 and 60 minutes. Cityline is the first talk show I ever watched growing up. I do not remember the name of the current host but I remember Dini Petty's name. I think the new host is Tracey Moore.

I have joined a couple dating sites, Match and Our Time, and they are awful! I am trying to find someone at the encouragement of my caseworker trying to keep it real. But I find myself comparing them to Gary and yes, the way I remember George.

I wrote in my previous book that I was feeling sexual feelings I had never felt before while watching Gary and that I wanted him to make it that I did not have them until we were together. I could say that he did that but in reality it is the drugs. Rexulti made me feel alive. I was also a take charge woman. Now I do not feel sexual nor do I feel as confident being on 10 mg of Olanzapine. I definitely prefer the creative and energetic side of me when the medication is not working.

I have been having problems with my left arm. It hurts when I use it and have limited mobility. If I move it the wrong way it will ache. It will go all the way down to my hand. I had X-rays and my doctor feels the problem is coming from my neck so he has suggested physiotherapy and is ordering an MRI. I go for an ultrasound on December 6. I have arranged for Physio for next week.

I currently weigh 157.4 lbs. I have been a member of Weight Watchers since August 9. I started at 158.8lbs. I have only lost 1.4 pounds. I was a lifetime member years ago so I know it can work. I so want to lose weight for my nieces wedding in June.

I have come a long way from depending on George to living on my own. From having no friends to having many, a couple of them close. I thank God for encouraging me to take the first step and attend one of the dinners with the Newcomers group where I met Danielle. I have met so many different ladies through her. I also thank him for giving me the courage to attend the coffee gatherings in my building. I also thank him for having my friends willing to listen to me.

I think that is what George and I were missing, friends, that we could socialize with.

Thursday, October 18, 2018

Today Julia came to my place and the first thing she asked me to think about is how I would like my cover to look like. I think it should have a picture of me with my brain exposed with all my colours exposed with the names and words they represent on top and of course with my title. A Mind Awakened: My Colour Coded Life.

I suppose I cannot have a picture of me since names have been changed unfortunately…perhaps a silhouette.

Julia believes that I can use my own name as the author. She believes that my ex-husband cannot stop me from doing that, I hope so.

Julia and I worked on finding publishers. Funny how that worked out for several years ago I found nothing. Anyhow we found one named Caitlyn Press and left a message but I have more faith in the second one located in Victoria called Heritage House.

Next week we will go to the library and print off my book, so that I can mail it to Heritage House along with all their requirements like a synopsis of the book, a marketing summary stating who my target audience is and why I think it will sell, photograph suggestions, and what qualifies me to write this book.

I was listening to "I Believe" by The Tenors on Spotify which now displays itself as soon as I sign into my computer. It was the perfect song for today for I would really like someone to say to me that they believe me about all my concerns that I have about George.

Tomorrow is an exciting day. Cassie turns 9 and George and I will be spending the day with her. She has a Pro D day. We have bought her a bike and she has no idea. I, of course, will get there for 7:00 am while George will be getting there around 10:00 a.m.

Sunday, October 21, 2018

Even now while I look at my ex-husband I do not see how he has aged. It is like I missed several years with him. I keep comparing him to that picture Paula showed us and I do not see it, even George did not say anything when he saw it. I do recognize him when I look back on all the photographs I have of him.

Cassie did not seem that excited by getting a new bike. That could have been because her surprise was spoiled by George listening to Paula's voicemail in the car where she said to George, "Make sure you take a picture of Cassie with her new bike". Big fail on George's part!

Wednesday, November 7, 2018

Julia and I printed my book and I put it in a binder. Is it ever daunting to look at! She will be coming over tomorrow and we will together begin to go through it.

Saturday, November 10, 2018

We started the book and I realized since we only got to page 8 that it was a futile effort. I will reread it on my own. I have made a goal of reaching page 100 by our next appointment.

On another topic I feel I will never be free of my colours. As I watch YouTube and they present me with new artists and videos, their colours scream out loud to me!

I am so happy that they are presenting new videos to me. I am now seeing more of Beyoncé!!

Maybe all these musicians do believe in me. But if that is true maybe my medication is not working. Yet as I watch Beyoncé her outfit during the same song changes from green and black to solid black.

As I swig back my rum and diet cokes tonight, I think of how easy they go down and how now I am starting to drink alone which is scary. So I will stop.

Even though it does not make sense, I feel I am a part of something bigger. As I look over my photos there are pictures of a past principal and other teachers I first taught with, but I never took their pictures. Why aren't there pictures of those at my other school?

Friday, February 15, 2019

It has been awhile since I have written anything because I have been so absorbed with my book and changing names and ensuring everything is in it that needs to be there.

Today I saw Kay, my caseworker and I broke down. I have not been my happy self. Several of my friends have noticed. It could be the result of many things:

- † Beginning to take calcium and vitamin D. Maybe there is some conflict with it and the Olanzapine
- † My unhappiness with my weight. I joined Weight Watchers in August hoping I would go from a large to a small again, but I only have been going up and down a couple of pounds. Very disappointing.
    - † At home I try to only eat zero point foods, so getting pleasure from food is hard. Although I manage to get cookies in but I am honest with the points.

† I'm recovering from a hairline fracture of my right foot therefore I have been unable to do Zumba or go to my music classes because of all the stairs. I have to refrain from these for another month.
† Not being able to celebrate Jessica's birthday. Her not communicating with me and needing to have her sister present whenever she sees me.
  † I expressed my fear of being alone with her because I do not know what to say that will not cause her to withdraw more. I am afraid but I am willing to face that fear.
  † Kay is going to call Jessica next week and ask if she'll come in to talk…the three of us.
† George and Darcy's family are renting a house together in South Saramin where George will be living in the basement. There's a whole story behind this and so I guess putting it in this spot of the book seems logical.

A while back Darcy and I had lunch and she asked me if I would consider selling my condo and investing in a house where I would live in a basement suite. I would still be mortgage free because they would assume the mortgage. Apparently, George had planted this idea in her head. I told her I had reservations but I would look into it before making my final decision.

So, I contacted my financial planner who verified my thoughts that it was not viable. We would need a mortgage of at least $500,000 and the kids would not be able to afford it. I also discussed it with Kay. She verified that Duncan Mental Health had geographical boundaries and I would have to find a new health team.

There was also the friends I have made in the building and in the community. I just was not willing to give that up…plus I look out my window and I feel grateful every day!

Although Darcy felt that if they were true friends they would come to visit, I just like my life here. Plus, I did not want to be abused with babysitting because of my proximity. It is only now that I am learning to say no to things.

So, if you have not guessed, although I was afraid of the conversation, I told Darcy it would not work. She was totally fine and said she totally understood.

In December, George and I met at Blue Angel Cafe to discuss how best to automate the deposit of the alimony cheques. What was very odd and really wreaks havoc with my mind is that George seemed happy to see me and agreed with me that it was crazy for me to think I could buy a house with Darcy. He acted like he never suggested it to her. I am not yet able to confront him when what he says conflicts with what I know.

I know my brother had suggested that if he thought it was such a good idea why doesn't he do it by renting with her. I honestly can't remember if I passed that suggestion on to him during our lunch.

Funny though, for a guy who thought he knew everything about real estate and budgeting why he is not in the market and is now having to pay $1,600 in rent. I am grateful for my choices.

Because of the scare of being sued by George if I published my book without changing names, I have been referred to a defamation lawyer.

The stars seem aligned for the lawyer is willing to work with me through email. So I have sent it to him. Now I wait.

Actually the first publisher I will be trying to send my book to will be, Arsenal Pulp Press.

Dear Mom and Dad,

I hope that while your deaths make no sense to me, you are happy with the decisions I have made and feel I have invested your gifts well.

There are so many times where I need to express myself to you. I really need to print a picture of you guys but I have so few of you together.

Although I shouldn't I have this hope of Gary Barlow coming into my life. He is a musician I've become fascinated with on You Tube. But honestly wouldn't it be like a Cinderella story. He is so much younger though so honestly I need to stop thinking about it.

I believe wherever you are that you are helping me. I tried to thank you for what you did for me by your song dad and your knitted blanket mom. I hope you felt the love behind it.

MY COLOUR-CODED LIFE

I never knew how powerful those words "I love you" were until George caused me to wake up and realize that he only initiated saying it once to me and that was before we were married. He phoned and said "I just called to say 'I love you' just like Stevie Wonder's song at the time. Hence it became our song.

In 2005, I told him I needed to hear him initiate it. I told him all that I needed, like affection shown during the day to help me want to be intimate at night. It was my psychiatrist that suggested I express myself to him.

Cassie, whom you'd love, and I have a thing. We take turns saying I love you first, then respond, I love you more, then the other says, I love you most, then the other says, not possible. Cute, right? I just love it!!

I am an emotional wreck tonight. I help Darcy and Royce with their move. They moved into the new place today.

George is renting with them and living in the basement suite.

Maybe with the publication of this book some of my other dreams will come true. But at least my girls will know that I am strong. I just pray that they are strong enough to read and not be hurt by the contents or revelations this book provides.

On that note Darcy posted this beautiful touching expression on Bell Let's Talk Day on Facebook that emoted how she felt about me. I had no idea that I made that kind of impact. I hoped to print it and frame it so I could read it when feeling sad. So I saved it on Facebook and frequently reread it. I have decided to retype it so you can read it too.

> *"My mama has always been one of my best friends. One whom I can talk to, tell everything to and receive no judgement back. She is forever loving, caring and strong as f*ck. Mental health has rocked our family back and forth on a rollercoaster for over 15 years, some times are much harder than others. But this rockstar has come out shining every time life throws her a curveball. I am so proud of her for overcoming so many steppingstones and I will always be here to be her back catcher."*

Speaking of Darcy, I remember George always saying to us that he knew David Foster and Sam Feldman and he would use this connection to help her with her singing career. I think it was bunk, for he never did.

I love you both. You may have kept mom on a strict budget dad, which I thought /think is awful, but, you always celebrated mother's day at The Board of Trade at that awesome buffet. I usually had to organize my own mother's day once the girls grew up.

My spirit has been broken and I am trying to get it back. It was me that got the girls to their events and it was me that found Jessica's talent agent. After a while because they started to be during work hours George had to take over. Then he acted like it was all him and her.

It always hurt me when he refused to take Darcy when the agency asked for her. She was never asked again. I firmly believe had it been Jessica he would have taken her.

It bothers me you guys how he talks negatively about them behind their back, yet they adore him.

Please kiss Poppy for me. Dad I picture you sitting on the edge of my bed and hugging me while I cried. Thank you both, your conversations helped a lot. Tell Poppy that I have never forgotten her.

I know I am sad tonight but I really have come a long way.

Love,
#2

Tuesday, February 19, 2019

Well Darcy and Royce and George moved into their new residence on the 15th, which was a Friday. I helped them on Saturday, Sunday and Monday which was family day. It appears that it is an open-door policy between their respective places.

We all had dinner on Family day together. I did mention to Darcy again that I worry about how I will fit into the mix and that I may not see her now as often as we used to. She said I had nothing to worry about.

I see Dr. Jake on the 26th. Frankly I am going to tell him that I am not doing so well. Seeing George and Jessica this weekend, really threw me off my game. Jessica just came for a visit. I still look at them searching for differences in their faces. Jessica's looks longer than I think it should.

Even something Darcy said to me one day at her place at work when I took her to lunch while on Rexulti has me wondering. When I admitted to her that I thought she was a double, she said, "Well I think I have her cheekbones." I never questioned her on it though.

In addition to all of this, I am feeling somewhat depressed. I am wishing that I was stricken with terminal cancer or something because I am getting tired of this fight to get mentally well that I am on. My friends have also noticed it and they have only heard my voice over the phone. I think it may be more than just missing Zumba and music lessons.

I am nervous about the meeting between Jessica, Kay and I. Jessica has the ability though when she and I do get together with other people of making it seem that there is no strain between us.

It seems I still cannot look at past pictures. Many do not make sense to me for I do not recall ever taking them. I must remember to tell Dr. Jake this.

Adele's songs seem to emit feelings that I feel, especially "Rolling in the Deep" and "When We Were Young".

If I hadn't had Darcy, I do not think I'd have gotten this far.

Wednesday, March 6, 2019

The defamation lawyer has offered specific advice. I made the changes he suggested. Frankly, now I feel better about publishing my book.

He was gracious and did the work via email, so I did not have to drive far. He said we could meet face to face if needed.

Julia suggested to me that the lawyer and I could meet at the new Tim Horton's that opened up. I think I will suggest it to him because I want to thank him in person for taking my project on.

Listening to my music lately has me believing again that my school board and the Catholic Church are helping me publish this book and taking action. It only makes sense to be true because it is hard for me to believe that they would ignore me without a reason.

I am afraid, when I see Dr. Jake on March 12 that I will have to tell him I am slipping.

I think my four favourite songs by Elton John is the one he rewrote for Lady Diana, The Circle of Life, Your Song and I'm Still Standing.

I've been working on my first book making all the changes the defamation lawyer suggested but the file got AutoSaved. So I made the changes to that instead of the original document. I had no idea which was better to update. So now I hope my computer will somehow correct this. I will have to ensure that I send the right one. I like the original one because it is easier to read.

Monday, March 18, 2019

I had my appointment with Dr. Jake and I was honest how I felt I was slipping. He gave me a choice because he said I was in the driver's seat. He gave me 3 choices.

A. Keep the medication the same
B. Increase the Olanzapine
C. Add 1mg of Rexulti

I chose the third option. So we will see how it works for a month. I started taking Rexulti in addition to 10 mg Olanzapine on March 13. The pharmacist said it causes wakefulness so it is best to take it in the morning.

I will discuss with Dr. Jake perhaps it did not work for me when I was being transitioned over to it last time because I was taking it at night, hence losing sleep.

Friday, July 12, 2019

The combination of 10 mg of Olanzapine and 1 mg of Rexulti has been the best yet. However, in August my psychiatrist is planning to reduce the Olanzapine to 7.5mg.

Since I wrote in here last I went to Tinsel Town on Friday June 21, 2019 for my niece's wedding on the Saturday June 22nd. While there Sam was kind enough to drive me to Aurora to visit and stay with my girlfriend for a few days. I also saw some of my grade school friends thanks to Amy for hosting. On the 26th I had a date with Derek!!! We had been chatting on messenger every day for a couple of months I think. The date was like a dream because I was with my high school crush!!

I shared with him all about my mental health and he seemed fine with it. We had coffee on a park bench then had lunch in Newcastle on Rose Petal Lake. He asked me if there was anything I wanted to do, so I told him I would like to see the house he recently bought, so that I could picture him when he texted me. He drove for about an hour to get there. He gave me the grand tour. We talked, then went to a restaurant there called Becky's. The day lasted from 11:00 am to 9:30 p.m. He greeted and left me with a big hug!! The heart-warming part was when we walked around the Lake and sat on a park bench…he pulled me closer.

I worried that after he saw me that our communication would stop but it has not. In fact last night he agreed that once he gets familiar with his new job which he starts on the 18th we will plan getting together during his two week vacation. Where and when is up in the air.

Thursday, July 25, 2019

I had asked Derek if he would be willing to talk to my caseworker. He said he would be willing if I felt it would help me. I said yes, so I gave permission to Kay to speak with him. She called him yesterday and they spoke for 10 minutes. I needed to know how Derek felt, so I texted him telling him that Kay had told me she reached him, and my stomach was consequently in knots. I asked him if she scared him off or if we were still ok. He said nothing had changed between us.

They make stories about relationships like ours!! I thank God every day for bringing Derek into my life again, for giving me Darcy, for all my friends, and for the beautiful condo I own.

Thursday, August 29, 2019

I met with Kay and my psychiatrist on August 27. Since I am doing so well we have decided not to make any change to my medication. Apparently, lowering the dose of Olanzapine from 10mg to 7.5 would not have any effect on my weight.

I have signed up for a Women on Weights program and a Learn to run a 10K program. Both will help me use the equipment better in my building.

I have stopped going to Weight Watchers because I have not lost a thing. Even when I asked the instructor to look at my record of what I eat she had no recommendations because I was doing everything right. It just goes to show the need for the drug companies to focus on developing anti-psychotic medications that do not cause weight gain!

For me the form of art therapy that worked best for me was listening to music, especially the lyrics, specifically watching musicians perform on stage. That which I could listen to provides the path for me to find my inner strength.

One thing I have not mentioned is that I believed and now hope that all the musicians that I have been exposed to on You Tube are performing to raise money for the dream of my online school.

Another thing that hospital wards for those suffering from a mental illness should offer, is access to earphones and access to YouTube. This should be offered as another form of art therapy. I struggled having access to music during my last stay at the hospital.

This ends my book for you knowing that finding the right medication can take a lifetime. Although mine is working well now Dr. Jake worries about me being on Olanzapine long-term. So I may have changes up ahead.

I can dress myself, eat properly, sit on furniture, listen to and play music, go shopping, trust technology, and go out by myself. Essentially, all those things which were crippling are now in the background. However, my life will never be the same for although the colours do not scare me anymore I am quite aware of what each one stands for. I have many new friends, and a hopeful romance. In the lyrics of Elton John's song "I'm still standing better than I ever did, looking like a true survivor." As well as Whitney Houston sings, "I Didn't Know My Own Strength" Although I have lost respect for my religion, I have not lost my faith in God. It is in my conversations with him that guided me to where I am now. I have decided to go with FriesenPress and self-publish this book at the suggestion of a literary agent I spoke with. They have helped me rename my book, *My Colour –Coded Life – Living with Schizoaffective Disorder*.

Please do not feel ashamed to seek help from a psychiatrist if you, a family member or friend think it wise. When my family suggested I go to the hospital I went with the thought I would prove them wrong. Agreeing to go was my saving grace. My psychiatrists from Duncan Mental Health did converse with me, if yours does not, find another. My first psychiatrist, Dr. G. recommended by my family doctor was awful. She spent the entire time looking at her papers and writing copious notes. I told George I would not return. He found Duncan Mental Health. Also, insist on talking with someone every week. My lifelines were my caseworker and community support workers and any friend that would listen to me. I did not have access to a psychologist when I asked for one and I do think everyone should be offered their service. There should be no difference in seeing a psychiatrist than seeing a specialist in any other area. Their profession is stigmatized just like the mental health illnesses are. There is no denying that my medication is working for me.

CPSIA information can be obtained
at www.ICGtesting.com
Printed in the USA
LVHW081041120122
708408LV00012B/273